Anyone Can...Arts
DRAWING MAGIC
Guidebook 2

By Peter Kraus

Anyone Can...Arts Publishing
www.anyonecanarts.com

ACKNOWLEDGEMENTS

My many, many thanks to the following people for their valued support and encouragement.

Karen Higgins
Angie Harris
Debbie Nelson

ANYONE CAN...ARTS
DRAWING MAGIC
Guidebook 2

ISBN 978-1466454125

Published by Anyone Can...Arts
www.anyonecanarts.com

Printed in the U.S.A.

GREETINGS
from Professor Pencil

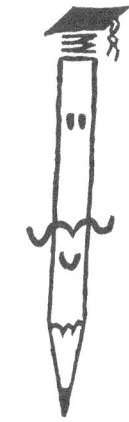

Did you know...
DRAWING SKILL
CAN BE LEARNED?

Think about this. Did you always know how to tell time, or did someone teach you? Did you know how to form letters of the alphabet without help, or were you taught? Did you just pick up a book one day and begin to read, or did you receive instruction?

The same goes for drawing. You have the ability, but you have to be shown how to use it. If you are taught the basics, isn't it reasonable to assume that then you will produce better results? That's what this book is all about. In simple language, *DRAWING MAGIC* will teach you the fundamentals.

Extra care has been taken to choose subject matter beneficial for conveying useful principles and elements. While having fun replicating the pictures, you will be amazed by your quick improvement. Whether you are a beginner or advanced, there is something for everyone. Since each chapter builds on the lessons from the previous, I recommend following the course in sequence.

Now get ready to enjoy yourself and prove that indeed,

ANYONE CAN DRAW.

HELPFUL HINTS

The following suggestions are very important. Please, pay close attention.

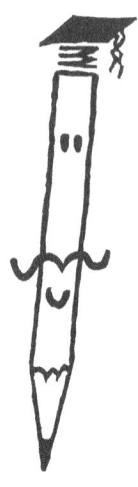

1. Read directions carefully and stick to the program.
   Principles mesh. It's unwise to skim or skip around.

2. Be sure you don't miss the follow-up after each chapter.
   These summarize and shed further light.

3. Finish only one exercise in any one period, and let the lessons sink in.
   Should you feel rushed, confused or fatigued, stop and regroup. Then, resume when refreshed.

4. For review, by all means refer to previous chapters. Repeat all, or parts, as often as you like.
   Consult the glossary (at the back of the book) whenever you need word clarification.

5. Your attitude is important. If bored, angry or frustrated, it's not a good idea to press on, or
   to tackle something new. Wait until you're relaxed and your positive outlook returns.

6. Avoid talking on the phone, watching TV, or some other distraction.
   Budget an hour or two, just for you, and focus on drawing without interruption.

7. Whenever you begin a new segment, or continue where you left off, always put your favorite
   music on and your cares aside.

8. Don't hurry. Move at a comfortable pace. FORGET ABOUT TIME.
   Your thoughts should be on your drawing, NOT on how long it takes.

9. ELIMINATE preconceived notions and pressures like how good you think your results should be.
   To expect your work to absolutely match the printed illustrations is impractical.
   Strive for knowledge.

10. Remember, you're learning. Those of you who set your sights mainly on the final outcome, rather
    than on the steps that get you there, are apt to miss the mark.

11. While doing the exercises, you may find one subject matter will seem more to your liking than
    another. But please keep an open mind. Each lesson offers valuable experience. Stay receptive
    to all possibilities. If you must judge, rate your success AFTER you've completed the entire course.

12. If you haven't already done so, please see *"Greetings from Professor Pencil,"* on the previous
    page, and take his words of wisdom seriously. Most of all, enjoy yourself.

Draw for pleasure.
The fun is in the doing.

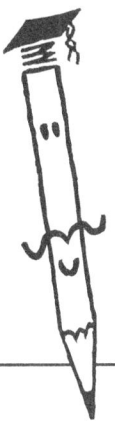

Here are some other
points to keep in mind.

1. Each chapter introduces a different facet of drawing. By replicating select subject matter, you are able to learn and apply concepts and procedures easily. To make things even easier, clear written explanations, plus hundreds of tips, hints and illustrations show you what to look for, what to do, how to do it, and when to do each step from start to finish.

2. Always remember to rely mainly on your vision. You may use your pencil readings for assistance, but your eyes and thinking cap should ultimately decide when you are on target.

3. Since you are going to be working FREEHAND (without a ruler), you should not expect your drawings to turn out as accurate, or as neat, as the printed drawings in the book. Student examples are included.

Be sure to also get acquainted
with the following symbols.

When you spot these 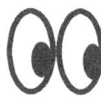 study and observe.

This 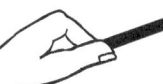 means draw.

This 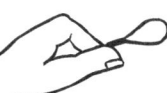 means blend.

This 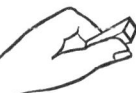 means erase.

MATERIALS

Standard Size (8 1/2"x 11") **White Unlined Paper**

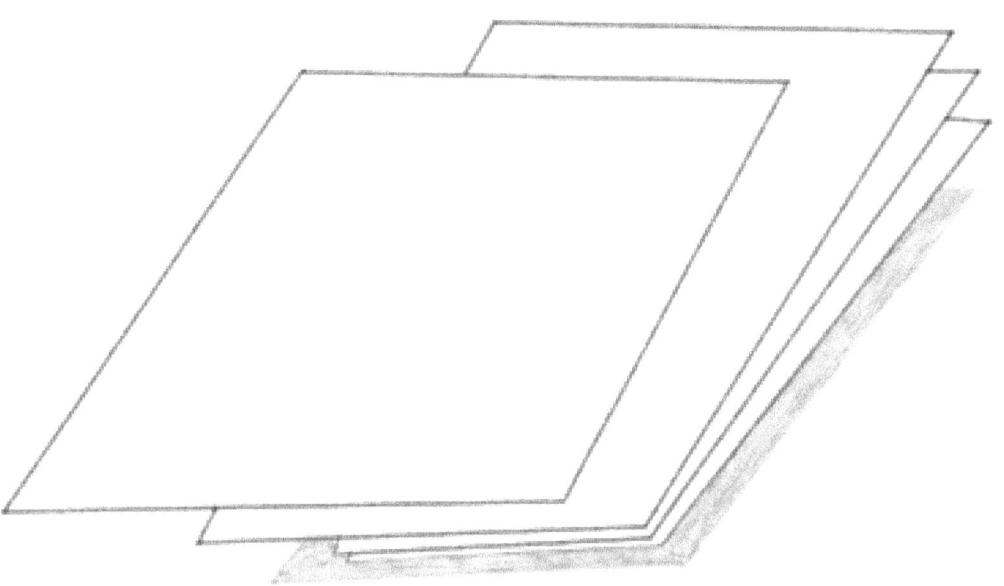

A couple of standard #2 pencils

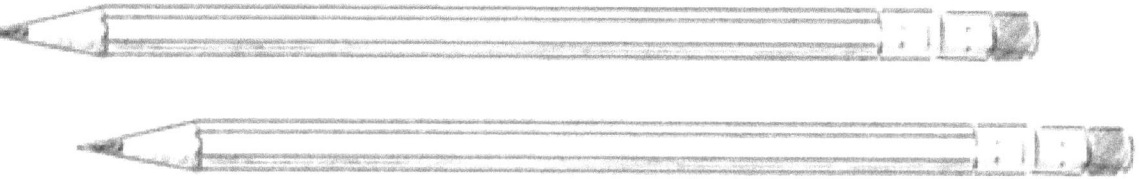

Blender (or Cotton Swab)

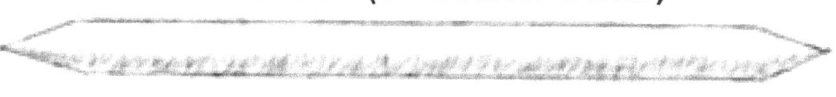

Kneadable Eraser

Pencil Sharpener

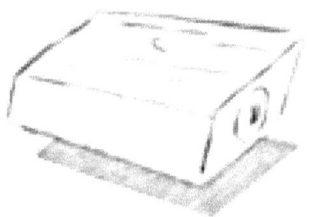

CONTENTS

*EACH JOURNEY BEGINS
WITH THE FIRST STEP.*

Enjoy your odyssey.

*Take delight in your voyage
as well as your destination.*

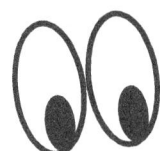

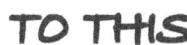

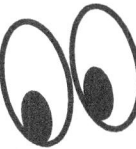

FROM THIS

TO THIS

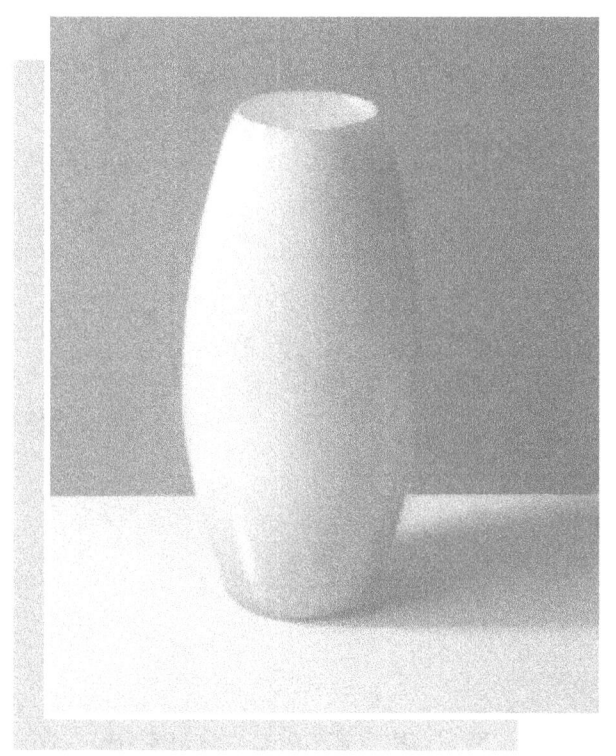

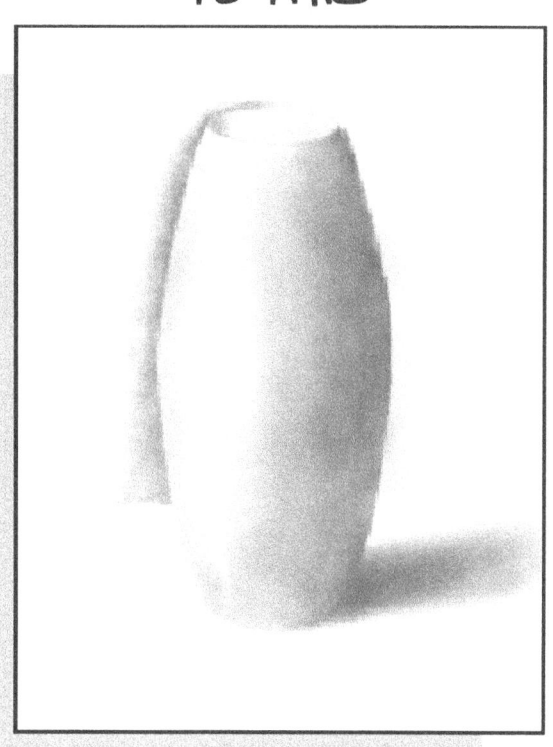

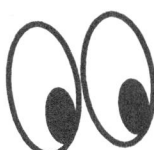

BEGINS HERE

Before you reach for your pencil, please... get acquainted with the situation.

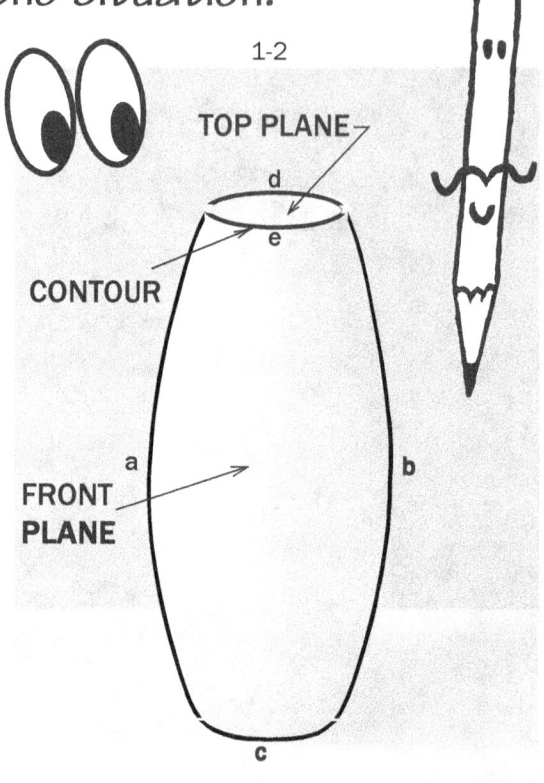

1-1

1-2

TOP PLANE

d

e

CONTOUR

a   b

FRONT PLANE

c

Whether your view is of a real object or a snapshot, such as example 1-1, the thought of drawing it may be a little overwhelming. However, if you *squint* (close your eyes half way), then visualize (make believe or picture in your mind), you can separate the object into manageable components (1-2). For instance, the sides (a & b) are just two long vertical (upright) curves. One short horizontal (sideways) curve (c) forms the base. Another curve (d) forms the *back* portion of the top. As for curve (e), it stands not only for the *front* part of the top, but also for the boundary, or *contour* between the front and the top. Equally important: these two curves (d & e) help form a narrow *ellipse*. Why an ellipse? From a bird's eye view, the top is *circular*.

In this case however, our view (or *perspective*) is mostly frontal and slightly from above. This gives us a *plane* (or surface) view of the top at an *angle* which causes the circle to appear *elliptical*. As indicated by the examples on the right, lowering the line of sight on the object makes the *top elliptical plane* appear to shrink in height (F). By raising the line of sight, the same *elliptical plane* seems to grow taller in scale (G). Eventually, it would become a circle (viewed from directly above). Because visual changes like these occur, and since ellipses have a great impact on drawing, it's wise to learn their secrets.

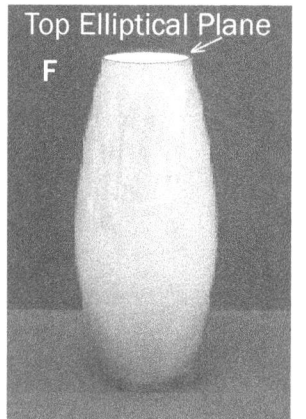

Top Elliptical Plane

F

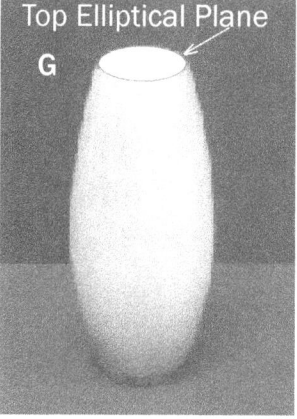

Top Elliptical Plane

G

TIP The word PLANE in drawing may sound complicated, but it's just another way to describe the surfaces of something, as they appear in your perspective (or line of sight). For instance, looking at the corner of a box at eye level, you see two side *planes*. CONTOUR in drawing basically refers to the boundary between planes. The corner of the box is an example.

ELLIPSES

WHAT IS AN ELLIPSE? An ellipse (or oval) is not a rectangle with rounded corners because an ellipse does not have any straight lines (1-3). An ellipse is a circle which has been compressed (squeezed), much the way a balloon changes shape when pressed between your hands. With *equal* pressure centered from above and below, a horizontal, even (symmetrical) ellipse would result (1-4). The same thing would occur when pressing at both sides, except a vertical ellipse would be the outcome (1-5). If the balloon were held at an angle, squeezed stronger from below and closer to the right end, then an uneven *(asymmetrical)* angular ellipse such as 1-6 would be formed.

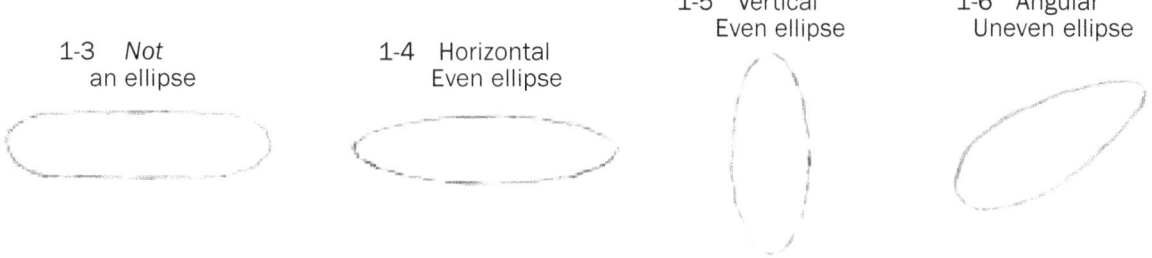

1-5   Vertical
Even ellipse

1-6   Angular
Uneven ellipse

1-3   *Not*
an ellipse

1-4   Horizontal
Even ellipse

ELLIPSES CAN BE CONSTRUCTED. Upright, lying down, or at a slant, ellipses can be shaped with a choice of four, or six curves. Plus, they can be fashioned with imaginary or boxed-in guide lines and a mid-line. These helpers make it easier to see the amount of bend in the curves, as well as the reverse shapes they create. In turn, this enables you to replicate ellipses more accurately. For instance, horizontal/symmetrical ellipse 1-7 consists of 6 curves. Please note the reverse shapes indicated in gray. Next, observe that symmetrical ellipse 1-8 was formed with only 4 curves. Then, study the 6 curves that created angular/asymmetrical ellipse 1-9.

> ***TIP*** ACCURACY in drawing means *visibly* close.   What looks reasonably similar is fine.

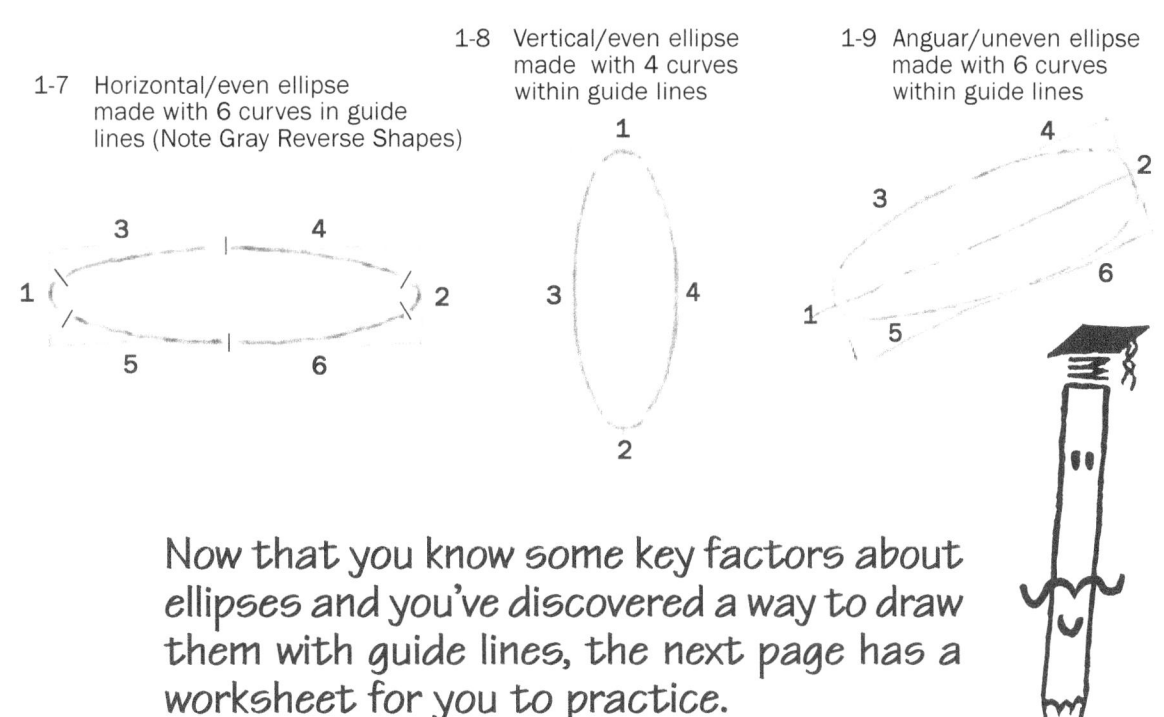

1-7   Horizontal/even ellipse
made with 6 curves in guide
lines (Note Gray Reverse Shapes)

1-8   Vertical/even ellipse
made with 4 curves
within guide lines

1-9   Anguar/uneven ellipse
made with 6 curves
within guide lines

Now that you know some key factors about ellipses and you've discovered a way to draw them with guide lines, the next page has a worksheet for you to practice.

Worksheet　　Duplicate ELLIPSES with Guide Lines

DIRECTIONS: Following are pairs of guide lines. One set contains an even or an uneven ellipse. Your job is to reasonably match each ellipse example inside the empty boundary nearby. You can alternate, using the continuous line (sample A-1) or sketch line (sample A-2) techniques, with your choice of four or six curves. LIGHTLY draw your curves *slowly*, one at a time. Be sure to glance back and forth between the model and your advancing curves, as you steer the pencil. This will enable you to adjust as you go. The reverse shapes (or negative spaces), like those shown in gray, are also helpful references (A-3). You must not turn the worksheet for convenience. The goal is to exercise your hand in a variety of ways. "Lefties" may invert the page only to keep from blocking the view of the example. After you have finished, I recommend that you draw some more ellipses on a fresh page, the way you would normally create large, narrow and wide letter O's. Vary the sizes and angles, as well as tilts. Box them in (without a ruler) and place a center line. Then, lightly trace your boxes on another sheet and replicate your own ellipses.

TIP A continuouos line means once you start, you do not lift the pencil until *that line* is done. A sketch line is made with short, overlapping strokes by lifting the pencil between each mark.

A-1 6 Continuous Line Curves　　A-2 4 Sketch Line Curves　　A-3 Reverse Shapes (gray)

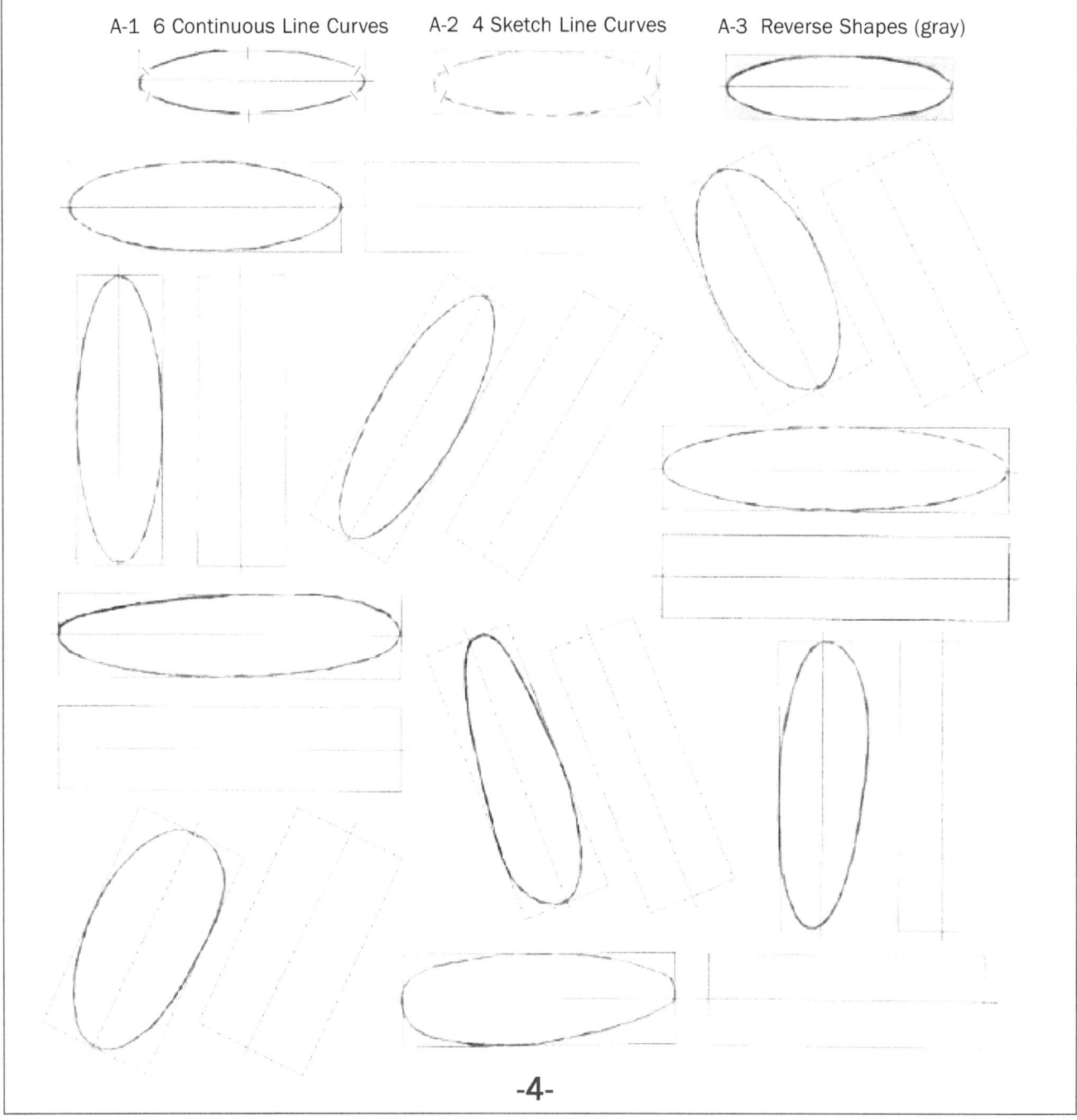

ELLIPSES CAN BE FORMED WITH LAPS

One of the main reasons why people tend to become frustrated when drawing ellipses is that they expect each stroke to be accurate on the first try. When this doesn't happen, out comes the eraser and the cycle repeats with new starts and ersures, over and over again. In order to prevent this from happening to you, please understand: drawing is a process of gradual development and refinement. Adjustment is part of the program. After you draw the *entire* ellipse the way you learned, you can modify the parts that need it. Or, you can also apply the modification principle in another way.

TRY THIS. Take your pencil gently in your hand, like you normally write, but place your fingers twice as far back from the point. On a fresh sheet of paper, *lightly* form a large *narrow* letter "O" with three or more quick *continuous* laps, *in one direction*. That means, either advance clockwise or counter clockwise *without stopping* until you have completed your travels (1-10). Do the same thing, *sideways,* and also at an angle. Your three shapes will appear like ellipses similar to mine (1-11). Next, using your ellipses as a reference, draw over them with four or six curves, one at a time, with continuous or sketch strokes in order to refine your ellipses (1-12). When using this method, it is not only permitted, but encouraged to rotate your paper occasionally to vary the view of your ellipses, as you refine. Why? Because this enables you to reduce the effects of *astigmatism*. After you are reasonably satisfied with your results, erase your excess marks and make a few minor adjustments for the final outcome.

TIP Astigmatism is uneven curvature of the eye lens, causing view distortion.

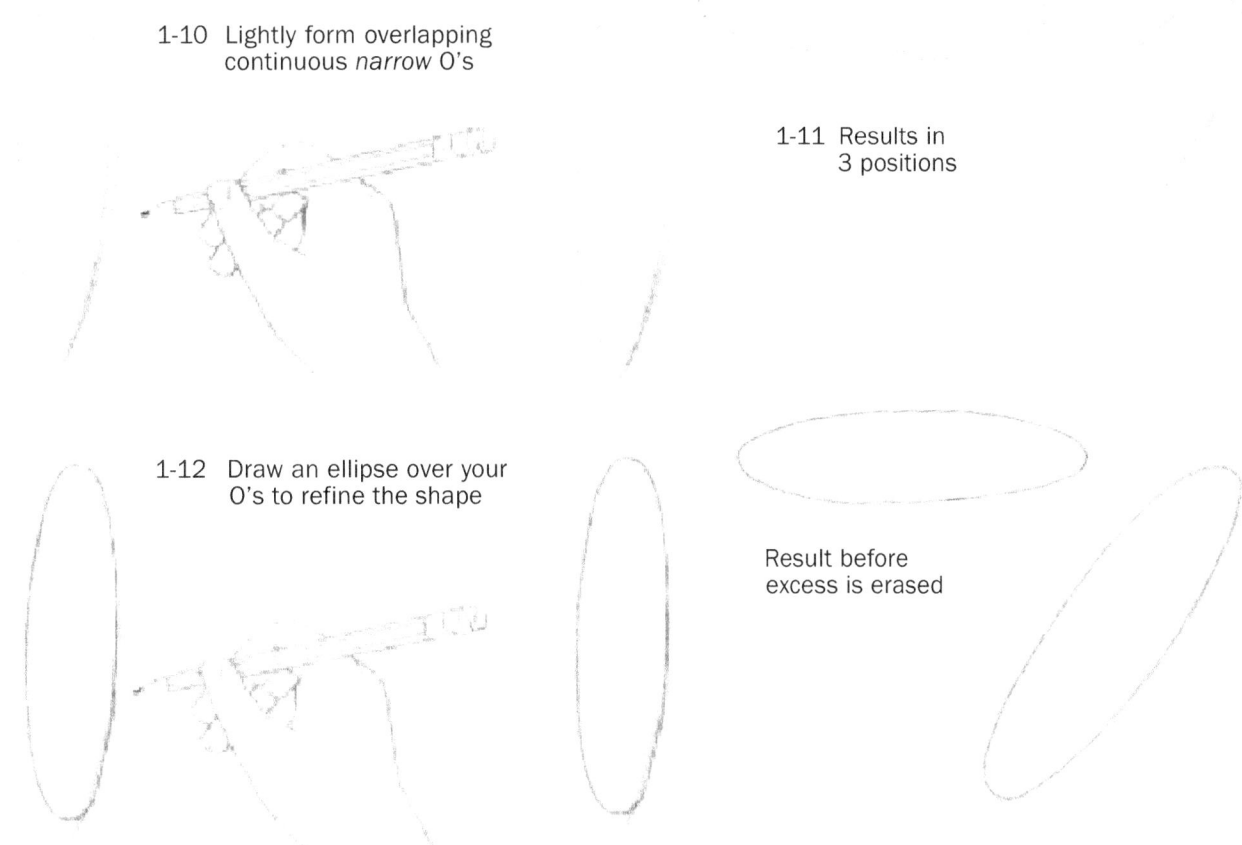

1-10 Lightly form overlapping
continuous *narrow* O's

1-11 Results in
3 positions

1-12 Draw an ellipse over your
O's to refine the shape

Result before
excess is erased

ALSO TRY THIS.   Repeat what you did, except this time, *lock* your wrist. Allow only your arm to move when you make your laps. Although the technique may feel awkward at first, you will be able to create larger sizes, and with practice, you will find your lines will be more fluid. Plus, your eye-hand coordination will improve, and in turn, so will the quality and accuracy of your shapes.

It's time to Begin Drawing the Figure

STEP 1 **HOW and WHERE to START?** The answer is right in front of you, if you take time to *observe.* The instant you begin to see things simply as shapes, based on what I call the TRUSTY SEVEN, you will discover that drawing can be organized into easy, manageable stages. Let's look at the figure's horizontal (sideways) extent, for example. When we estimate it visually (by eye) or take a pencil reading, then compare it to the vertical (upright) span, we see that from the top (ellipse center) to the bottom curve's base line, the distance is roughly DOUBLE (1-13). And the point is? We get a basic idea about the figure's *overall proportion* (maximum height compared to width). This valuable finding can serve as a foundation that starts your drawing. So let's get underway. On a fresh sheet of paper, begin by LIGHTLY centering two squares, stacked one on top of the other,as suggested by illustrations 1-14,15 and 16 (shown on the next page). When completed, you will have a rectangle that is twice as tall as it is wide. A word of caution though: it's smart to PLAN AHEAD. Said another way, if you choose a rectangular size that is too small, you may end up with a tiny figure. It's also not a good idea to start so large that there will not be space to add the curve below, the ellipse above, and still have room for a pleasing finished appearance.

1-13   Distance from ellipse *center* to bottom curve *base line* is about twice the figure's horizontal span

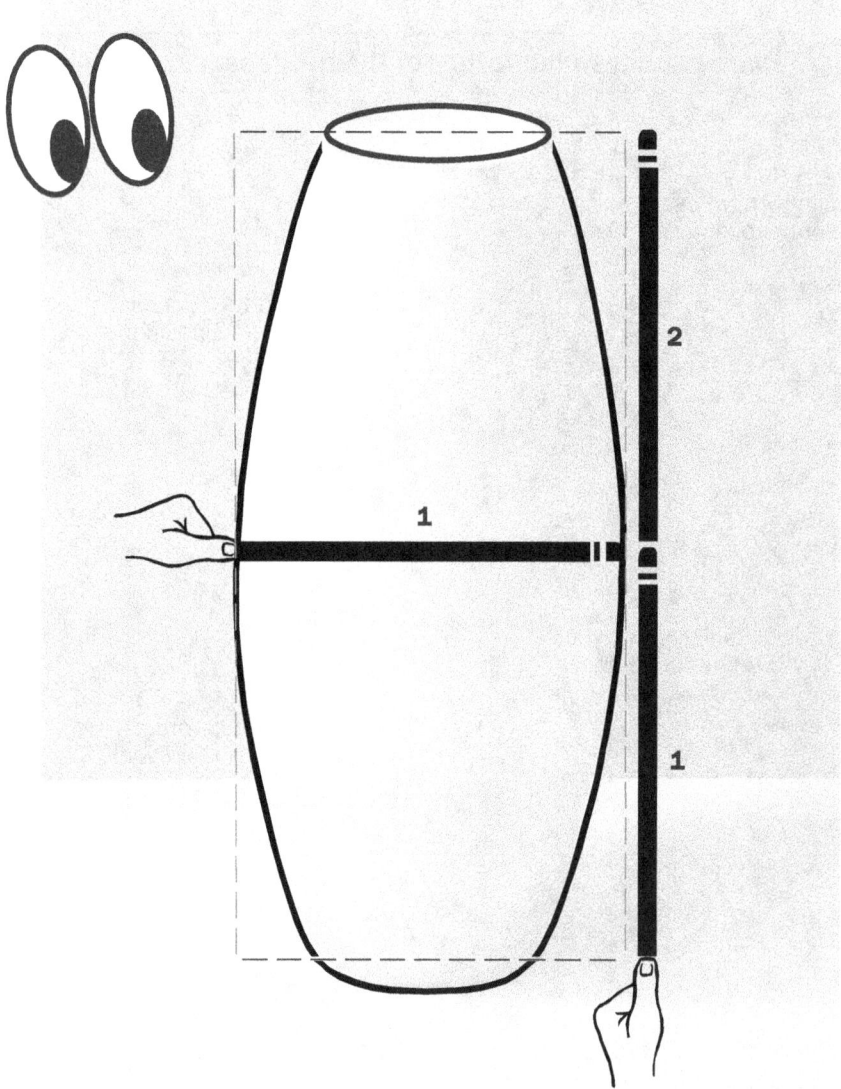

1-14 LIGHTLY center a square near the upper half of *your* paper

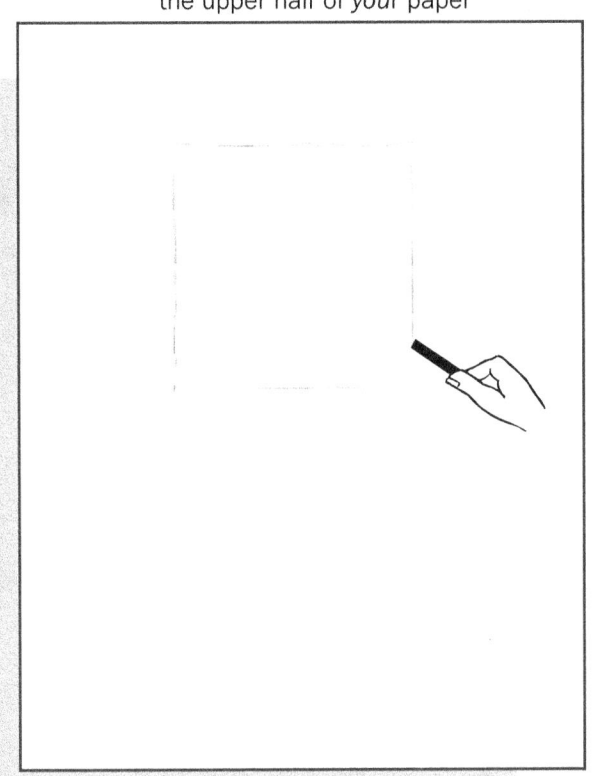

1-15 LIGHTLY attach a square of equal size to the bottom of your upper square

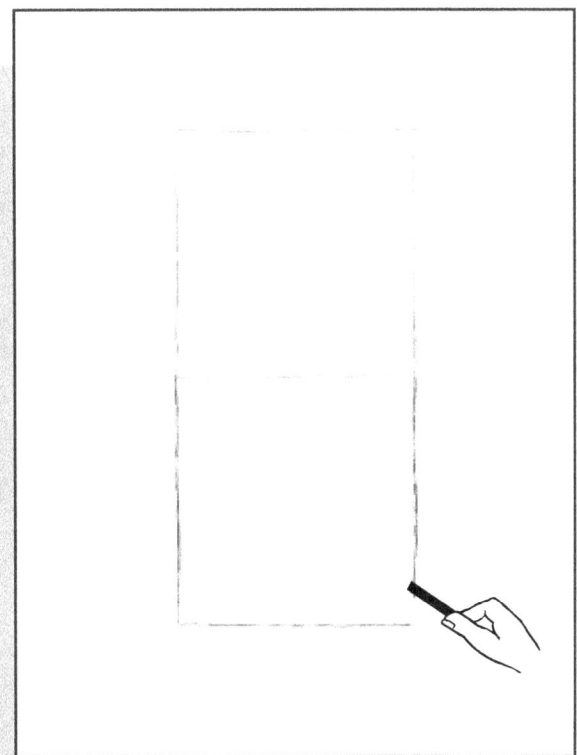

1-16 Erase middle line to make two squares into one rectangle

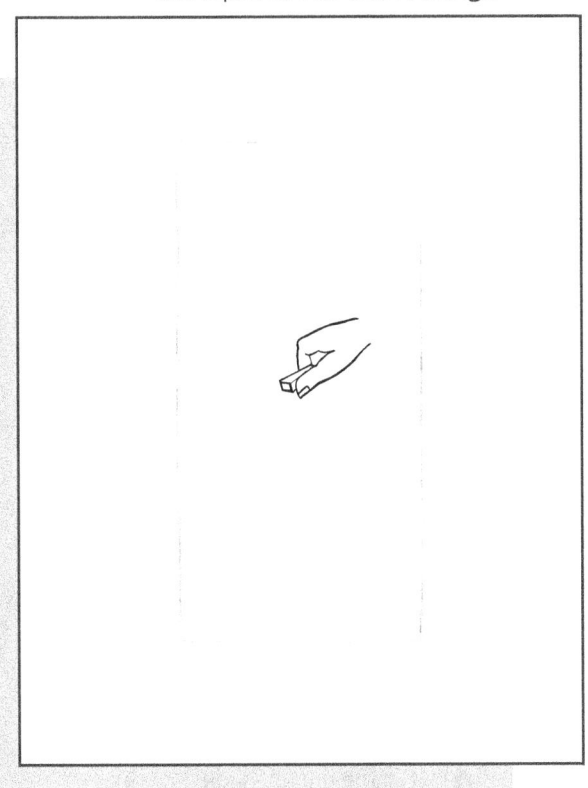

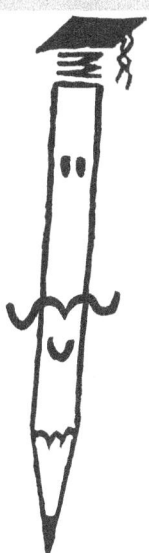

Did you draw lightly so you can easily erase? And did you plan ahead? If your rectangle is too big you will run out of room. If your rectangle is too small, your finished figure may end up being too little for your liking.

STEP 2 As illustration 1-17 indicates, please take a lateral (sideways) pencil check (or a visual) of the top ellipse. Then compare that horizontal unit of distance to the base curve. You will find that both spans are the same length. When you compare that to the figure's middle, you will discover another important feature. The distance extends slightly *past* center. You can convert (adapt) these observations *proportionally* to fit your drawing. Simply visualize, or take a horizontal pencil reading, slightly beyond half way across YOUR rectangle (1-18). Center that distance on the top of your rectangle and LIGHTLY mark it with two dots (1-19). Then do the same thing to the bottom of your rectangle (1-20).

1-17   Ellipse and base are equal distance across and
slightly longer than half way across the figure.

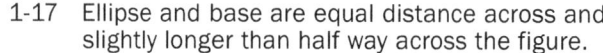

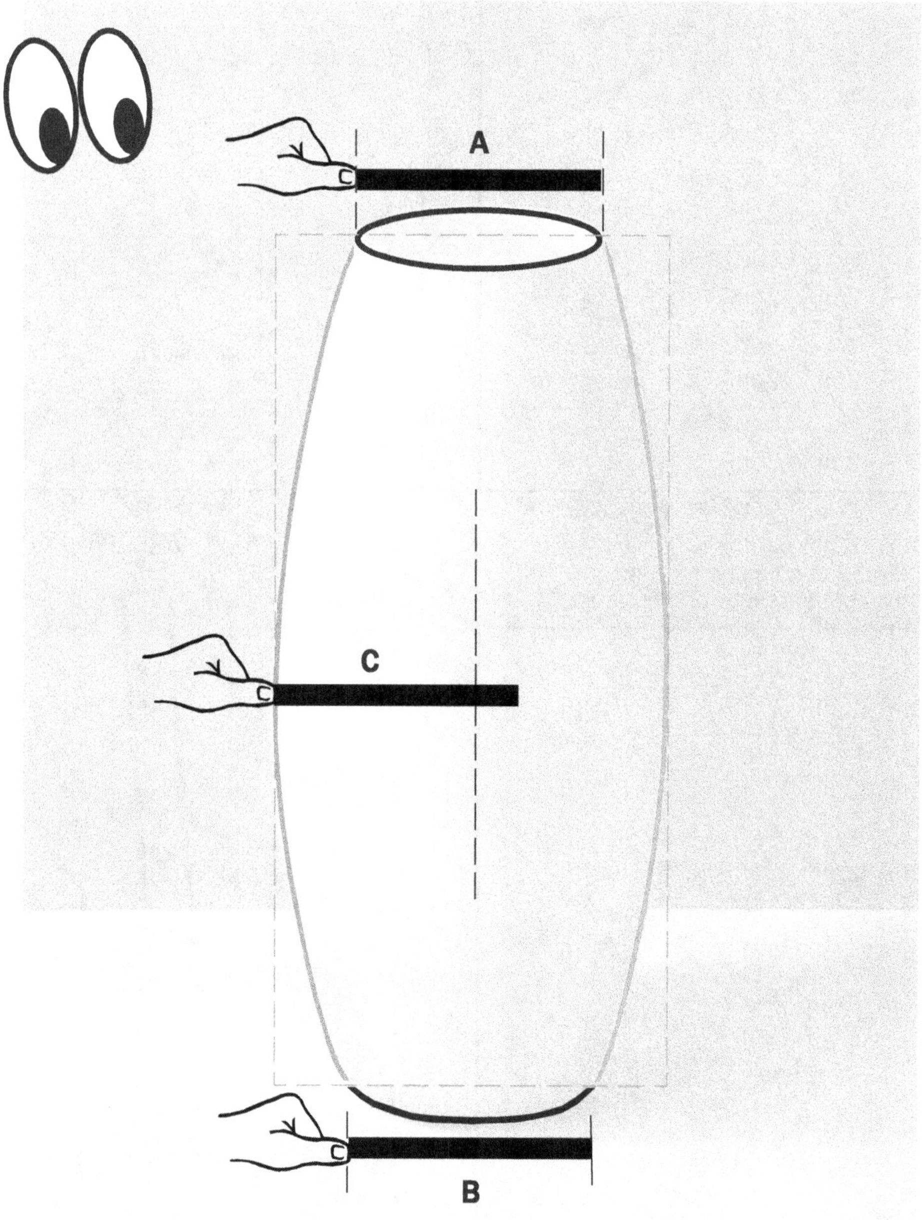

A

C

B

1-18 Estimate the horizontal distance slightly past center across your rectangle

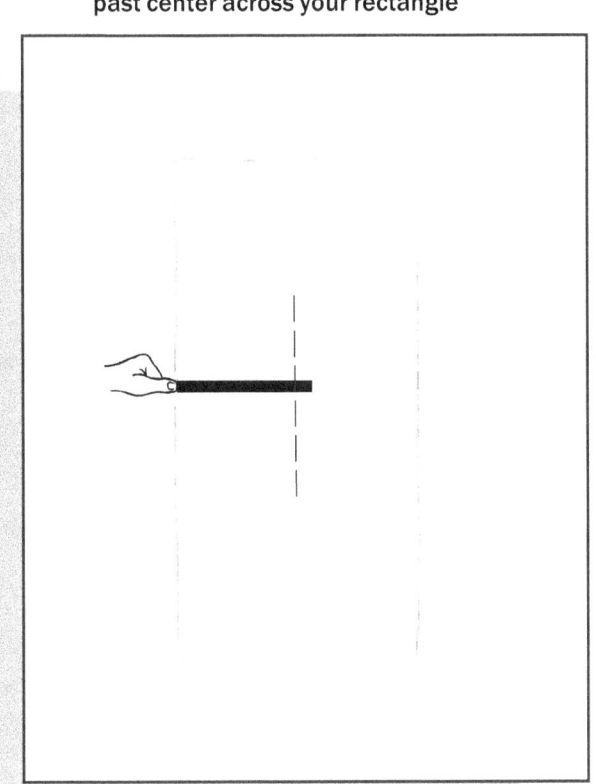

1-19 Center the span on the top of your rectangle and mark the distance with **2** dots

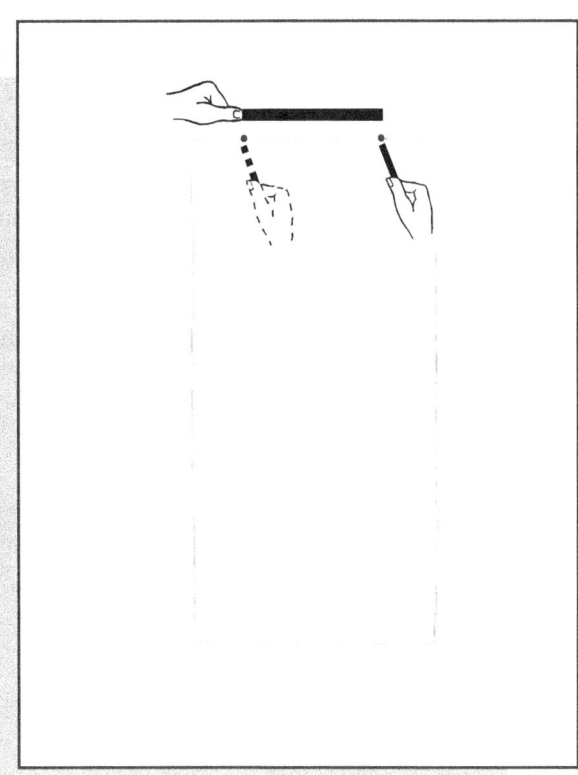

1-20 Center the span at the bottom of your rectangle and mark it with **2** dots

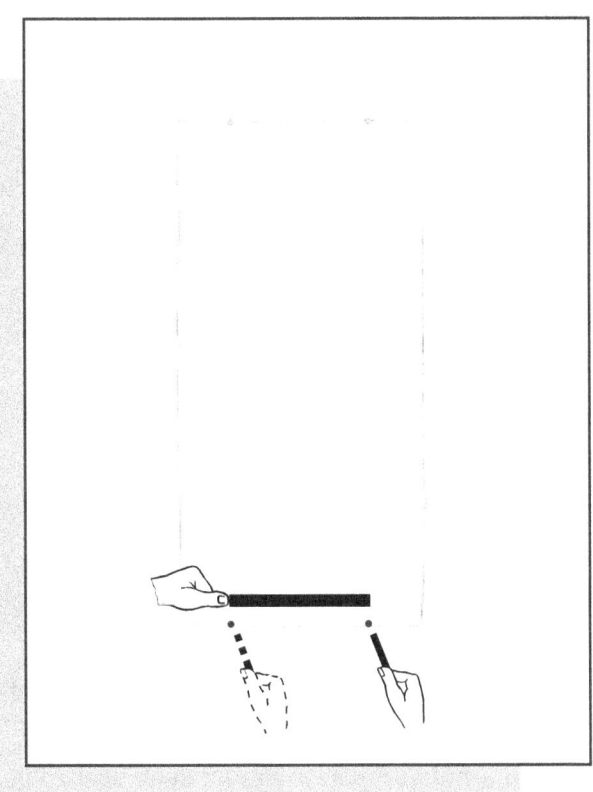

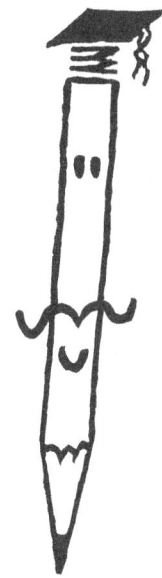

Please keep in mind that visual and pencil check distances are ESTIMATES. They are not exact measurements. That's why accuracy means visibly close. As your drawing develops, you can adjust it any time.

STEP 3 Illustration 1-21 shows us that even though we know the figure's *top* has a *front* and *back*, its proportion can be estimated *vertically* and *horizontally*. By doing this, we discover that the *height* of the top ellipse is about one fourth unit of distance compared to the length. The *base curve* height is about *half* that. You can apply these findings proportionally to suit *your* drawing. Begin by taking a visual, or pencil check, to find a quarter of the way between your two dots located on the *upper* part of your rectangle (1-22). Center the distance *vertically* above and below your left dot and mark it with two more dots. Next, using *half* that distance, position it at the *bottom* of your rectangle, beside your left dot. Mark the span with one more dot (1-23). These procedures will help locate your top ellipse and base curve in step 4. Beforehand though, you may want to *lightly* box-in the areas with guide lines (1-24).

1-21   Top Ellipse height is about 1/4 the length
Base curve height is about 1/2 the ellipse height

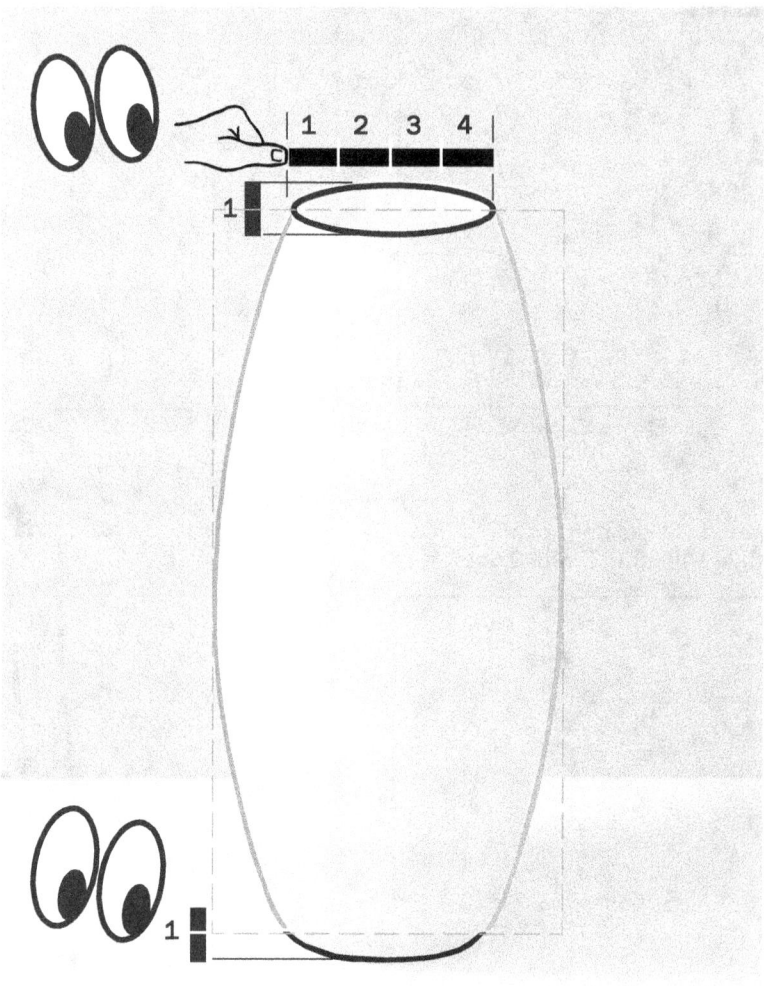

TIP As I mentioned at the outset, our view of the figure is mainly frontal, from slightly above. This makes the top *plane* appear to be elliptical, even though it's actually circular. In turn, there is a natural tendency to draw the ellipse wider than it looks, in an effort to convey the third dimension, known as *depth*. There is also a powerful urge to draw the *lower* part of the ellipse very narrow, thereby indicating it is closer to the front. At the same time, there is a strong desire to depict the *upper* part of the ellipse with more bow, trying to represent that it is in back and farther away. It's very important to remember however, that just like a conventional photo, your paper is flat. What am I implying? Simply that when drawing on a flat surface, you must keep switching three dimensional planes (surfaces) to *two dimensional* terms (horizontal and vertical).

1-22 Eyeball or pencil check 1/4 span
(bisect and subdivide)

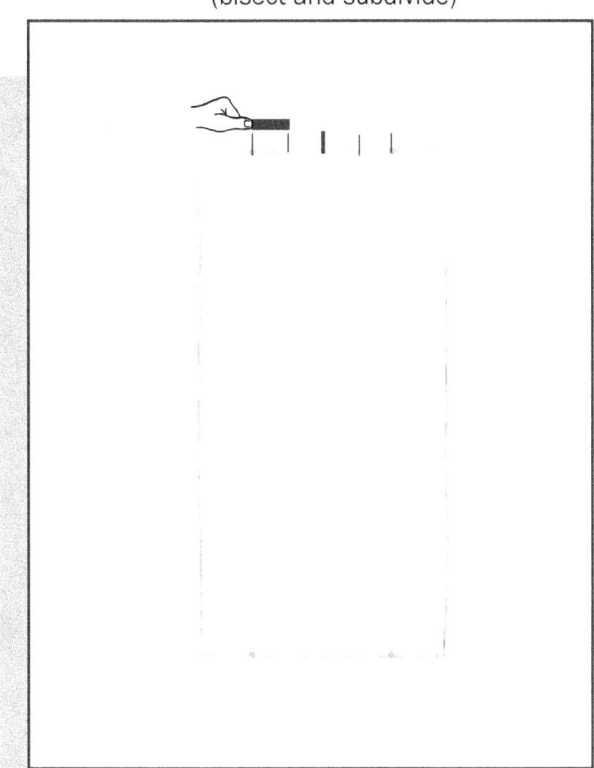

1-23 Center 1/4 span upright on top with 2 dots
Mark half of 1/4 span from bottom with 1 dot

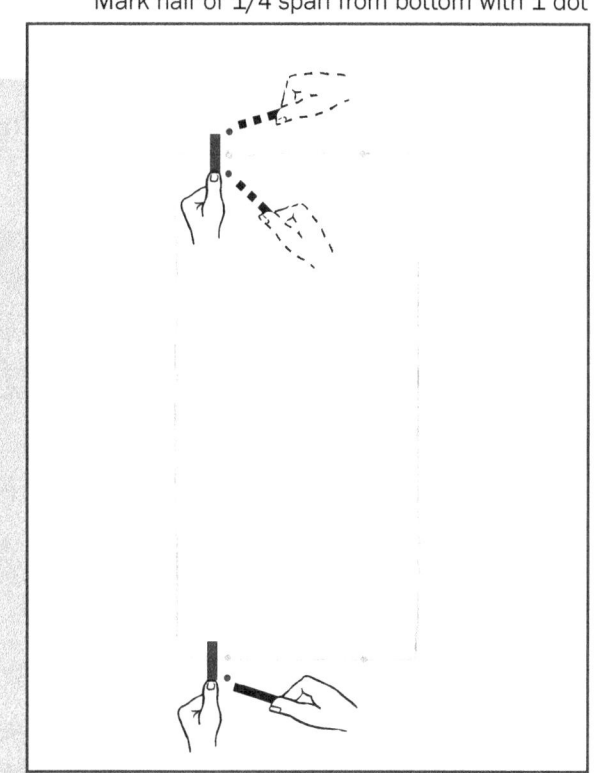

1-24 LIGHTLY box-in divisions with guide lines

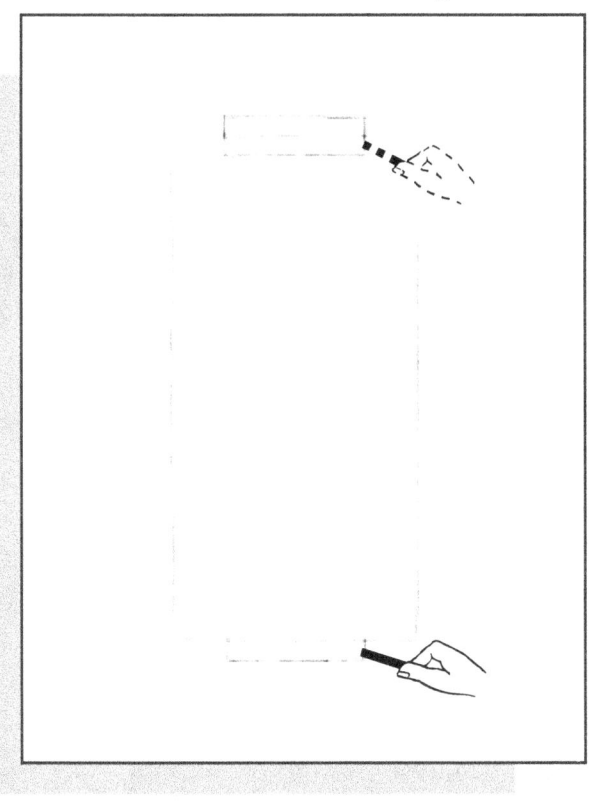

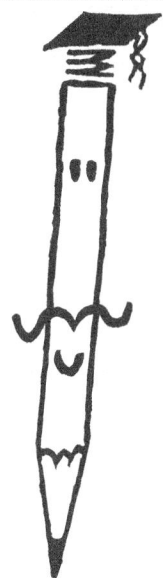

Occasionally, it is helpful to stop drawing in order to do a side-by-side double check. When you compare your work to the book illustration and your attention is directed only to observing, you will likely spot needed adjustments more easily.

STEP 4 Using illustration 1-25 as reference, lightly form *your* top ellipse to scale within your designated area. You can choose either the structural four or six curve method, or the laps/refinement method you practiced (1-26). Next, proceed to lightly draw your figure's bottom curve proportionally (1-27). If you have chosen to include guide lines, you may now erase them (1-28). Those of you who did not want guide lines, you only need to erase the mid-line in your ellipse, and the base line of your bottom curve.

1-25   Guide lines can help you form the top ellipse and base curve

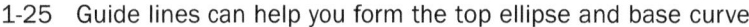

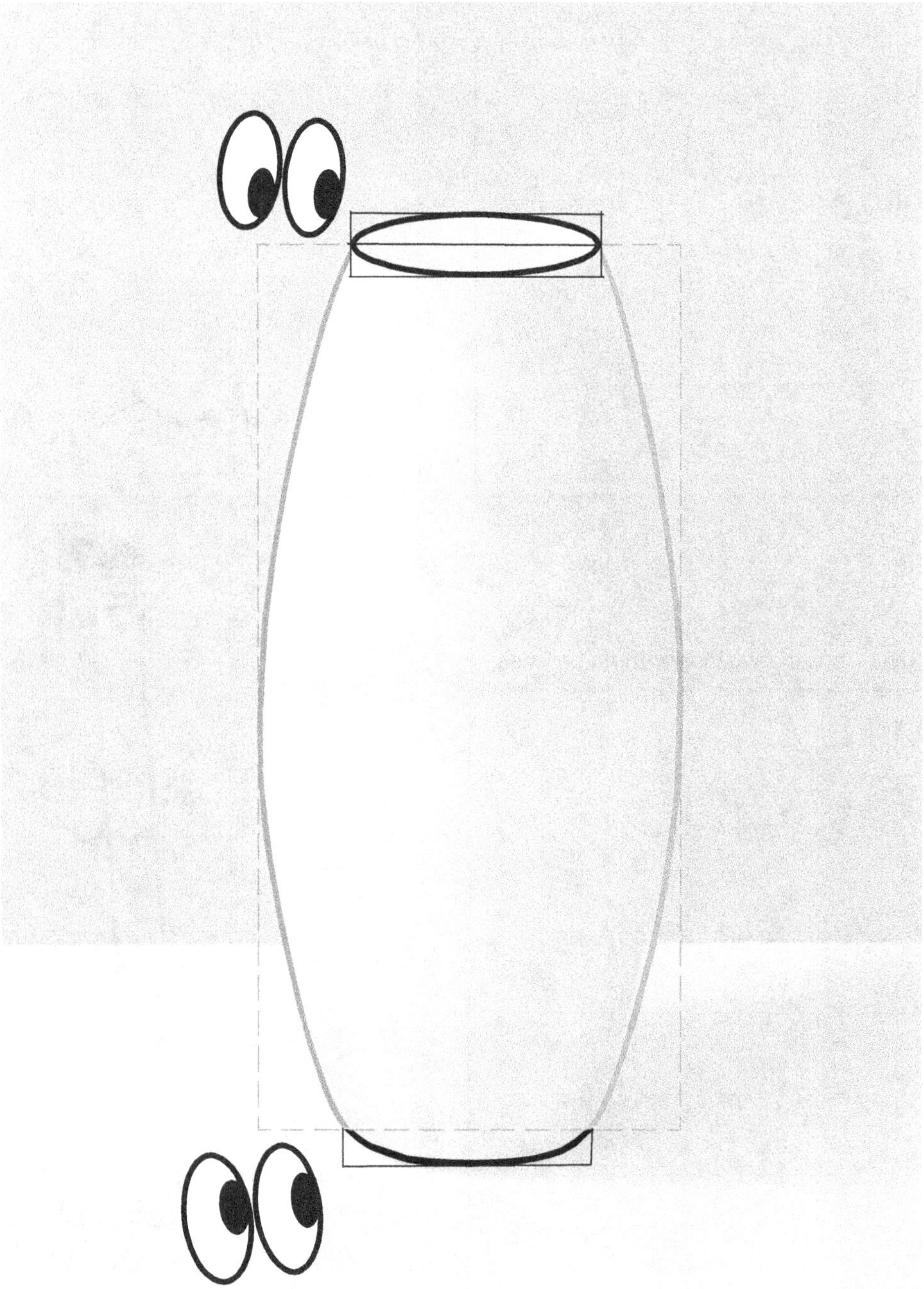

TIP Remember to also check the reverse spaces as you form your shapes.

1-26 *Lightly* draw top ellipse with curves
or use the lap/refinement method

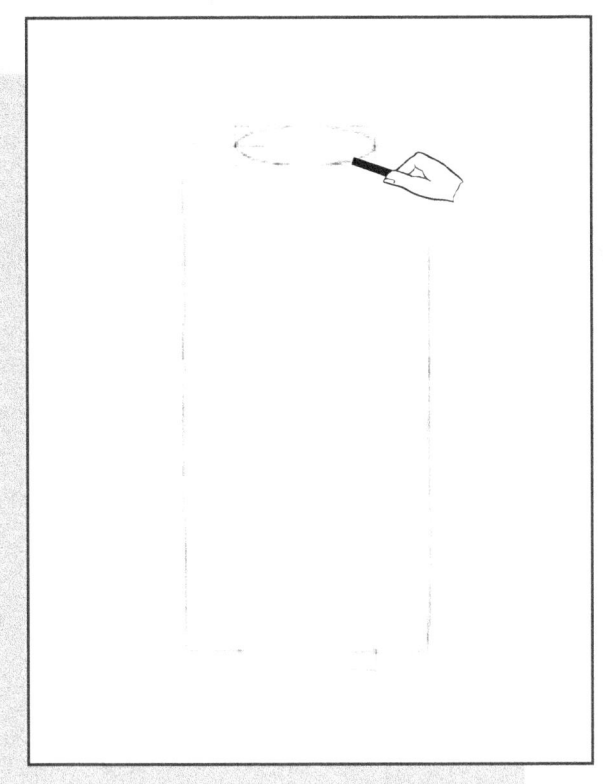

1-27 *Lightly* form the base curve

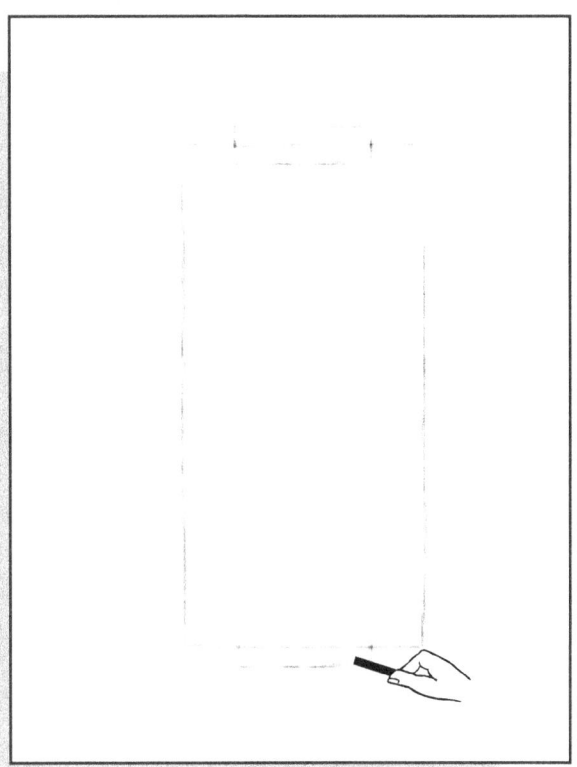

1-28 Erase guide lines

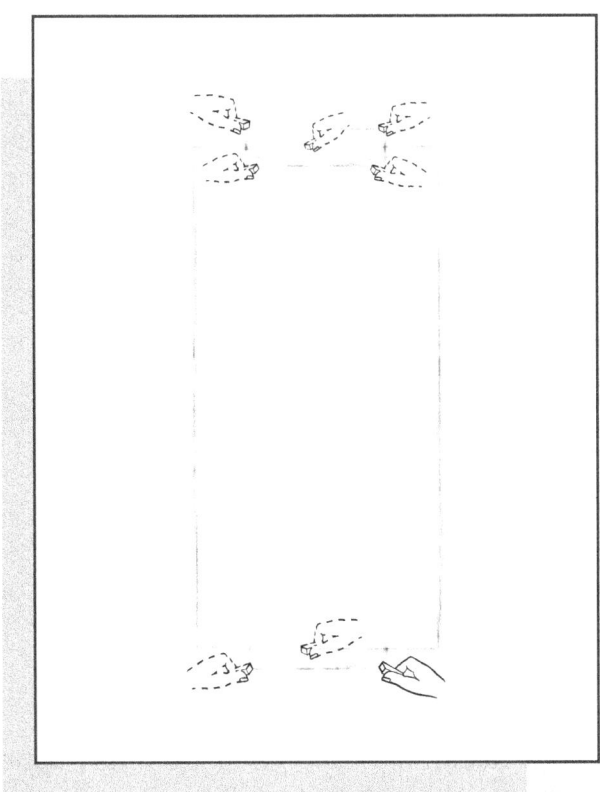

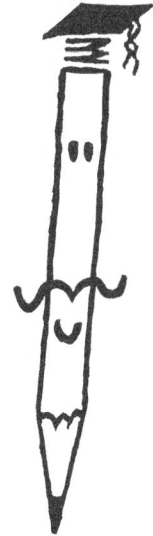

At times, you may find it a good practice to turn your paper and the book sideways in order to compare from a fresh point of view. If you will recall, this tends to reduce the visual effects of astigmatism and helps form your ellipse more accurately (visibly close).

STEP 5 Please note the reverse spaces shown white on illustration 1-29. They will serve as a helpful reference, enabling you to see the amount of bend more clearly, as you fashion your figure's sides, *one curve at a time*. You may use the *continuous line or sketch line* method (1-30,31,32). Afterward, go ahead and erase your guide lines (1-33).

1-29 The reverse spaces bordered by guide lines help you see
and draw the amount of curve in the figure's sides

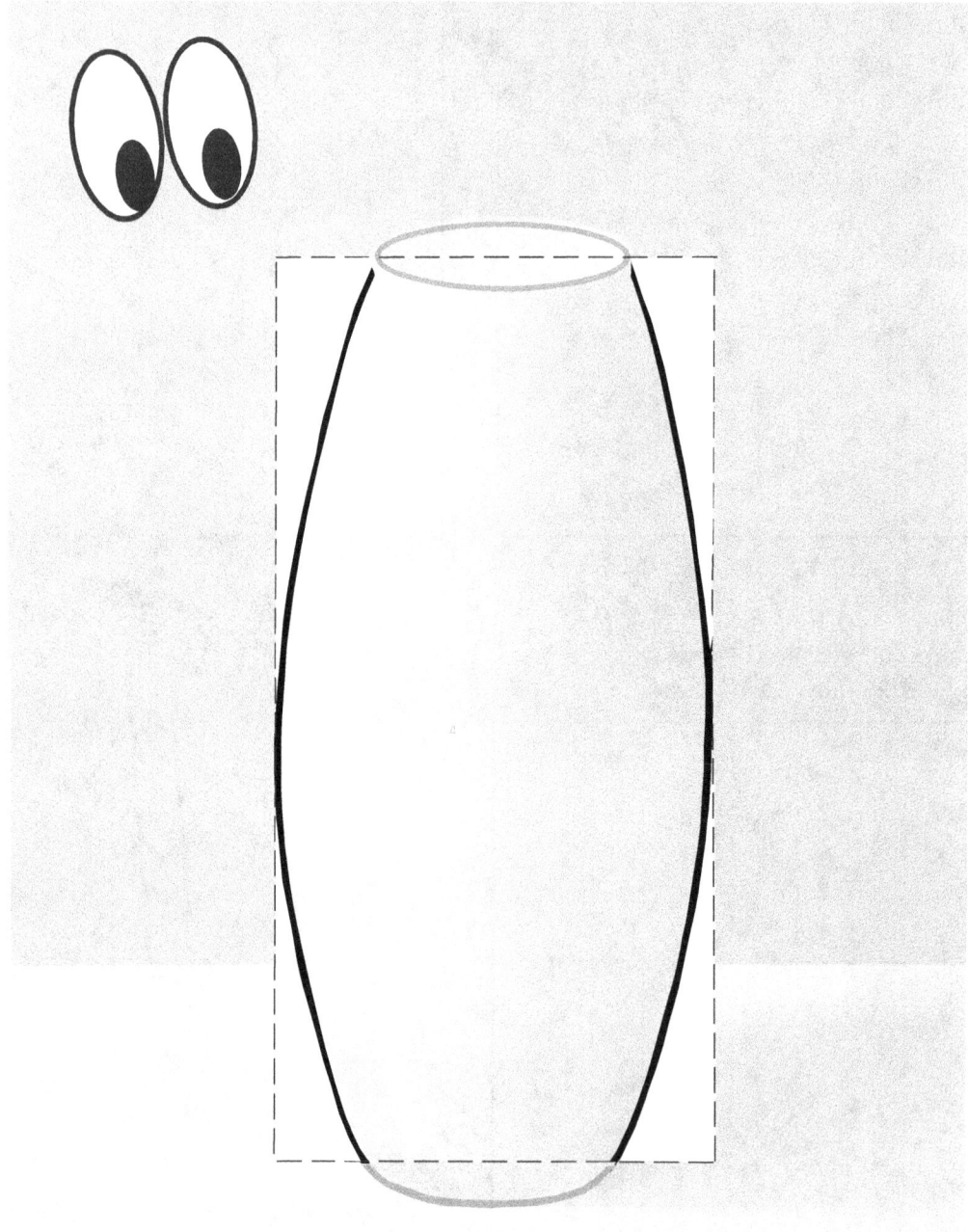

TIP A continuous line means once you start, you do not lift the pencil until *that line* is done. A sketch line is made with short, overlapping strokes by lifting the pencil between each mark.

1-30   Draw the upper half of the left side

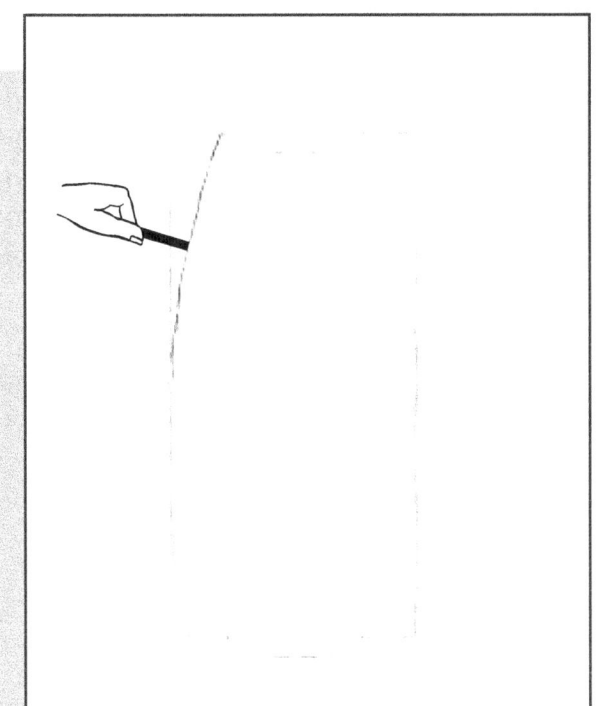

1-31   Fashion the lower half of the left side

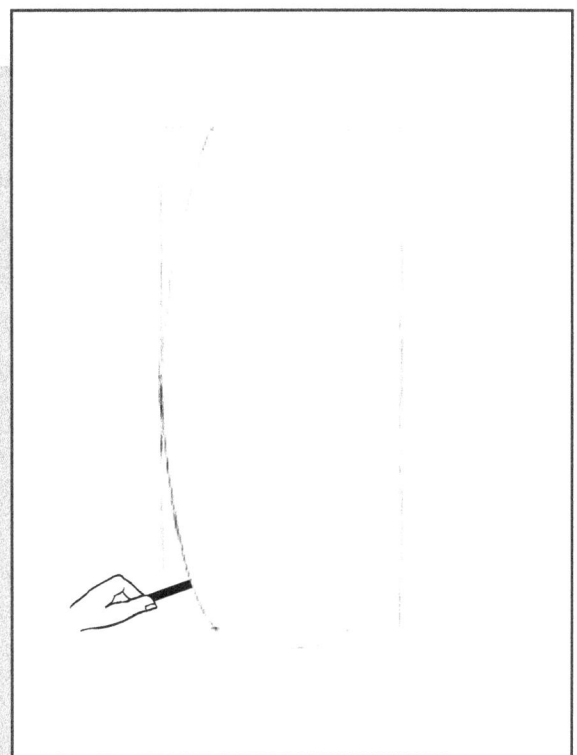

1-32   Form the upper & lower halves of right side

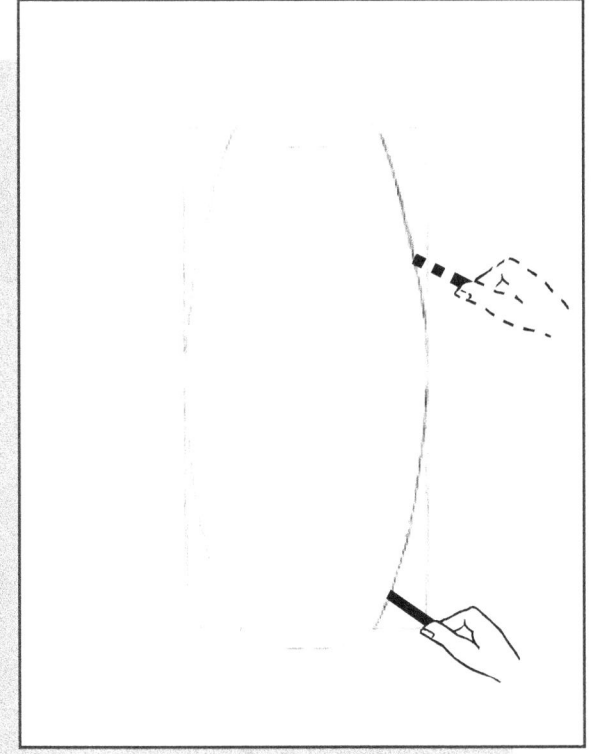

1-33   Erase guide lines marked "x"

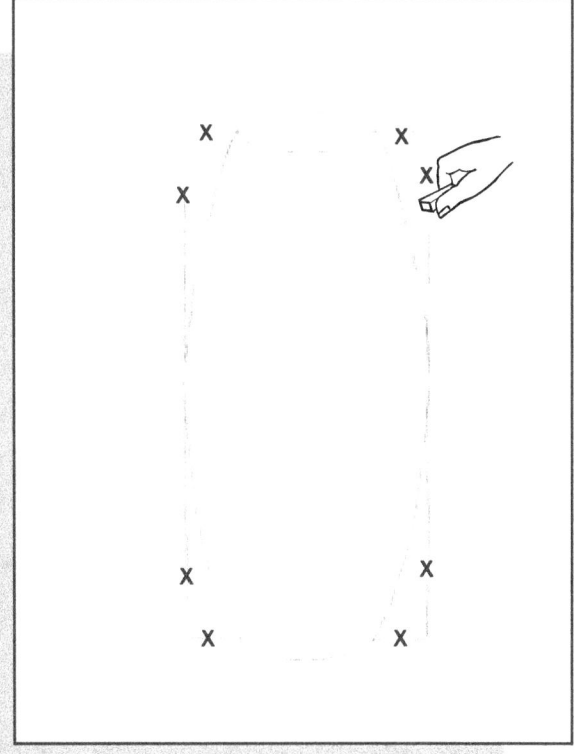

-15-

STEP 6 Pretend you have x-ray vision and imagine that you can see through the figure. Eyeball (estimate by eye) or pencil check where the back of the table would cut across the figure. The distance is about one quarter of the way up from the base to the middle of the top ellipse. In order to apply this observation, mark the respective *mid-point* on YOUR figure's side with a dot. Bisect the lower half and place another dot to locate the *quarter* span (1-35). Next, draw a level line from one edge of your paper to the other(1-36). Then erase the *excess line inside* your figure (1-37). The extra step may seem unnecessary, but it assures that your two remaining lines are aligned.

1-34 Line representing table edge locates 1/4 distance up from base to ellipse center

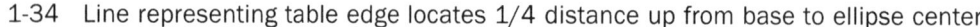

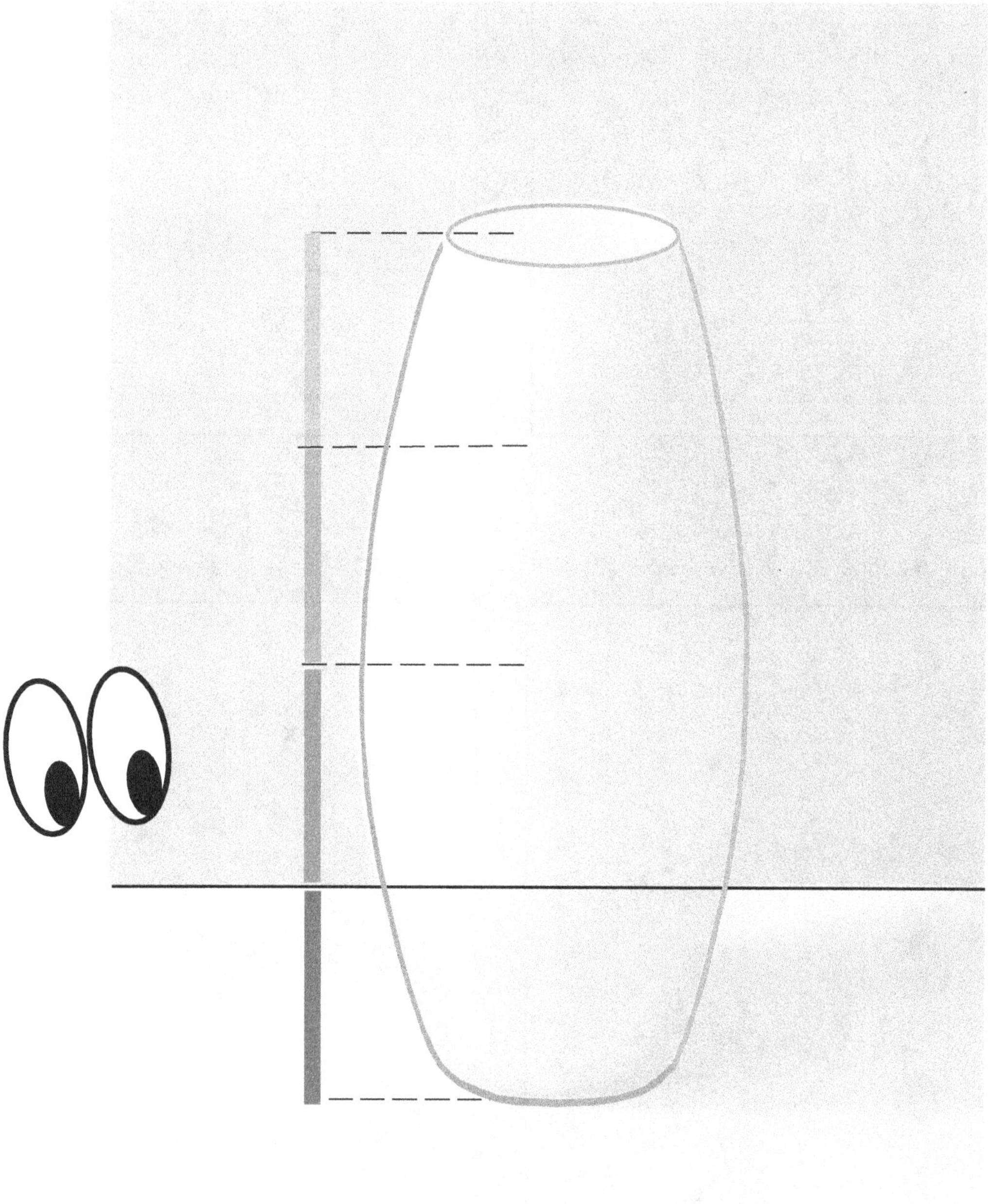

1-35 Mark 1/2 way between base & mid-ellipse
Subdivide lower 1/2 to find 1/4 distance

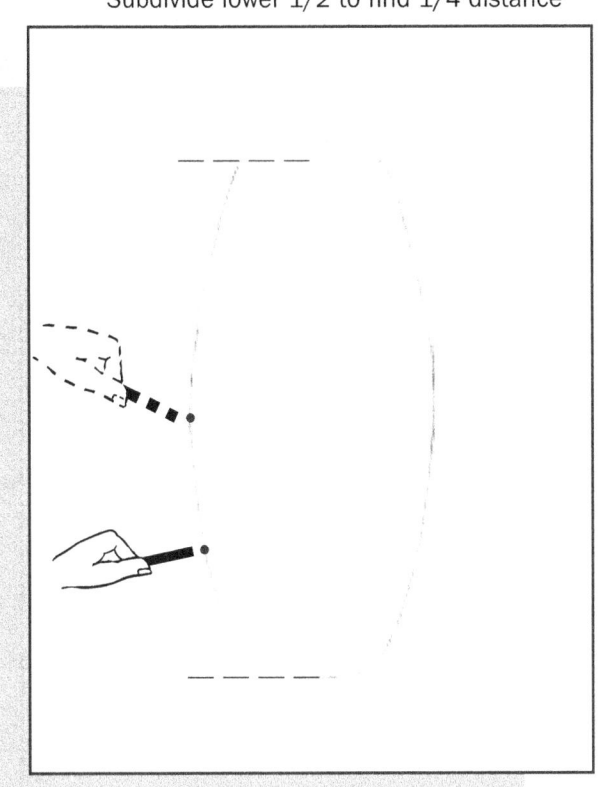

1-36 Lightly draw a level line paper edge to
to edge through your 1/4 distance mark

1-37 Erase excess line *inside* your figure

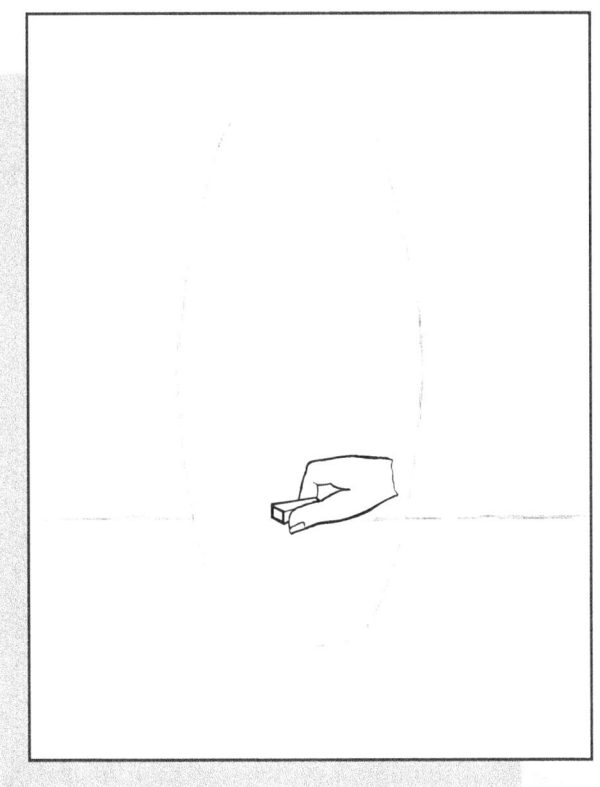

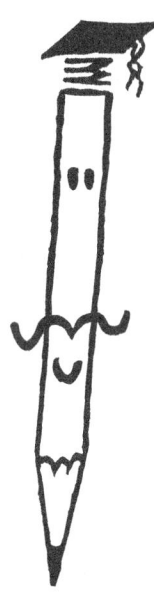

Bravo! Your line drawing is
nearly finished. The next
page reveals one more very
important step.

STEP 7 I'm sure you agree, it's smart to pause now and again to study your work in progress. This enables you to concentrate entirely on possible revisions. After all, nobody is perfect. And when it comes to drawing, virtually everything is a *visual estimate*, not an exact measure. Evaluation/modification is part of the routine, both while drawing *and* afterward. For instance, you can stand your picture beside this page and compare them side-by-side from a slight distance, by glancing back and forth (1-38). You can also rotate your drawing and this page, and do the same thing for yet another view. Plus, you may choose to use a mirror for an inverse (backward) look. Unexpected differences will surprisingly seem to stick out, providing you with valuable opportunities to verify accuracy.

1-38 Example side-by-side comparison with book illustration reveals ellipse in drawing is proportionally too tall

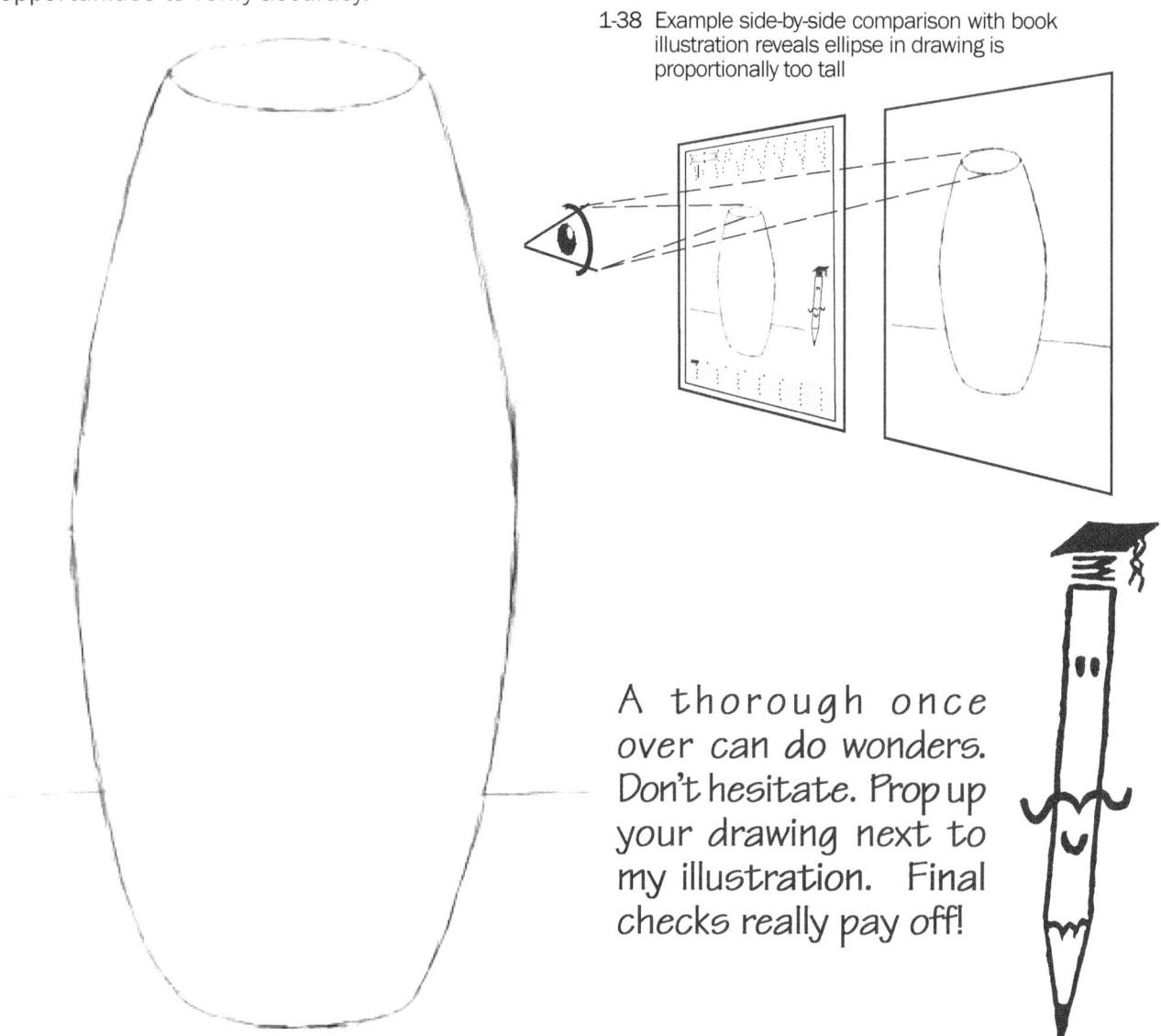

A thorough once over can do wonders. Don't hesitate. Prop up your drawing next to my illustration. Final checks really pay off!

TIP It's important that your shapes are accurate. For just as it is unwise to add walls to a house with shoddy framing, shading shouldn't be applied to a poor line drawing. To help find where adjustment may be necessary, look for the OBVIOUS first. Begin with proportion, then possible tilting and curvature irregularities. Although you may feel the urge to tally everything and rush to modify all your findings at once, please resist the impulse. *Search for one thing at a time.* When you spot something amiss, *adjust* and *verify* (make certain the change improved your drawing). Then, repeat the cycle. As you do, keep in mind that you are *not* searching for "mistakes." You are seeking to make *improvements.* Choosing to be content with less than you are capable of, because you might spoil what you have, cheats your potential. On the other hand, continuing to modify when your revisions do not make much difference could do more harm than good. For a practical solution, I recommend the following rule. *When your drawing appears reasonably accurate to you, that's a sensible place to stop.*

Ellipse is proportionally too tall & not wide enough

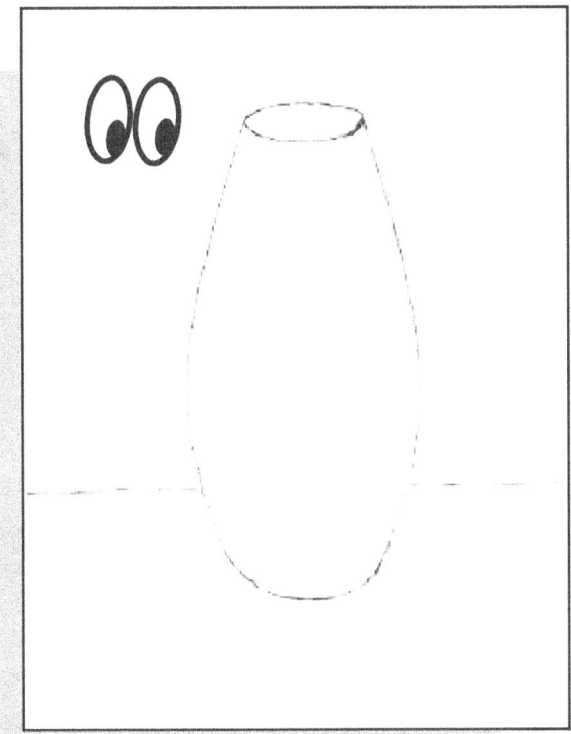

Result after ellipse was changed proportionally

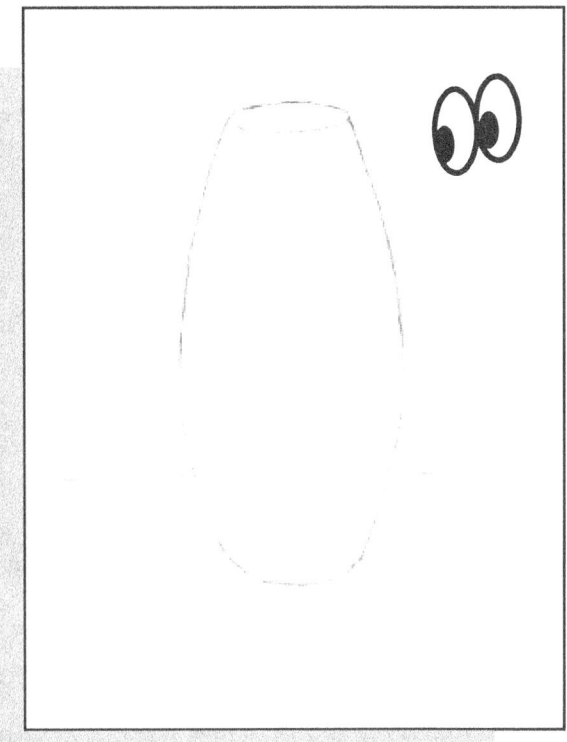

Proportionally, figure is too short or chubby

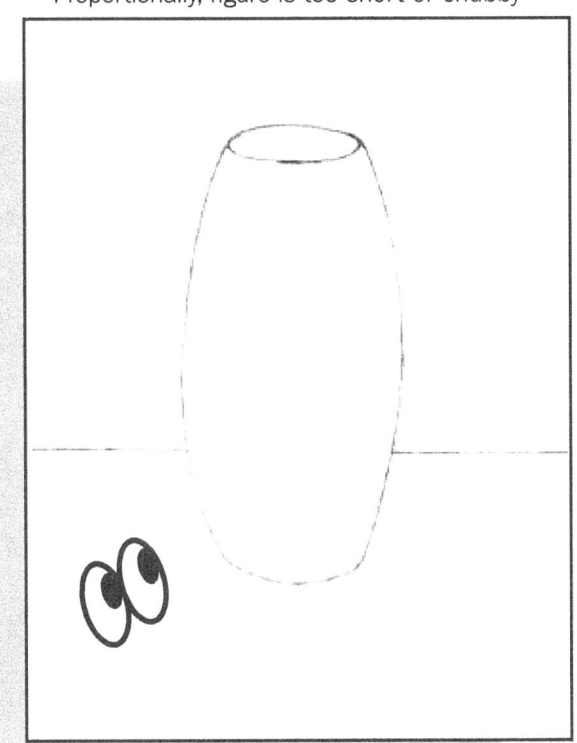

Result after base was lowered

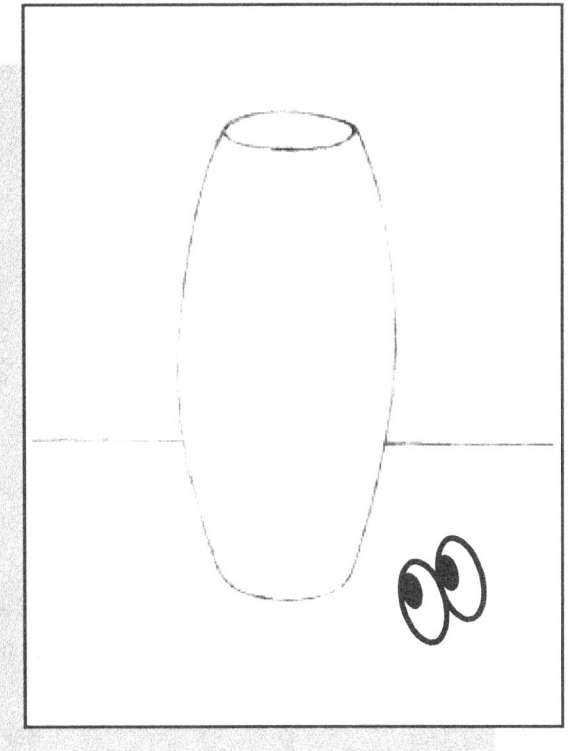

TIP Having studied the samples, I trust you learned from them. You see, the true measure of your achievement is not whether you think your drawing equalled or exceeded these. It's what you learned that counts.

Chapter 1
FOLLOW-UP

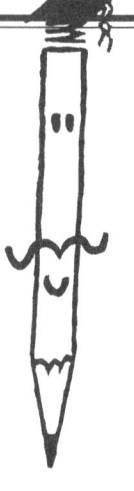

You've learned a lot, haven't you? Let's recap.

1. Becoming familiar with your subject BEFORE you begin to draw is very helpful.

2. Shapes can be taken apart with your eyes.

3. Squinting (partly closing your eyes) helps to see basic shapes more easily.

4. Much of what you are searching for is right there in front of you, but you have to take the time to look.

5. When drawing on flat surfaces, it is important to see shapes in two dimensional terms: horizontal and vertical.

6. Drawing is a process which can be organized into manageable steps and stages.

7. At the start, it's sensible to plan ahead by taking placement and size into consideration. Otherwise you might run out of room, or end up with a drawing that is smaller than you may have wanted.

8. Drawing lightly is smart because you can erase guide lines and make adjustments more easily.

9. Real or imaginary, guide lines are a worthwhile means by which to "map out" (or chart) a course for shape.

10. With either guide lines or the laps method, you can form ellipses more accurately.

11. The TRUSTY SEVEN, namely reference points, alignments, straight lines, angles, curves, proportion, and reverse space are fundamental ways to observe, draw and adjust shapes.

12. Whether the model you are working from is real or a picture, pausing to stand back and make side by side comparisons is not only a smart practice during the drawing stages, but afterward as well.

All told, this is quite a tally, indeed.
Now that you're off to a marvelous start, always remember:

Successful drawing doesn't stem from able HANDS alone.
It also comes from skillful THINKING and OBSERVING.

Chapter 2

FROM THIS

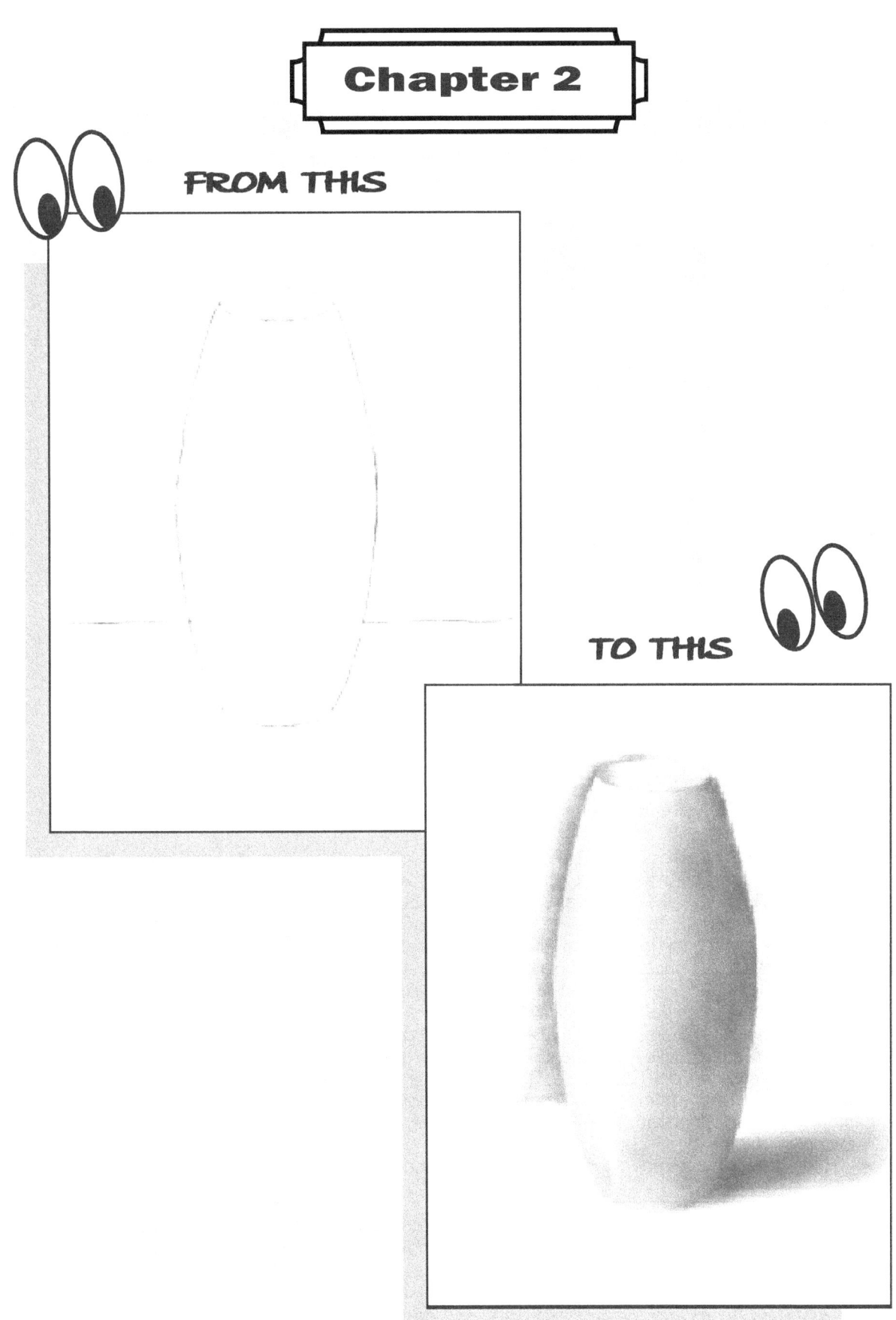

TO THIS

It's nearly time to apply tones, but first let's see how their VALUES affect the scene, namely: BACKGROUND, FIGURE and GROUND.

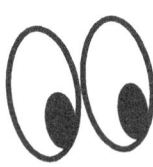

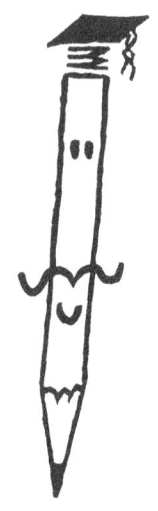

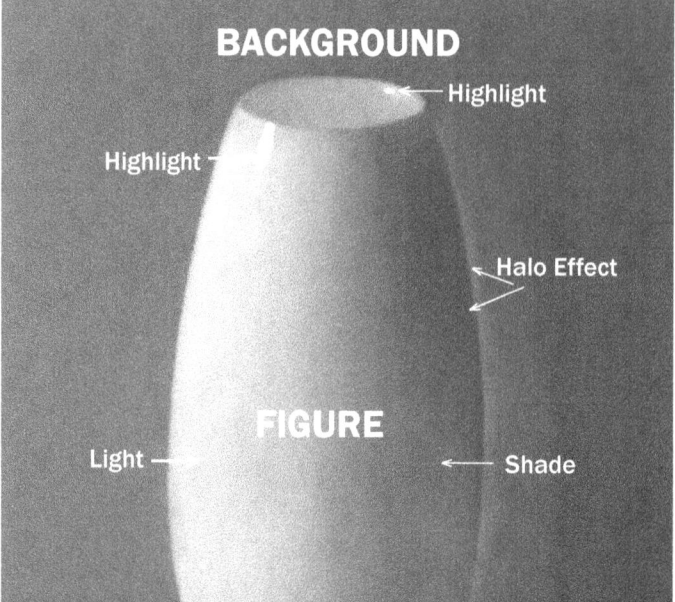

BACKGROUND

→ Highlight

Highlight →

← Halo Effect

2-1

FIGURE

Light →

← Shade

Highlight →

Cast Shadow

GROUND

The tones on the FIGURE where light is most intense are called *highlights*. In our view, *light* is coming from the left. It can't reach the figure's opposite side, causing that part to be in *shade*, nearly black like the BACKGROUND. The GROUND (probably a table top), as well as the side of the figure facing the light, are both essentially a medium gray. As for the *cast shadow*, it is about the same *VALUE* as the figure's shade side. In general it's fair to say then that there is very little difference, or *low CONTRAST*. Because of that, in some places boundaries are especially difficult to see. Even the faint *halo effect*, making the shade edge seem just a little darker and the background edge beside it seem a little lighter, does little to help the visibility (2-1). Must we tone our drawing likewise? Of course not. We have choices and can play a game of "what-if." For instance, imagine what would happen if the ground and background darkness were *decreased* slightly. The change would make the figure stand out a little more, although maybe not enough (2-2). On the other hand, causing *high CONTRAST* by leaving the background and ground white as the paper, appears excessive (2-3). An effective third alternative might be a medium gray tone bordering the figure's edge before fading into the white background (2-4). Get the hint? How a real scene or a photograph appears doesn't require that we make an identical copy. We can improvise by exercising options and create our own unique version. That's how we can make something ordinary appear extraordinary.

TIP CONTRAST means *difference*. Here they are tones. *VALUE* is the *intensity* (strength) of tones. This make them visibly different. For instance, a strong light tone compared to a very dark tone shows *high contrast* because we can see a big difference between the *values*. Tones that are close in *value* (all fairly dark or all very light) bring about *low contrast*. Where the boundary between form and space meet, the tone edges seem to *intensify*. I call this the *HALO EFFECT*. You can see it bordering the above figure's shade side and the background. Study the edges of each figure on the following page. Notice the changes in the halo effect due to various *contrasts* between figure, ground and background.

2-2 Option A. Make background tone somewhat lighter than in photo

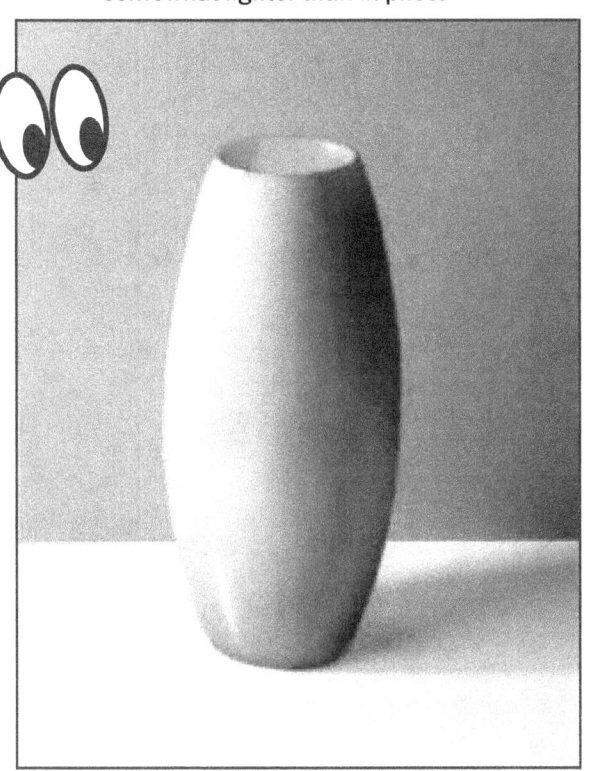

2-3 Option B. Background & ground stay paper tone white, separated by a line

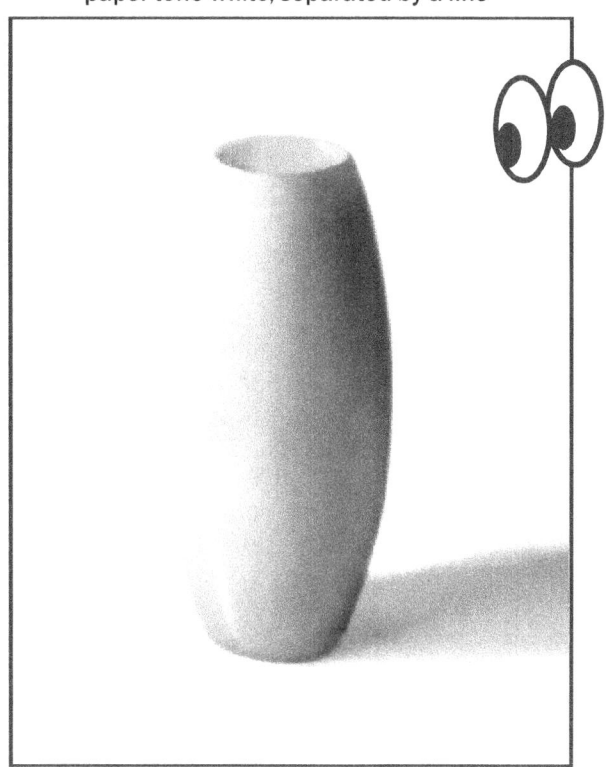

2-4 Option C. Ground stays paper white Background fades from gray to white

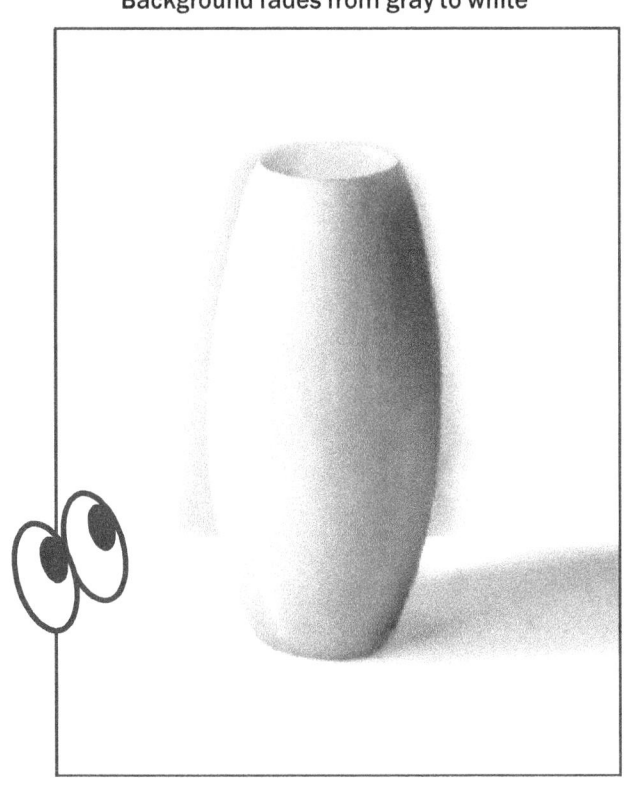

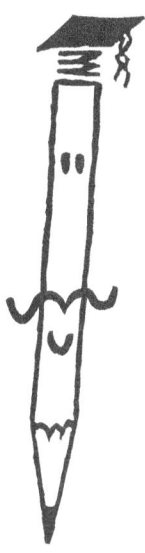

Option "C" seems favorable. Now, we are ready to do some toning, or what is commonly referred to as "shading."

Let's Begin Toning

STEP 1 **WHERE SHALL WE START?** I think the background is the best place to start toning, rather than starting with the figure. Why? Because, if you tone your figure *before* the background, you could be in for a shock. Due to visual mixing called *"assimilation,"* the tones on your figure may look fine against the white of your paper. However, they would probably appear too low in contrast *after* background tone is applied. With this in mind, whether you are a "righty" or "lefty," I suggest you practice first. On a sheet of paper, create several different consistent tones of gray, preferably with the underhand method, so your hand doesn't block your view. The technique might feel a little awkward, but soon you will get the hang of it (2-5). Once you feel confident and ready, begin toning your *background* by placing the side of the pencil point slightly above center on your top ellipse. Stroke gently with even pressure, only *RIGHT-TO-LEFT, not back and forth.* This will help keep the strokes from invading the figure. As soon as your marks reach the upper side (your left) vary the distance occasionally, for a more fluid appearance. Continue down until your reach your horizontal line representing the back of the table top and stop (2-6). In order to tone the background area bordering your figure's *right* edge, switch to a *LEFT-TO-RIGHT* direction and reduce pressure a bit (2-7). Next, using the background tone for contrast, prepare to tone your *figure.* Since its shape is basically a cylinder with a bulging middle, you will need to indicate the curved surface, or plane. How? It's simple. Start on the shade side (your right). With increased pressure and *RIGHT-TO-LEFT* strokes, begin slanting *downward* and limit the lengths to about one fifth of the way across your figure. By the time your strokes reach half way down, they should level out and gradually start tilting upward, all the way to the base (2-8). After having completed the shade area, use the same method and tone another stripe of equal width beside it (to the left). *Reduce* pressure because this part is the *mid- tone* between the side facing shade and the side facing light (2-9).

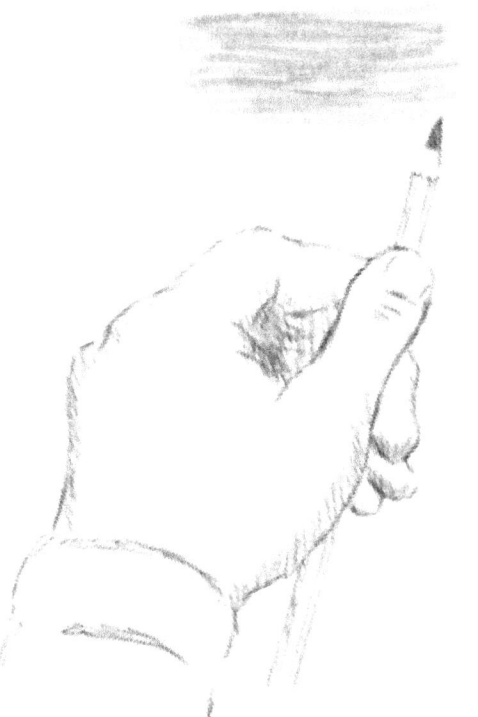

2-5 Right handed or left handed practice stroking *underhand*

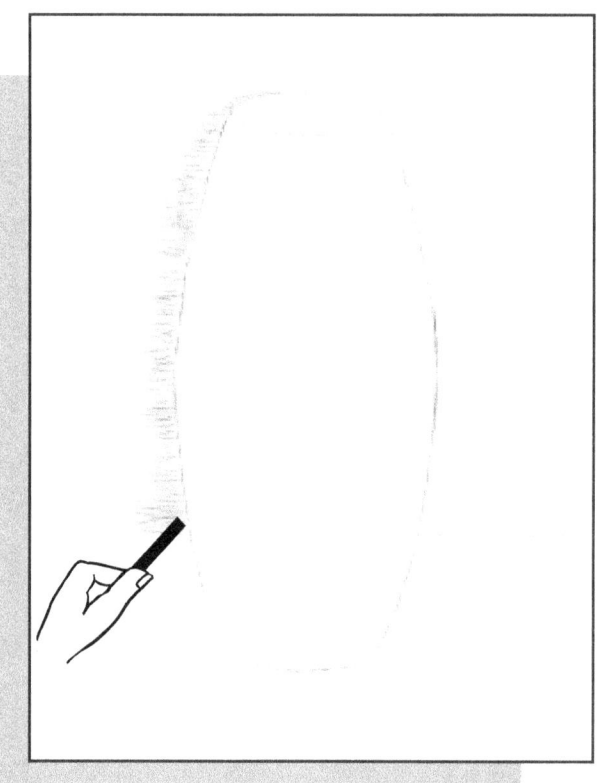

2-6 Tone background bordering figure on *your* left

TIP Do not erase if/when strokes go astray. Later steps will attend to them.

2-7 Tone *background* bordering figure on *your* right

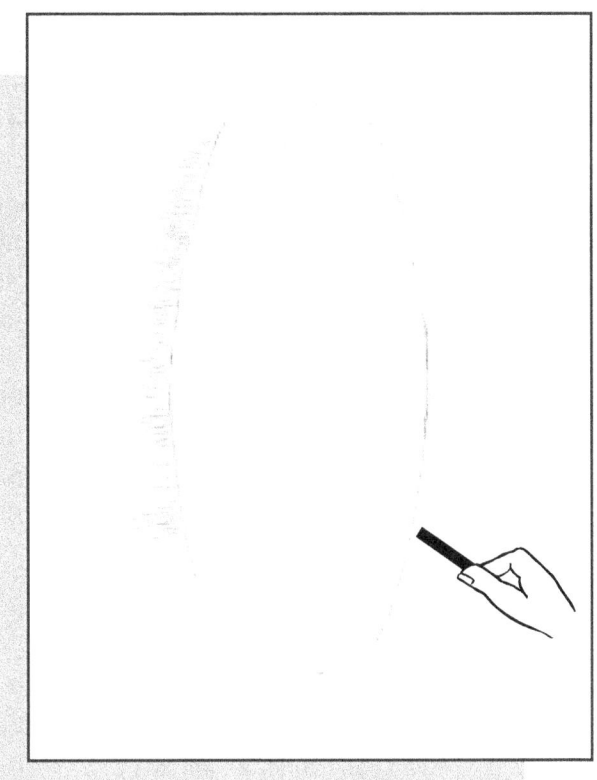

2-8 Tone the shade portion of your figure

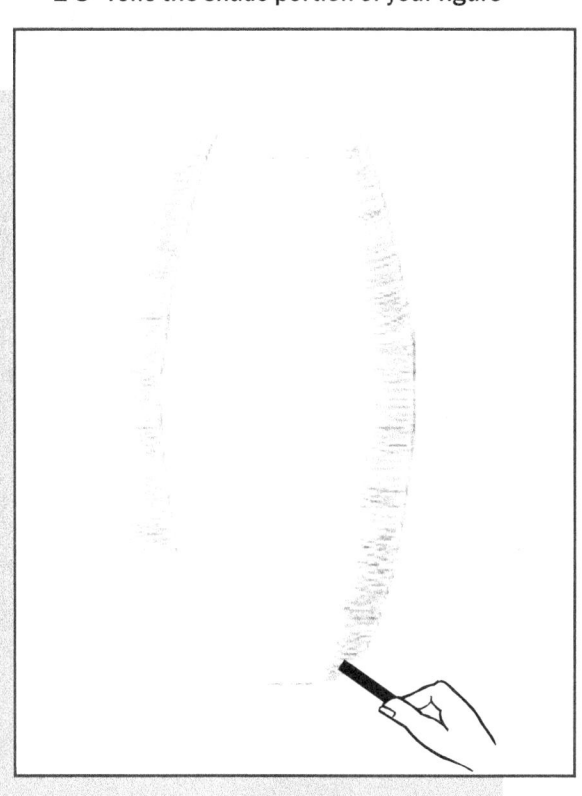

2-6 Attach the *mid-tone* beside your figure's shade area

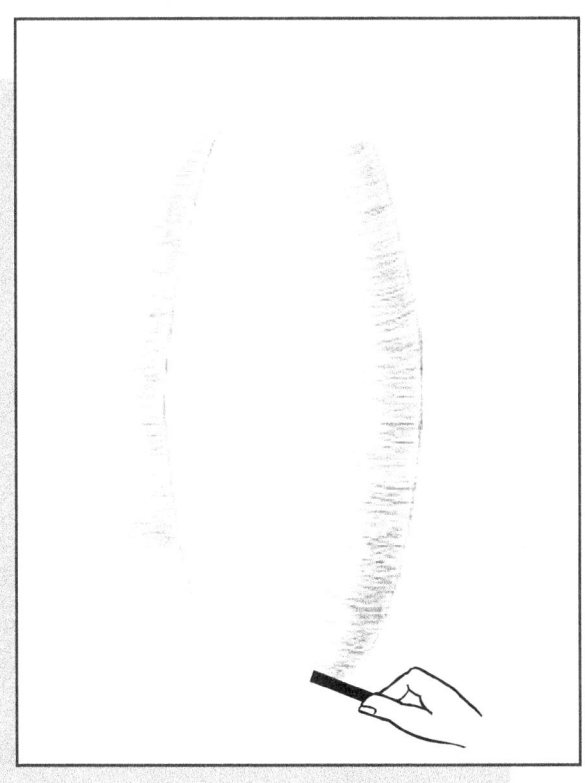

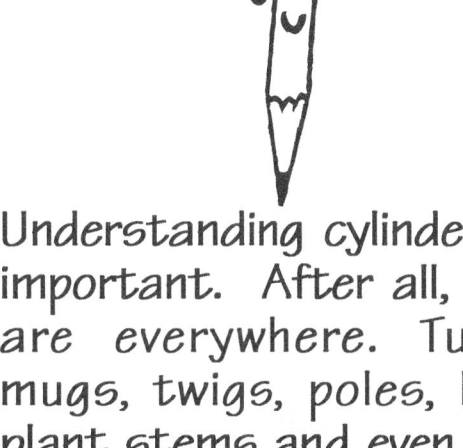

Understanding cylinders is important. After all, they are everywhere. Tubes, mugs, twigs, poles, logs, plant stems and even your arms are cylindrical, to name a few. Think how many other things are cylindrical.

STEP 2 For the figure's side facing your left, you will need a very light tone. The purpose is to indicate the curved plane where light strikes but not as strongly as the highlight. For this procedure, start below the top ellipse, stroke gently, *left-to-right*. Angle a bit downward, at first. By the time your strokes reach midway, on route to the base, they should level out, then begin tilting *upward* (2-7). Since less light strikes the *figure's opening*, represented by the top ellipse, proceed to softly tone that part as well. Use *back and forth* strokes (2-8). Then, darken the tone of the small inside portion on your left with a kind of letter "C" shape. This will indicate that even less light is able to reach there (2-9). Next comes the cast shadow. Closest to the figure, the tone should be as dark, or *slightly* darker than the shade side of the figure. It gradually becomes less dark farther away (where light begins to penetrate). To accomplish this effect, first apply a tone with soft pressure, preferably *left-to-right*, instead of back and forth. If you consider yourself "soft handed," keep your strokes closer together. If you are "strong handed" (tend to press hard) *leave some space* between strokes. The combination of your white paper and gray marks should visually assimilate, in other words, "mix" to the desired intensity (2-10). For the darker part of the cast shadow, use short sweeping motions to "feather" in some more tone. Increase pressure at the start of each stroke, then ease up as it moves toward the right, before you lift the pencil (2-11).

2-7 VERY GENTLY tone side on your left
varying your strokes angles

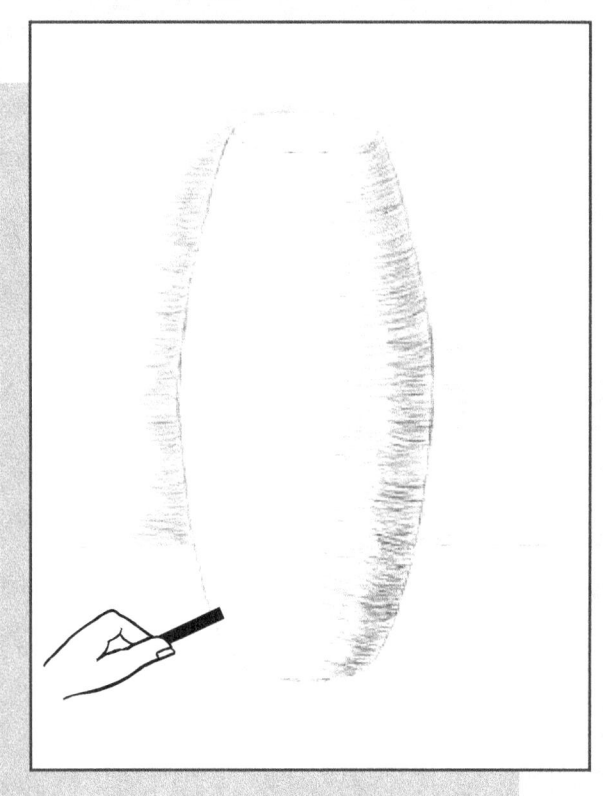

2-8 GENTLY tone your top ellipse
with back and forth strokes

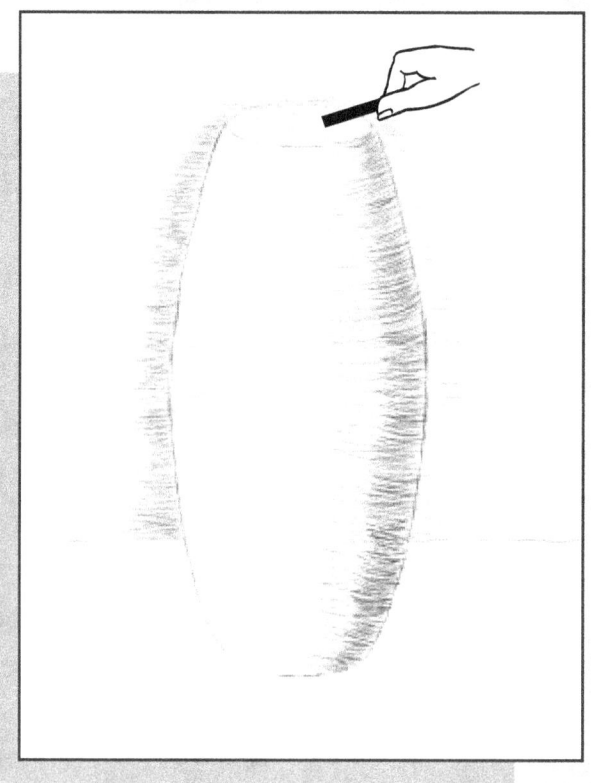

TIP When your pencil marks appear shiny, it's a sign you pressed too hard and applied too much graphite.

2-9 Add a "C" shaped darker tone inside top left of your ellipse

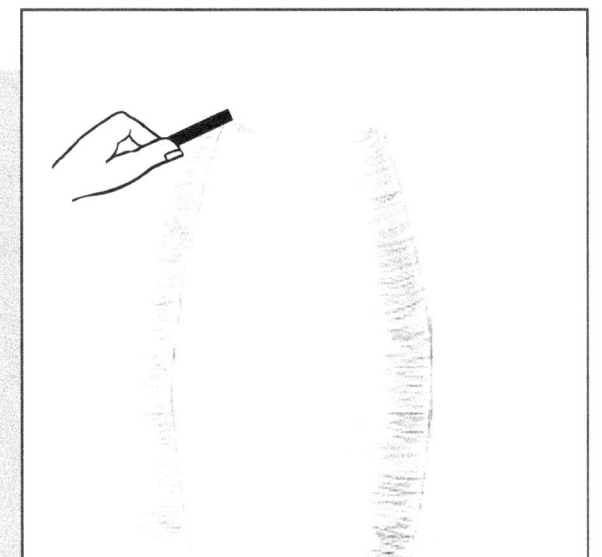

2-10 Tone the cast shadow with gentle pressure and left-to-right strokes

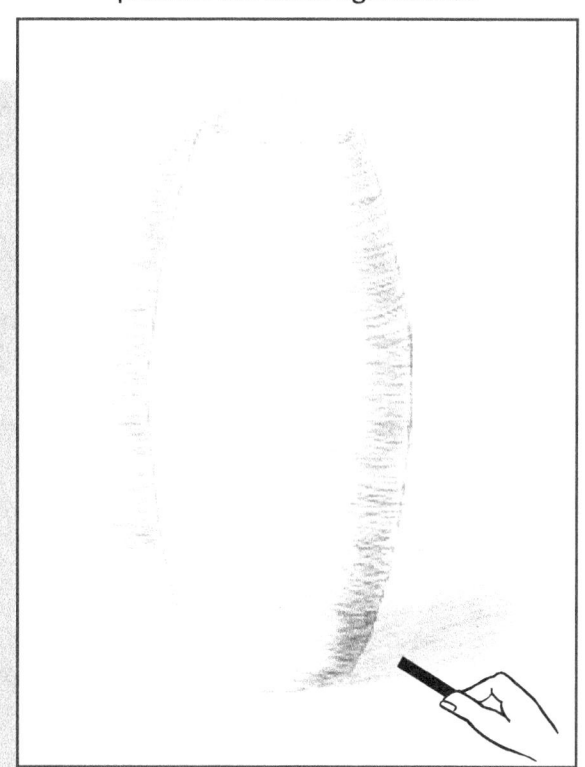

2-11 Darken cast shadow area near the shade portion of your figure

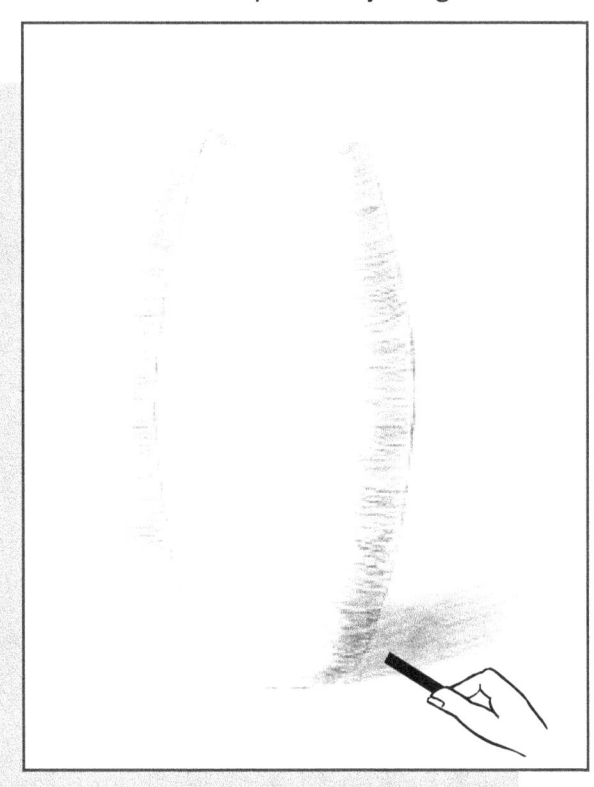

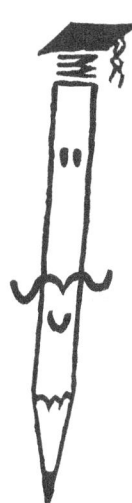

Prepare to blend. For this you will need a blender (paper wrapped stub) and your putty eraser, also called "kneadable rubber."

STEP 3 *Texture* (surface appearance) is a very important part of "shading". In order to achieve a smooth texture, the tones need to be blended. This is done by simply rubbing with a blender, your finger, or a cotton swab. There's just one hitch. A smooth figure may be too much contrast against a rough background. So, for practical as well as aesthetic (pleasing) reasons, let's also blend the background, and again, let's do it *first.* Why? Because, by clarifying the background, *then* the figure, it's easier to create the impression that the *figure* overlaps. The other way around, it would be difficult to keep overstrokes away from the figure. Assuming you're convinced, begin by blending half the background at a time. Start near the top center. Stroke *right-to-left* with a SWEEPING motion as you move downward. In other words, press hard and gradually *reduce* pressure prior to lifting the blender with each sideways stroke. Stop at the line that represents the table (2-12). Repeat the method on other half of the background, but switch to a *left-to-right* direction (2-13). The "feathering" technique will create a wavy effect of *fading* tones. Do not fret if dark and light spots appear. Later you will have the opportunity to refine. Meanwhile, having blended your background, move on to your *figure.* Initiate with the *shade* side using *right-to-left* strokes to fade the *shade tone* into the *mid-tone* (on your left). Vary the angles, the way you did when the tones were originally applied, but add the SWEEPING method (2-14). This includes fading the shade into the mid-tone, followed by the mid-tone into the white area, *within* your figure (2-15). Next, attend to the *line* that separates the figure from the ground, *on your left.* If your line is quite dark, reduce the intensity by dabbing your putty eraser, *then* blend to create a slightly fuzzy appearance called a "soft edge." The effect will indicate that the figure's curvature continues beyond your view (2-16). To form an intermediate range between the mid-tone and the light tone, connect them with small circular blending motions (2-17).

2-12 Blend background bordering figure on *your* left

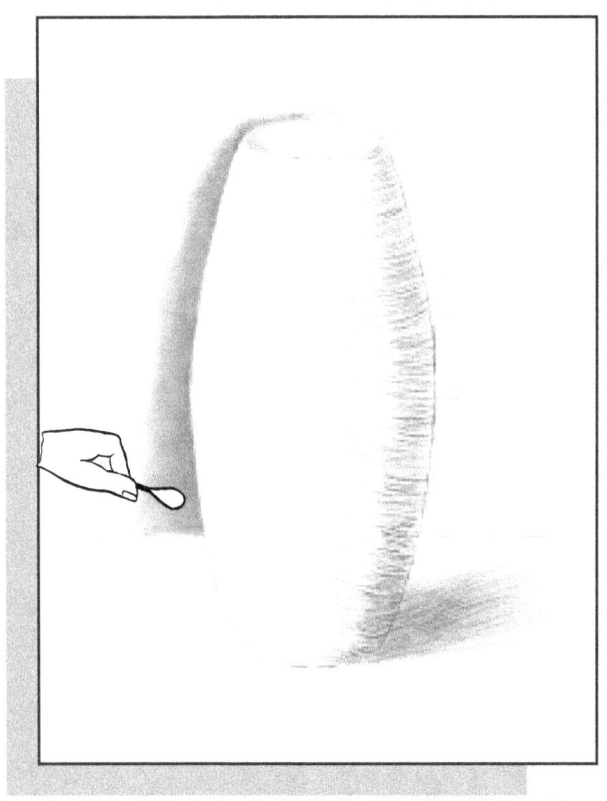

2-13 Blend background bordering figure on *your* right

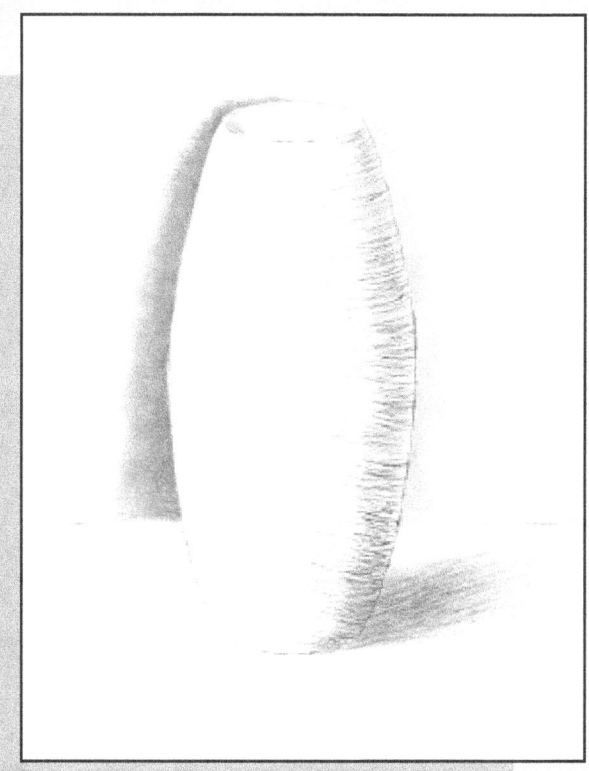

2-14 Blend figure's shade side on *your* right

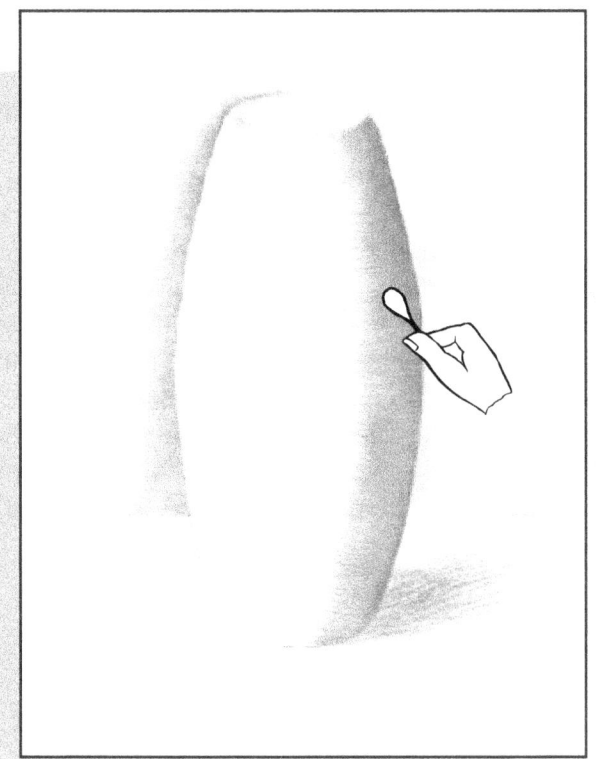

2-15 Blend mid-tone

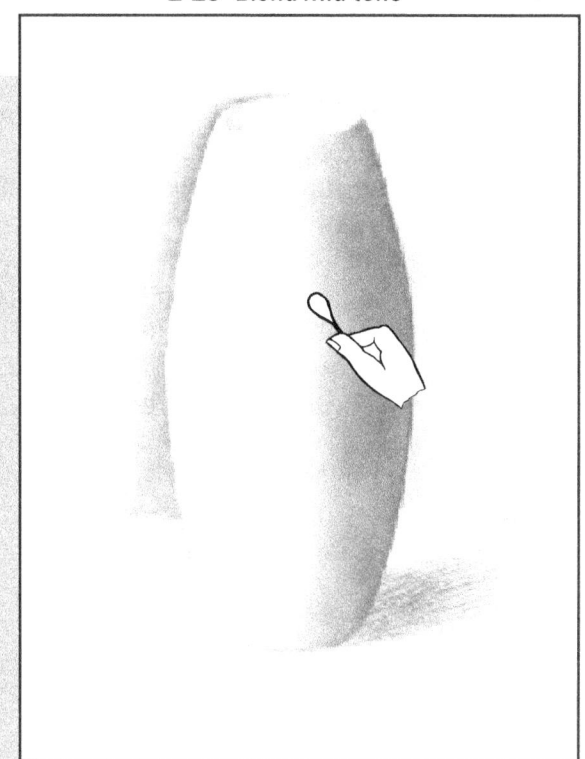

2-16 Blend light tone

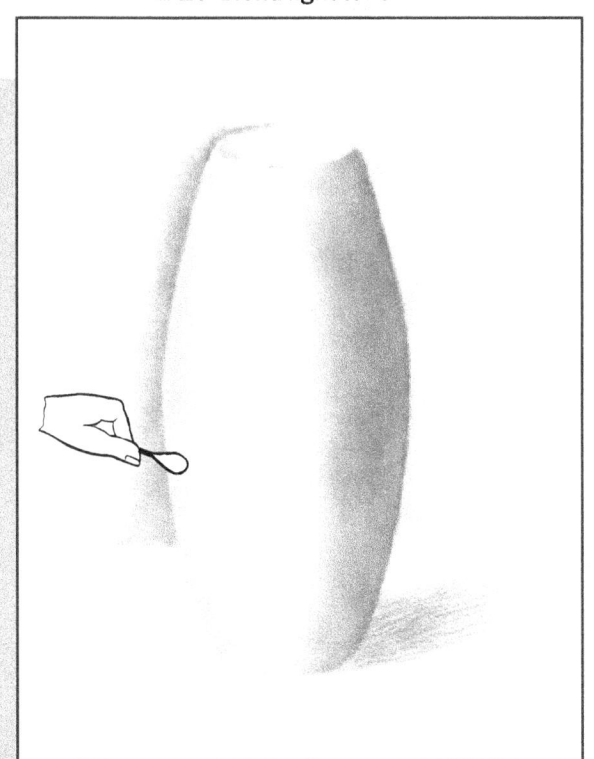

2-17 Blend mid-tone into light tone

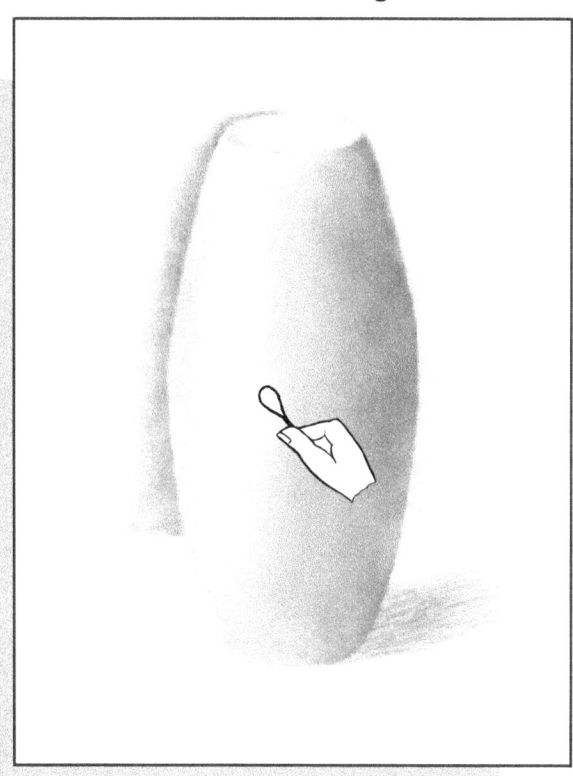

TIP Blending darkens tone because it fills spaces between strokes and the pores of the paper. If an area becomes too dark, *don't rub* with your putty eraser. This causes smears. Instead, *lift* using a dabbing motion. If an area appears too light, add tone with your pencil, or stroke the lead on the tip of your blender, then use it to apply

STEP 4 Continuing the blending procedure, please "feather" the cast shadow with short, gentle sweeping motions. After all, as you have observed, a cast shadow *gradually* changes from a dark tone to a lighter tone, as it spreads out closer to where light begins to penetrate. To achieve this visual effect, press harder at the start, especially in the dark part near the figure. Gradually reduce pressure to gently fade the rest of the tone into the white of your paper. The technique will help bring about a "soft edge" (2-18). Next, attend to the light tone in the top ellipse, using *back and forth* motions for an even spread. Do the same to the darker portion of the top ellipse, but switch to a *left-to-right* direction. Make sure to keep the "C" shape (2-19). Next, prepare for the *highlights*. For this, you will need to use your putty eraser as a *drawing tool*. How? Squeeze one corner into a dull point. With a quick motion, erase a small curve inside the upper part of your top ellipse, on your right (2-20). At the opposite side, vertically align your putty eraser with the dark "C" shape. Erase a small portion of the tone on the front of your figure in order to bring about a narrow upside down triangle shape (2-21). Then create the tilted vertical highlight near the base by simply erasing a thin white line with slow, slightly jerky motions (2-22). If you erase too much, replenish (put back) the tone and repeat the process with very narrow left-to-right strokes.

2-18 *Blend* dark tone in cast shadow, then soften the edges

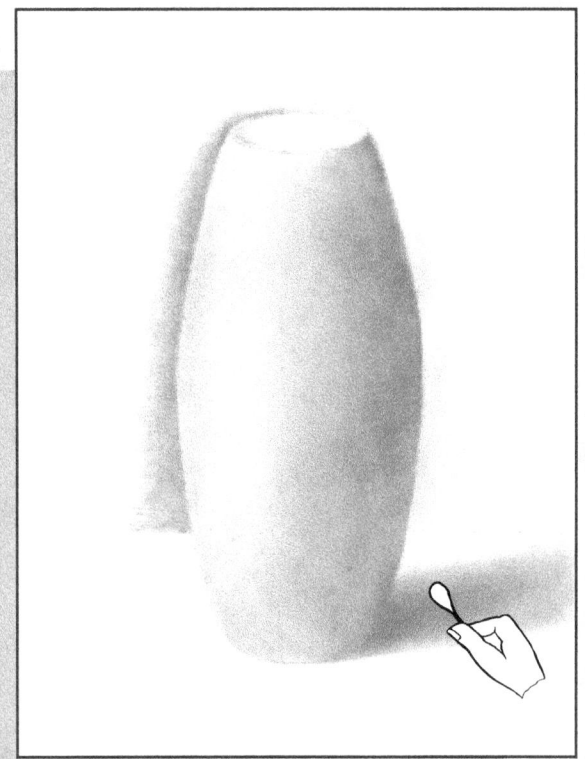

2-19 Blend light tone in top ellipse then blend dark part

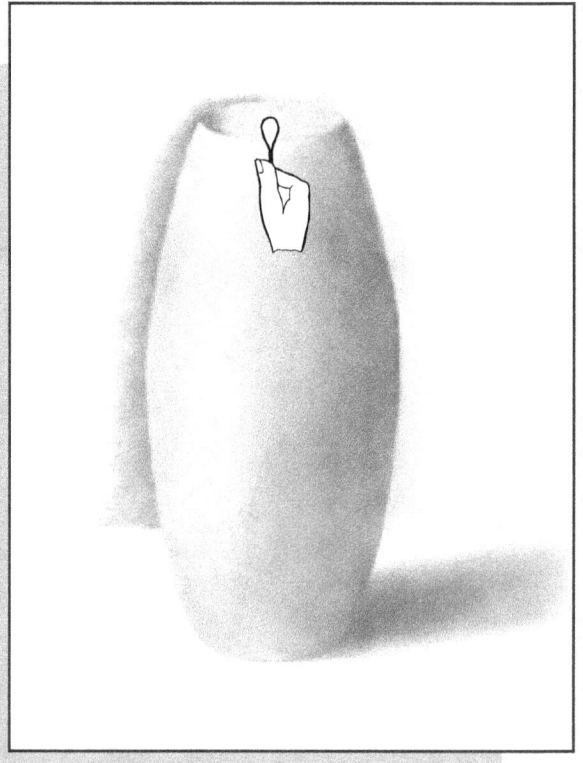

TIP Your putty eraser is "kneadable" and can be shaped. Try it. Before forming your highlights, apply tones on a separate sheet of paper and practice removing deliberate portions with your eraser. To *clean* your putty eraser, tear and push it back together, repeatedly. To remove tone from your *blender*, DO NOT use a pencil sharpener. Wrap the blender inside your putty eraser. Holding it in one hand, spin the blender with

2-20 Fashion a short curved highlight inside the top ellipse with eraser

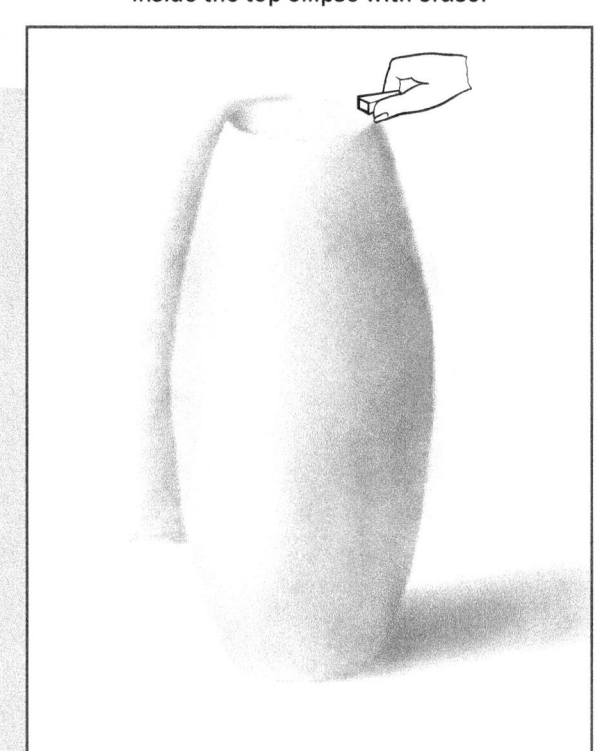

2-21 Form upside down triangle shaped highlight with eraser

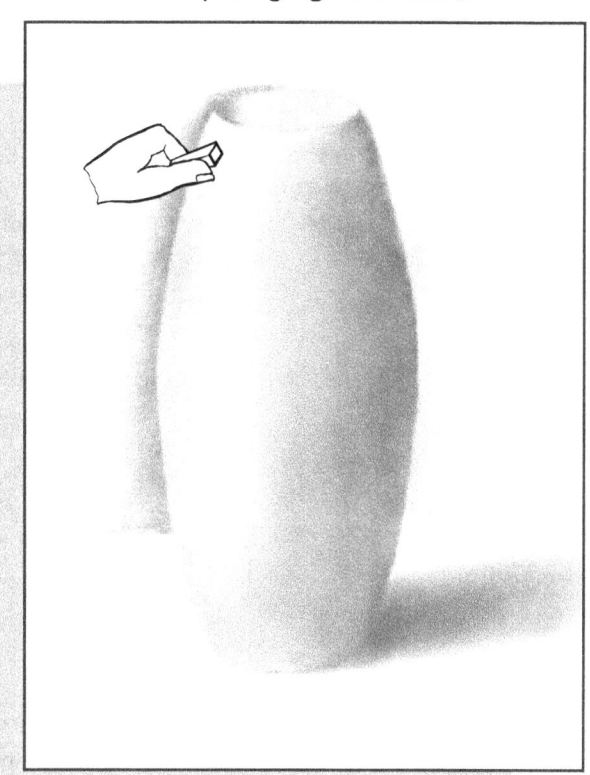

2-22 Create the narrow tilted highlight with your eraser

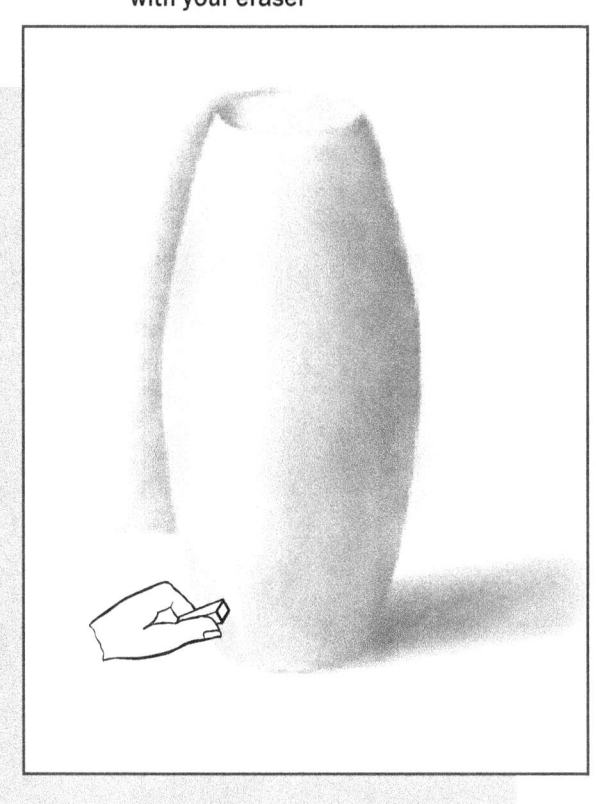

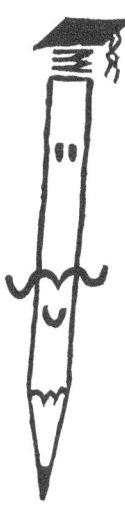

We're nearly done. Can you guess what's next? Yep! A check-up.

A ONCE OVER CAN DO WONDERS

STAY IN TOUCH WITH YOUR WORK. Periodic status checks are helpful. Your picture is nearly finished and now it's time to verify results, preferably from a slight distance. Why? Up close, we tend to see *parts* that make the whole. From a few paces, we are more likely to see the *whole* as a result of its parts. Plus, visual assimilation makes *BLOTCHES* easier to spot from a little distance.

WHAT ARE BLOTCHES? Blotches are uneven patches of tone (2-23).

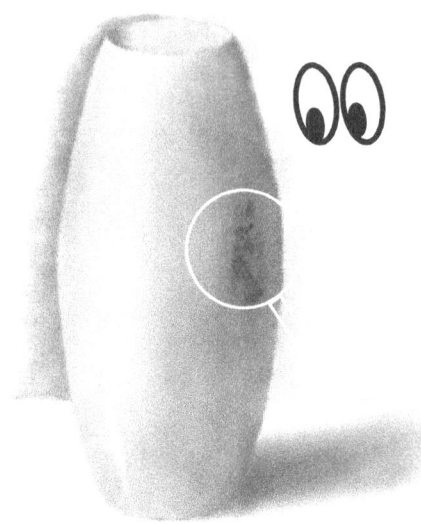

2-23 Blotch Example

HOW DO BLOTCHES OCCUR? A blotch forms when you stroke inconsistently by changing from hard to soft pressure within the same general area. Blotches are also caused by leaving portions of the paper showing through and darkening nearby.

WHAT CAN CURE BLOTCHES? There are two main options. **Option 1.** If you want to make a light tone dark as the dark *value* within it, carefully add tone using gentle pencil strokes, or put some graphite on your blender tip. Apply on the light area *without adding tone to the already existing dark part.* **Option 2.** In order to *eliminate* a dark spot, simply dab it with your putty eraser and lift as needed. Then blend until the tone evens out.

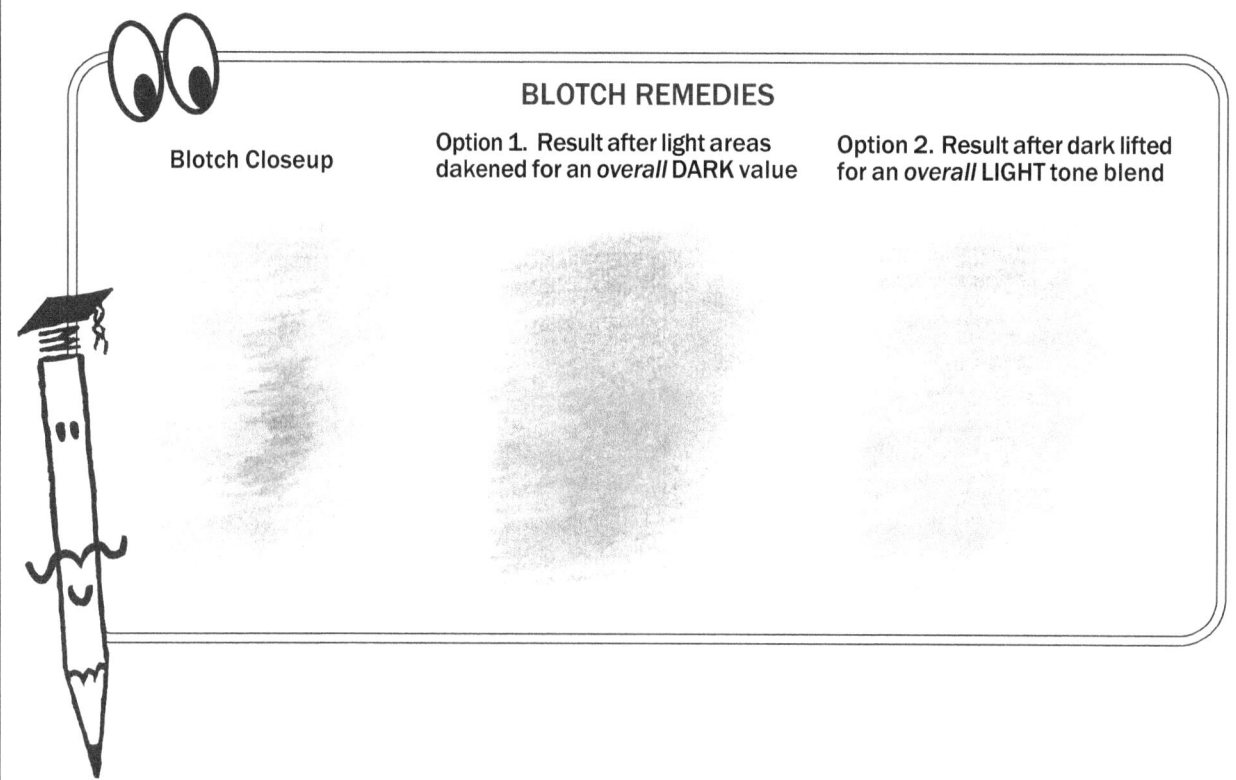

BLOTCH REMEDIES

Blotch Closeup

Option 1. Result after light areas dakened for an *overall* DARK value

Option 2. Result after dark lifted for an *overall* LIGHT tone blend

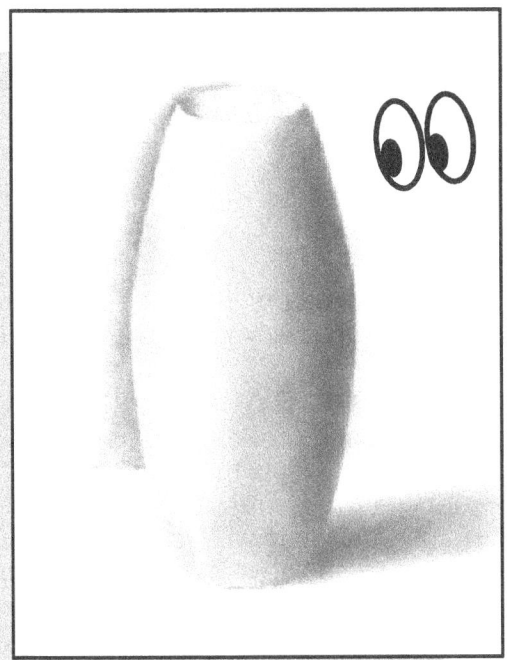

2-24 Drawing in present state
Observe low contrast-shade side

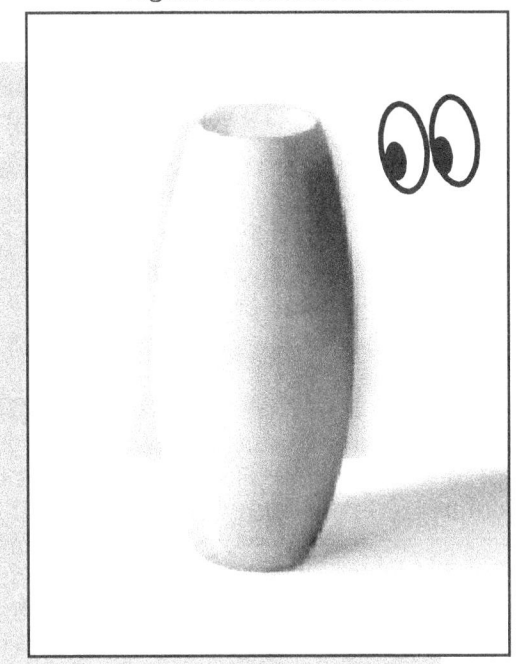

2-25 Intended outcome
Higher contrast-shade side

PLEASANT SURPRISES DO HAPPEN   What we set out to accomplish and what we achieve may turn out to be two different things. After having eliminated the blotch, I studied my work again (2-24). It didn't have as much contrast between the figure and background as I had intended (2-25). Was this a goof? Not necessarily. Just as we have choices at the beginning of a drawing, we have them during development. Case in point: my picture has a "quiet" appeal, don't you think?   On the other hand, more dark tone on the shade area would bring about higher contrast. In turn, the background would appear to be further back, and the figure would seem to be closer in front, practically popping off the page. I call this the *push-pull effect*.   The question is, should I apply the method? In situations like this, I advise my students to photocopy their work, or computer scan and print it, then draw on the duplicates. The option provides "painless" experimentation. Which version do you prefer; current state 2-24 or photocopy test 2-26?

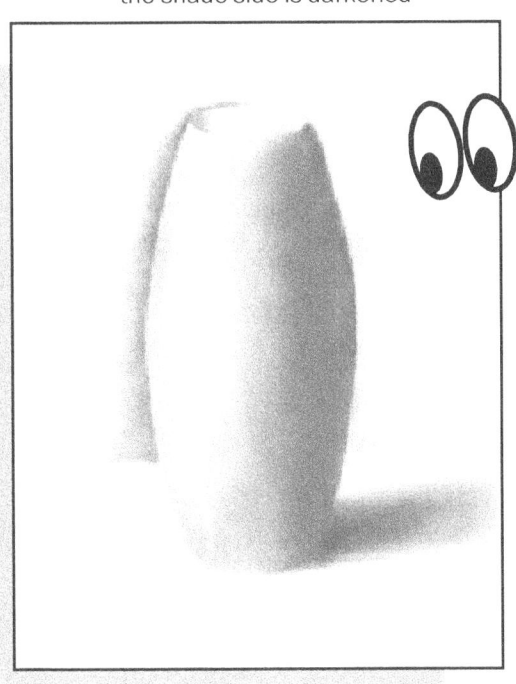

2-26 Drawing is photocopied and
the shade side is darkened

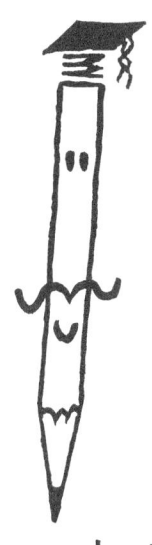

So now what?
Read on to find out.

TEND TO *YOUR* FINISHING TOUCHES

What are finishing touches?   These are things you do AFTER you think your picture is about done. Following are helpful suggestions.

1. Pretend someone else did the work. It's easier to be objective.
2. Check accuracy. During toning, boundaries may have gone astray. The TRUSTY 7 can help.
3. Check edges. Some edges may be vague, others may be too soft or too hard.
4. Check for blotches and attend to them.
5. Check for contrasts. Certain areas may have too much, while others may not have enough.
6. Keep refining until you decide your drawing is complete. And that brings up the age old question...

How do I know when my picture is finished?   If you set out to portray naturalism," meaning things are supposed to be recognizable and realistically represented, the general rule is that their likeness should be reasonably accurate. Plus, there should be at least FIVE distinct tones ranging from light to dark, thereby creating the impression you are looking at a three dimensional scene on a two dimensional surface. The method is called *Chiaroscuro*. Although the word may sound complicated, it's just a way to show what happens when light strikes an object. Instantly, highlight appears. Where light *cannot* reach, there is shade. Where light can *partly* reach, there are several in between tones. Does this mean that you must always have five obviously different tones (or more) to complete a picture? Not necessarily. Sometimes, you may want your drawing to have a subtle mood. In that case you would use *low contrast* by keeping all the values closely light, or closely dark. Examine the student work on the next page (top left). The highlights are vague. Once more tone was added (top right version), the highlights became more defined, but *high contrast* remained absent, due to the lack of very dark tones. Since preferences vary, either way is fine. But, as I said on the previous page, choices occur during both shaping and toning. Decisions are made and your picture undergoes many changes. That's why it is important to verify results and evaluate outcomes not only while you draw, but also *after* you think you have finished. Then you get to see what you really have. For instance, in the lower half of the next page, another student's drawing reveals something. This one has a crisp, dark line along the lower part, making the figure seem flat there. To create the artistic illusion that a form continues to curve behind, however, a "soft" edge is a nifty device. Notice the change, after the dark, "hard" line was removed. Next, the tone was blended by fading it in the figure and into "ground."

Apparently, even after both students thought they were done, their drawings still had room for adjustment, didn't they? Not that I am implying they had to be perfect to be called finished. On the contrary. I recommend that before judging your picture complete, simply double and triple check. This offers the opportunity to advance your skill as well as your work a little more (within reason of course). In Chapter 1, I mentioned it is wise to find a balance between being too lax and being too strict. That's good advice. Don't accept less than what you can handle, nor hold back, fearful you might ruin what you already have. At the same time, don't demand too much of yourself. After all, your eye-hand coordination is constantly improving. When you see further refinement is needed, but your hand can't deliver, be fair to yourself. Modify only to the extent you feel capable, based on your present experience.

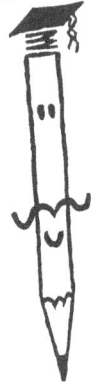

OK. It's your turn. Give your work a final once over. Modify as needed according to your present capabilities. Tend to the adjustments one by one and check each result. Then study the student examples on the next page.

Front highlights are not clearly visible

Front highlights are clearly visible

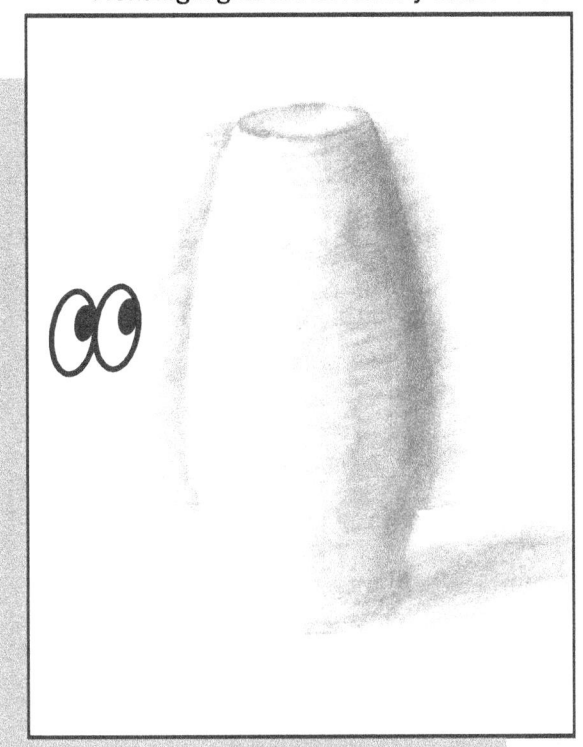

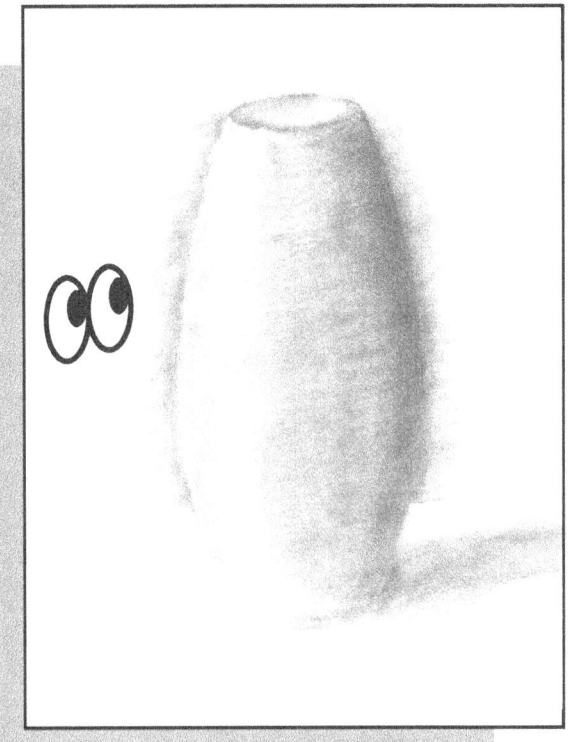

Hard edge suggests figure does not curve behind

Soft edge implies figure continues to curve behind

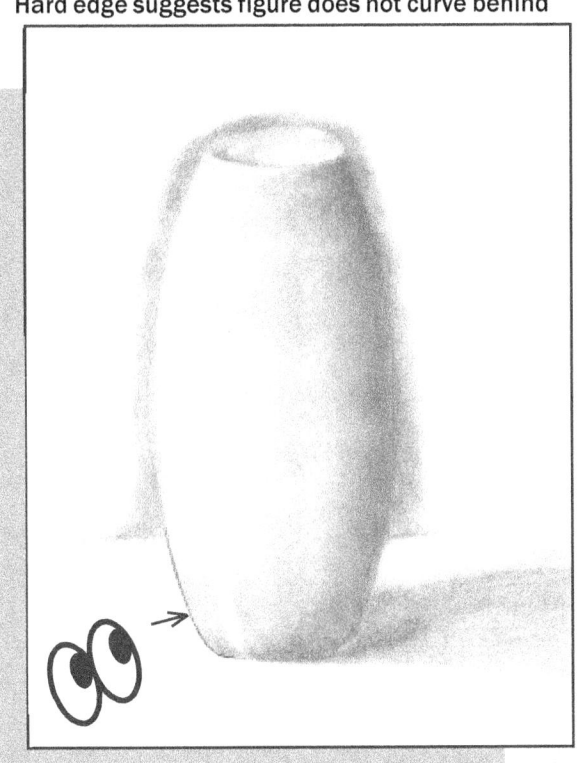

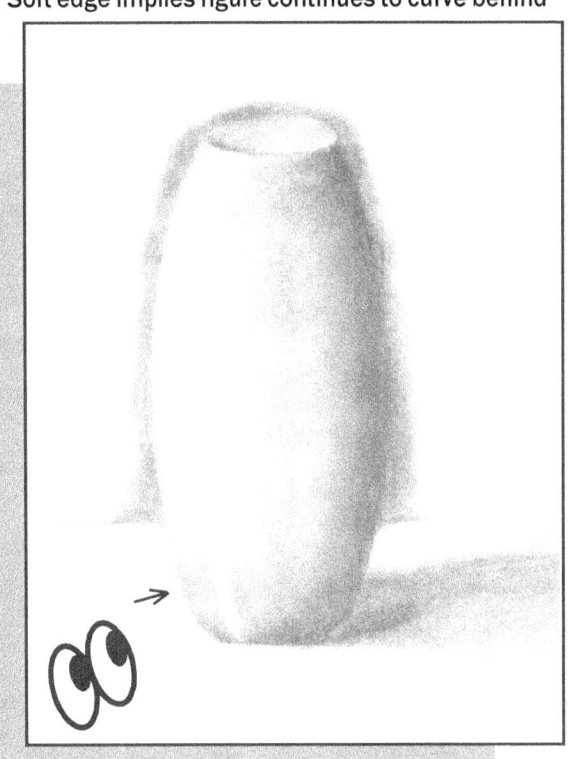

These versions are impressive, even before the changes, don't you think? Be content with your accomplishment, too. Prize what you learned as much if not more than what you drew.

What makes a drawing unique?   Usually, it's not the subject matter but rather how it is portrayed, wouldn't you agree? Even a simple scene showing a cylindrical object can be creative.   Equally exciting, no matter how many people draw it, and no matter how many times, each would be different, each brimming with special attraction.

How is such an amazing feat achieved? One secret is in the manner by which the effects of light are depicted, not only on figures, but also on the ground or surface they occupy, and the background that surrounds them. To accomplish this, tones are an effective method.

Tones, as you know, are simply marks that are applied in a variety of ways. For instance, you can create *values* by simply changing the pressure of your pencil strokes. You can go over the same area more than once. Various blending techniques can also be used. Even the eraser serves as both an adjustment tool and a drawing tool.

Above and beyond that, other factors come into play. Stroke direction can suggest a plane, its surface and its contour.   Soft edges, hard edges, contrasts and textures can also affect appearance.

What is the purpose for learning these elements and principles? Primarily to be able to create a convincing likeness of something that seems to be solid and three dimensional, even though it is pictured on a flat two dimensional surface. Photos give us this kind of illusion. And while it's challenging and rewarding to make a drawing appear almost as realistic as a photograph, I think ultimately that should not be the goal. After all, we have excellent machines that already do that. Concentrate on your own personal touch. That's the key.

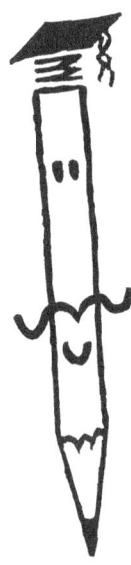

Now, take a break. Then get set for more thrilling adventures in drawing.

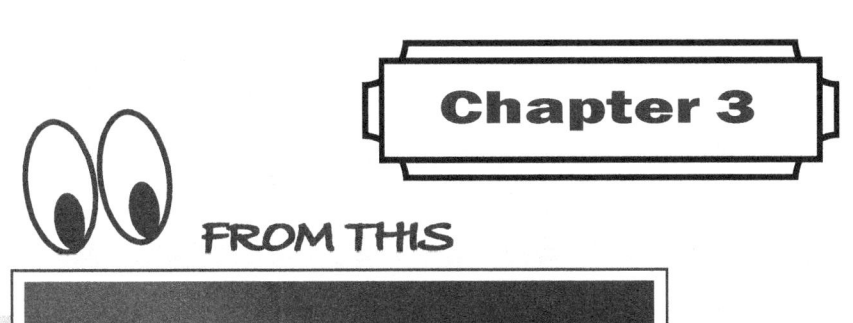

Chapter 3

FROM THIS

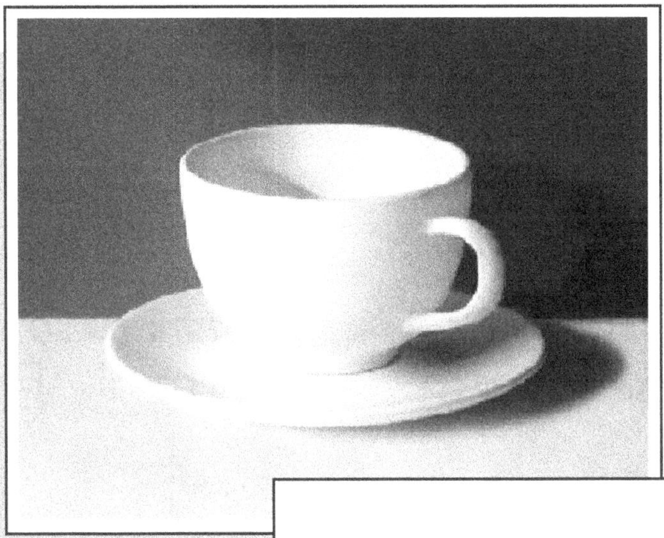

TO THIS

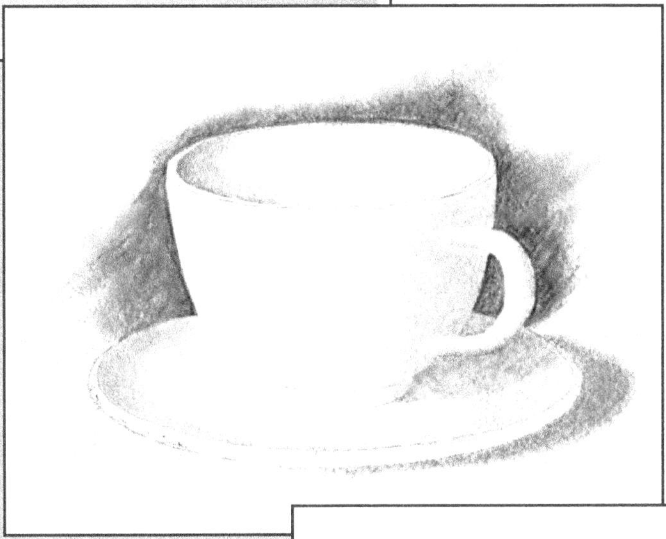

BEGINS
HERE

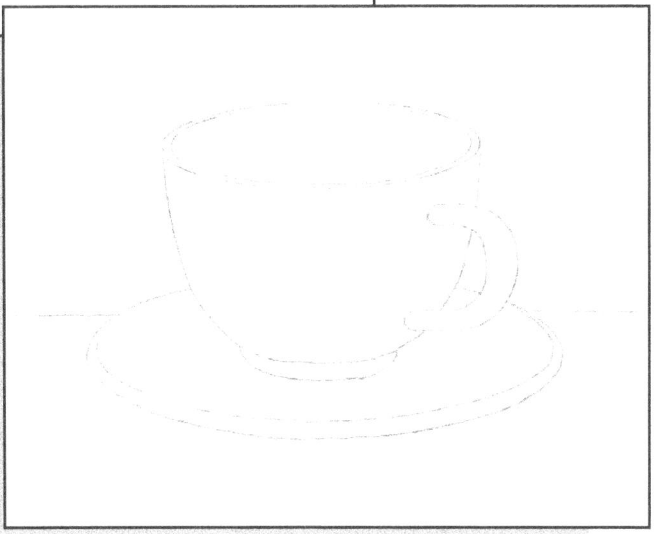

STEP 1 LET'S GET ACQUAINTED WITH THE SITUATION. Initially, the subject matter may appear overwhelming, but a closer look provides helpful clues. For instance, when we take an *overall* pencil reading, or a visual check, vertically from the cup's opening to the saucer, then compare that to the *horizontal* span, we find it is about a *half* span *longer* (3-1). We can apply this observation by forming a proportional rectangle to serve as the foundation on which to build our drawing. First though, we must *plan ahead* by deciding how large the rectangle should be, and we must determine placement. If we go too large and/or locate the rectangle off center, as our drawing develops we may discover the shadow will not have room (3-2). Should we elect to start with a very small rectangle, we may find the picture will turn out too small for our liking, and perhaps too difficult to draw within the cramped space (3-3).

3-1 Overall proportion is 1/2 span longer than tall

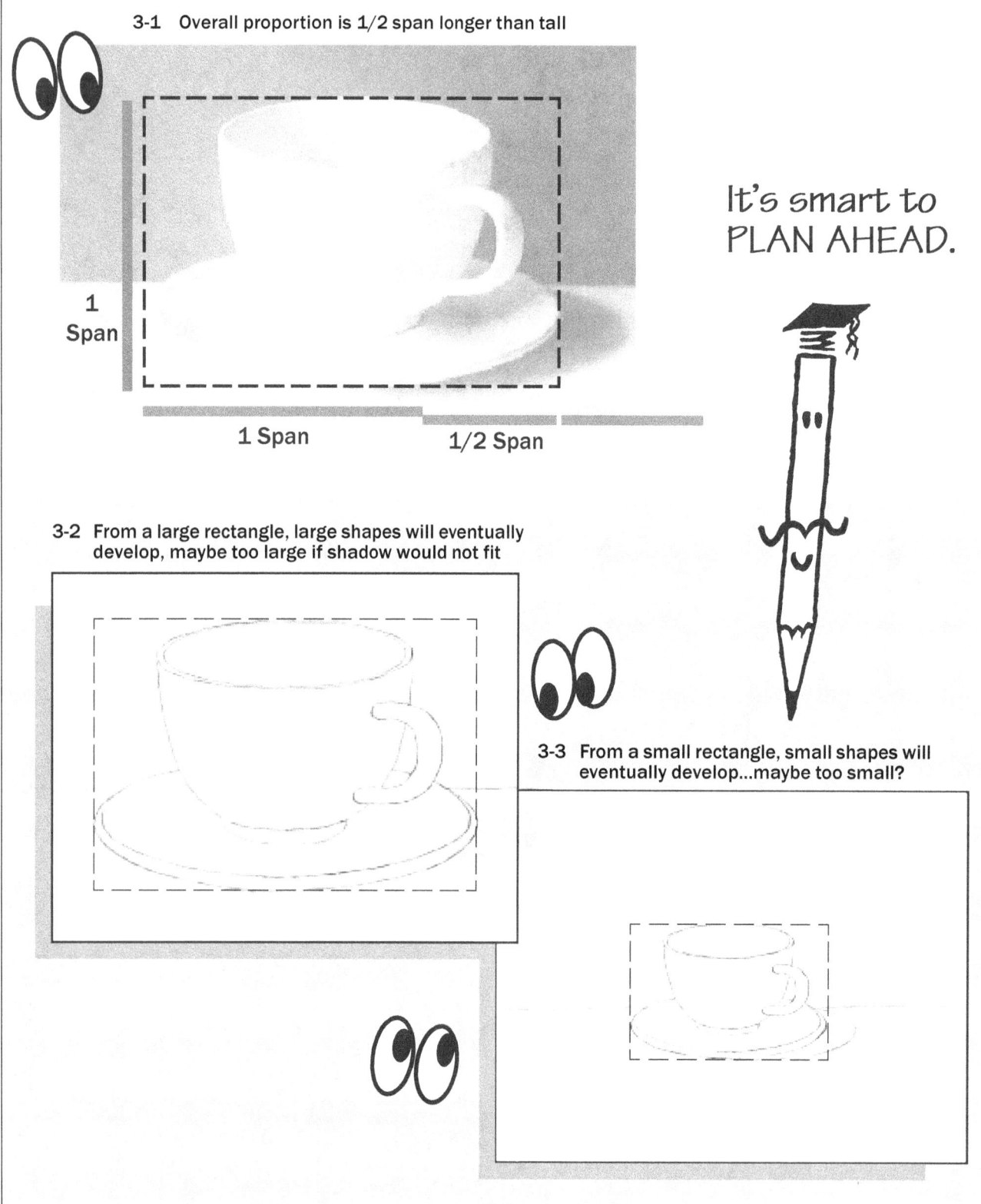

1 Span

1 Span

1/2 Span

It's smart to PLAN AHEAD.

3-2 From a large rectangle, large shapes will eventually develop, maybe too large if shadow would not fit

3-3 From a small rectangle, small shapes will eventually develop...maybe too small?

Select a proportional size that is both aesthetic (suits your taste) and feasible (works for you). Start by making sure your paper is set in a horizontal format. That means the short side should be upright and the long side is sideways. Next, make believe your rectangle is already positioned and visualize your figures within it. This preliminary procedure is useful because it gives you the opportunity to test options in your mind. Having made your size selection, *lightly* place a *vertical* line to represent the left side of your rectangle (3-4). Take a pencil check, or a visual estimate, of its length. Next, lightly attach one *horizontal* line that same length to the top of your vertical line and one from the bottom (3-5). Thereafter, using *HALF* the horizontal distance, lightly add it to each of your *horizontal* lines. This will form the desired ratio, namely *one span tall by one and a half spans long* (3-6). In order to finish your rectangle, lightly close the right side with a vertical line (3-7).

TIP Draw LIGHTLY. Adjustments can be handled more easily. Please do not use a ruler. Practice your freehand skill. It's the route to your unique, personal touch.

3-4 Visualize your figures in the rectangle, then lightly draw left side to start the foundation

3-5 Lightly attach *horizontal* lines to the top & bottom of *vertical* line (equal to its length)

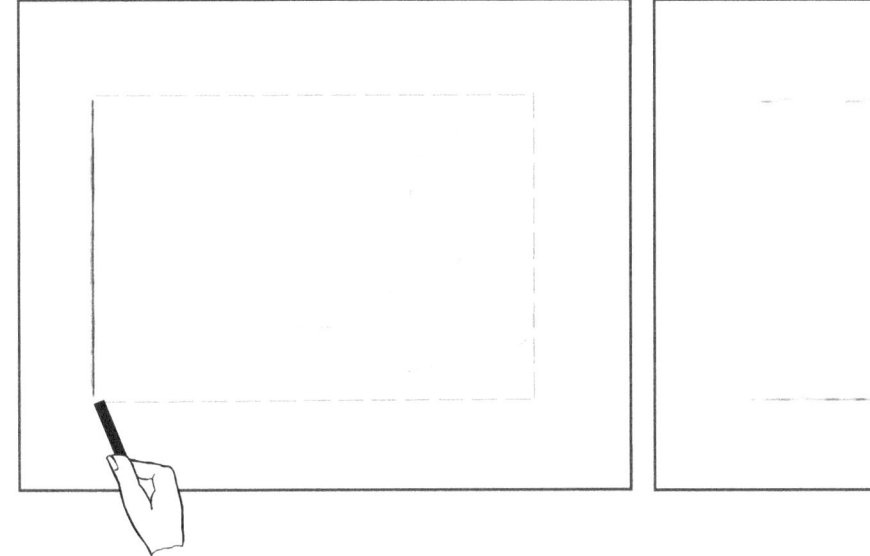

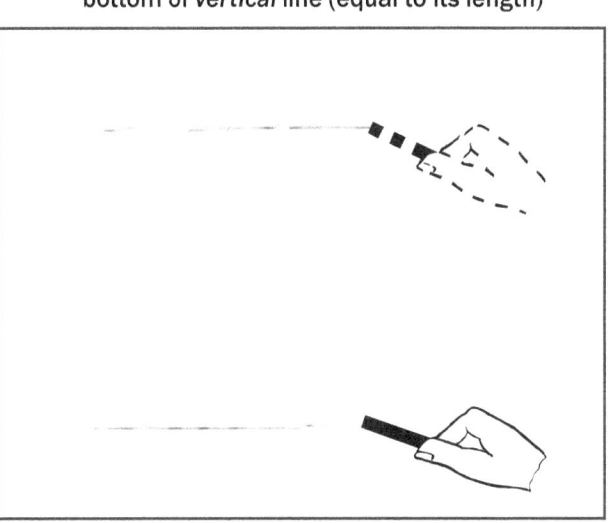

3-6 Extend your horiztonal lines by *half*

3-7 Close right side of rectangle with a vertical line

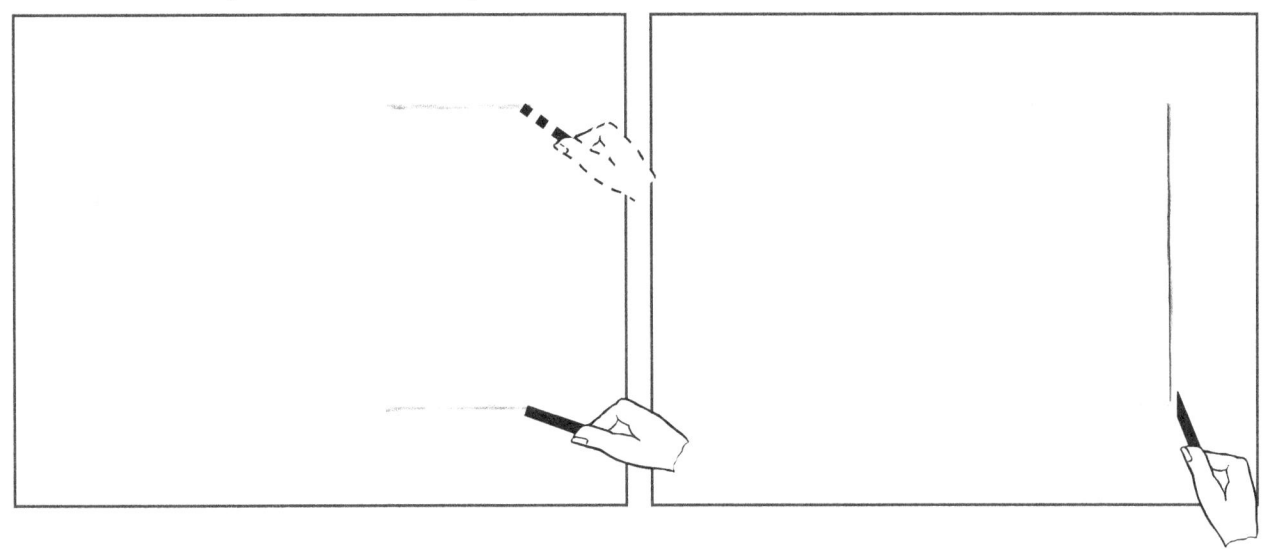

STEP 3 In order to continue making proportion assessments, we need to improvise a little by using our x-ray vision. Pretend you can see through the cup to the back of the saucer. Take a visual, or a *vertical* pencil reading, from there, as shown by "A" in illustration 3-6. Then compare that span from the cup opening as shown by "B." The procedure enables you to convert the three dimensional figures (height, width, depth) into two dimensional terms (height and width). Observed this way, the height of the saucer's ellipse takes up half the vertical distance of the cup and saucer *combined*. This finding can be adapted to fit your drawing proportionally, by simply drawing an ellipse within the lower half of your rectangle. Use illustration 3-6 for reference. It will help you form the curves more accurately. Or, if you prefer, you can work with guide lines and follow along with me. Begin by bisecting your rectangle with a horizontal line (3-7). Then divide the lower half with another horizontal line (3-8).

3-6 Observed with make-believe 2 dimensional x-ray vision, the saucer's elliptical height is about half the cup and saucer height put together

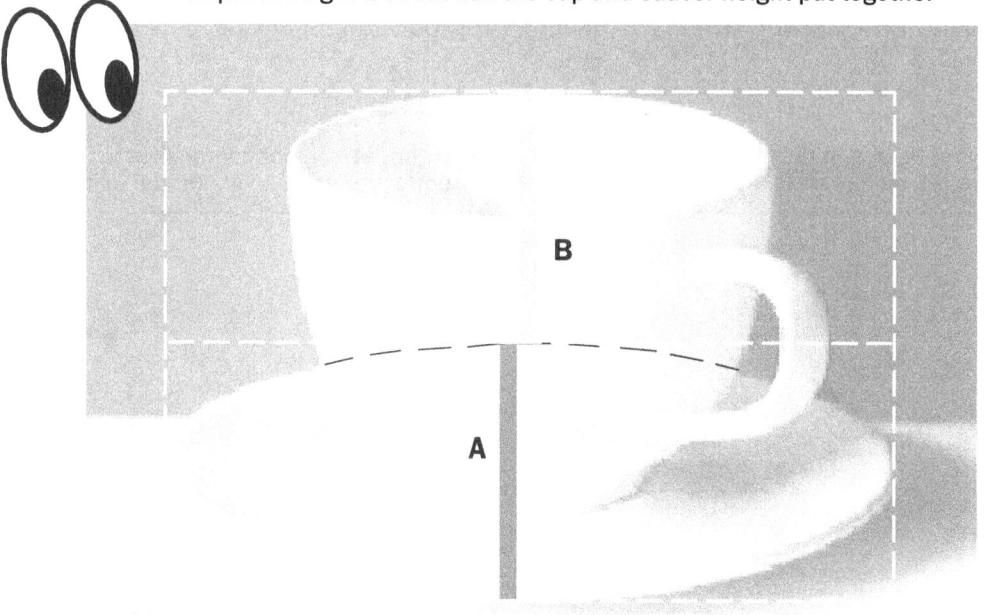

3-7 Bisect your rectangle with a horizontal line

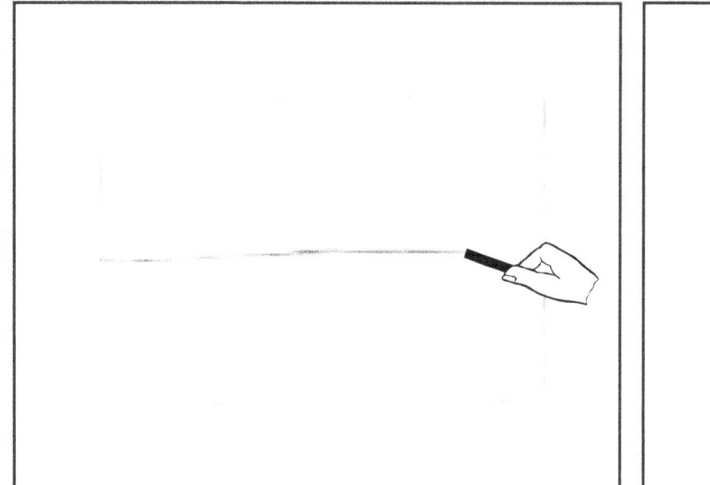

3-8 Bisect bottom half of rectangle with a horizontal line

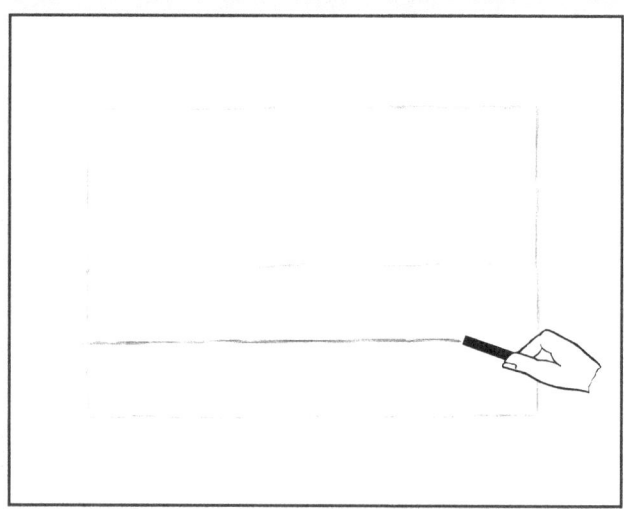

STEP 4 By using your guide lines, you can construct your ellipse with either four or six curves, the way you learned in Chapter 1. Be sure you refer to illustration 3-6, to help match your curves proportionally. Start with the two small side curves (3-9). Next, lightly draw the left half of the *upper* horizontal curve and the right half of the *lower* horizontal curve (3-10). Then lightly form the *left* half of the lower horizontal curve as well as the *right* half of the *upper* horizontal curve (3-11).

TIP The practice of dividing an ellipse into several sections, and switching from convex to concave strokes has its advantages. It reminds us to look closely at every curve and study how *each* contributes to the entire shape. For instance, in this case we have an ellipse that is symmetrical, with fairly short vertical side curves and narrow upper and lower horizontal curves. But as you know, both symmetrical and asymmetrical ellipses come in all kinds of shapes. So it's important to stay alert and flexible.

3-9 Lightly form the two small side curves

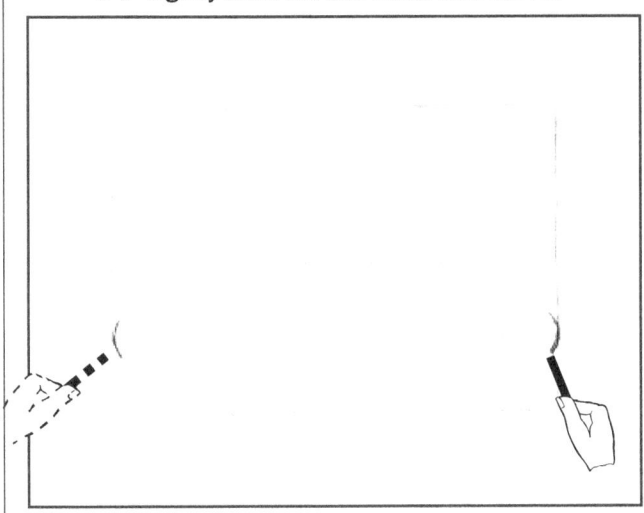

3-10 Lightly draw the top left and bottom right curves

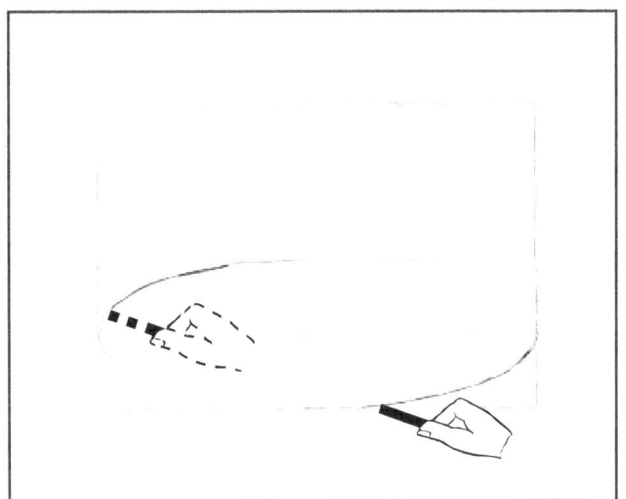

3-11 Lightly draw the top right and bottom left curves

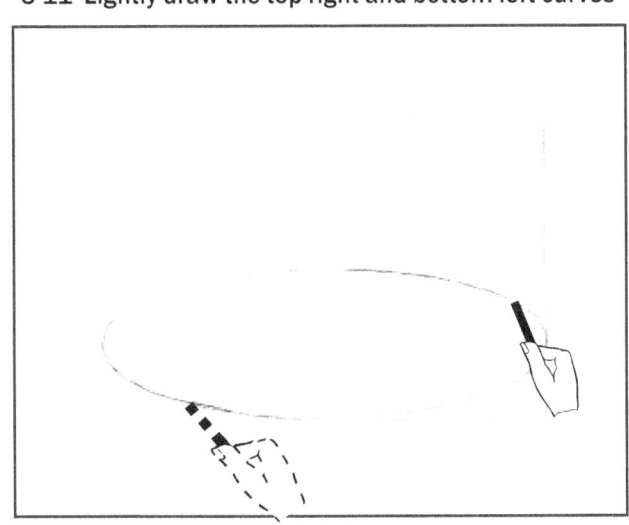

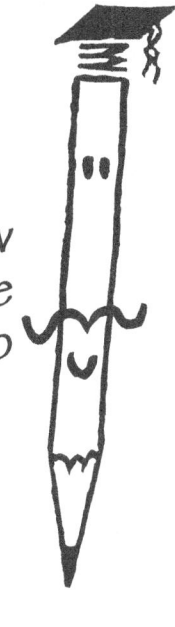

Remember to draw lightly. Dark lines are hard to change into soft edges.

STEP 5 Let's study the cup's opening. I've outlined the shape to show that it is an ellipse. Please take a vertical pencil check of the height, or estimate the span visually. The distance is about half way to the saucer's elliptical top, agreed? Next, by turning the span sideways, we see the same distance applies to the left and right *ends* of the cup's opening. They are vertically aligned with the saucer's respective ends (3-12). To apply these findings to *your* drawing, begin by bisecting the top half of *your* original rectangle, horizontally (3-13). The cup's opening will be in the uppermost part. Estimate that vertical distance by eye, or take a pencil reading and use the span to locate the sides with dots as shown in illustration 3-14.

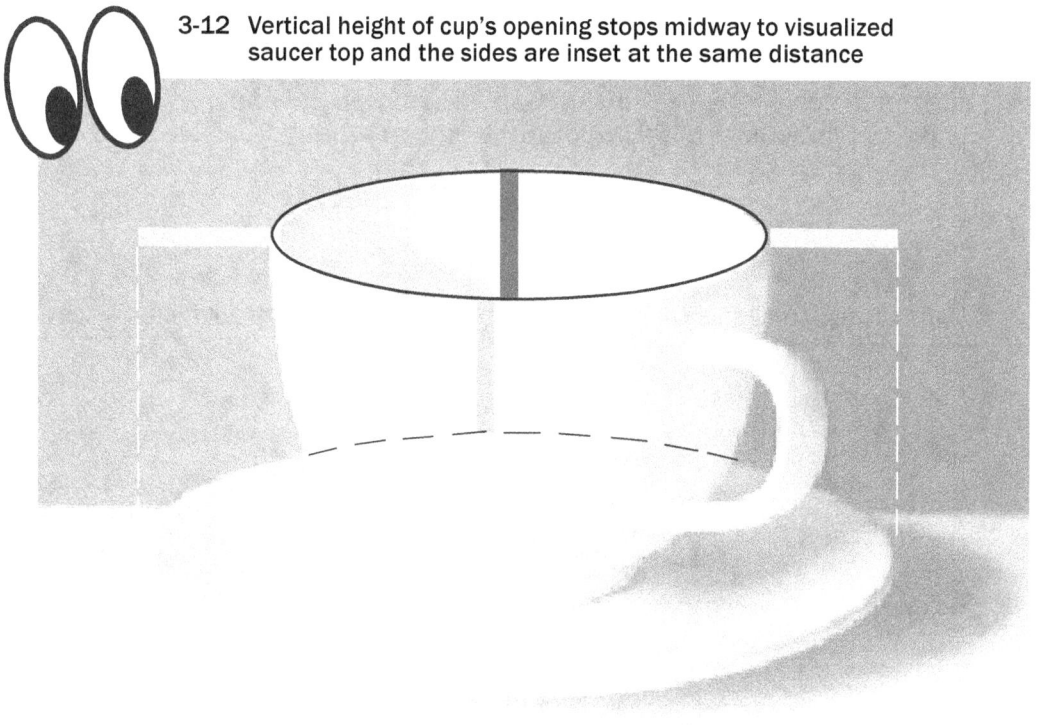

3-12 Vertical height of cup's opening stops midway to visualized saucer top and the sides are inset at the same distance

3-13 Bisect rectangle upper 1/2 with a horizontal line

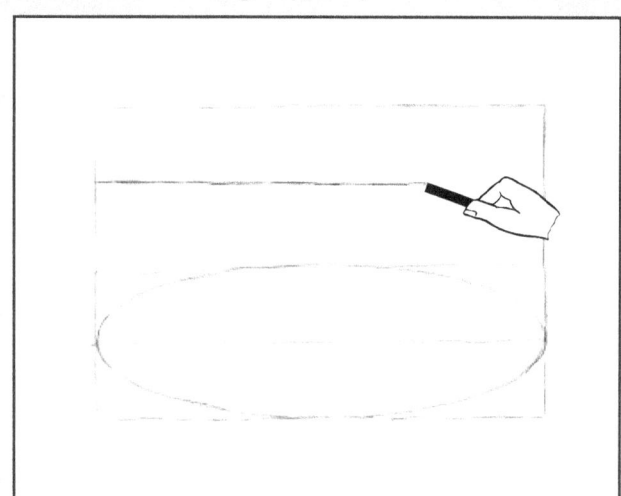

3-14 Use span to locate ellipse sides

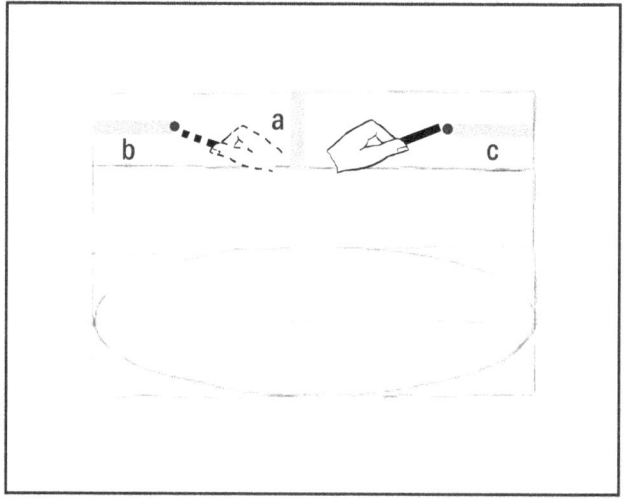

STEP 6 Having designated the space in which your cup's elliptical rim is to be located, you can now draw it freehand. Or, you may use guide lines to help form the ellipse. Simply box-in the area with a couple of *light vertical lines* that cut through your two dots and bisect with a *light horizontal line* (3-15). Then draw the ellipse with four or six curves (3-16). Afterward, erase all the guide lines *except* the mid guide line within the large ellipse. The outcome should resemble illustration 3-17).

TIP Whether you choose to use guide lines or not, please refer to illustration 3-12. It will help you duplicate the elliptical shape.

3-15 Lightly form guide lines for the small ellipse

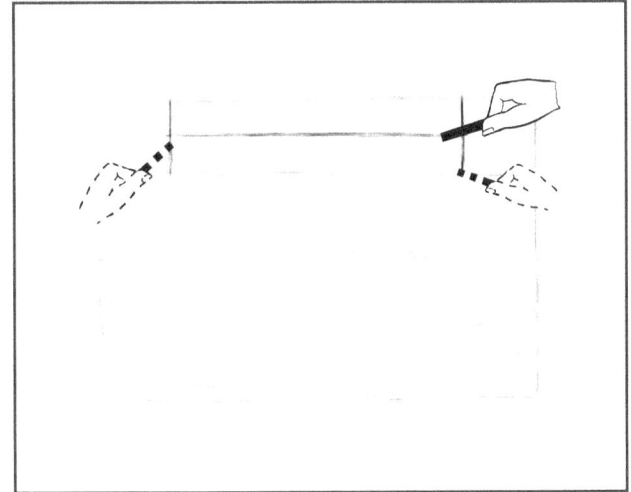

3-16 Form the small ellipse

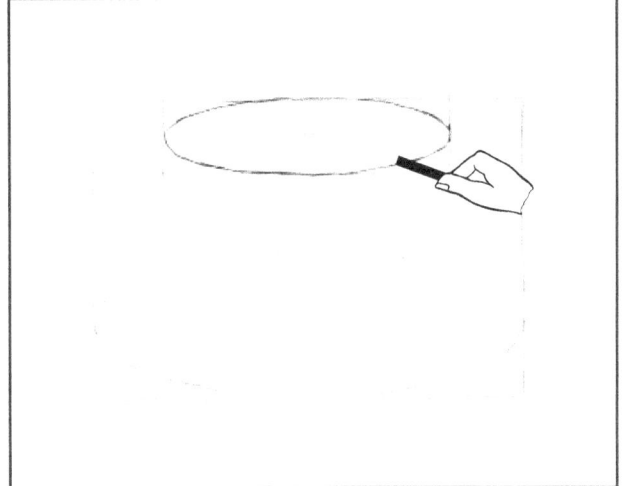

3-17 Erase all guide lines *except* within large ellipse for a result as indicated

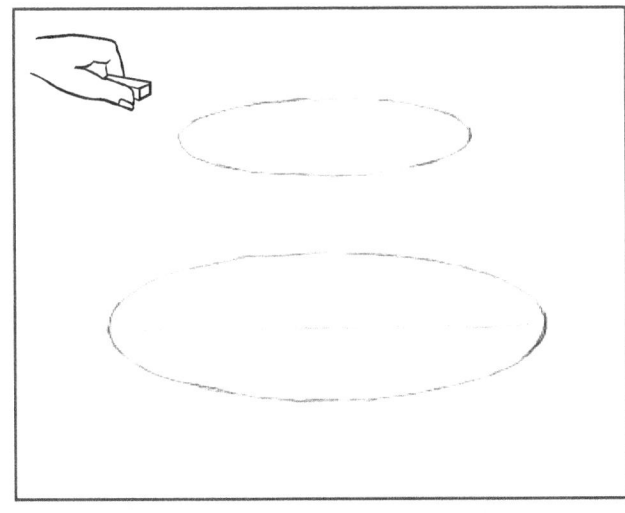

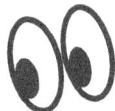

You're not watching TV or on the phone while drawing, are you? Your attention should not be divided.

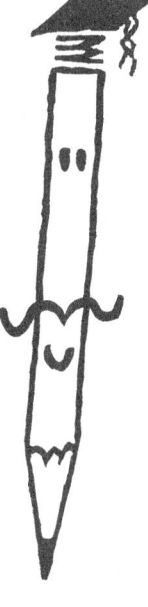

STEP 7 Please focus your attention on the curve that forms the cup's *base* in illustration 3-19. As you can tell, the *base* ends are inset from the *cup* ends at a rate equal to the cup's opening height. Plus, the widest part of the base curve drops roughly a third of the way below the saucer's middle. To apply these observations, determine the height of *your* small ellipse with a visual estimate, or a pencil check. Using that unit of distance, place a couple of dots inset from the plumb alignment of your cup rim ends (3-20). Center another dot about a third of the way down between your saucer's mid guide line and the bottom. Then, using illustration 3-19 for reference, lightly form the base curve (3-21).

TIP A plumb alignment is vertical without tilt and parallel to the sides of the paper.

3-19 Base curve *ends* are inset from cup rim ends according to opening height. Base curve *bends* one third of the way down from saucer middle to bottom

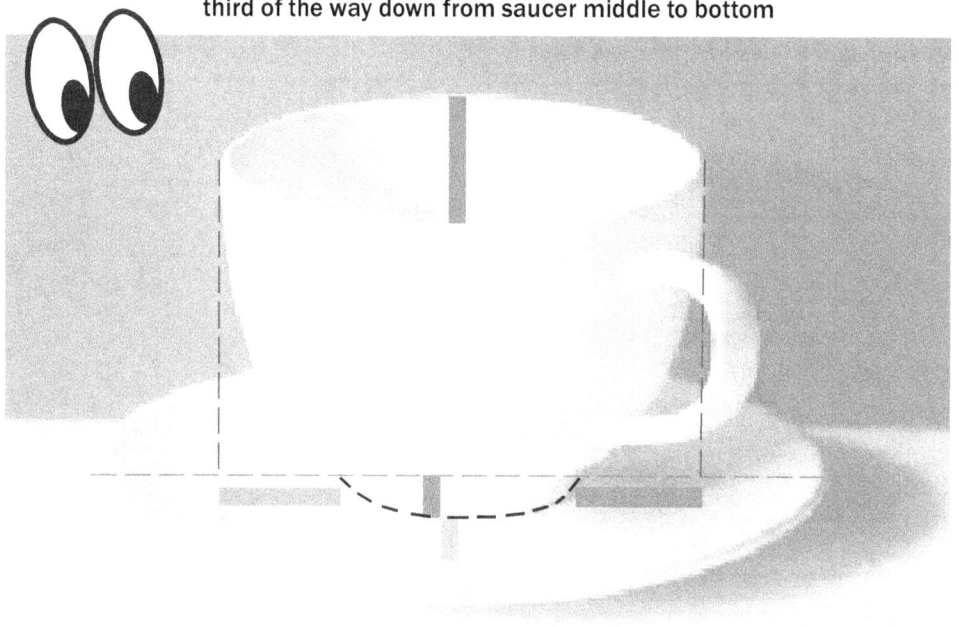

3-20 Use height of your small ellipse to locate reference points for the base ends

3-21 Center a dot 1/3 span below your guide line and draw the base curve

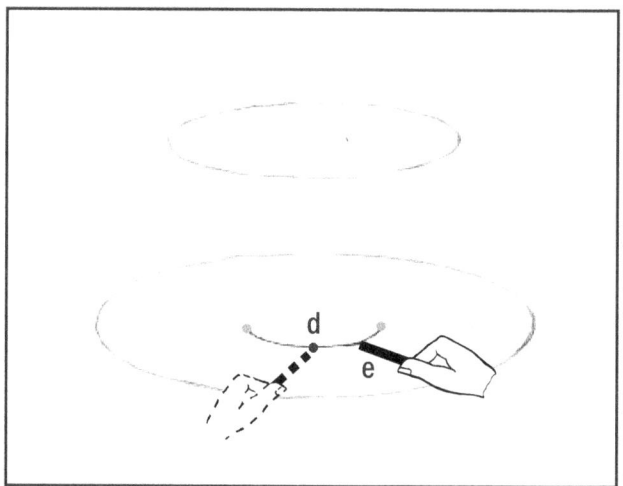

Picture in your mind two respective guide lines connecting from the cup's rim ends to the base. Also, make believe you have x-ray vision enabling you to see through the handle (3-22). This helps to observe the curvature forming the cup's *sides*. Next, visualize or place actual guide lines on your drawing. Then refer to illustration 3-22 as you replicate the side curves (3-23). After that, erase existing guide lines. At this point your primary shapes are visible and should resemble illustration 3-24.

TIP Guide lines are helpful. Please use them.

3-22 Visualized or drawn, guide lines connecting from cup's rim ends to base ends help you see the curves that shape the cup's *sides*

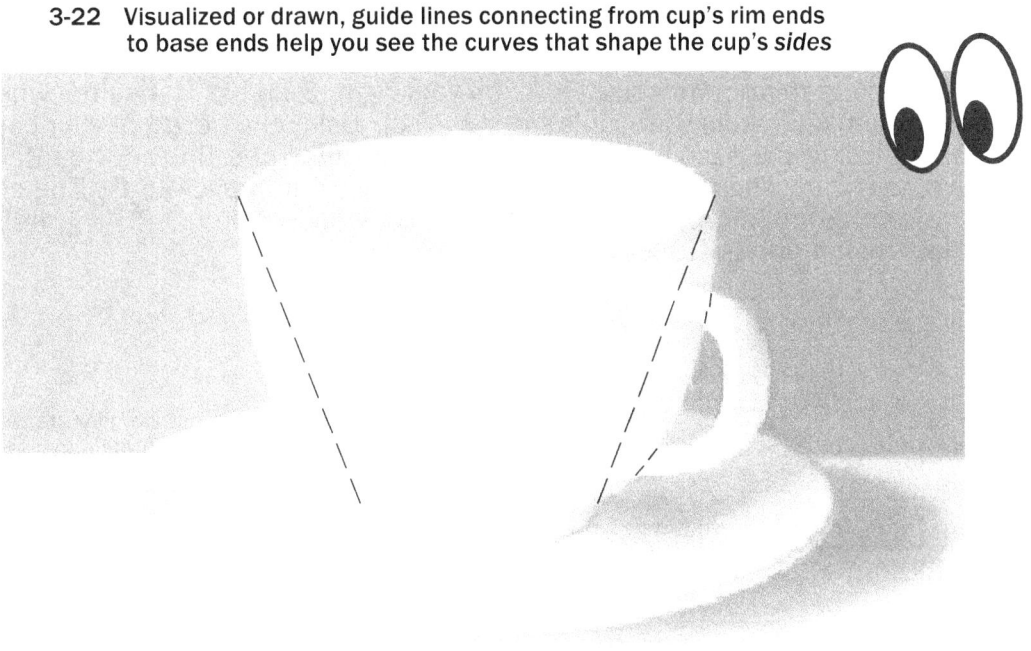

3-23 Draw sides with visualized or actual guide lines

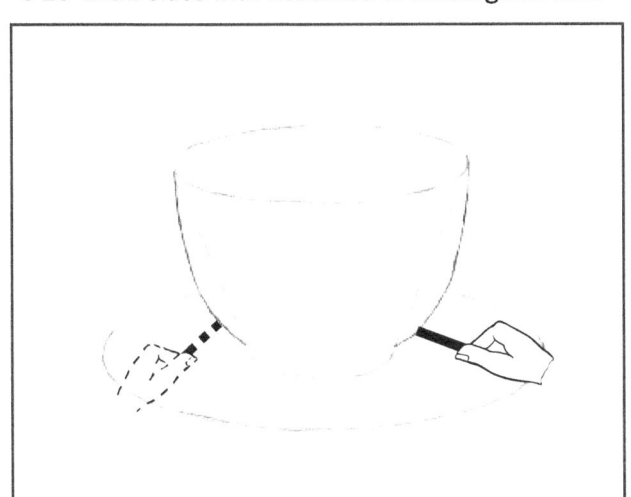

3-24 Result after guide lines are erased

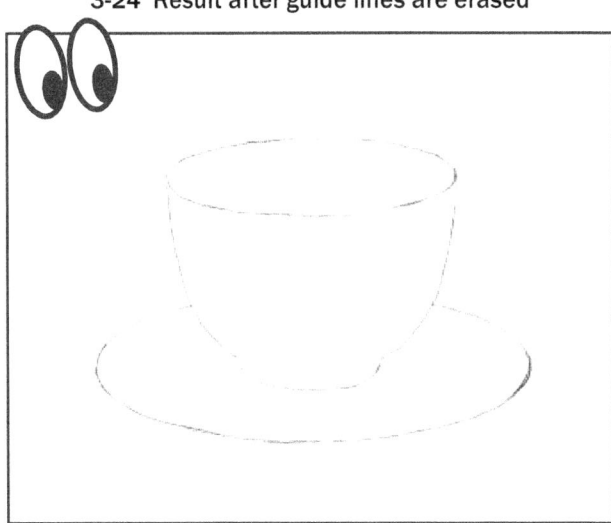

STEP 9 It's time to address the cup's handle. Since it is turned toward us, there is a natural urge to draw the shape bigger to indicate that its front is closer. However, as you've discovered, shapes at an angle in your line of sight appear to *narrow* with respect to *planes*. You observed this with the cylinder's top in Chapter 1 and the cup's top plane in this Chapter. The proper word for the visual effect is *foreshortening*, although I like to call it *forenarrowing* because it's the *narrowing* that tells us something is at an angle in our view. Observe that in Example 1, the handle opening is *circular*. However in Example 2, the handle is at an angular *plane*, and the circle seems to have *narrowed* to an *ellipse*. As you can see, here's another reason why you should convert three dimensional shapes to just horizontal and vertical terms when drawing. With this in mind, let's study illustration 3-25. Take a vertical pencil check, or visual of cup top"A". Compare the distance to the *handle's* vertical opening, or reverse space "B." The spans are nearly identical, aren't they? Next, observe where the bottom of the *handle* opening intersects the *cup's side "C"*. It is aligned midway at position"D," based on the cup's opening inset from the edge and turned sideways. As for handle opening "E" on the opposite side, the mid-point vertically aligns slightly *beyond* the cup's end. To apply these *sub-proportions*, begin by using *your* cup's opening height (3-26-a). Rotate the distance horizontally. Estimate half that span from your cup's end, on your right (3-26-b). Mark a dot where a plumb line from that point intersects your cup's *side* (3-26-c). Using the height of your cup's opening again (3-27-d), locate the second dot (3-27-e). To the right, the third dot centers between the first two, vertically aligned slightly past the side of your cup (3-28-f). The combination including reference points, optional guidelines, plus illustration 3-25 will help you form your handle's inside curve with confidence and ease (3-29).

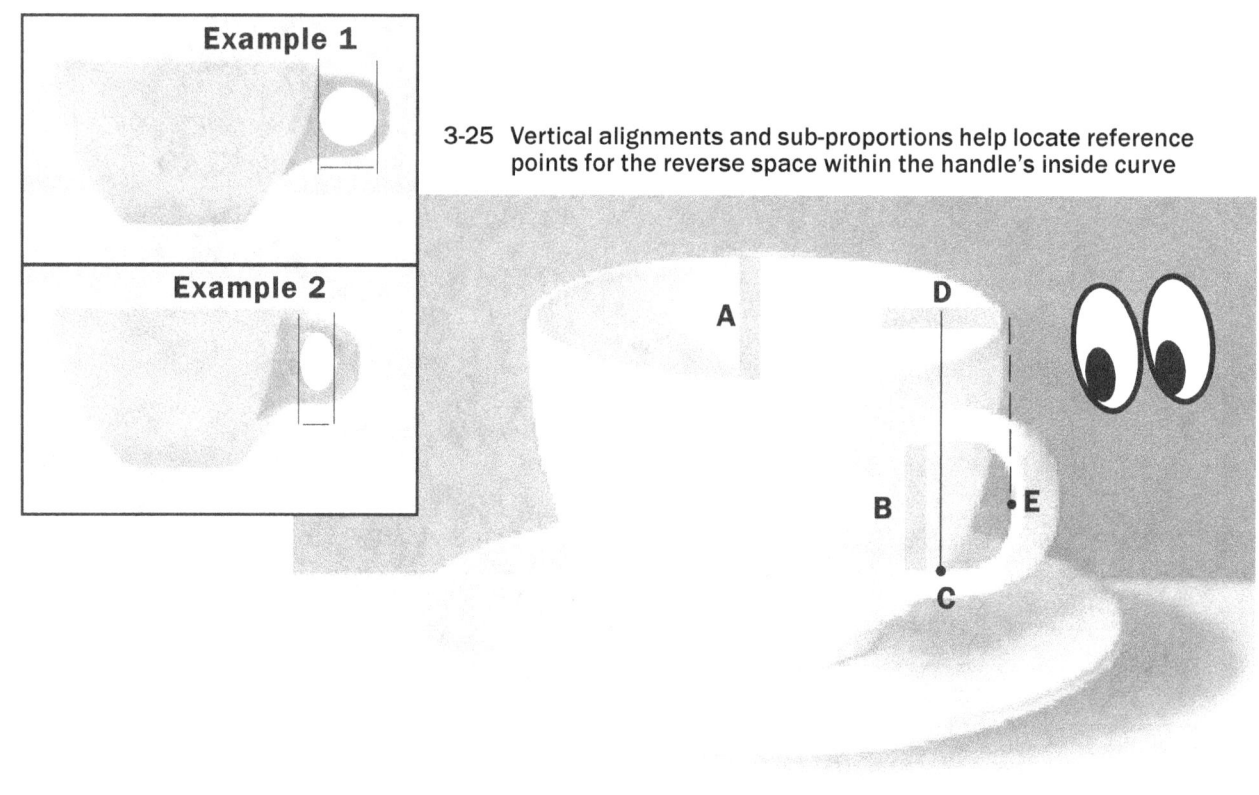

Example 1

Example 2

3-25 Vertical alignments and sub-proportions help locate reference points for the reverse space within the handle's inside curve

---

TIP
- *SUB-PROPORTION* is a comparison of one span in a shape/figure to another part of the shape/figure.
- **ALIGNMENT means two or more reference points line up straight.**
- **REVERSE SPACE (or negative space) is the area that borders a figure.**

3-26 Mark reference point on cup's side using relative proportion and vertical alignment

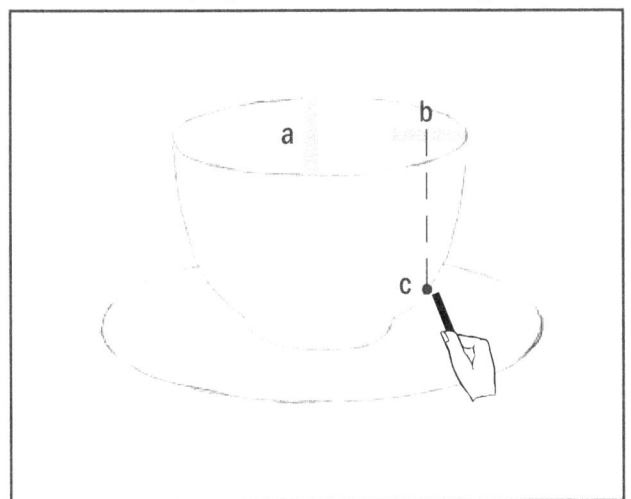

3-27 Mark reference point using relative proportion

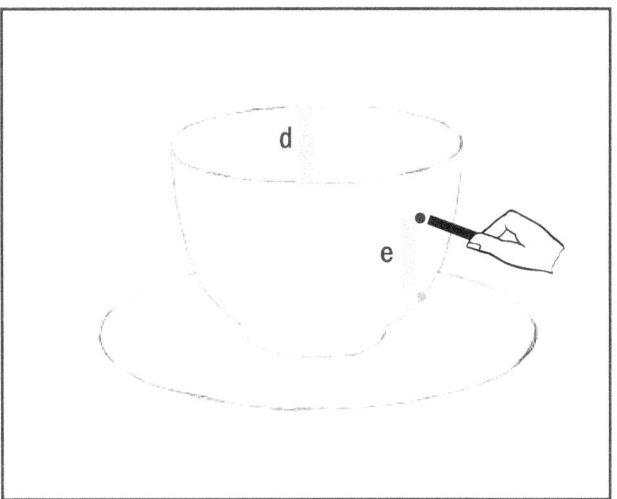

3-28 Mark reference point using alignments

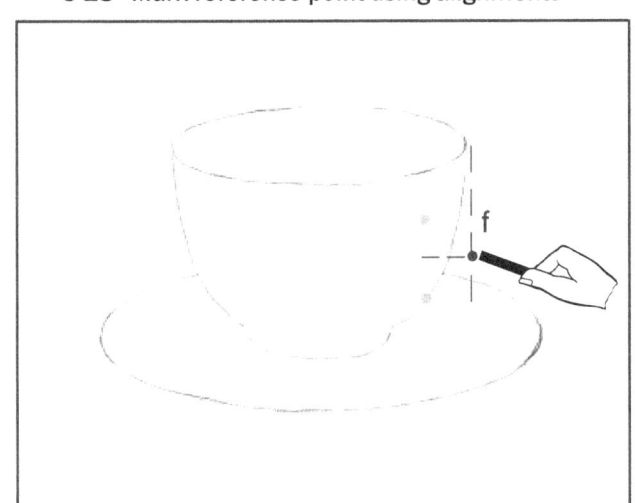

3-29 Draw handle's inside curve

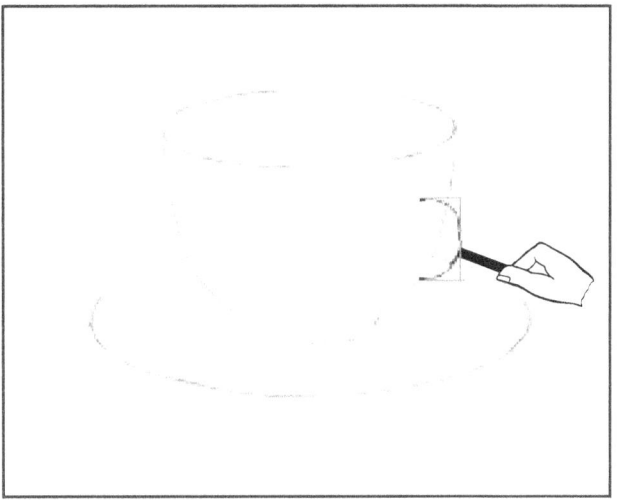

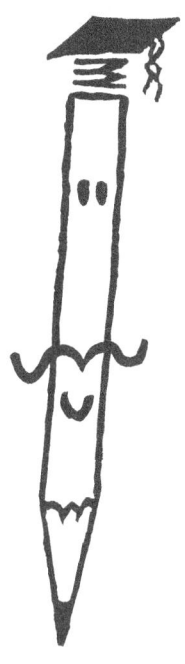

Pretty nifty, the way we formed the inside of the handle by drawing its negative space, don't you think? That's why I prefer the term REVERSE space. After all, NEGATIVE space suggests something undesirable, when in fact, it is actually very useful.

STEP 10 Now, let's attend to the handle's *outside* curve. Please sight along the vertical alignment from reference point "A" to reference point "B" in illustration 3-30. Observe that reference point "A" locates a little below midway between the upper inside curve and the edge of the ellipse. Reference point "B" locates about half way between the lower inside curve and the cup's base. Reference point "C" extends horizontally to the right of mid-point "A" to "B" at roughly the same distance as the cup's opening height. These three coordinates can be applied to your drawing by following illustrations 3-31 and 3-32. Then use illustration 3-30 as your reference to help form the right amount of curvature.

3-30 Alignments and relative proportions locate reference points to help form the handle's outside curve

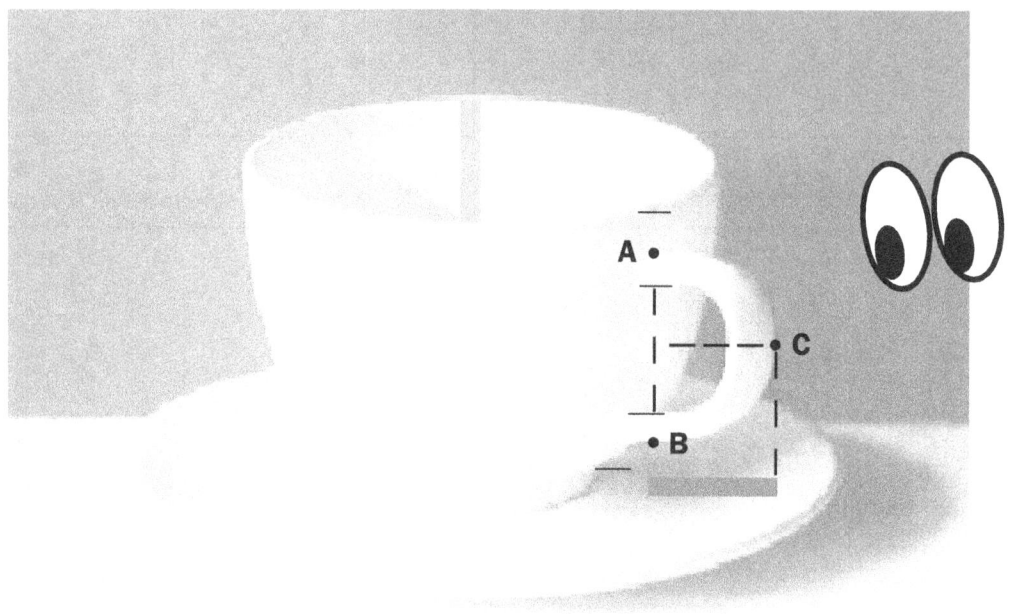

3-31 Mark reference points using relative proportions and alignments

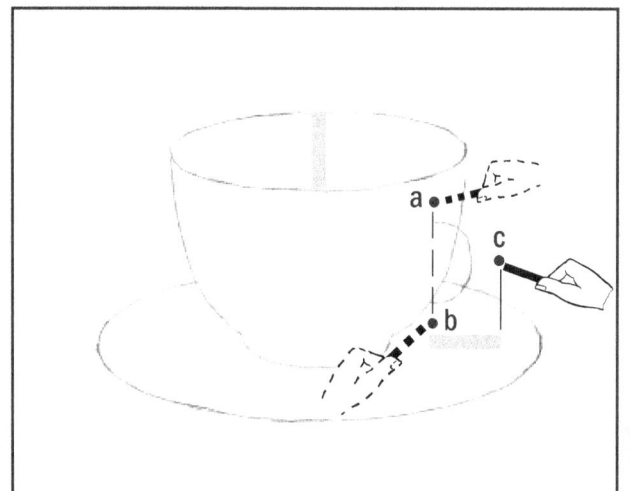

3-32 Draw handle's outside curve using reference points and optional guide lines

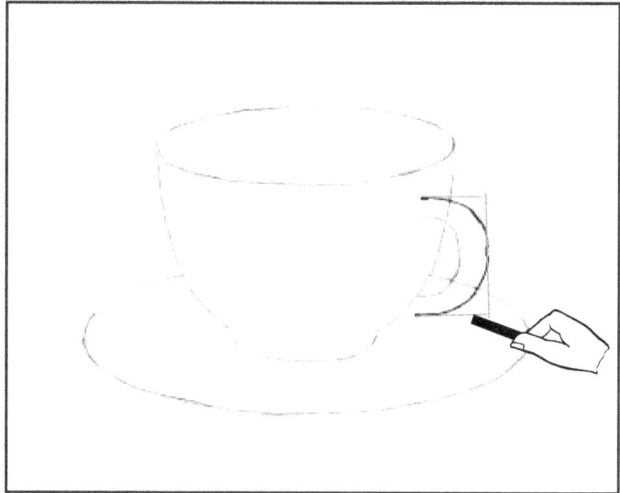

STEP 11 Please study the handle *ends* in illustration 3-33. Because I've outlined them for increased visibility, we can easily see that the upper portion closes with a simple curve. The lower portion also closes with a curve, but not before extending until nearly aligned with the cup's base. To complete the handle on *your* drawing, just elongate the bottom until it is about midway to the cup's base (3-34). Then lightly close the handle ends with a couple of "C" shaped curves (3-35).

> **TIP** Think of the handle as merely another *flat* horizontal and vertical shape.

3-33 Handle *top* connects with a small arc; *bottom* extends then
connects with a narrow arc, nearly aligned with the base

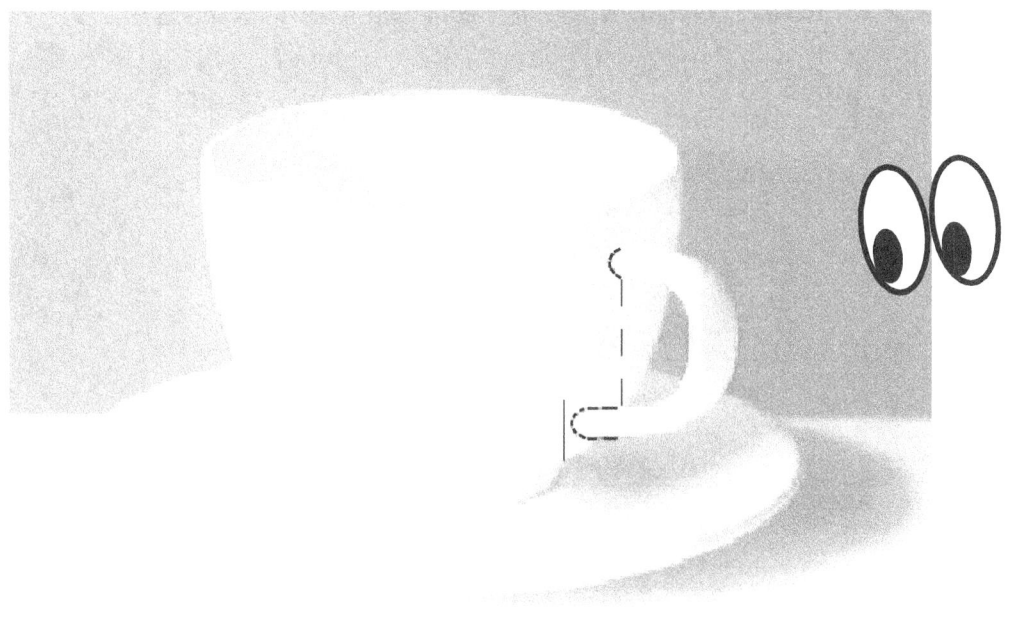

3-34 Extend handle bottom until halfway to cup base

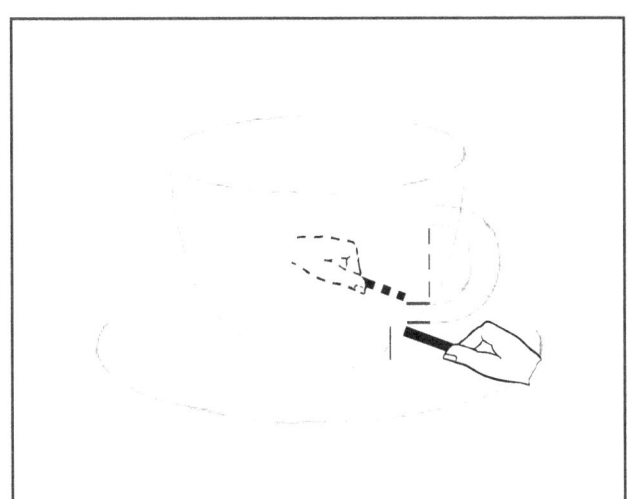

3-35 Close handle with a pair of curves

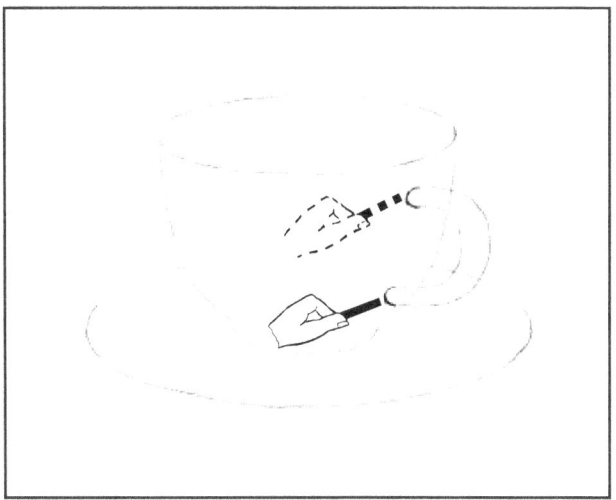

STEP 12 The secondary details are next. I have outlined them in illustration 3-33 for increased visibility. As you can tell, area "A" shows another ellipse. This one represents the rim's *inside* edge. From our view, the distance between the inside rim and the outside is about twice as wide at the ends compared to the the top and bottom. Line "B" indicates an edge of what is probably a table. Notice that by pretending we have x-ray vision again, we find that it appears to be *level* with the lower portion of the *handle's* opening. Moving on to curve "C," we notice it forms the cup's bottom and connects the base ends. Last but not least, partial ellipse "D" represents the *saucer's* inside rim. At the widest point (indicated by gray rectangles), the height is about equal to the cup's base. From there, it narrows until even with the outside rim at the "table" line. These observations can be applied to your drawing. Illustrations 3-34 through 3-40 will help guide you.

3-33 Relative proportions and alignments help observe secondary details

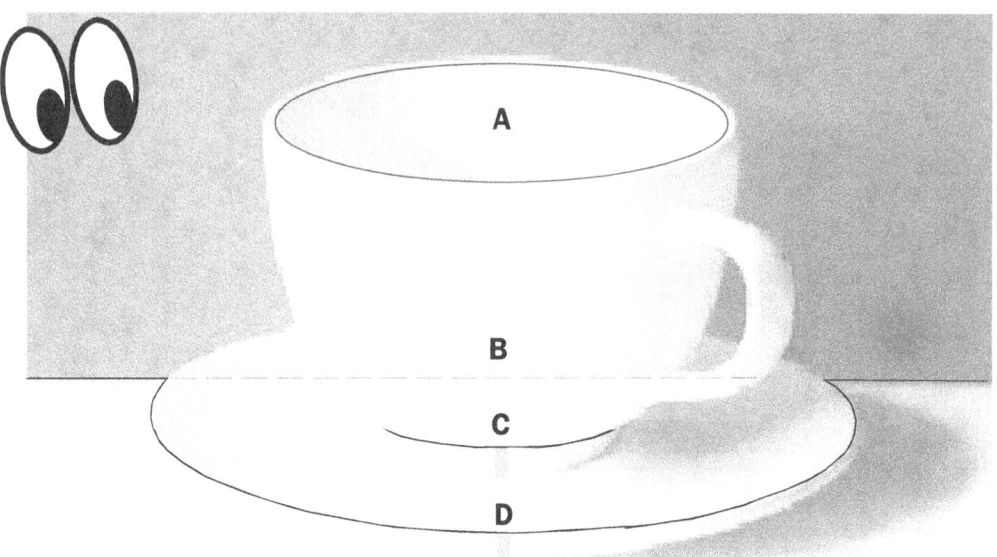

TIP Use illustration 3-33, along with reference points to help locate and form your curves. *Lightly* draw the "table" line level with the lower part of your handle from paper edge to edge (*through your figure*), to ensure that both ends line up. Then, erase excess lines. If you have notions of using a ruler or a straight edge, please reject the idea. Devices can become a habit and a crutch. I can't stress enough the importance of practicing freehand.

3-36 Draw cup's inside rim ends with 2 short curves

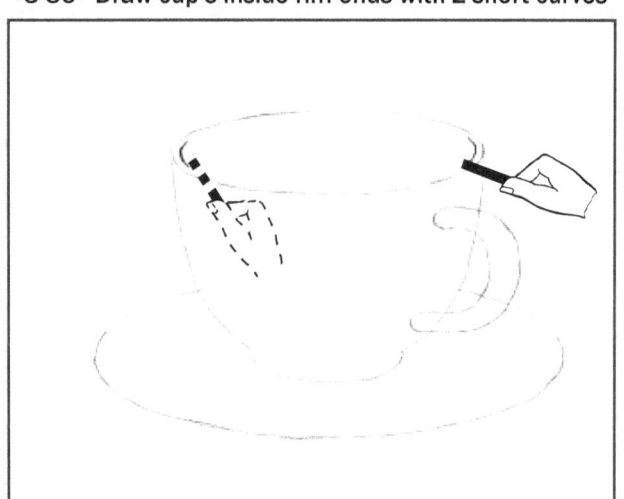

3-37 Draw top & bottom inside rim with 4 curves

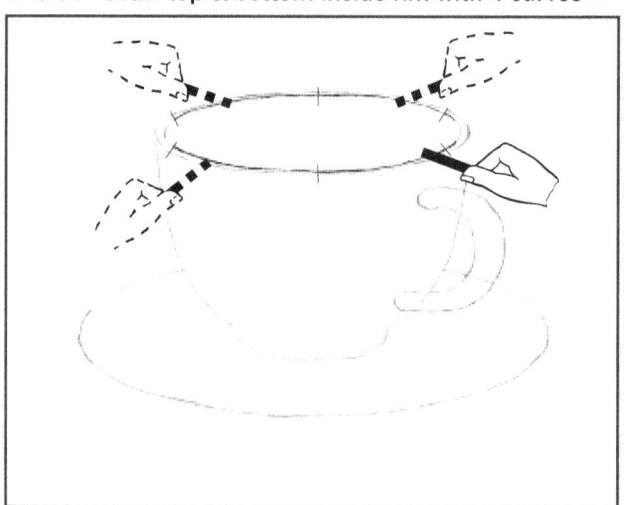

3-34 Draw curve forming cup bottom

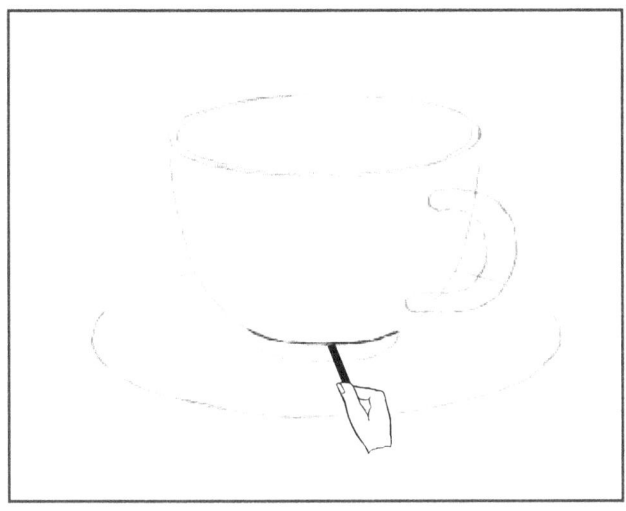

3-35 Draw saucer's inside left & right rim ends with 2 curves

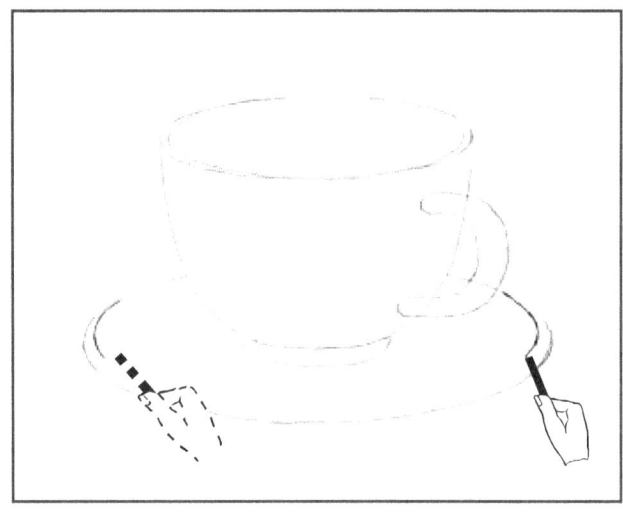

3-37 Draw saucer's bottom inside rim with 2 curves

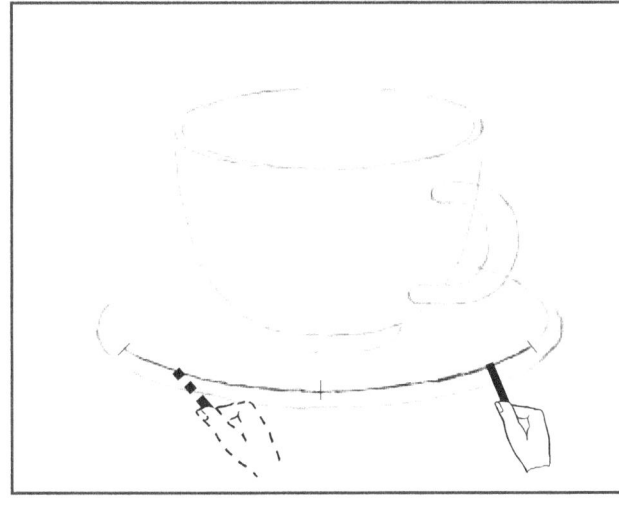

3-38 *Lightly* draw a level line even with bottom inside handle from paper edge to edge

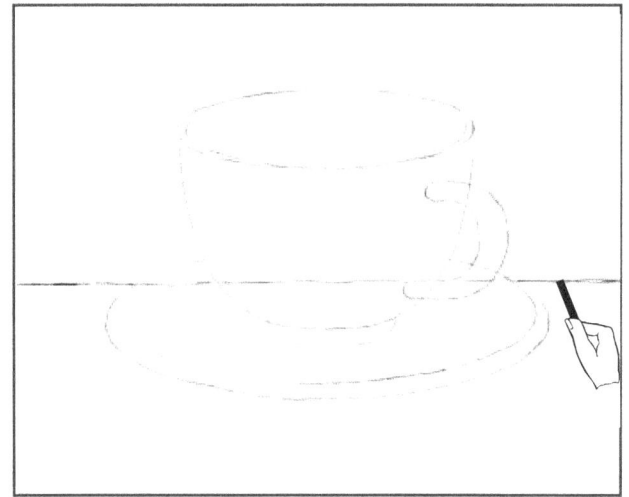

3-39 Erase excess lines within the figures marked "x"

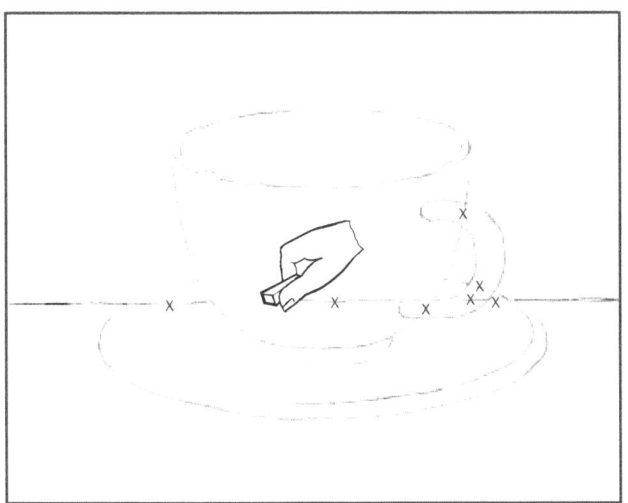

3-40 Result after excess lines are erased

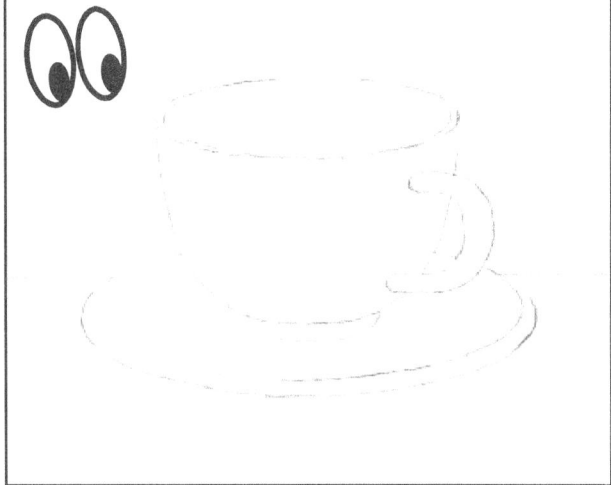

It's time for a check-up. As you know, a thorough once over can do wonders. Here's your opportunity to make final adjustments. Prop up your drawing next to my illustration. Then compare and contrast from a slight distance.

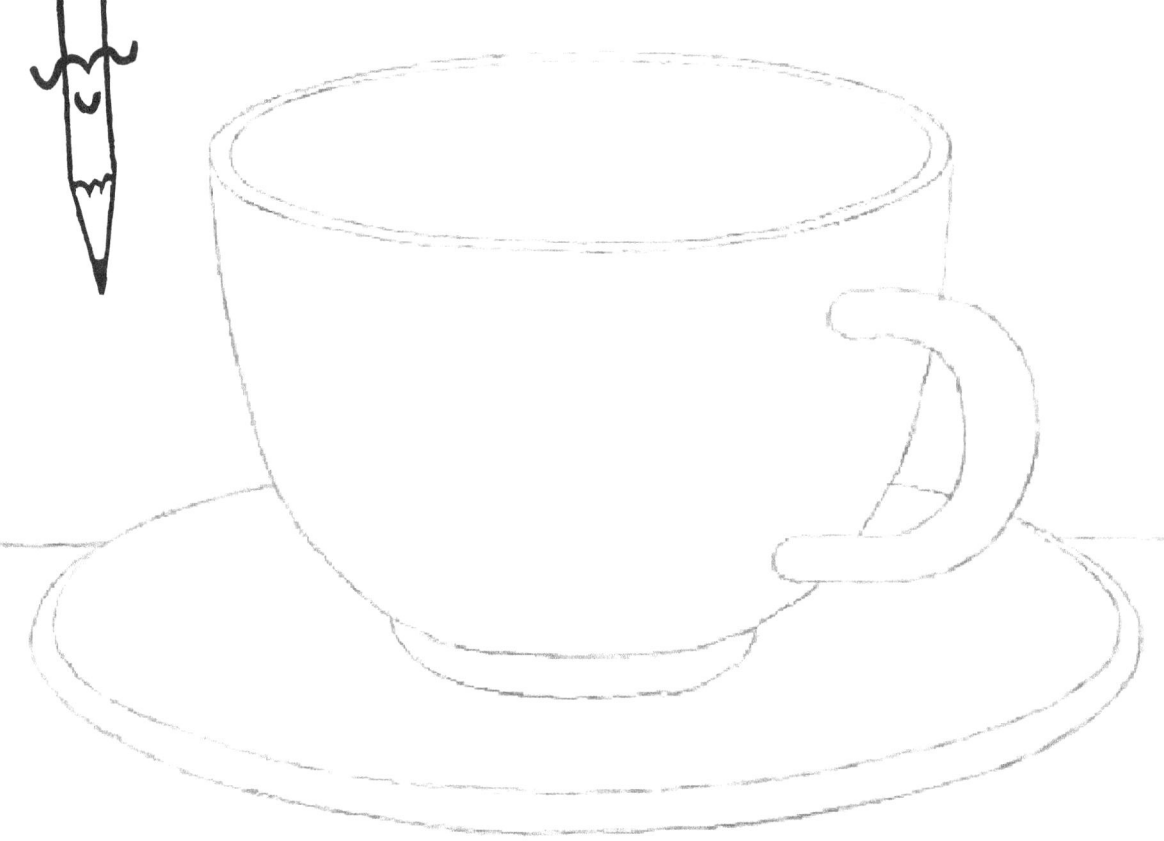

TIP Don't be concerned about minor stuff. Look for major things such as possible tilting and curvature irregularities. Overall and relative proportion is another important factor. Remember that your version doesn't have to be an exact match. If this sounds new, please refer to page **18** and page **34**.

Example A
Left side needs more angle and curve

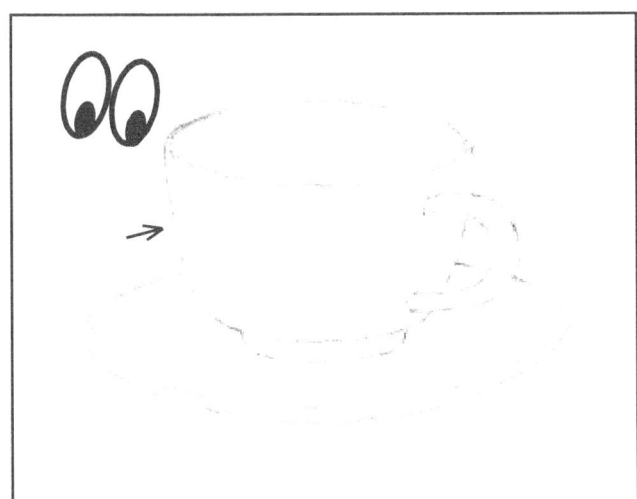

Result after left side angle and curve increased

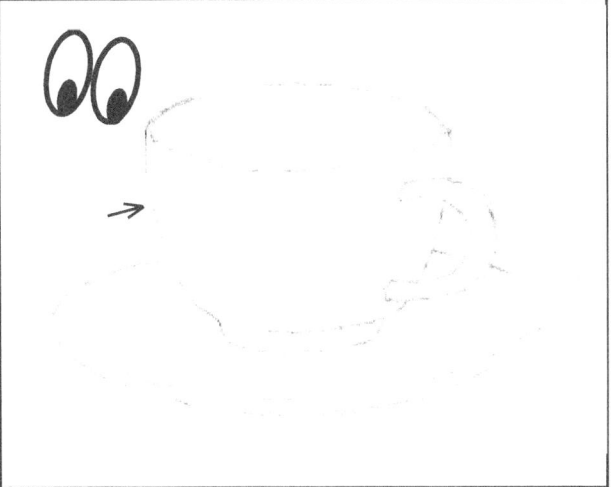

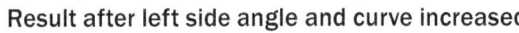

Your goal should not be to see whose picture is the best. Strive for knowledge through your experiences, and by studying the works of others.

Example B
Saucer rim is too thin

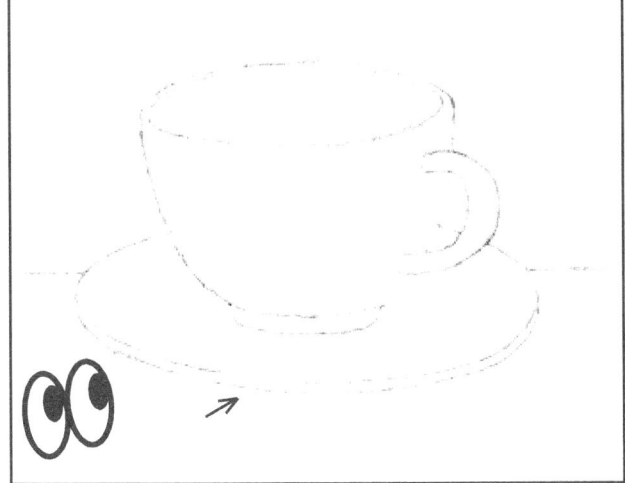

Result after rim is widened

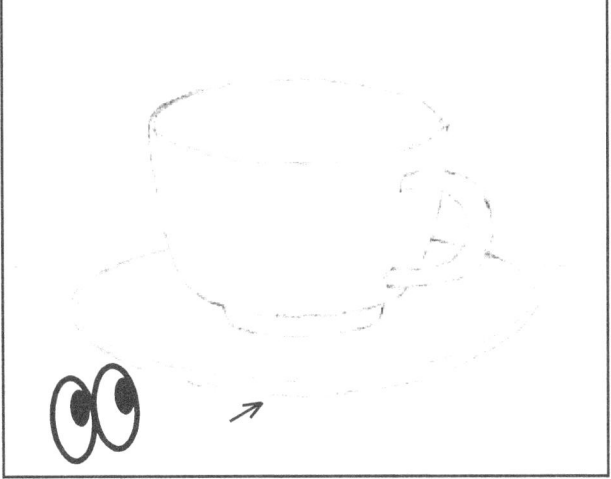

Chapter 3
FOLLOW-UP

The cup and saucer was a worthwhile exercise, wouldn't you agree? It heightened your practical experience working with ellipses, planes and contours. Equally rewarding, with the offshoot called *foreshortening,* you advanced your knowledge.

An easy way to describe ellipses is to think of them as even or uneven egg shapes. Planes, if you will recall, are the surfaces as they appear in your *perspective*, or point of view. These are commonly referred to as front, top, bottom and side planes. As for contours, they are the boundaries between planes. When planes (or surfaces) are in your line of sight, at an angle (like the cup's opening and the handle), the shapes seem to narrow, or *foreshorten*.

Although such apparent change occurs, it is not difficult to manage. Just the opposite. Planes, contours and the illusion of foreshortening are easy to operate in perspective, providing you remember to convert your three dimensional observations into two dimensional terms. Hopefully, you are beginning to appreciate this more and more.

I trust you are also developing a greater respect for the need to plan ahead, and for the ability to pretend you have x-ray eyes. After all, whether you work from a photo or from the real thing, perception (understanding by observing and analyzing), along with visualization (picturing in your mind), as well as improvisation (clever thinking), are skills that really come in handy.

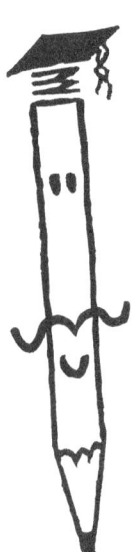

Next, get ready to add tones to your cup and saucer drawing. Did you work lightly? If not, simply flatten your putty eraser like a pancake and press it on your drawing, dabbing instead of rubbing. This will help lift some of the graphite without smearing or eliminating your lines.

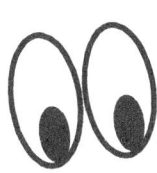

FROM THIS

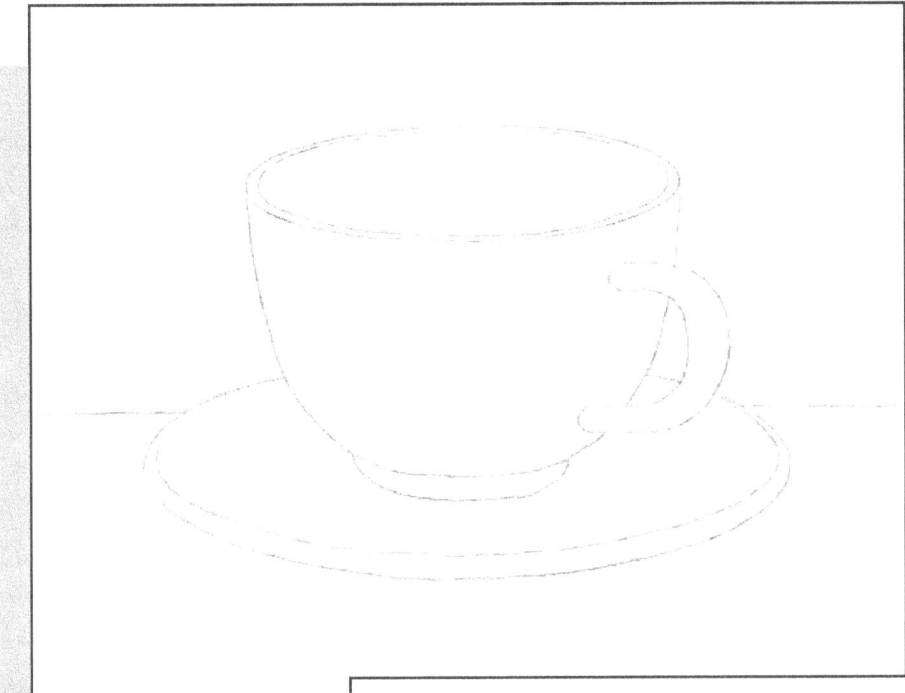

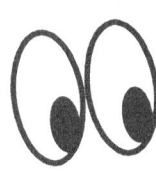

TO THIS

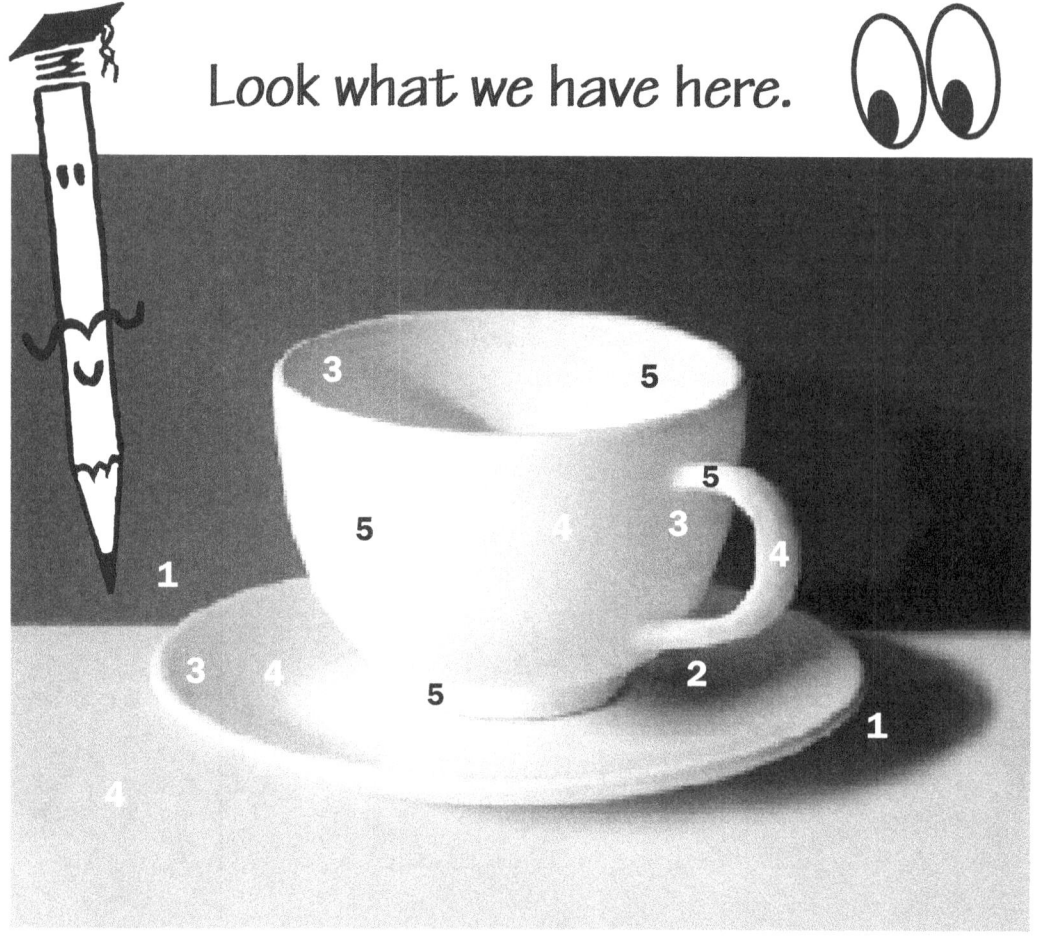

This photo is your reference for the next phase, namely to add tones to your line drawing. For the most part, there are just five main values and the numbers help point them out. As you can tell, background 1 and ground shadow 1 are very dark values. Saucer shadow 2 is not quite as dark. Cup opening shade 3 is slightly lighter in intensity. Table 4, saucer shade 4, cup shade 4, and handle shade 4 are a little lighter yet. The other areas, designated as number 5, are mostly bathed in light, and therefore nearly as white as the paper. With the five clearly different tones we get the impression the figures are three dimensional, even though they are shown in a photograph. If you recall, in Chapter 2 (page 34) I mentioned a minimum of five distinct tones are needed to achieve the principles of Chiaroscuro. However, when it comes to tone intensities, you have options. For instance, you can copy the tones pretty much as they appear or, by exercising *creative freedom*, you can change things. I often like to point out, it's not the subject matter that makes the artist. It's the way the artist makes the subject *matter*. In other words, you have the opportunity and the invitation to create your own unique *rendition*. What is a rendition? It is an interpreted version. Just as there are many ways to say something, so it is with drawing. Instead of a verbal description, a picture depicts the scene, in your choice of style. When finished, your pictorial expression would be called a *rendering*. The next page illustrates three examples. Each has individual characteristics and attractive qualities. Version 1 was made with oodles and oodles of dots. The technique is called *stippling*, and takes a lot of time as well as patience. Curved and straight *lines* brought about Version 2 which demands a great deal of pressure control. Version 3 resulted by spreading tone, followed by blending. The dual (two part) procedure is similar to the methods you have already experienced, except the values are applied with larger, more aggressive strokes.

TIP *Value* in drawing refers to the intensity (strength) of a light or dark tone.

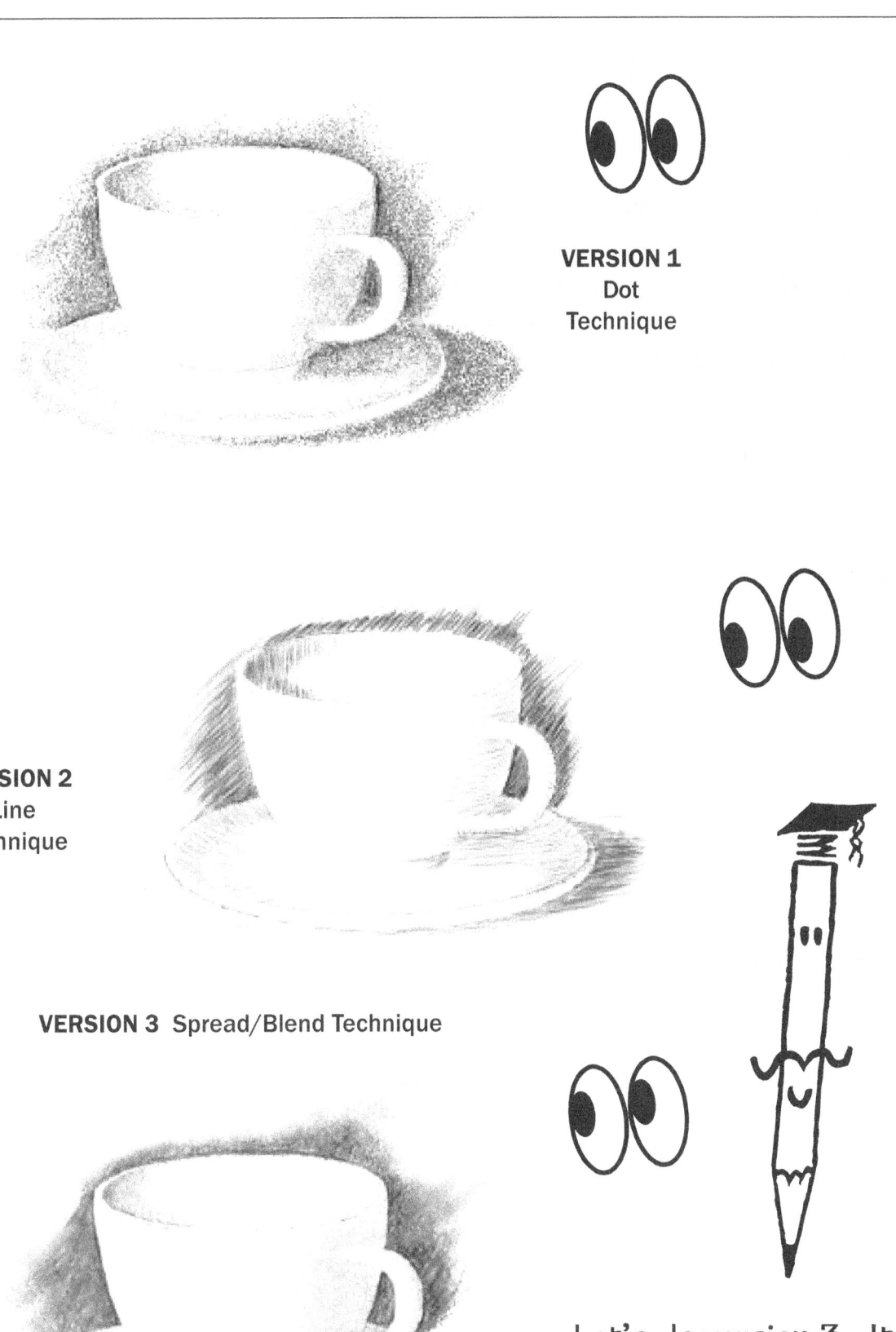

VERSION 1
Dot
Technique

VERSION 2
Line
Technique

VERSION 3 Spread/Blend Technique

Let's do version 3. It expands on the methods you have used. The steps begin on the next page.

STEP 1 Your completed cup and saucer line drawing from Chapter 3 should now be ready for toning. I trust you remembered to work lightly. If your lines turned out quite dark, please make them less visible by dabbing with your putty eraser. Then proceed to fill areas with tone. I recommend using the underhand method, with a variety of pressures, stroke lengths, thicknesses and directions. These techniques will help bring about a range of values, styles and lively effects, plus enable you to cover large areas (4-1). You may want to practice on another piece of paper first. As soon as you feel confident, begin with the background. Start from the center of your cup's top opening and stroke at an angle, *left-to-right*. Apply strong pressure for a dark value and vary your stroke lengths as you make your way across and down. When you reach the the left side of the cup switch by stroking right to left (4-2). Repeat from the top center, around the right side at the same angle. Proceed with *left-to-right* strokes again (4-3). After you reach the edge, stroke *right-to left.* The change in direction, but not the angle will maintain consistency and help reduce the number of unwanted marks that invade the figures.

4-1 TONE EXAMPLES USING A VARIETY OF STROKES

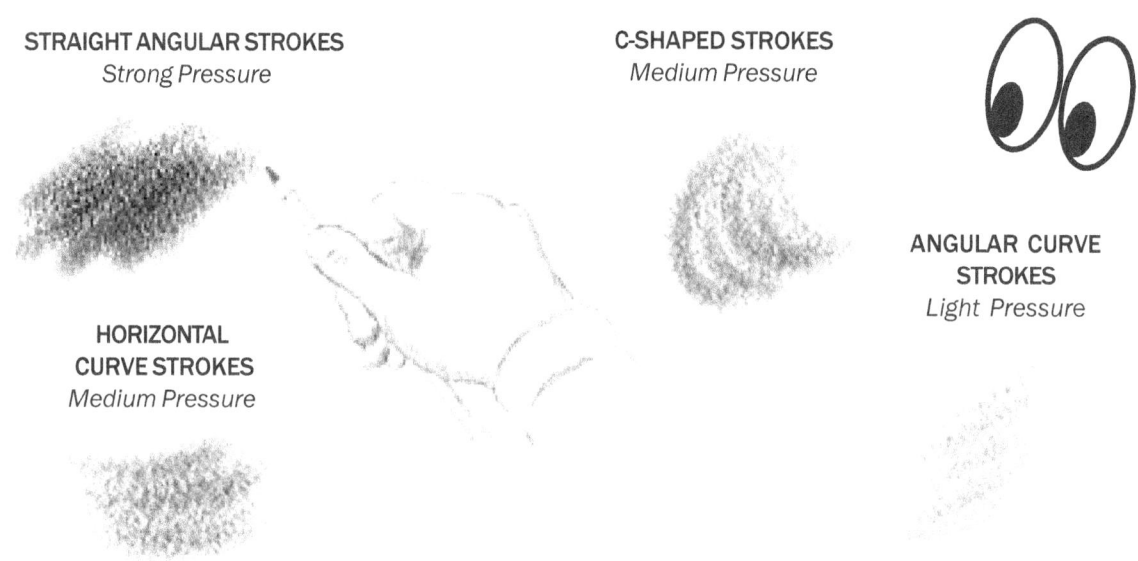

STRAIGHT ANGULAR STROKES
Strong Pressure

C-SHAPED STROKES
Medium Pressure

ANGULAR CURVE STROKES
Light Pressure

HORIZONTAL CURVE STROKES
Medium Pressure

TIP If your tones have a shine, you are overstroking and/or applying too much pressure. If absolutely necessary, dab shiny areas with your putty eraser. Blotches, smears and strokes that invade figures can be remedied later.

4-2 Tone background left half with angled strokes

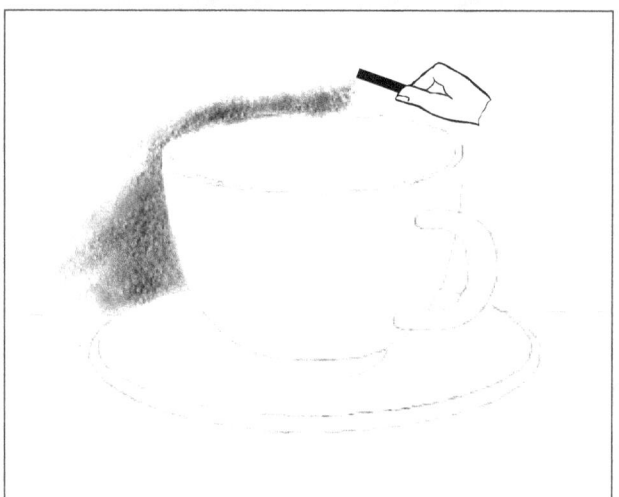

4-3 Tone background right half with angled strokes

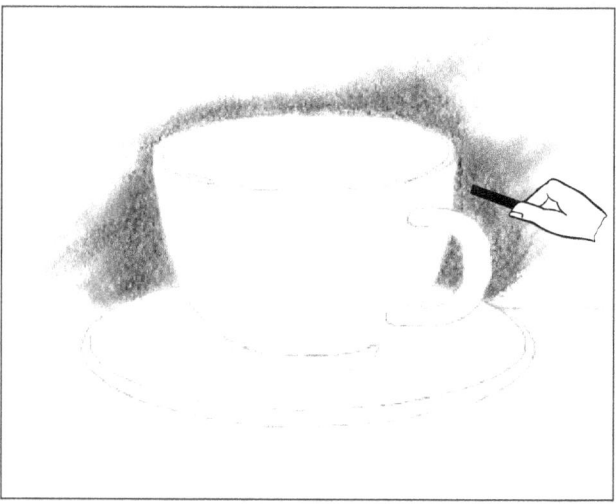

STEP 2 Continuing with the underhand toning method, proceed to the ground area (table). Instead of angle motions however, you should switch to a *horizontal* direction to indicate the flat surface. Start a little under the lower middle part of your saucer. Stroke *right-to-left* along the left edge. For a more random appearance, try to keep your marks somewhat uneven (4-4). Then repeat the process by beginning from the section below your saucer's middle again. This time advance toward the right with *left- to-right* strokes (4-5).

4-4 Tone ground on left with horizontal right- to-left strokes

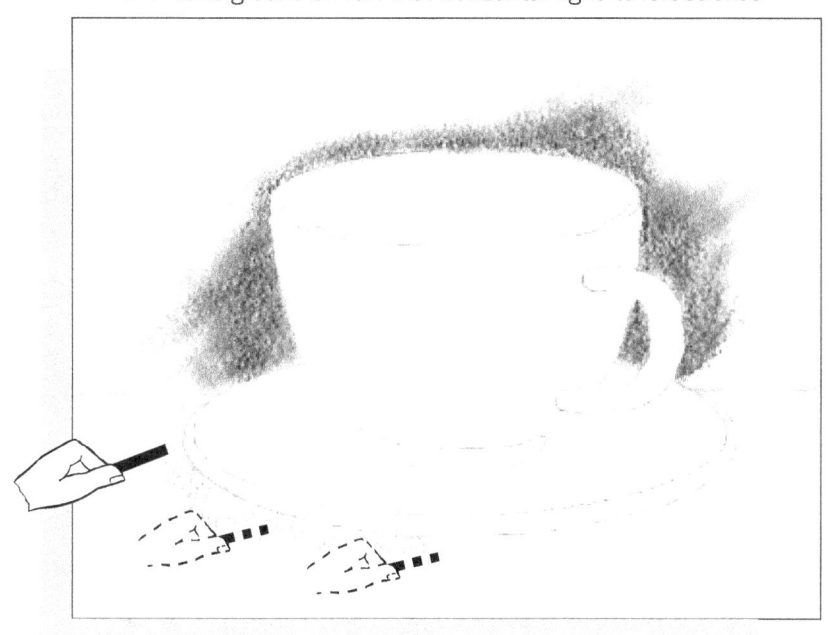

4-5 Tone ground on right with horizontal left-to-right strokes

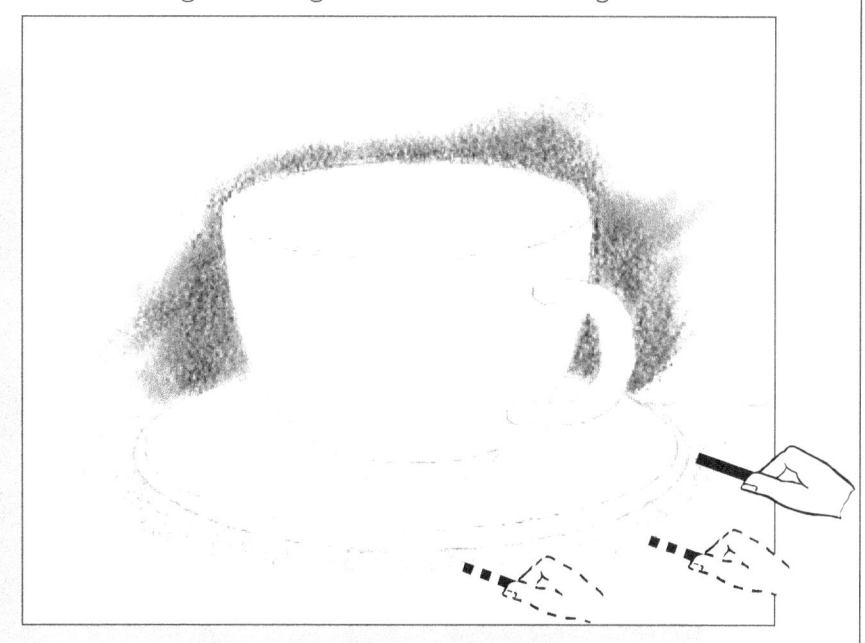

TIP Are you wondering why the background and ground areas were picked for toning *first*? Please re-read page 24 in Chapter 2.

STEP 3 Shade the values in your cup's opening with "C" strokes to indicate the surface curvature. Start on the left inside rim. Apply pressure, then ease up with a sweeping motion (4-6). Place additional strokes next to each other to the right, with decreasing pressure. The gradually softening appearance and tapering (narrowing) effect will suggest that the shade gradually fades into the light (4-7). For your cup's shade side (handle side), apply a medium gray tone, curving from right-to-left to indicate the rounded surface. Advance only about a *quarter* of the way across the entire cup. The value should be dark enough so the lines forming your *handle ends* disappear into the tone. If your lines are too dark, they should be erased until only faintly visible *before* you apply the tone. Be sure to shade a small part of the base as well (4-8). Then, add a lighter tone beside your cup's shade tone for a fading effect that extends halfway across your cup. Use *right-to-left* sweeping angle strokes that follow the curved surface (4-9).

4-6 Shade inside rim with a "C" stroke

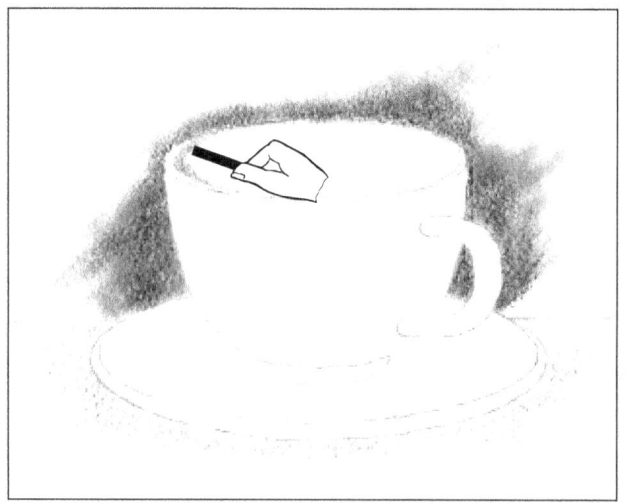

4-7 Shade inside rim with more "C" strokes
fading gradually by decreasing pressure

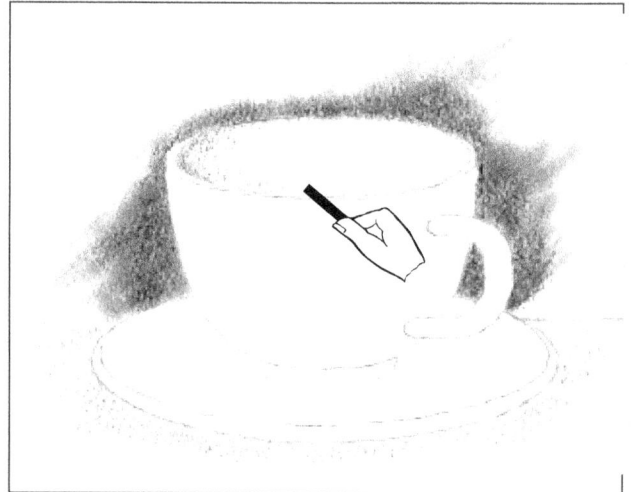

4-8 Tone cup's shade side and base

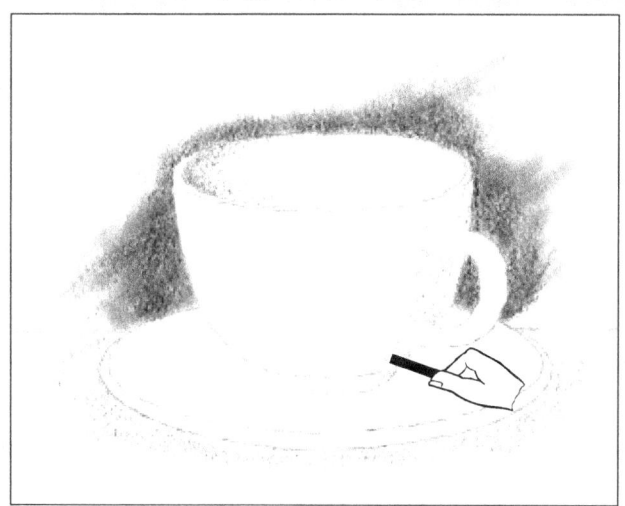

4-9 Fade shade to the left with less pressure

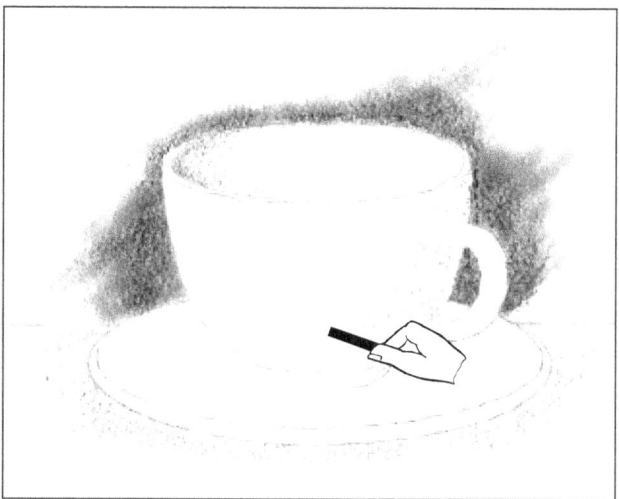

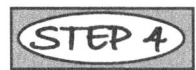

Now, let's tone the handle. It's simple when you understand how light affects the shape. As illustration 4-10 demonstrates, the handle can be seen as basically just a bent tube. If we were to cut sections away, we would see the upper and lower segments lie *horizontally* before turning to connect with the *vertical* portion. Equally important, since light is coming from the upper left, and since the shapes it hits are *cylindrical*, the *bottom* side of the *horizontal* sections are in shade. On the *vertical* section, however, shade is on the *side* facing your right. With these helpful observations, you can tone your cup's handle. Start *gently with your pencil point* at the bottom end. Move toward the right with slightly curved vertical strokes. These show surface curvature as you make your way around. When you reach the lower turn in the handle, your strokes should gradually angle left. By the time you reach midway along the vertical portion, your strokes should level out. From there, your strokes should gradually tilt downward, stopping near the end of your handle's upper curve (4-11). In order to shade your handle's remaining top portion, start again from the left end, on the *underside*. Advance right with short vertical curves that halt at the upper turn (4-12).

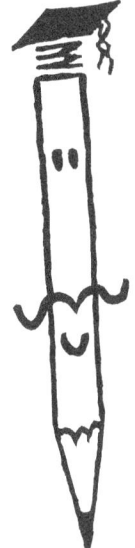

Many shapes are cylindrical. The handle is yet another example.

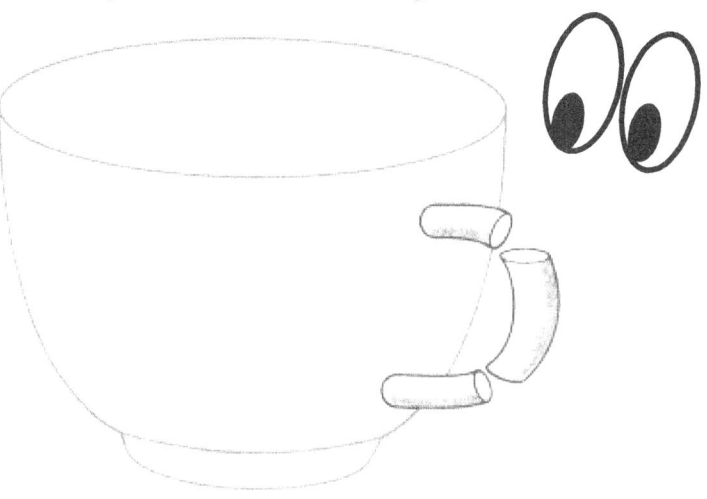

4-10   The horizontal handle sections receive shade on the bottom. The vertical part receives shade on the right side.

4-11 Tone handle *bottom* and *inside right edge* Stop at upper curve

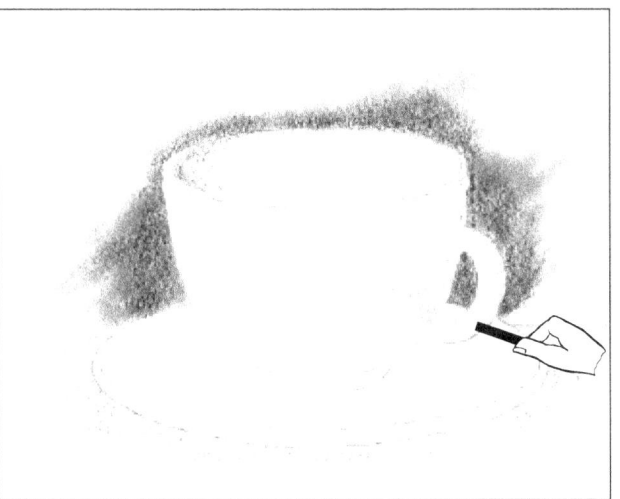

4-12 Tone lower portion of handle top Stop at curve

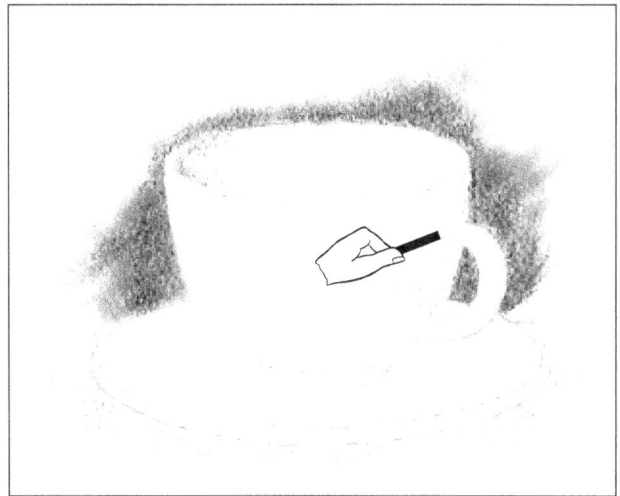

STEP 5 The cup has cast a shadow on the saucer. To indicate this, begin toning the visible area through the handle. For contrast, the value should be *DARKER* than your *cup's shade*, but *LIGHTER* than your *background tone* (4-13). Next, you should apply *left-to-right* strokes and a little more pressure under the handle and against the cup's edge. Then ease your strokes as they move away from the figure to express a natural fading effect (4-14). As for the inside of the saucer rim, since it has depth, there is *shade*. In order to tone the area on your left and show the surface curvature, use "C" shaped strokes, like those you placed in your cup's opening, *although not as dark* (4-15). The remaining section (to the right) should be toned with a narrow strip which leaves some white space under your cup's base (4-16). Why? Because that portion is the saucer's bottom, bathed in light from above.

4-13 Tone shadow area on saucer visible through handle

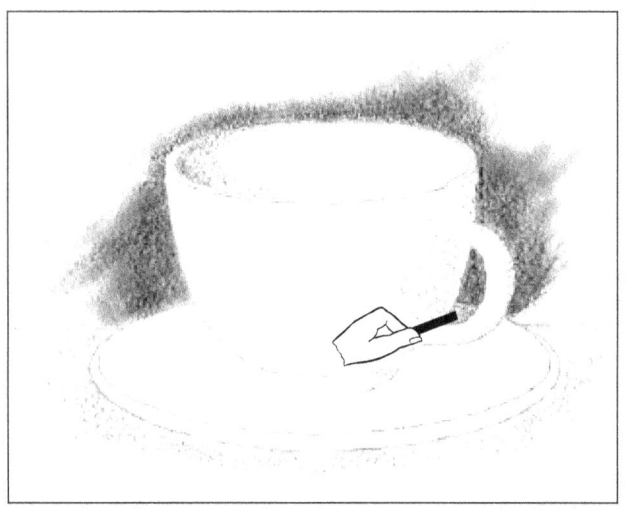

4-14 Tone shadow area on saucer below handle

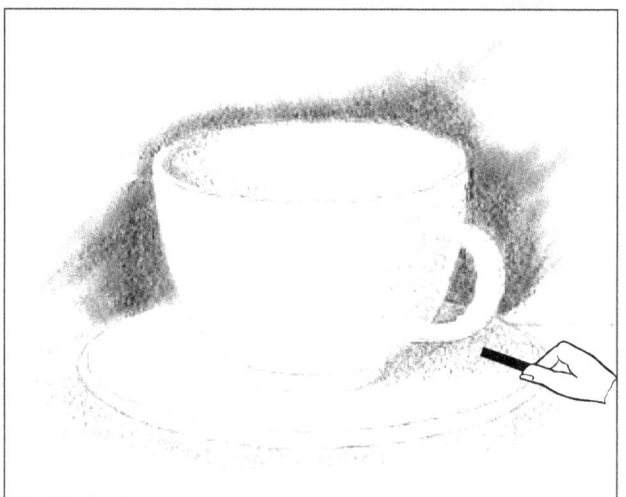

4-15 Tone saucer shade on left side

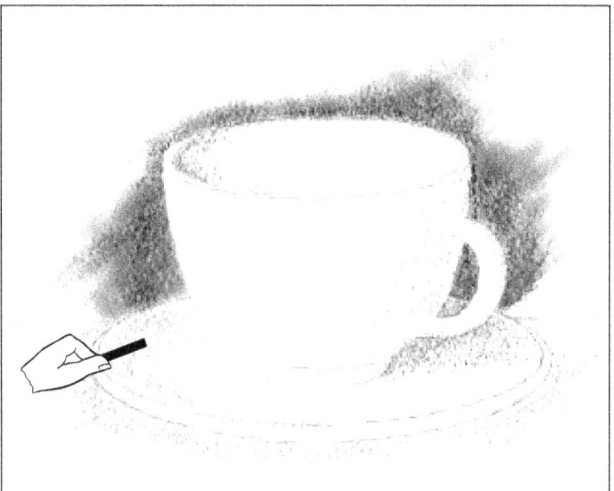

4-16 Tone saucer shade on right side

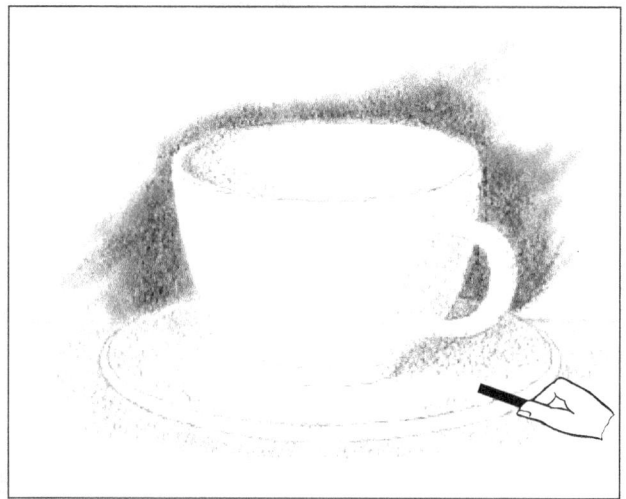

STEP 6 In Illustration 4-17, I've made a section more visible within the circular area to reveal something very interesting. The lower part of the saucer's *rim,* on the shade side, has a *lighter* tone within it. How is this possible? The answer is simple. *Light that strikes a surface can bounce off.* The phenomenon (observable event) is called *reflected light, and usually it is not as bright as highlight.* In this case, light hits the ground (table) and rebounds (bounces back) against the saucer's underside (losing intensity in the process). Using illustration 4-17 for reference, place your pencil on *YOUR saucer's top rim,* vertically aligned with the mid-point of your cup's handle. From there, make your way to the right, with short, gentle, downward vertical strokes that reach only about half way to the rim bottom. Your marks should shorten proportionally according to the narrowing of the rim, and stop where it turns away from view toward the back (4-18). Next, with the help of illustration 4-17 again, prepare to tone the *ground shadow.* Start a little to the right of center. Advance toward the right, applying underhanded *left-to-right* strokes to form the shadow's elliptical shape. Ease pressure when nearing the outer edge to achieve the natural fading appearance of a *soft edge* (4-19).

4-17 Light strikes ground and bounces back reaching lower rim

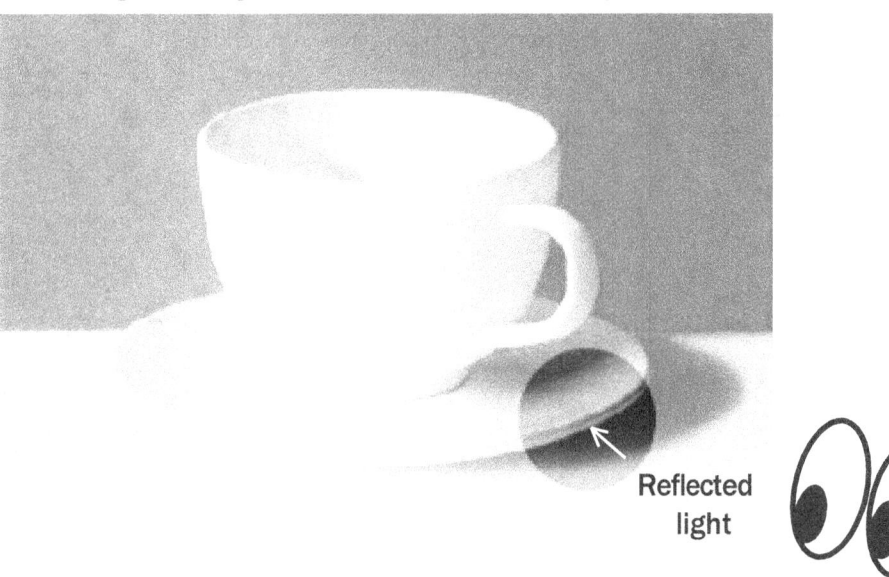

Reflected
light

4-18 Tone top half of saucer rim in shade

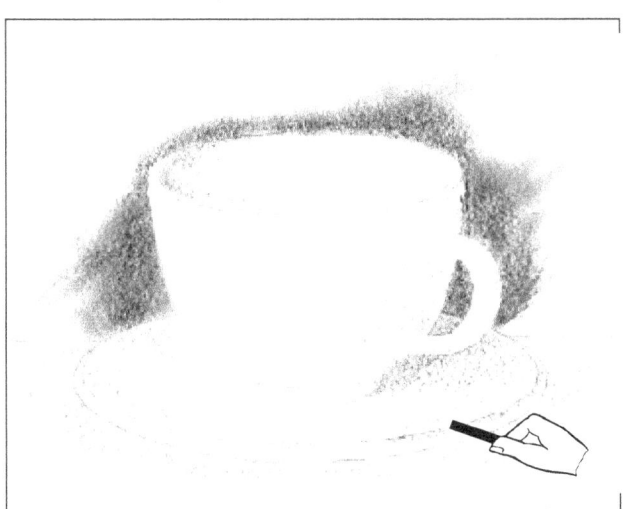

4-19 Tone ground shadow cast by the saucer

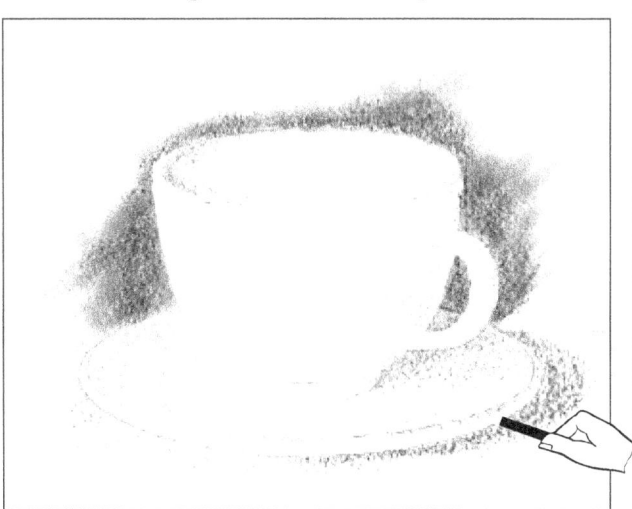

IS THE DRAWING FINISHED?

I'm sure you've discovered it's wise to keep track of your progress by stopping occasionally to do a side-by-side comparison between your work and your model (preferably from a slight distance). The overview opens the possibility for pleasant surprises. In other words, it provides the opportunity to discover where some results may not have turned out as planned, but may possibly be more desirable. You can also determine whether goals were accomplished, according to your present ability. Plus, you can decide whether anything requires further modification.

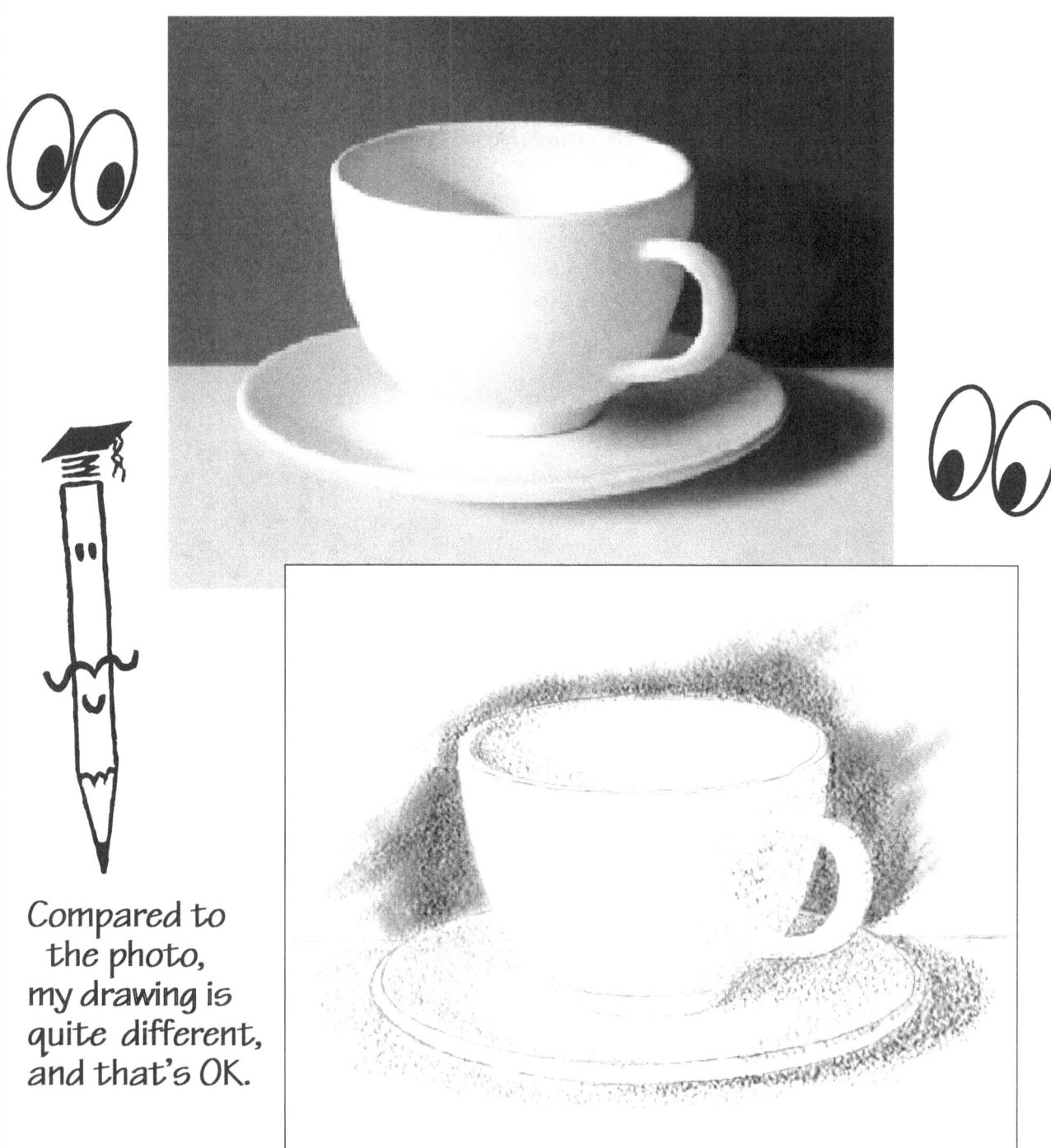

Compared to the photo, my drawing is quite different, and that's OK.

As you know, renditions do not have to be like a photograph. By comparing the examples on the previous page, we can observe that the figures in the drawing are depicted fairly accurately and convey recognizable, three dimensional objects, wouldn't you agree? The "shading," or chiaroscuro technique, is reasonably convincing, is it not? From what I can tell, the style is consistent and the values effectively give the impression that the forms are solid and bathed in light, coming from the left. If you can say the same about your work, we both have brought about what is generally considered a creative interpretation. Sure, my drawing is currently in a rough state, and yours is probably too, but this can be charming and appealing.

Some people may disagree, of course. They might say my rendering is incomplete and they may see the changes I made as flaws. For example, on my drawing the *saucer's* cast shadow is not as dark, nor proportionally as long as it is in the photograph. Granted, but I think the shadow in the photo is too close to the edge and the very dark tone is distracting because it takes attention from the figures. Given a choice, I'd rather leave my shadow be. On second thought, perhaps some blending couldn't hurt. And another evaluation couldn't do any harm, either.

Now let's study just the *drawing* on the opposite page. Since all the tones are in, we can examine their contribution to the picture. We can also allow the effects of *assimilation (visual mixing)* to reveal things that may not have been apparent before. Case in point: my background along the cup's rim seems to float on top. Also, many of the boundaries between the figures and the background appear to be a bit vague. Plus, there are some blotches in the cup's shade area under the handle.

Time to play *"what-if's."* For instance, imagine what would happen if the background was darkened for higher contrast and the edges of the figures are defined to make them more prominent (stand out). Next, what if the blotches were eliminated and select areas were blended for a smoother texture; would the picture be better? A tough judgment call, right? Tastes vary, but personally, I recommend we take the plunge. In this case, the gamble could favorably change the outcome. Take a look at the following version *(including* the suggested modifications). Is it an improvement to the drawing on the previous page? I think so.

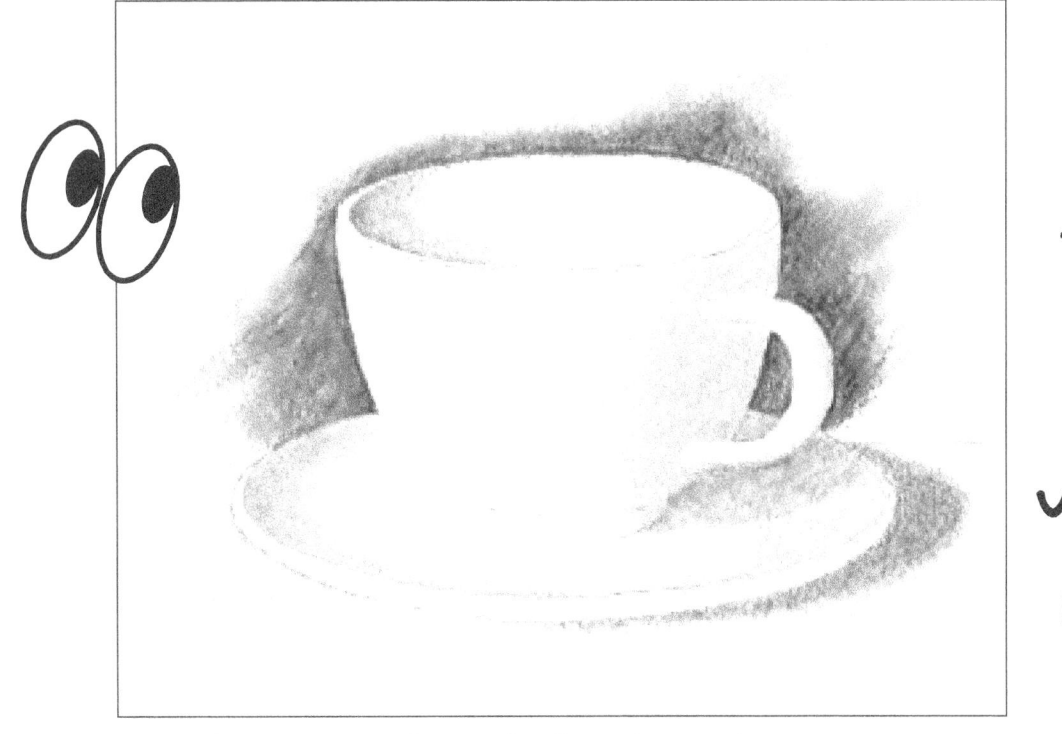

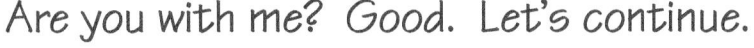

Are you with me? Good. Let's continue.

STEP 7 Earlier, I mentioned that overstrokes which may have invaded your figure can be remedied later. That time has arrived. Once you have erased unwanted marks, carefully draw a slightly darker line along your saucer, cup and handle edges where they meet the background (4-20). Then, fade your newly formed lines into the background with your blender (4-21). This will help clarify the boundaries, eliminate hard lines, as well as darken the background. In turn, the higher contrast will make the cup and handle more visible.

4-20 Darken edges bordering your figures in background

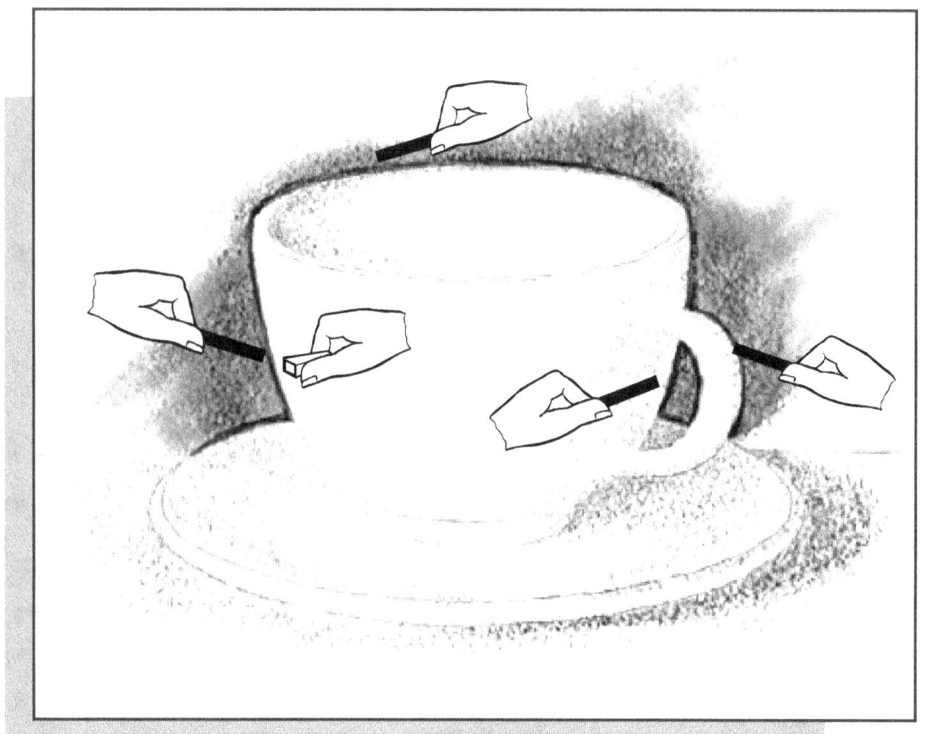

4-21 Blend to fade darkened edges into background

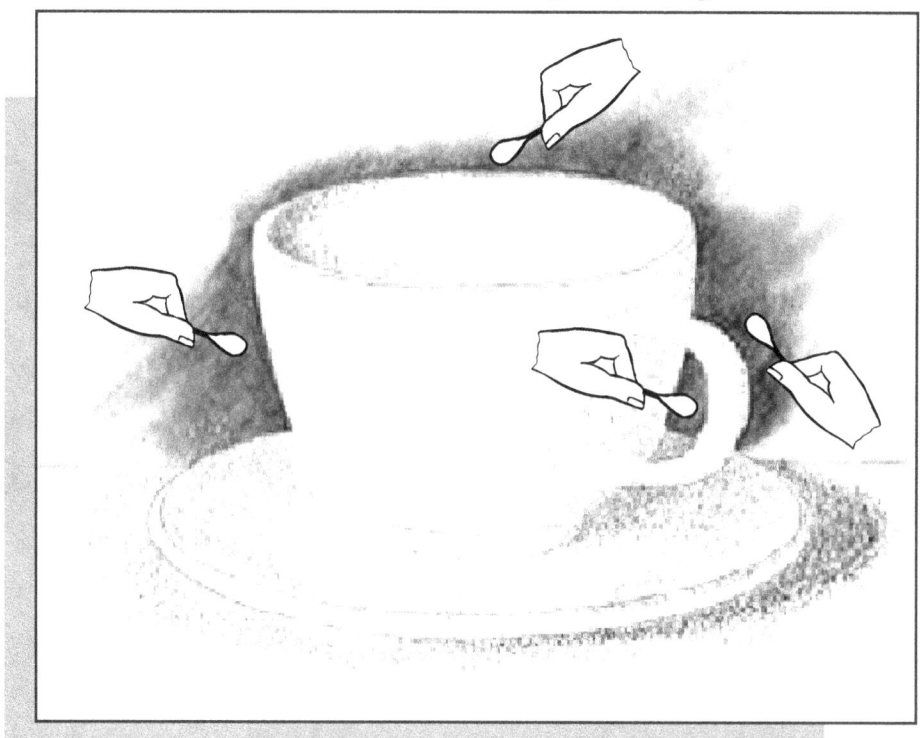

STEP 8 Sharpen the edges along the small part of your cup's cast shadow made visible through the handle by using the point of your blender. Use the same method for the remaining cast shadow area under the handle. With *left-to-right* strokes, spread the tone evenly. Apply less pressure and sweeping strokes to soften the edge and tilt it upward to indicate the saucer's sloping bowl (4-22). Next, blend the saucer's cast shadow to soften the pitted (porous) appearance and clarify the boundary. Be sure to reduce pressure for the fading effect (4-23).

4-22   Blend cup's cast shadow to soften and clarify figure edges

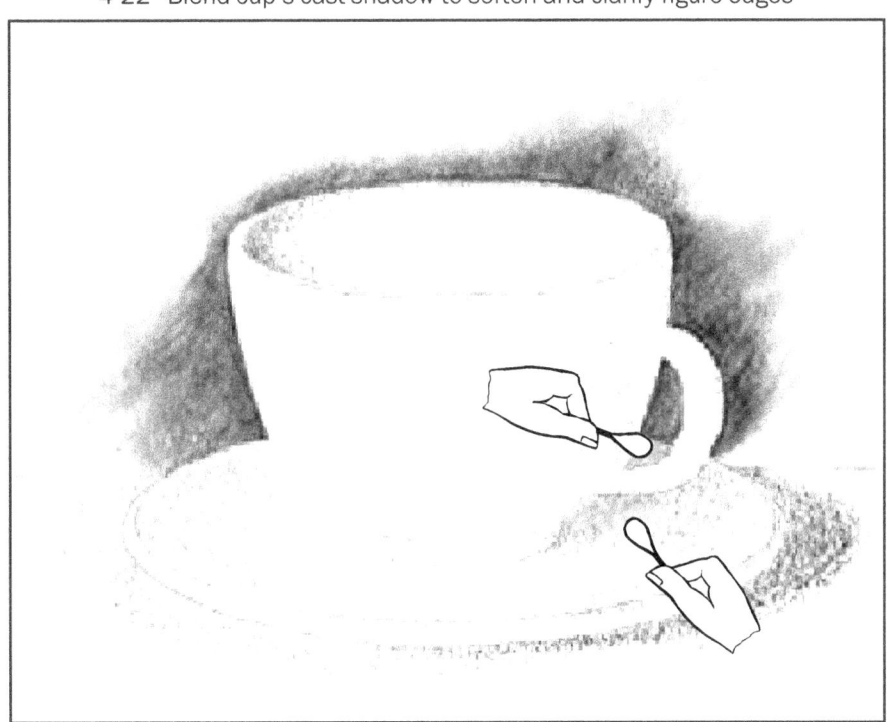

4-23   Blend saucer's cast shadow to darken and clarify saucer boundary

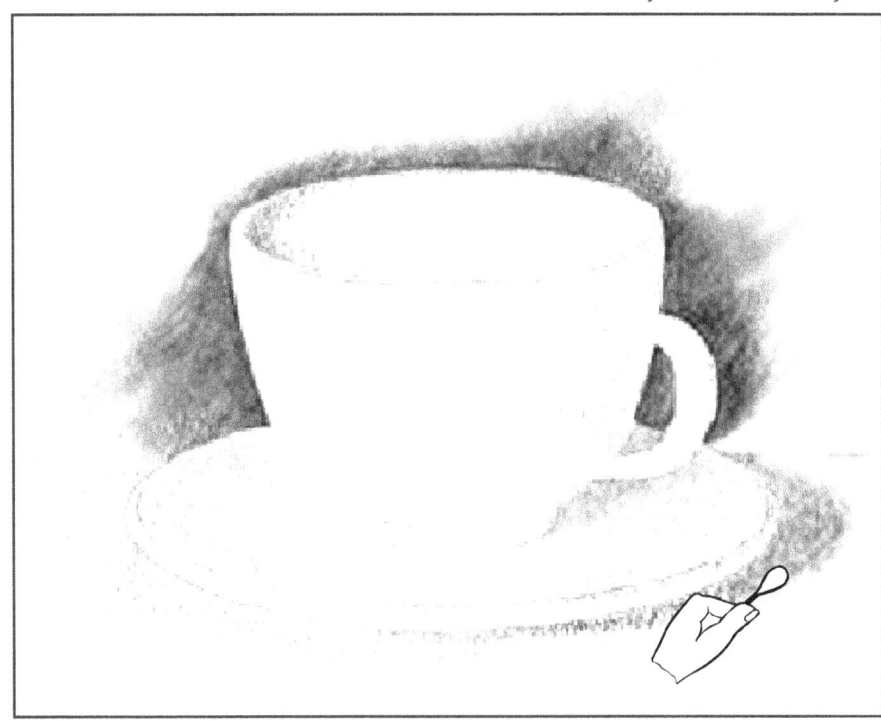

With sweeping "C" shaped strokes, sharpen the shadow edge along the left side of your cup's rim (4-24). Reduce pressure to fade the tone until its boundary practically disappears into the light area toward your right (4-25).

4-24 Blend rim's shade edge with sweeping "C" strokes

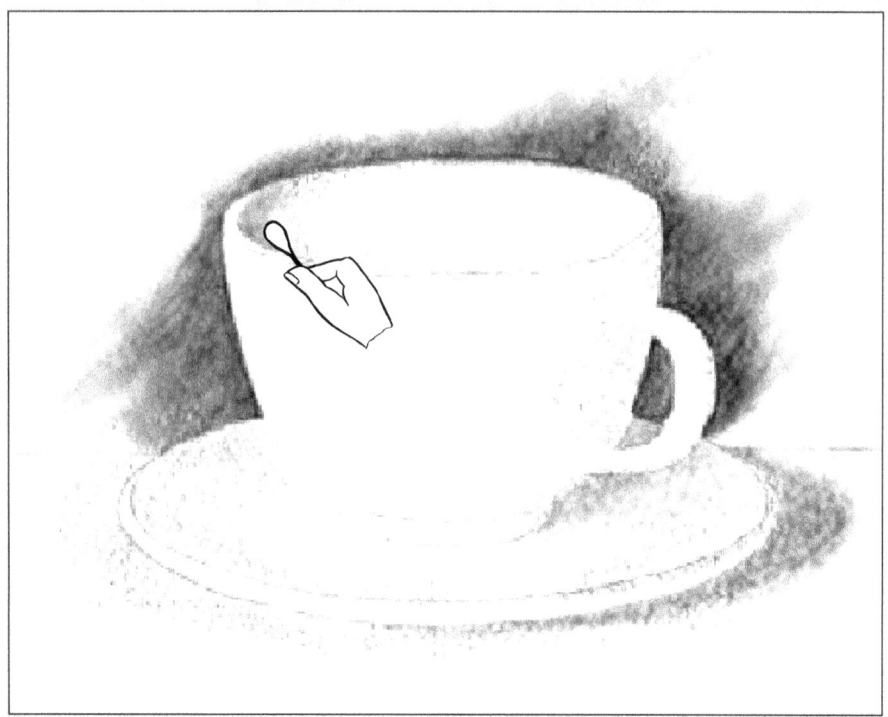

4-25 Reduce pressure to blend & fade shade into white with sweeping "C" strokes

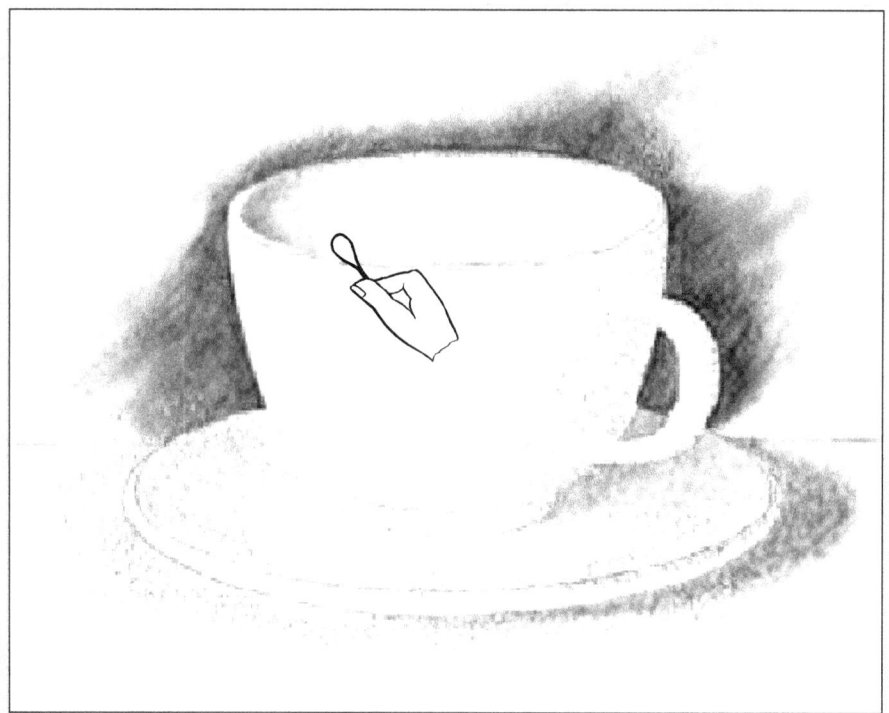

STEP 10 If you find blotches (uneven dark and light patches) in your cup's shade area, I recommend that you eliminate the spots. Otherwise, they will likely just become darker during blending. Illustrations 4-26 and 4-27 show the before and after. How did I remove the blotches? I dabbed the dark spots with the corner of my putty eraser, and filled-in the light portions with very gentle pencil strokes. Alternating between the two procedures, I kept working until the tone resembled the surrounding value. If this technique sounds alien to you, please re-read page 32 in Chapter 2.

4-26 BEFORE blotches are removed

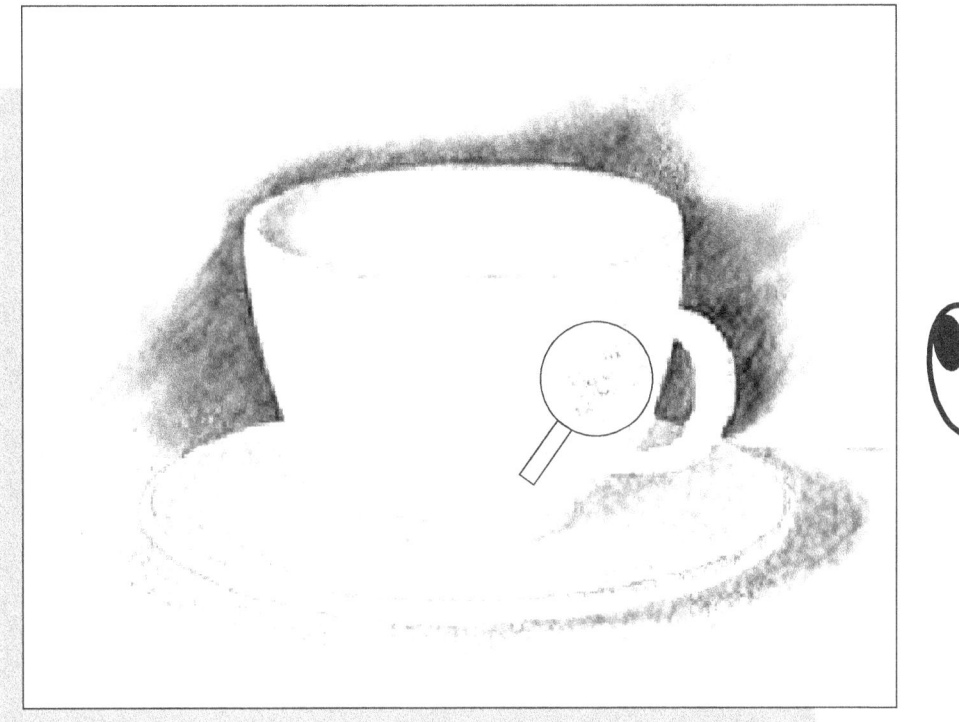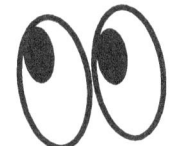

4-27 AFTER blotches are removed

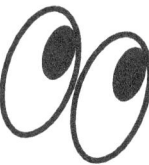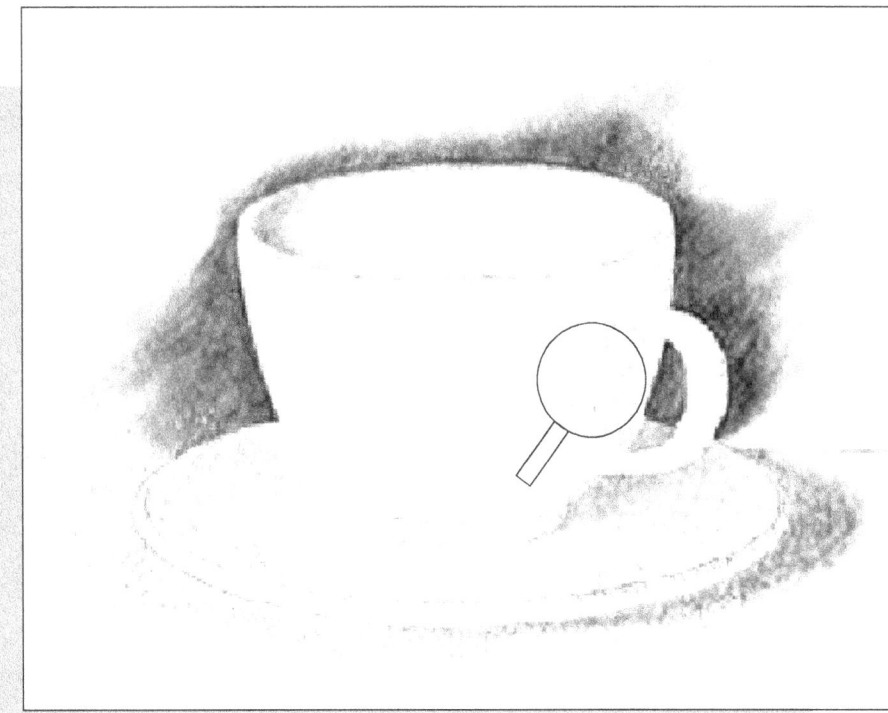

STEP 11 Blend your cup's shade area, including the base. Start from the upper portion bordering the rim. Use downward curved sweeping strokes that follow the *contour*, or surface curvature, as you advance right-to-left. Blend only the darker half of the shade area (4-28). Gradually reduce pressure to fade the remaining tone until it practically disappears into the white of the paper to your left (4-29).

4-28 Blend dark portion of cup's shade area (including base)

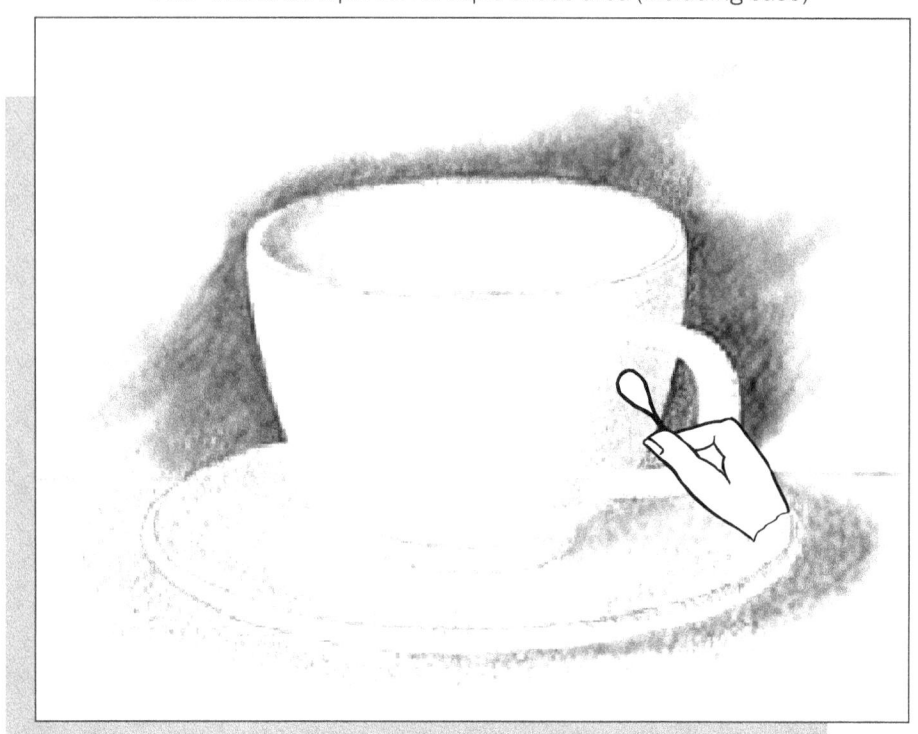

4-29 Blend and fade cup's lighter shade area into white (including base)

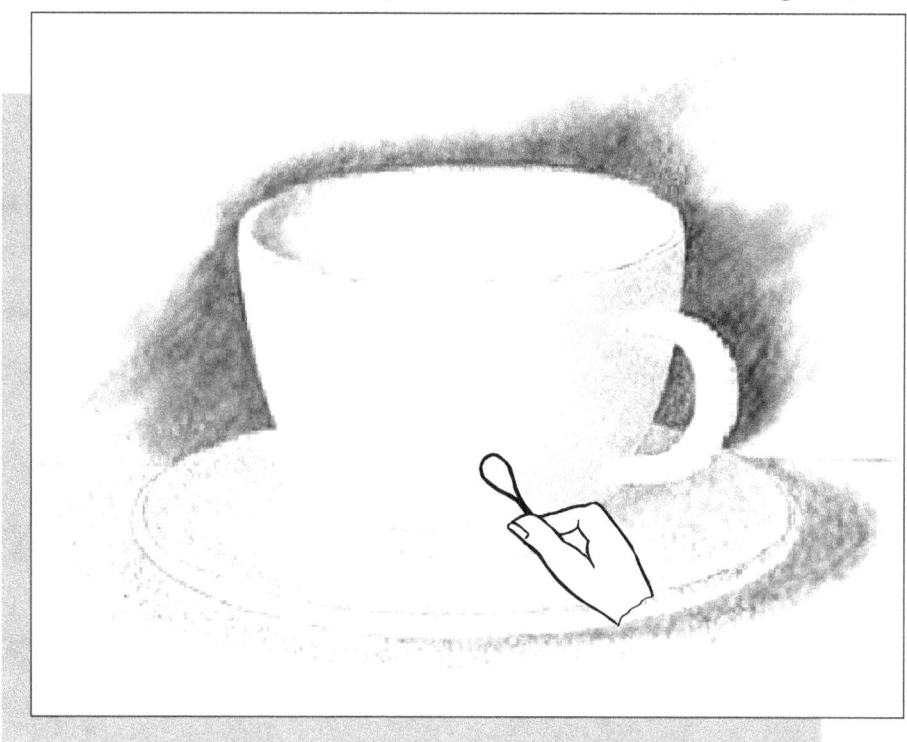

STEP 12 Blend and fade the shade areas along your *saucer's* inside rim. Be sure part of it remains white to indicate the bottom where light strikes more strongly. Start with sweeping "C" shaped strokes on your left. Then, using side sweeps, blend the middle and right end (4-30). Next, blend the shade portions on your *cup's handle*. Begin on the lower portion with *upward* strokes and gradually tilt them toward your left. When nearing your handle's vertical point, your strokes should be leveling out and gradually tilting *downward* to the left, stopping at the top curve. To fade your handle's remaining shade area, use upward blending strokes, advance right and stop at the top curve again. Then blend and fade your saucer's rim on the upper half of the shade side. Leave the lower part lighter to indicate reflected light (4-31).

4-30 Blend and fade tone inside your saucer's rim

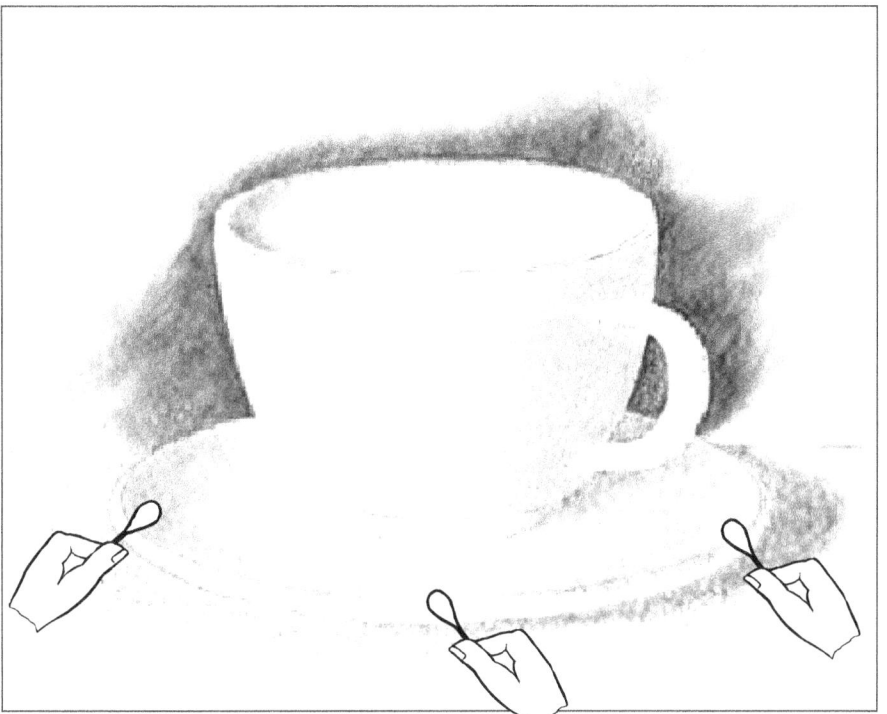

TIP

If you have blotches in your saucer, eliminate them first, then blend.

4-31 Blend and fade handle's shade & saucer shade into white areas

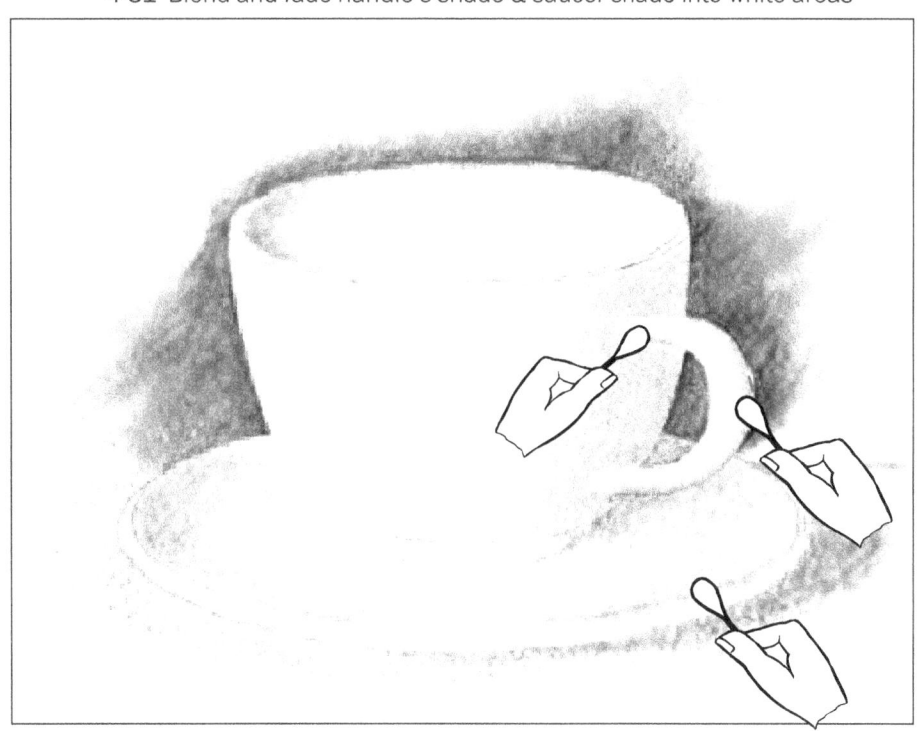

While scanning, I discovered smudges in my saucer's rim.

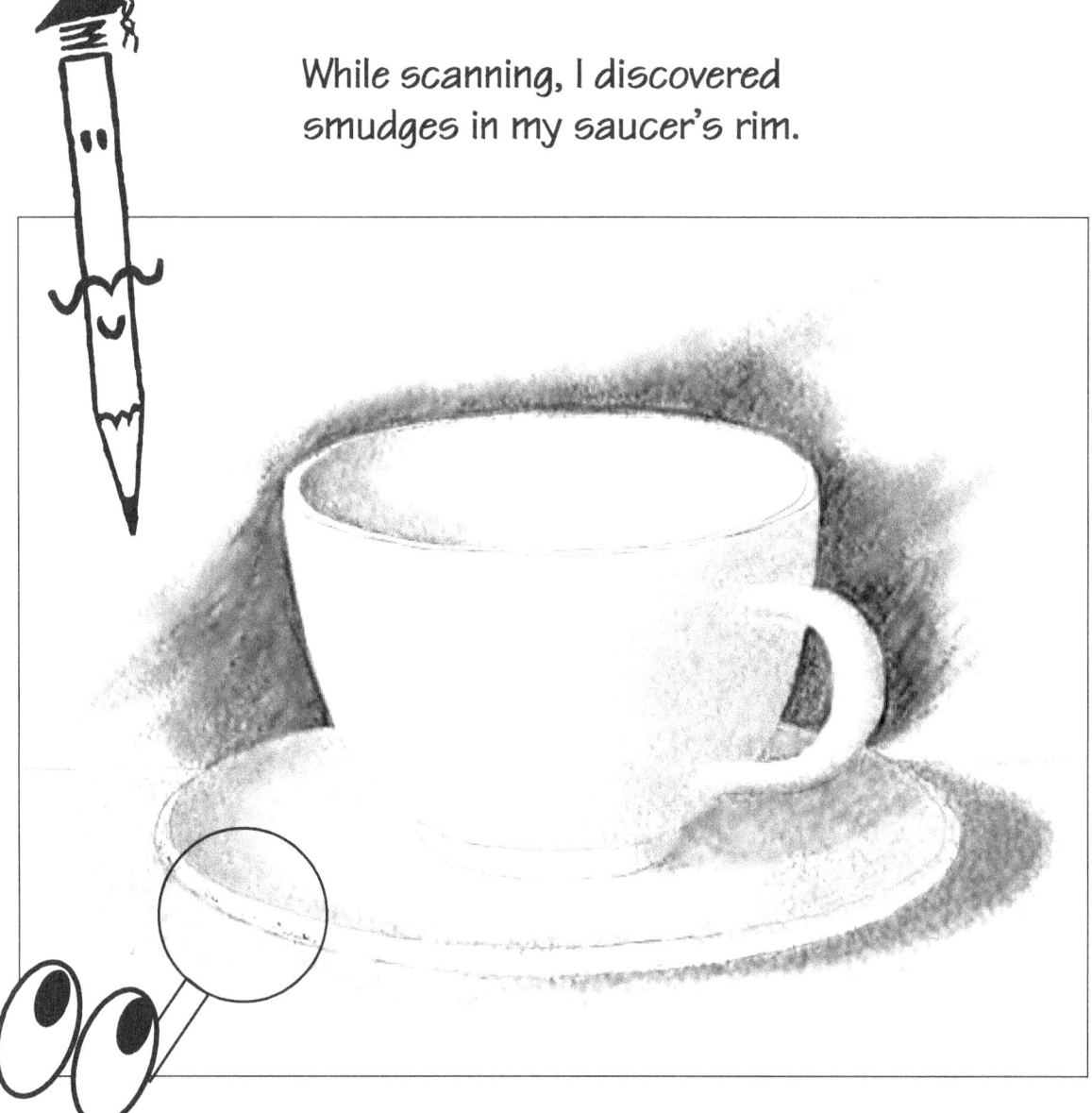

Give your rendition a final once over, too. Look at your drawing upright, then sideways and even backwards by using a mirror for alternative views. Or maybe set your picture aside for awhile. Having seen it through many stages and for long periods, eye fatigue may have set in and you may not be as observant as you could be. On another day, with fresh eyes, you may decide a few minor adjustments are appropriate. But don't get carried away. You could become a slave to your picture. If you like to sign your work, I suggest you make that your last step. Thereafter, you should not modify any more. Instead, move on to a new adventure. Why? Because currently this is the best you can do in your development. Be content with what you have achieved. Of course you will be able to do better next week, next month, next year. Meantime, for a breather, divert your attention to the student examples on the next page. And please remember, they are not competition. They are for you to learn from.

STUDENT SAMPLES

Example A

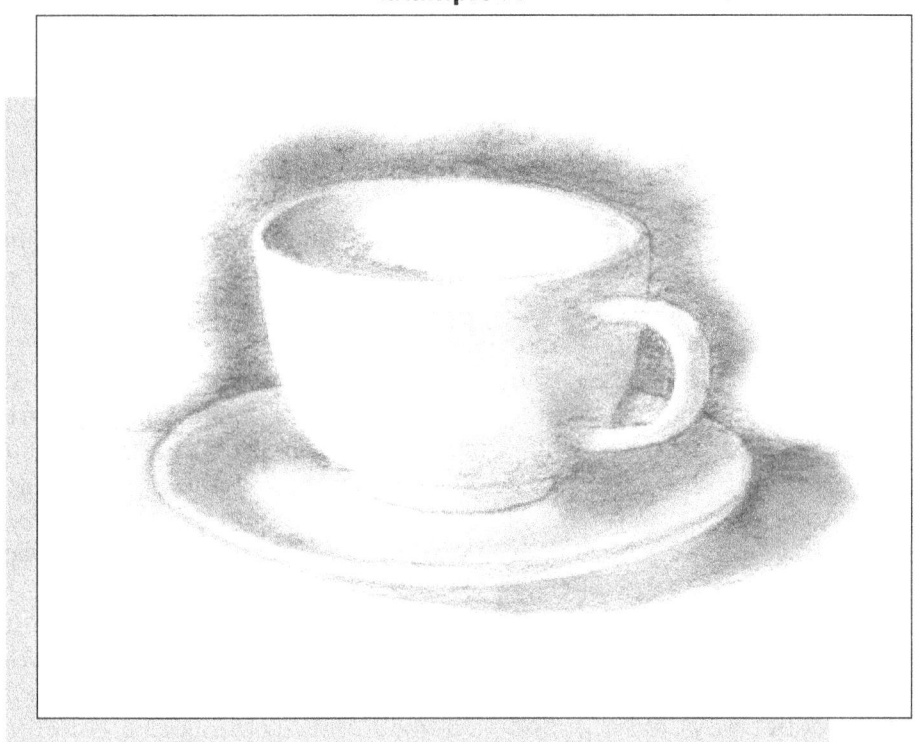

Example B

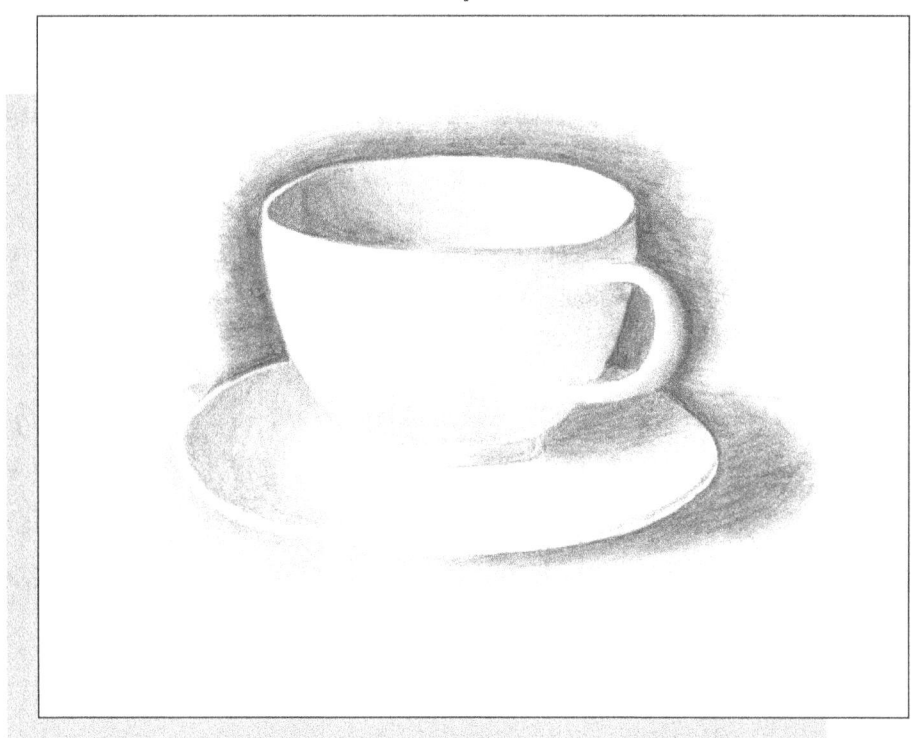

Chapter 4
FOLLOW-UP

Congratulations! You have truly come far, and to achieve this required a great deal of talent. Yes, *talent*. When you stop to ponder, you realize the term is just another word for skill, and skill is merely refined ability.

Take the ability to speak, for instance. People have the potential, but it doesn't become a skill or talent until they begin to practice and develop a vocabulary. In the preceeding exercises you have been developing your ability to draw and steadily advancing your talent.

To depict figures accurately, you have learned to put the structural components of the TRUSTY 7 to work, along with the concept of *planes* and *contour*. As you know, when drawing, the word "planes" does not mean aircraft. *Planes* refers to surfaces in your line of sight. Commonly, there are four planes known as *top, front, side* and *bottom*. These can be directly in your line of vision or at an angle to you. *Contour*, an offshoot of planes, essentially refers to the divisions where planes meet. For example, in a room where two side *planes* come together (such as walls), the division (or contour) is known as the corner. Elementary as this sounds, having managed the concept of planes and contour, you have been harnessing features of *perspective*. In so doing, you have been portraying the impression of three dimensional surfaces (length, width and depth), on a two dimensional field. All in all, that's really quite a feat.

Equally commendable, by using the side of your pencil lead, you showed *flair*. Above and beyond that, you also increased your understanding of *figure, ground* and *background* factors to create your own version of a scene. Of course, all these ingredients are not always necessary, but they are effective ways to help render (bring about) a complete picture.

Toning is yet another facet. During this phase, you indicated many types of strokes techniques, not to mention a variety of blending methods. Where things didn't quite turn out right the first time, you also may have employed blotch remedies. Plus, you learned about *reflected light* - the effect which occurs when light strikes an object, then bounces off and hits another area of the same object, or another object nearby.

Going further, you took full advantage of the effects of *assimilation* (often called visual mixing) and discovered it is very useful, especially when all your tones are blocked-in. At that point, seeing them together, you are able to sensibly and aesthetically determine which tonal values are too dark, or too light, and whether they are sharp enough, or too vague.

Indeed, you have much to be proud of. What you learned not only applies to still life, but virtually everything else. Think about it. Shapes, textures and tonal values are all around us, and guess what? With these, you can draw just about anything.

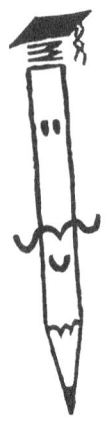

Now, I bet I know what you are thinking. The book spelled out the steps, but you're wondering whether you would be able to plan your own stages and carry them out. Fear not. The next chapter will put your concerns to rest.

Chapter 5

HOW WOULD YOU PLAN, ORGANIZE AND THEN LAYOUT THIS STILL LIFE?

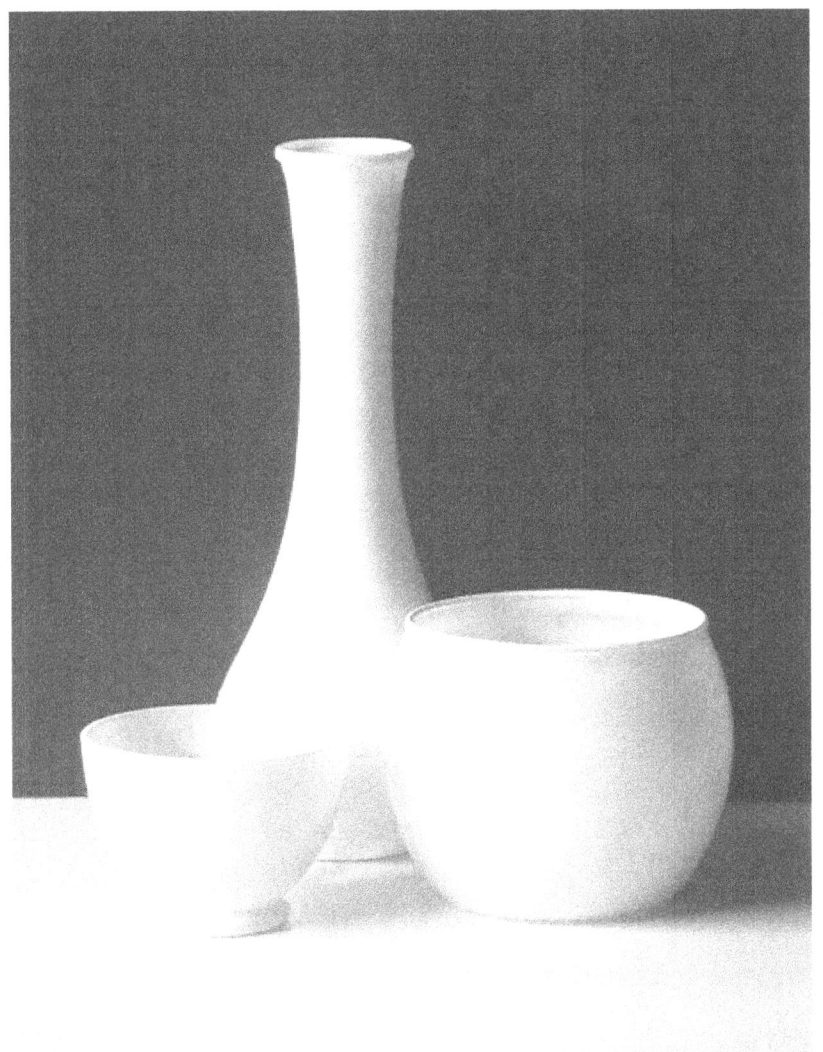

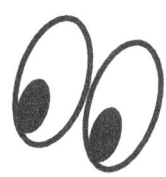

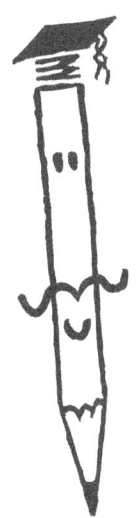

Let's explore several possibilities.

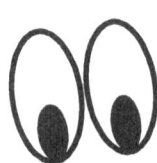

Please set your pencils aside. In ths chapter we will only observe and use our thinking caps. And that brings us to a question.

How do we get from this...

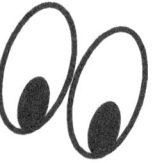

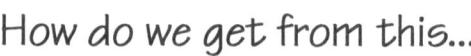

...to this?

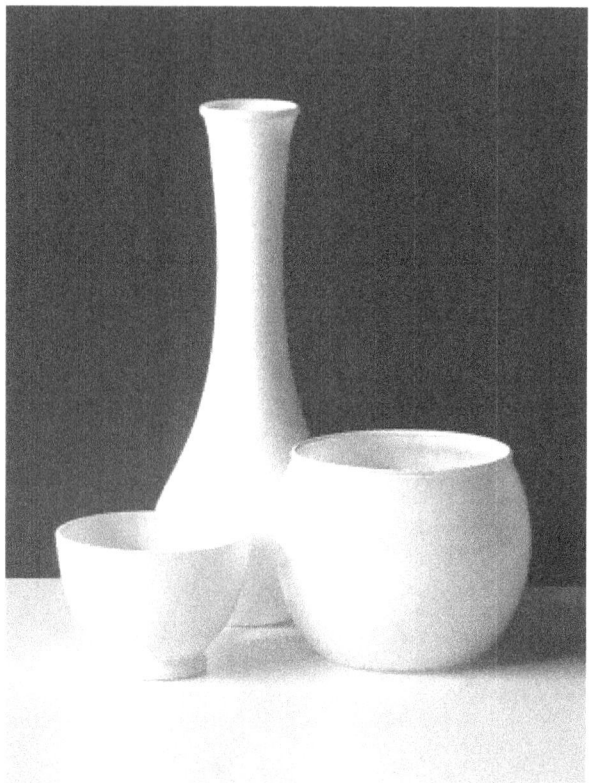

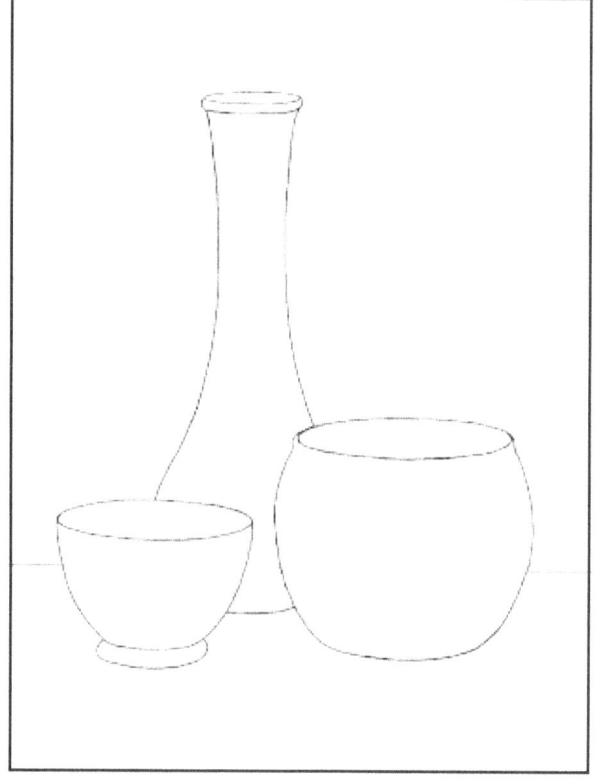

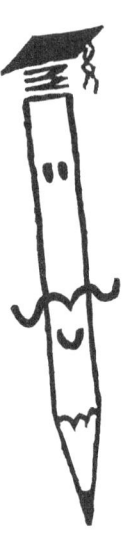

The answer is simple. We need a plan and a way to carry it out. The key is perception. In other words, we must first observe the subject matter and see how it's put together. This is important, because when drawing, essentially we take things apart visually, then reconstruct their likeness on paper. That means we are both architect and builder.

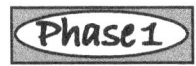 A plan calls for action, and that begins with looking and thinking.
The clues are right in front of you, but you have to take the time to find them.
Following are 3 helpful ways.

1. When first observing a scene, think of the figures as *unfamiliar* forms. This encourages you to examine more carefully. Even though you will usually know and recognize what you are viewing, you will be more likely to look for individual shapes that combine to make the complete figures.

2. Squint at the outset, meaning close your eyes half way. This is an easy technique that trains your mind and eyes to search for just the basics. If you are working from a photo, you can place tracing paper or wax paper over the photo. Since details become less visible, you can see the main shapes more easily (A).

3. Imagine the forms as already outlined, including *contour* lines which border the planes (B).
  - Notice, *below eye level,* the figure on the left shows a tall opening.
  - *Further up*, the figure on the right seems to have a proportionally more narrow opening.
  - *Near eye level,* the height of the opening on the middle figure appears to narrow greatly.

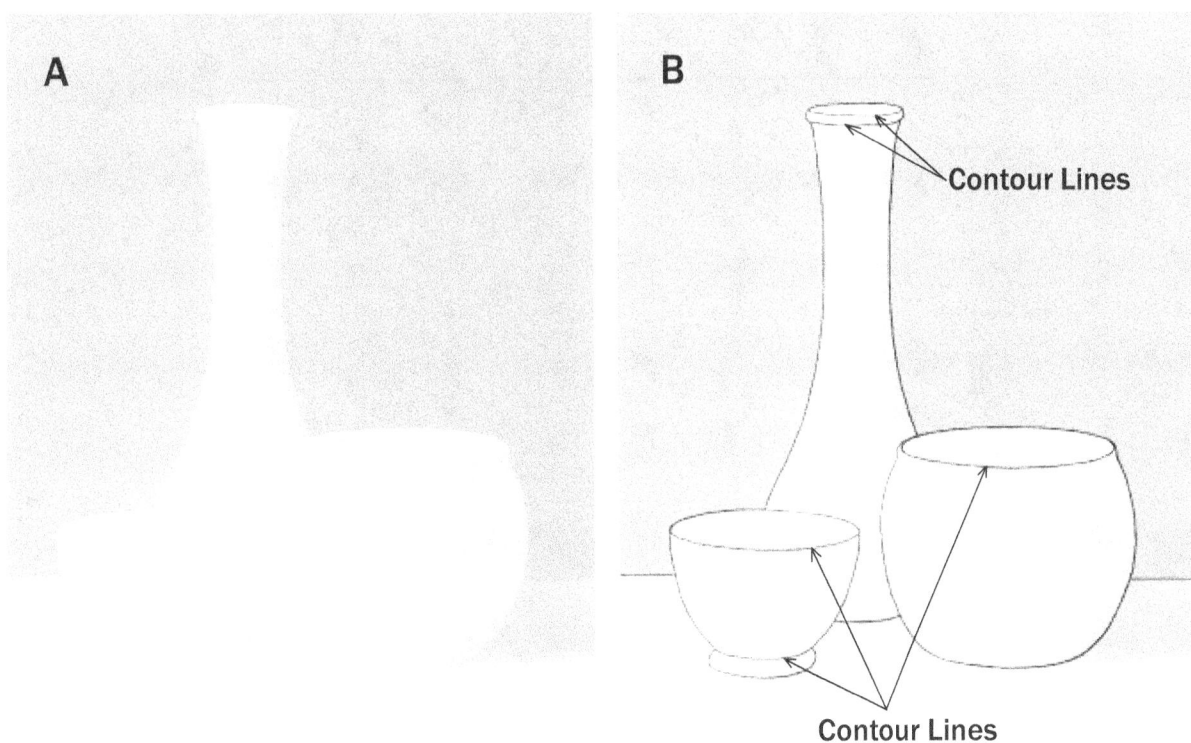

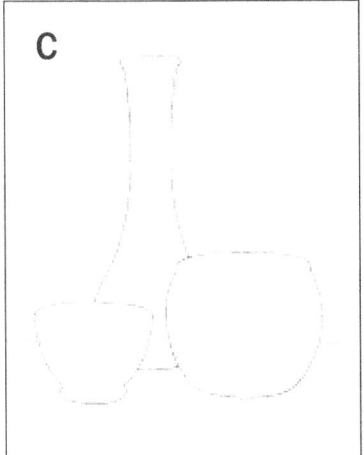

TIP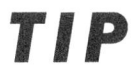
  - *Outlines* border the *outside* edge of figures.
  - *Contour lines* border the planes and appear as though they are within the figures.
  - Without contour lines, figures look flat (C).

Phase 2 Even after you have reduced the still life to an outline and contour format (in your mind) the blank page on which you intend to draw can be daunting. Thankfully, there are many fundamental drawing methods that act as tools to help you formulate a plan and carry it out. For instance, along with the seven structural components I call the TRUSTY 7 (page 6) you might opt for the OVERALL, the CRISSCROSS, the STREAMLINE, the RANDOM or the SQUIGGLE methods, to name a few. These can be used interchangeably and in combination. Let's begin by exploring the possibility of using the *overall approach*. This procedure is essentially the same method you applied in Chapter 3 and works from outside-in, so to speak. In other words, imagine that a rectangle frames the combined figures. As you can see, the vertical span is longer than the horizontal span (5-1).

5-1 Visualize the figures bordered by a rectangle

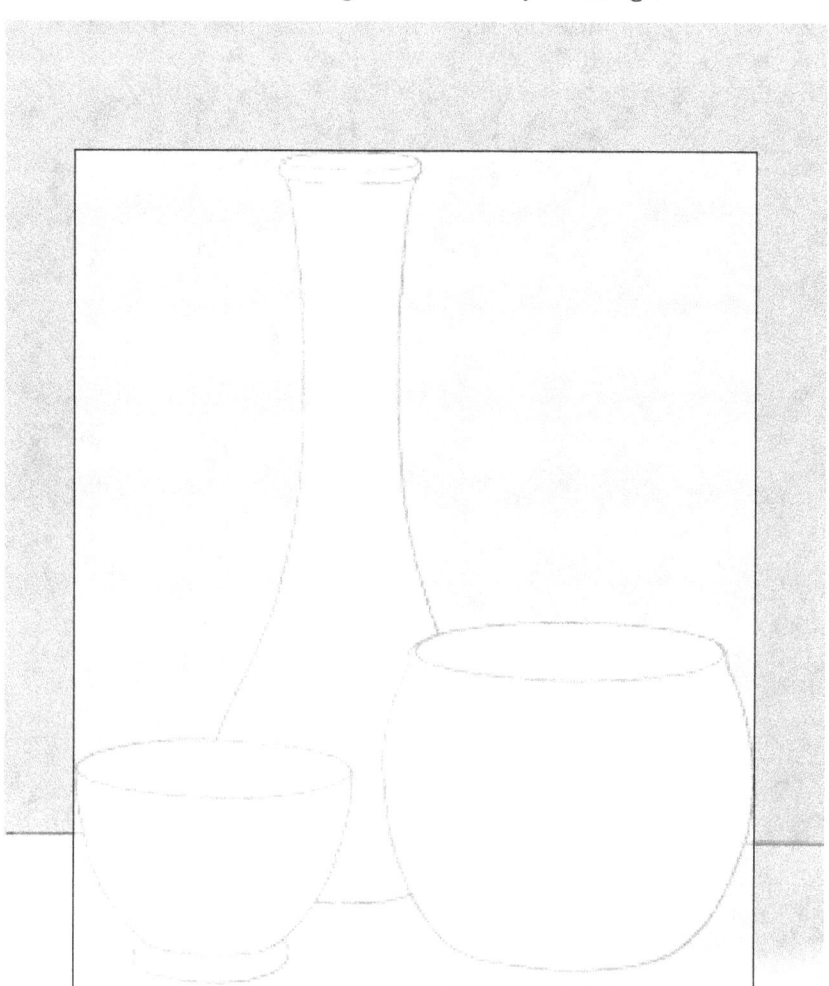

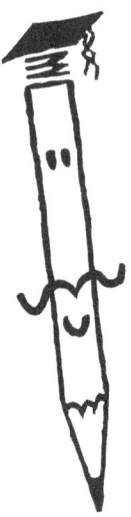

The overall frame can serve as a foundation.
But first, we need to determine its proportion.

Phase 3 Having discovered that the overall space for the figures requires more distance upright than sideways, you need to determine the difference. For this, I recommend using the square as a basic unit because it is equal in both length and width. By visualizing the square within the rectangle, you can see the remaining area (5-2). Next, by comparing the extra span to the square, you would discover it fits roughly five and a half times (5-3). That means, the combined figures require an *overall* space that is slightly more than one fifth longer vertically compared to the distance horizontally. *If you were drawing*, you would form your rectangle according to that proportion. The size could be large or small, as long as it conforms to scale. One easy way to achieve it would be to lightly center a horizontal line near the bottom portion of your paper. Two more lines of equal length would build the two sides. Next, using dots, you would bisect one side into five equal parts, or visually estimate the one fifth extra span. You would add that to the sides, plus a little more, and close up the rectangle. That easily, you would have your *overall* proportion.

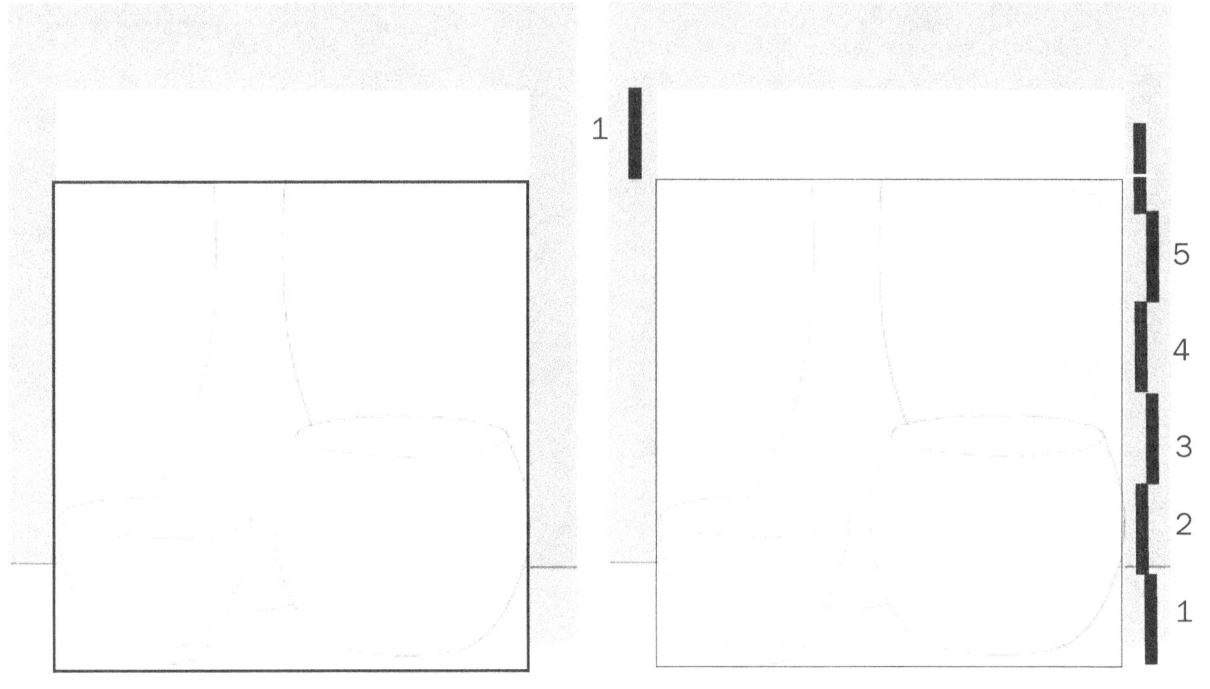

5-2 Visualize square in rectangle to see extra span

5-3 Compare extra span to square span

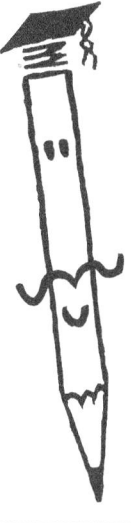

Since you're not really drawing, just going through the motions, let's pretend you have fashioned your rectangle and you are ready to proceed to your next observation. As both architect and builder, you would look, think and then draw.

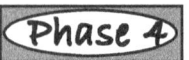 **Make believe each of the three figures *also* has a frame bordering it.** Due to overlapping, pretend you have x-ray vision as well (5-4). Next, imagine a horizontal and vertical line divides the overall frame through the middle (5-5). Bisecting *your* frame this way, you would be applying what I call the *CRISSCROSS METHOD.* With its help, you would refer to the nearest division to locate and fashion the smaller rectangles in *relative proportion* to one another and to the overall rectangle. Relative proportion is simply a comparison of one span in one figure to one span in *another* figure. Your choice of sequence would not alter the outcome. When completed, your foundation would have progressed to look much like example (5-6).

5-4   See each figure bordered by a rectangle on model

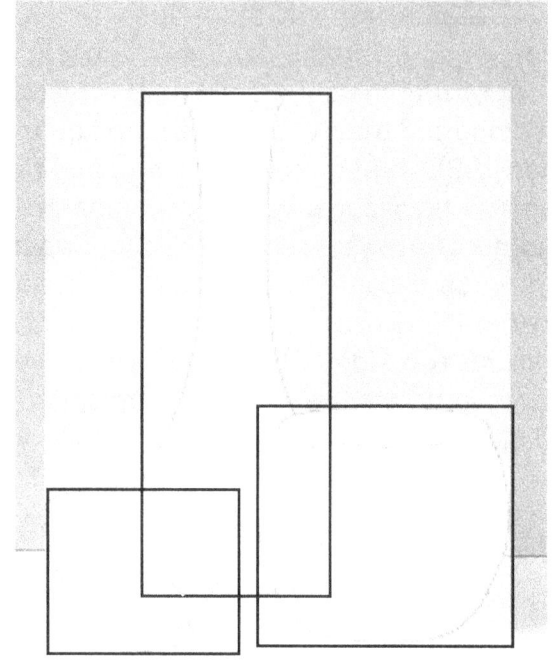

5-5 Visualize overall rectangle crisscrossed

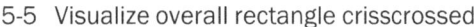
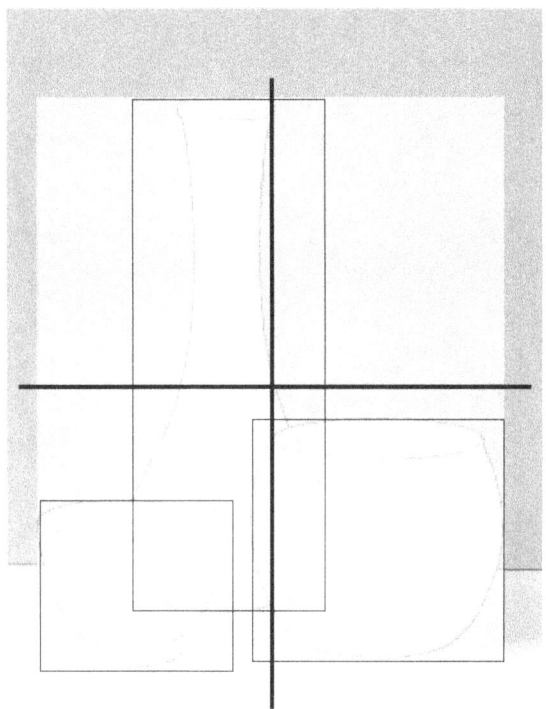

5-6 Foundation drawing example in current stage

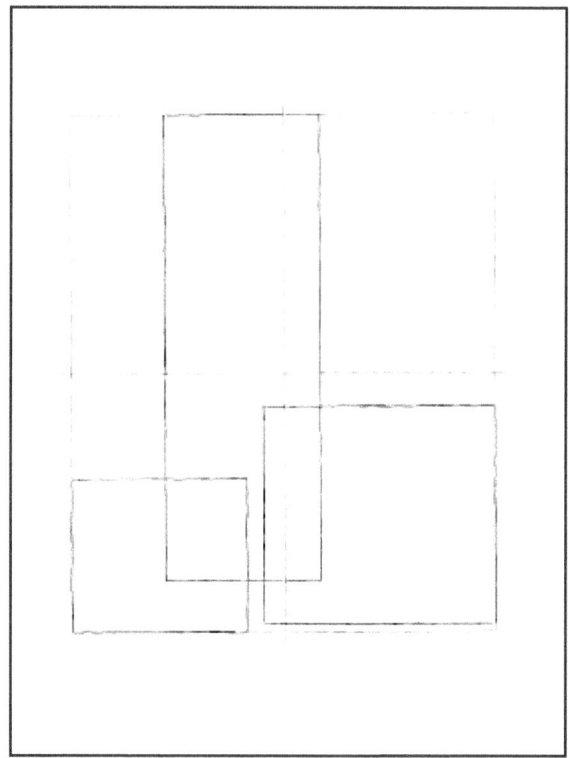

TIP Since drawing is mainly based on estimates, you would have the freedom to go inside or outside your guide-lines.

At this stage, assuming you were drawing, you could throw caution to the wind. While referring to the model, you could simply form the figures freestyle, with the aid of *reverse spaces, as* the gray areas illustrate (5-7). Or, you could continue to take the forms apart with your eyes by applying the concept of *sub-proportion* for each sub-section. *What does* sub-proportion mean? It is simply a comparision of one span to another in the *same* figure. Considering there are several divisions, I suggest opting for the latter by visualizing guide line separations on the model (5-8.) Then, in no particular order, you would locate them to fit your drawing in scale (5-9).

5-7 Figures can be formed with help of reverse spaces

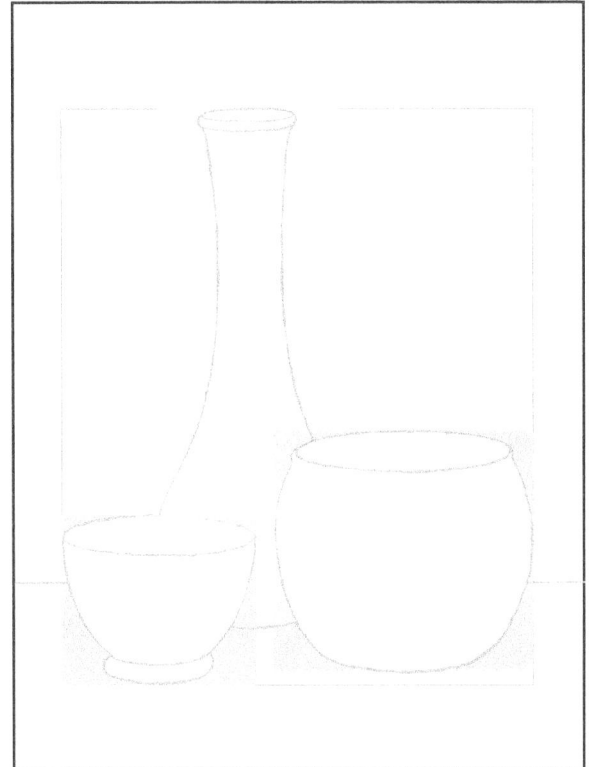

5-8 Visualize sub-sections bordered by guide lines on model

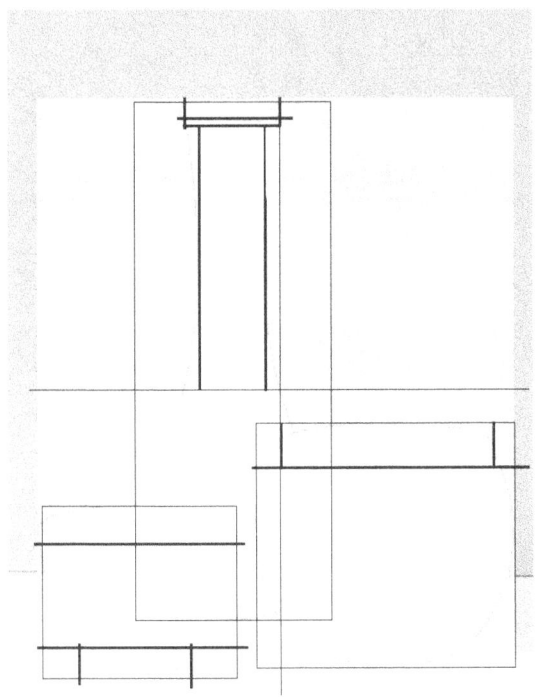

5-9 Foundation drawing example in current stage

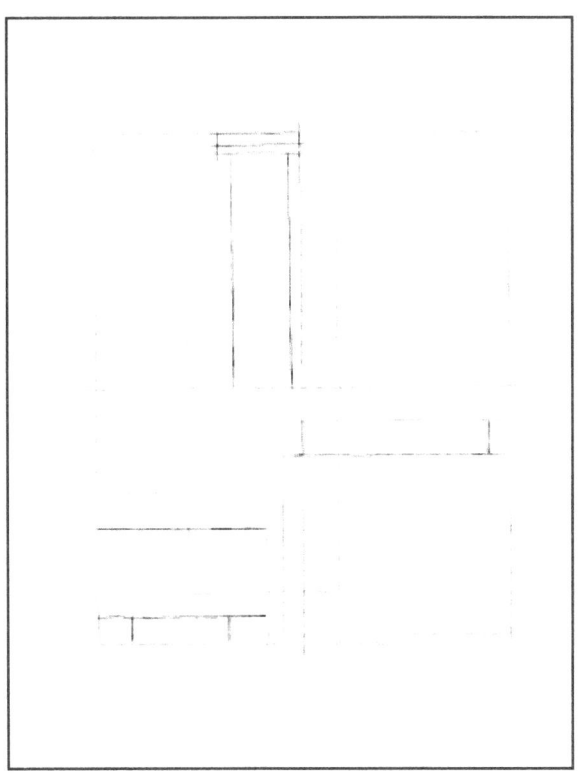

Remember: you are working hypothetically. That means you are playing "what-if" by imagining how things would be, if they happened.

Phase 6 While looking at the subject matter (or model), pretend that the curves have base lines. I've made them bold in illustration 5-10 so they would stand out. What are base lines? They are imaginary lines that connect curve ends to help you see the amount of bend. In your choice of sequence, if you were to apply base lines, they would work as guide lines and would eventually appear much like example 5-11. After having *lightly* placed the base lines, many of your original guide lines could be erased. Then your foundation would turn into a *streamline* format resembling illustration (5-12.

5-10 Visualize curves with base lines on model

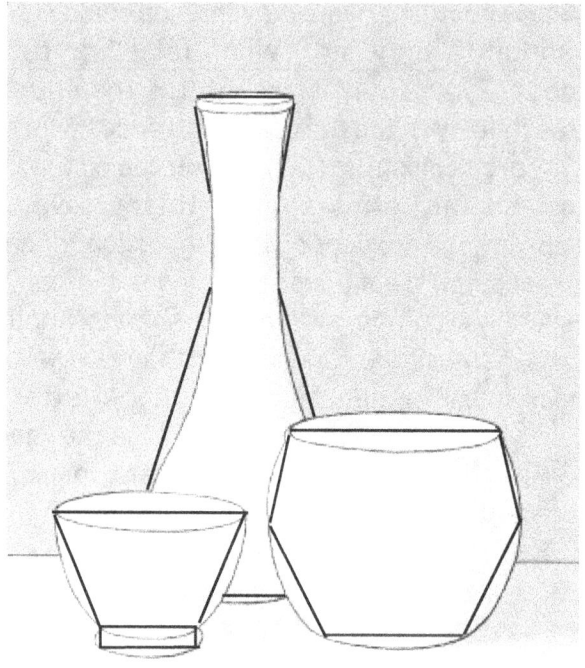

5-11 Drawing example *with* base lines

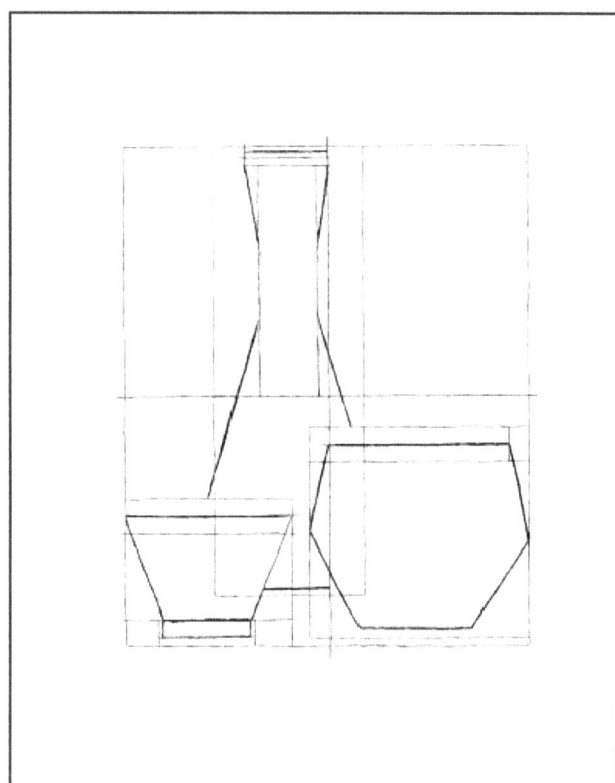

5-12 Drawing after excess guide lines erased

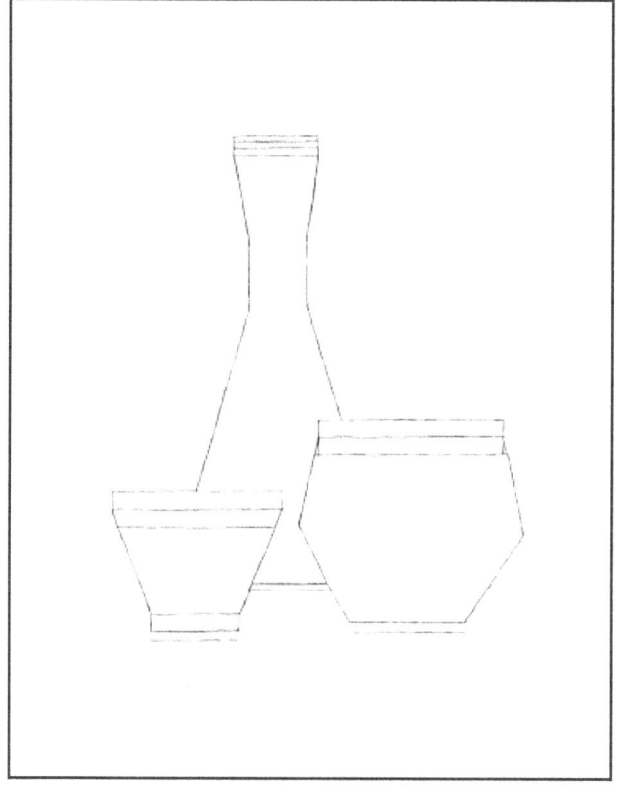

TIP You found straight lines where there weren't any. If you had been drawing, your figures would now be in a straight line format. This would be the time to stop and check your status. Curves would be easier to add once you made certain the basics were fairly accurate. For instance, you would look for possible tilting. You would also compare your forms to the model, as individual shapes that combine to make the figures, which in turn, make up the overall scene. In so doing, you might find some proportional adjustments are called for and you would attend to them.

Phase 7

Curves would come next (hypothetically speaking). In no particular order of steps, you would observe one curve at a time on the model including visualized guide lines and base lines (5-13). These would help you see the reverse spaces which aid in forming the bend in each curve more accurately. Then you would check your results by comparing your work to your model again. You would also use this opportunity to add the line that represents the back of the table (5-14). Next, you would erase remaining guide lines and do the finishing touches. After all is said and done, having elected to use the *overall, crisscross and streamline methods,* along with the help of shaping components from the TRUSTY 7, your final outcome would be an outline and contour drawing somewhat like example 5-15.

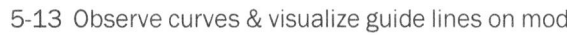
5-13 Observe curves & visualize guide lines on model

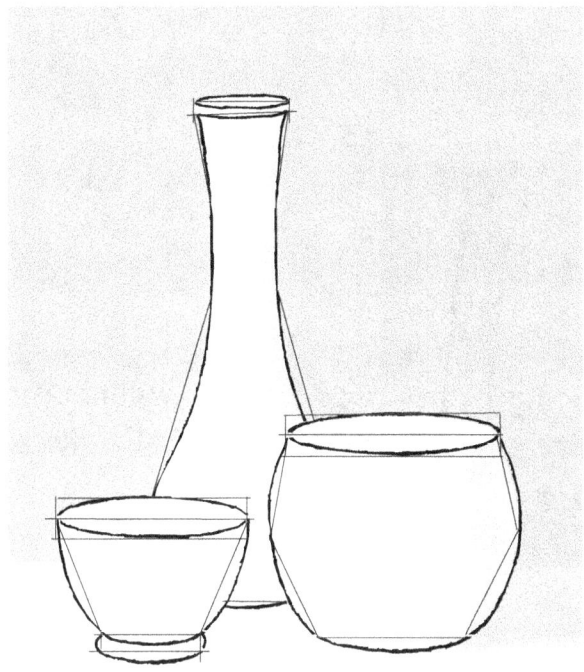

5-14 Streamling including curves & "table" line

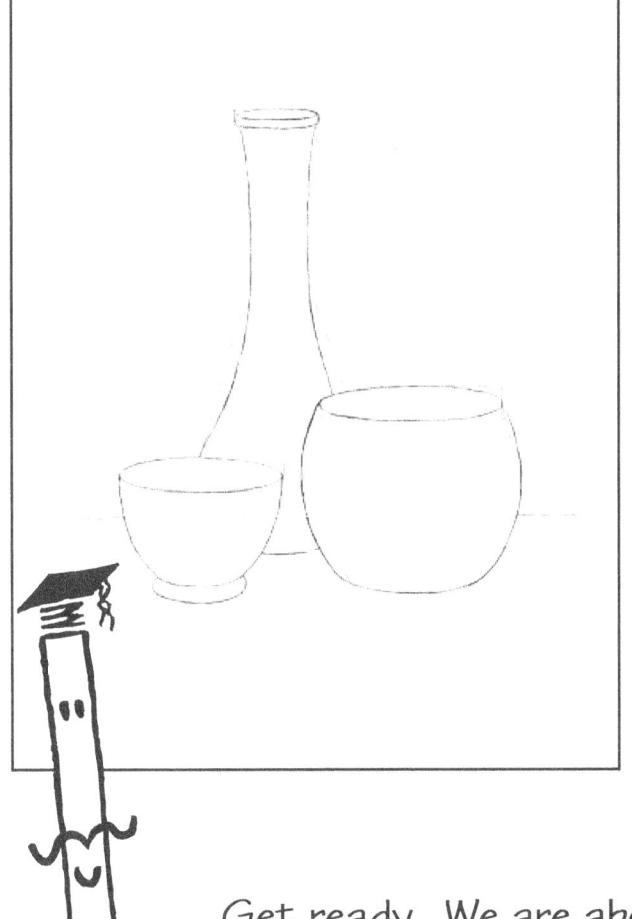

5-15 Finished outline/contour drawing example

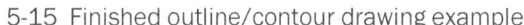

Get ready. We are about to take another set of methods on a dry run. Please turn the page.

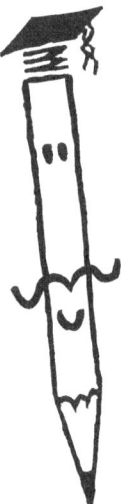

Continuing with the same still life, let's see how the RANDOM and ATTACH methods work.

Before we get underway, permit me to clarify the difference between the overall and crisscross methods (studied previously), as compared to the random and the attach methods we are about to explore. Put simply, unlike the overall method, which begins with a proportional frame that acts as a foundation for *all the figures,* the *RANDOM* method begins with one frame for *one* figure. The choice of where to start is by whim or impulse, in other words at *random*. You would proceed to *ATTACH* the other figures the same way. Even the lines that compose the figures could be formed in any sequence you prefer. But I recommend concentrating on one figure at a time, using *sketch lines* to make things less complicated. Once all the lines and parts eventually come together (in relative proportion), the forms could be refined to your heart's content. In this fashion, if you were actually drawing, you would start very basic as usual, but proceed from inside-out, as opposed to outside-in.

Remember: you are only going to be observing.

Suppose you chose to start with the figure on the right. First, you would visualize it already in outline and contour format, including frame (5-16). This would enable you to make an *overall proportion* survey to determine how much area the *lone figure would require* and still leave room for the rest. As you can tell, about one fourth of your paper near the bottom right would do nicely. Next, by comparing the right figure's horizontal span (a) to its vertical span (b), you would also notice that the figure is a little wider than tall. Based on these observations, assuming you were drawing, you would place guide lines to reserve the approximate area needed for the figure (5-17).

5-16   Visualize figure on right in a frame
and estimate its overall proportion

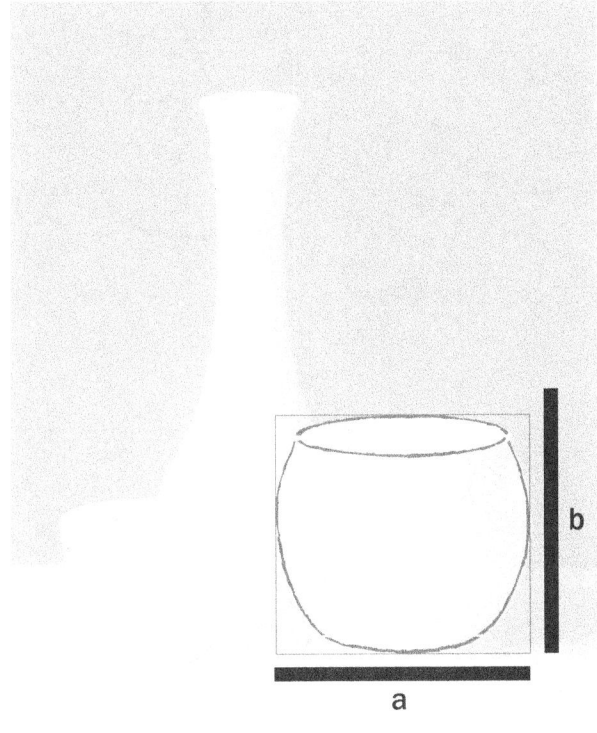

5-17   Rectangle guide lines for
right figure's foundation

TIP Guide lines are helpers but you could sketch one curve at a time, *without construction lines (as they are also called)*. The decision would be yours.

The figure on the right has two sections - the opening and the body. That means, you would need to determine the *sub-proportion* to find the division line, then decide which part to draw first. As you can tell, the upper segment (elliptical opening) is approximately one sixth of the figure's overall height (5-18). Armed with these observations, you would include a guide line to separate the area. Then, with or without base lines, you would sketch one curve at a time (see page 82). At this phase your lines would not even need to completely connect (5-19).

5-18 Right figure ellipse height sub-proportion

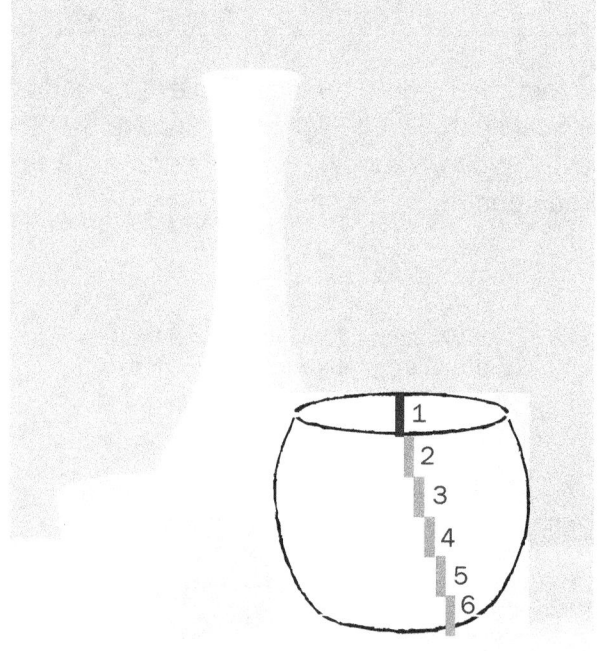

TIP

Sub-proportion is a comparison of one span to another span in the *same figure*.

5-19 Sketched figure within overall **and sub-proportion guide lines**

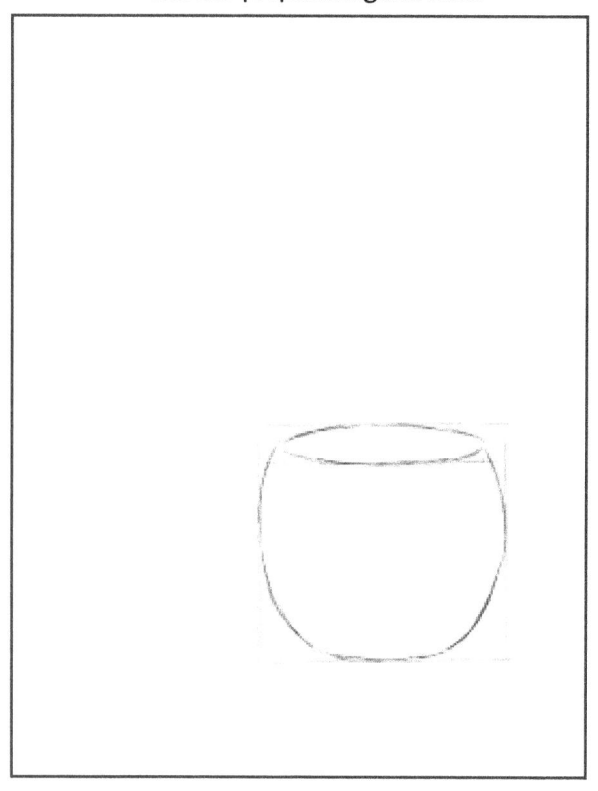

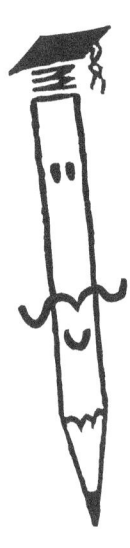

Which figure would you address next?

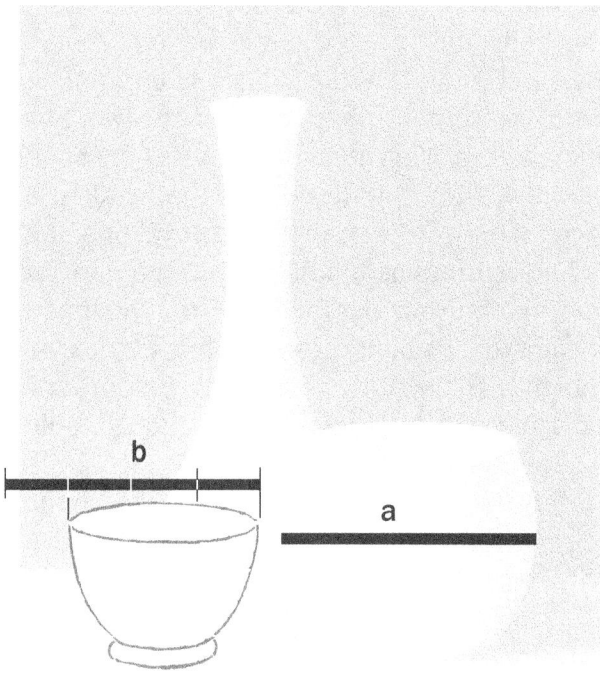

Phase 3 Suppose your next choice is to study the figure on the left? When comparing the overall horizontal length of the figure beside it (a) to the figure on the left (b), you would see it is smaller in relative proportion by about a fourth. Plus, there is a little space between the two figures (5-20). Next, you would also apply another structural component. I'm talking about alignments. As illustration 5-21 shows, the bottom aligns slightly below the figure on the right, and the uppermost part only reaches about two thirds of the way up. Using these observations, you would form a rectangle with four guide lines to locate the small figure's overall space (5-22).

5-20   Left figure's relative *horizontal* scale on model

TIP

Relative proportion is a comparison of one span in one figure to one span of *another figure*, in the same picture.

5-21   Left figure's position & relative *vertical scale*

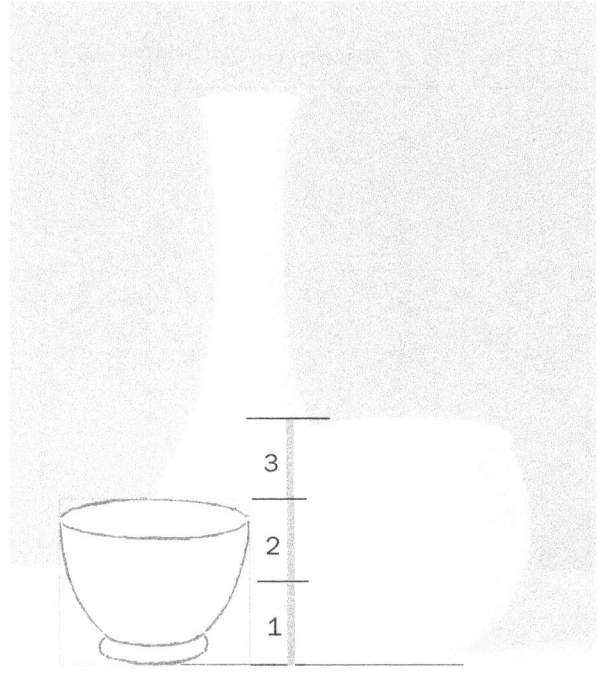

5-22   Left figure's overall foundation

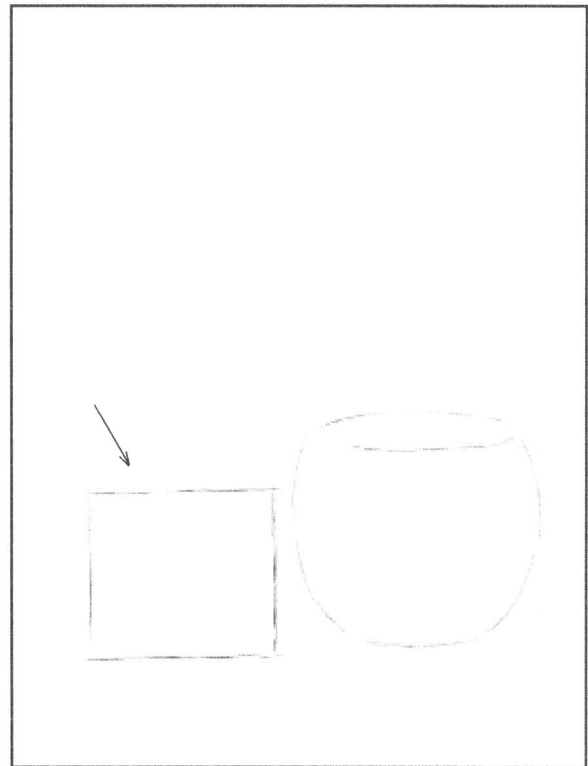

Phase 4 The figure on the left has three sub-sections - the base, the body, and the opening. These can also be surveyed with structural components. In this case, sub-proportions apply. For instance, in illustration 5-23 we see the base length (a) is slightly longer than half the overall horizontal span (b). The oval opening (c) appears to be a little less than a quarter of the figure's overall height. The base height (d), is about three quarters of the oval height. By locating these sub- proportions to scale with guide lines, your progress would resemble illustration 5-24. Next, while referring to the model, you would sketch the curves one at a time. When completed, your figure on the left would be in place (5-25).

5-23 Left figure's sub-proportions on model

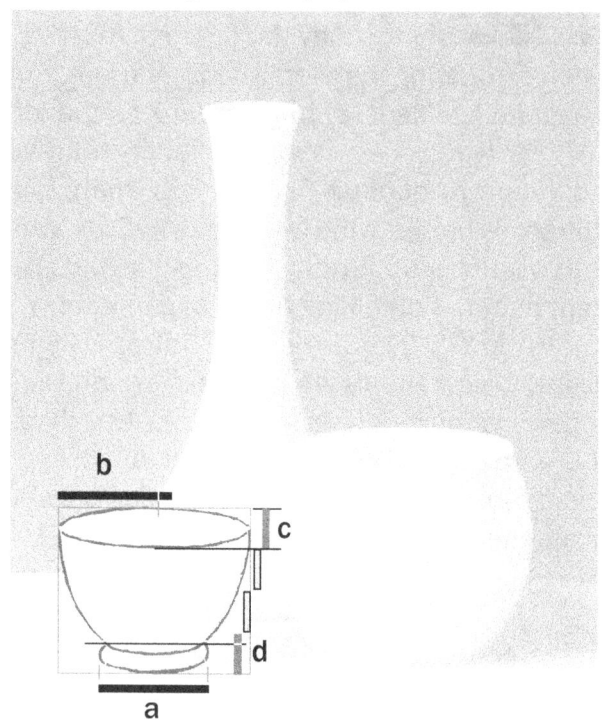

TIP Since drawing is based on estimates, it helps to work with basic sketch lines. After the figures are all in position, you would make necessary adjustments.

5-24 Left figure's sub-proportions located with guide lines

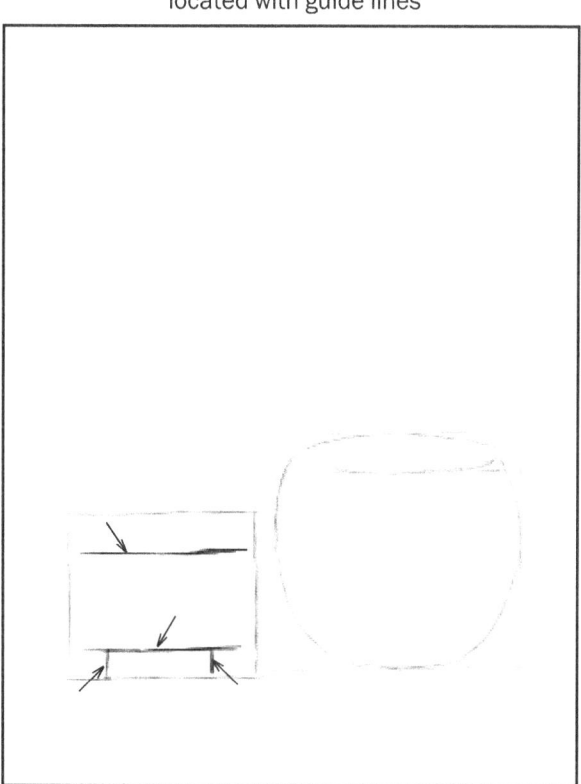

5-25 Left figure sketched within guide lines

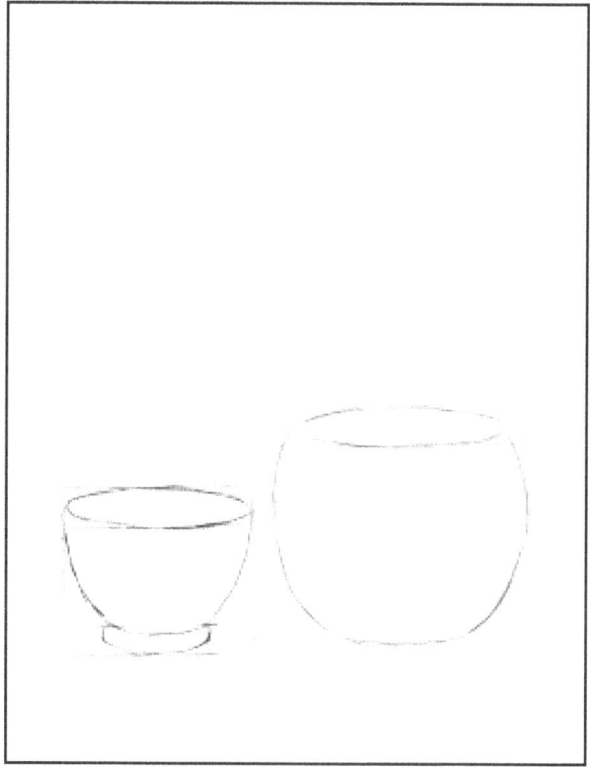

Phase 5 The middle figure also needs to be addressed. Here, relative proportion and an alignment check comes in handy. Using the small figure's *overall* height for size comparisons, you can see the middle figure's *top* extends nearly *three and a half times* more distance units up from the base of the small figure. The *bottom* of the middle figure *aligns* about a third of a span above the small figure's base. One end *attaches* to the figure on the left, the other end attaches to the figure on the right (5-26). If you were drawing, you would use guide lines to apply these coordinates in scale to locate your middle figure's top and base (5-27).

> **TIP** Instead of the left figure, the figure on the right could serve just as well for a relative proportion and alignment comparison.

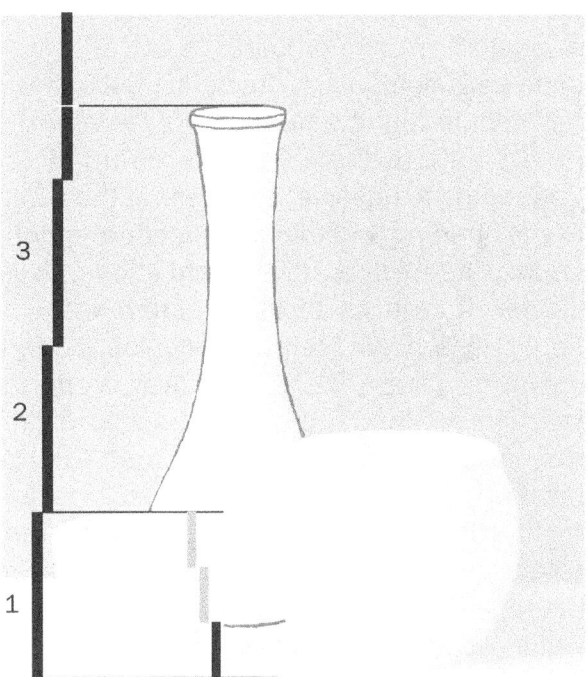

5-26 Middle figure's top & bottom in relative proportion on model

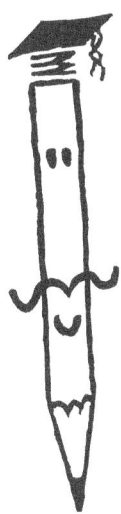

5-27 Sketch lines locate middle figure's top & bottom

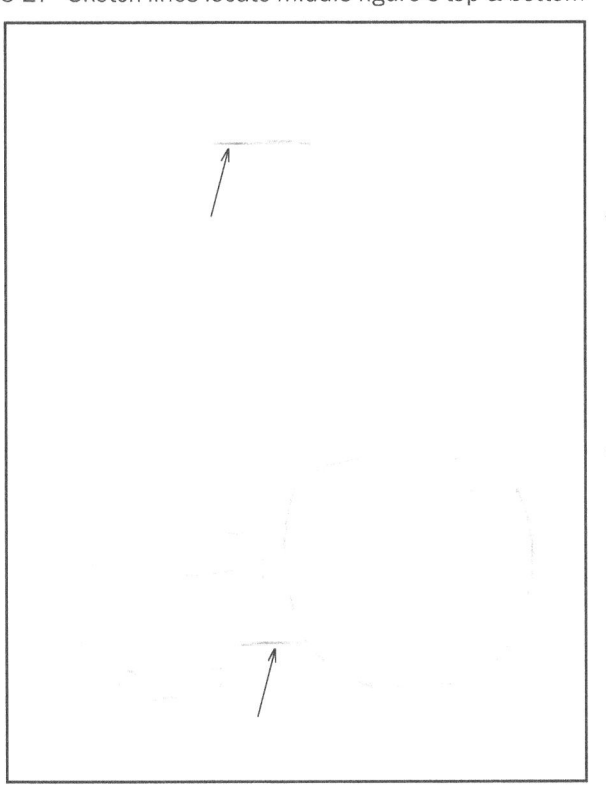

It's fun to imagine how a drawing could be developed by doing a rehearsal in your mind. This is just another facet to thinking ahead, and handy for helping to avoid possible pitfalls and needless reworking.

> **TIP** Seeing each phase is useful for learning to pre-plan, isn't it? Try the following method some time. Draw the first stage, trace it and add the next stage to the *copy*, then trace the outcome. Apply another phase to your newest tracing, making sure to include adjustments as needed. Trace that result and add the next part. Continue this way until your contour drawing is finished. Ultimately, you will have a visible record from beginning to end.

Phase 6 The middle figure also has sub-sections. In order to evaluate them, sub-proportions and alignment analysis is helpful. As illustration 5-28 shows, the middle figure's horizontal opening (a) is about half the left figure's opening (b). Continuing to observe, we see that the *height* of the opening and the rim height are roughly equal. The neck curves inward a little. Near center, it returns to *align* plumb with the upper edge. From there, the shoulders extend outward. One ATTACHES *midway* along the left figure's top. The other *attaches* on the top of the figure to the right at a rate that is inset about twice the narrow space between them. If you were drawing, guide lines and reference points would assist in locating these basic proportions (5-29). Then, curves would establish and refine the form in your choice of sequence (5-30).

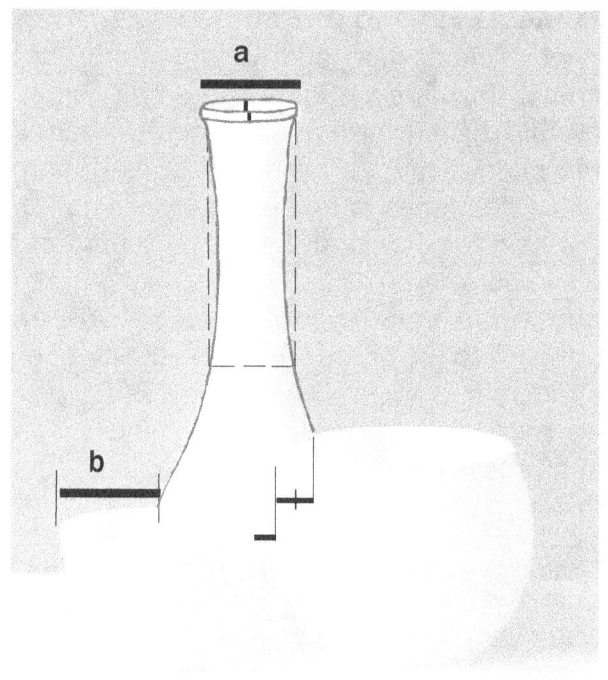

5-28 Middle figure's relative proportions on model

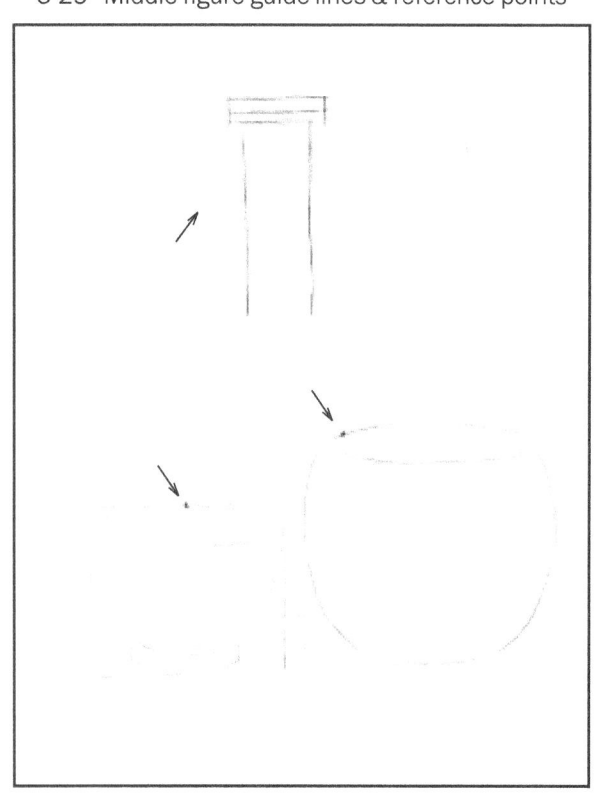

5-29 Middle figure guide lines & reference points

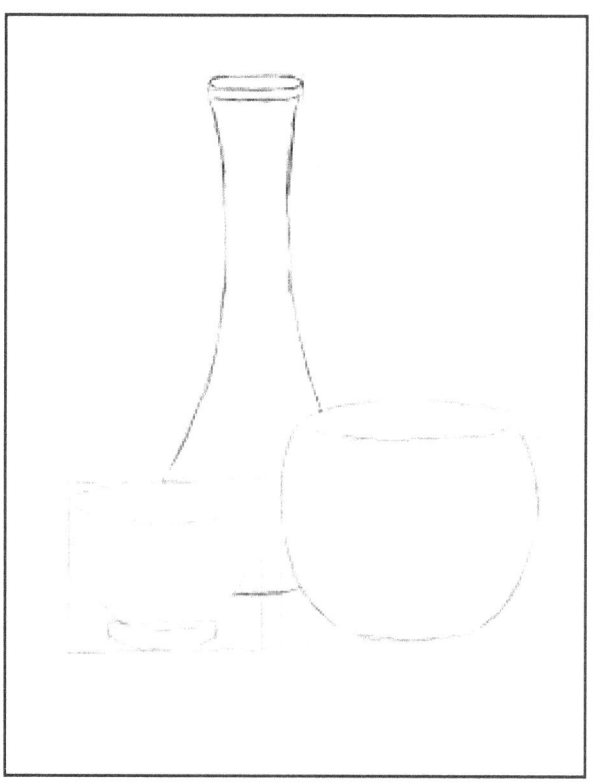

5-30 Sketched middle figure

Phase 7   At this stage, you would refer to the model (or photo) to help locate and add the line that represents the table (5-31). Next, you would erase your guide lines. With only your figures remaining, you would stop to verify your results by comparing them to the model again. Checking for accuracy, you would search for possible tilting and/or you would look for sections that may be out of proportion in your drawing. After making required adjustments, your finished sketch would resemble illustration 5-32.

TIP People's strokes and size estimates tend to differ. If you had been drawing, your figures would appear to have a unique quality of their own, and that's terrific.

5-32   Finished sketch example

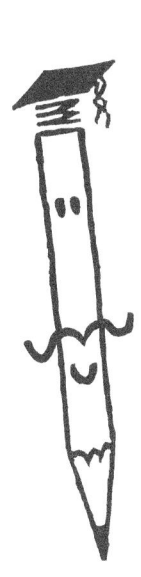

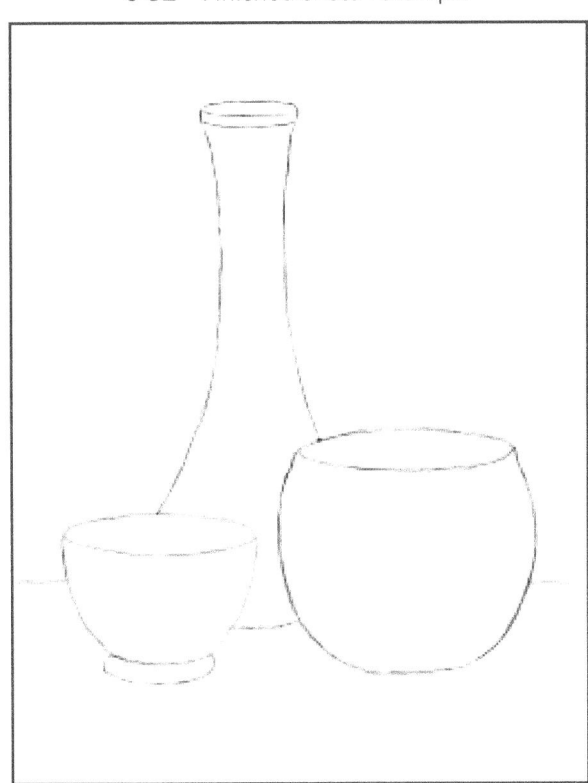

Gee! The random/attach methods and the overall/crisscross methods brought about similar versions of the still life, didn't they? After a break, we can explore another basic approach.

Would you believe this *doodle* will eventually look much like the other two still life drawings?

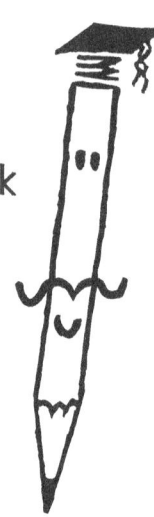

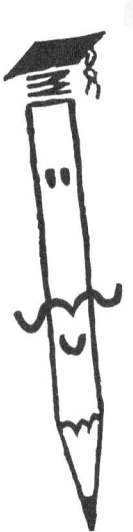

Let's turn back the clock and see the process from start to finish.

Phase 1   Imagine that a curved line borders all three figures on the model (5-33). While still fresh in your memory, you would quickly recreate the image on paper with a *very light* continuous line procedure. Your result would be a pear shape resembling illustration (5-34). And whether your line would have travelled only once around or several times (like my example), either way is OK. Being that you would have been applying a very flexible approach, I call it the SQUIGGLE method.

5-33 Visualize curved line loosely bordering figures

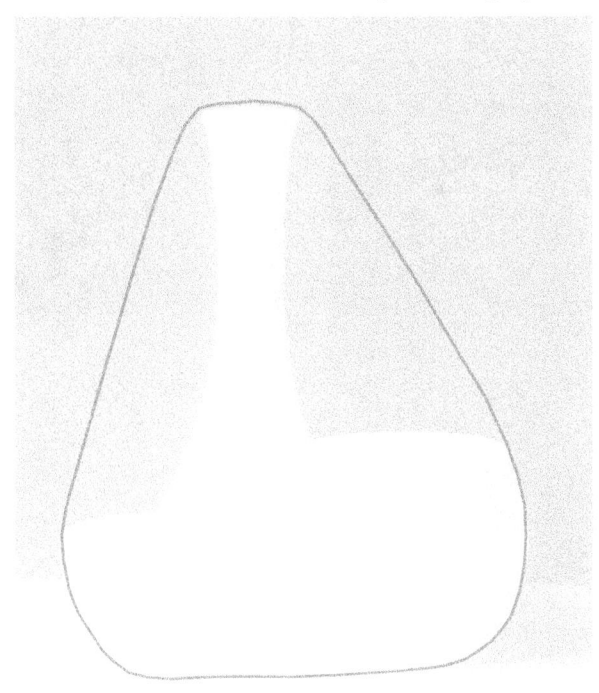

5-34 Squiggled border

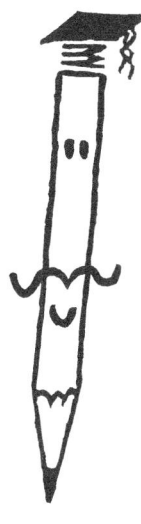

The squiggle method is like working with modelling clay. It can start as a glob and gradually develop.

Phase 2 Make believe a single line borders only the middle figure's general area (5-35). If you were drawing with the squiggle, you would allow your impulses to guide you. Working quickly, you would squiggle the basic form with respect to the overall boundary reserved for all three figures. Even if your lines went astray, you would not stop to erase, correct or redo. The exception would be if your lines veered *extremely far off course*. When completed, your drawing would appear something like example 5-36.

> **TIP** When applying the squiggle method you rely mainly on your intuition. This enables you to skip the overall boundary in favor of a very flexibile random approach.

5-35   Visualize loosely fitting middle figure boundary

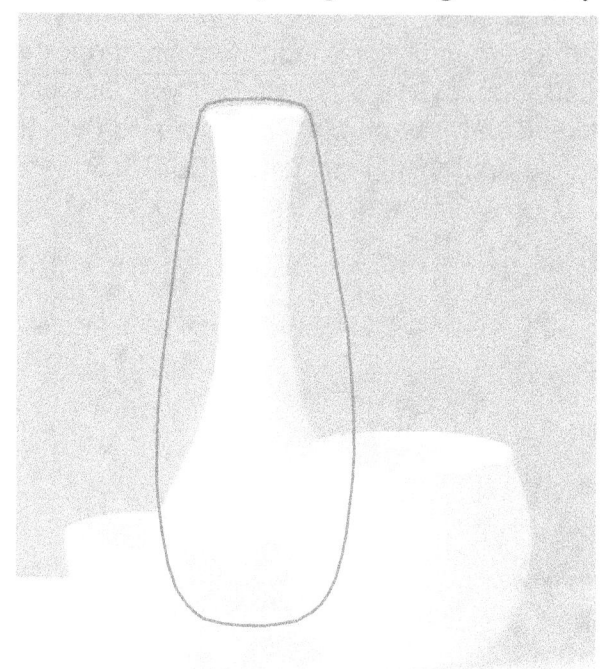

5-36   Squiggled middle figure

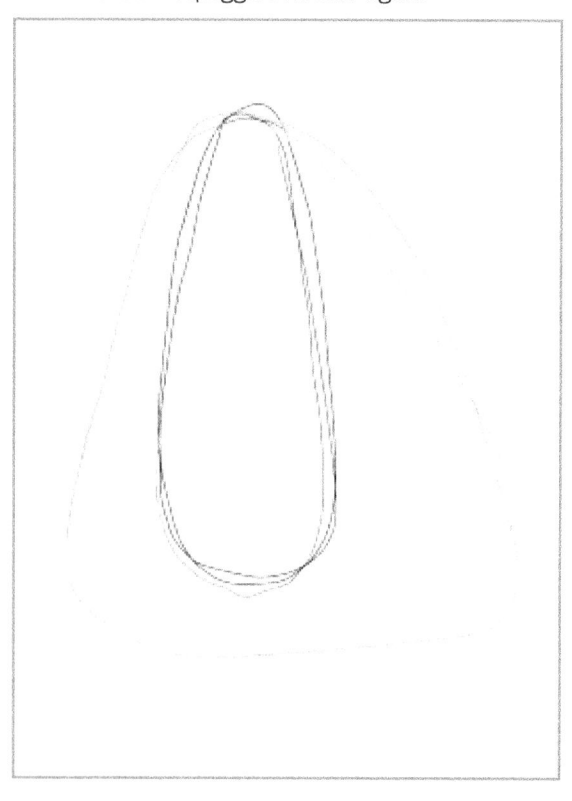

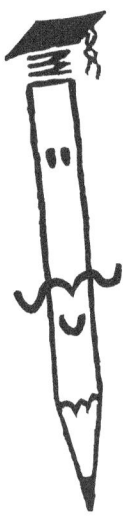

Sometimes it's good to plan things out. Other times it's fun to be spontaneous (act on the spur of the moment).

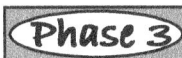 **Phase 3** Pretend loosely fitting lines surround the other two figures (5-37). You would squiggle them, one by one. Let's say you picked the figure on the right, and then the left. In both cases, size and location would be a factor based on the overall scheme of things, but once again you would let your intuition take over. As your eyes would scan the figure, your pencil in hand would form the general shape. After all, squiggles, or doodles as I also like to call them, are meant to be loose and flexible. Examples 5-38 and 5-39 illustrate.

5-37 Visualize left and right figures loosely bordered

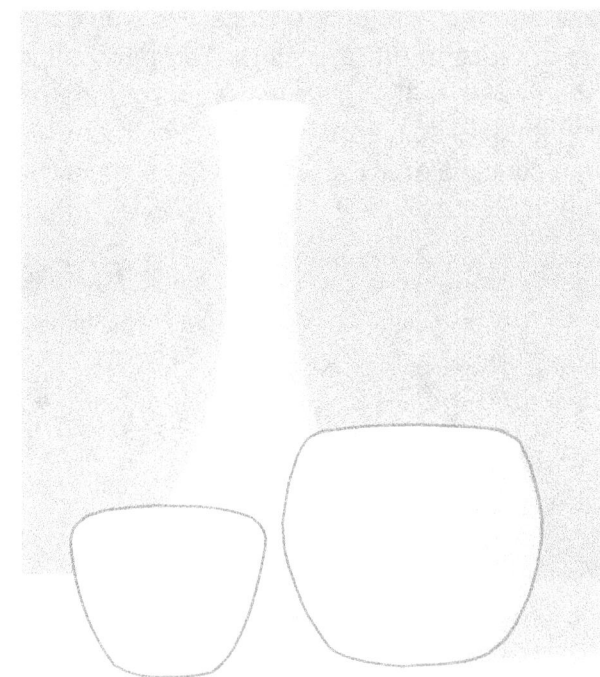

5-38 Squiggled right figure

5-39 Squiggled left figure

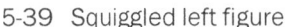

TIP Notice the figure on the right does not fill the right corner. Otherwise, it would end up being positioned out too far.

Phase 4 Since all three figures would have been done by impulse and would now be vaguely in place, you would stop to check your status. First, you would pretend there are loosely fitting lines that border the overall figure area, as well as the individual figures on the model (5-40). Then you would compare that image to your squiggle drawing. In so doing, you might find some areas need adjustment. For instance, the following progress check reveals that in squiggle drawing example 5-41, the overall size of the right figure is too large with respect to the figure on the left. Furthermore, the middle figure is not tall enough, proportionally,

PROGRESS CHECK

5-40 Model visualized with loosely fitting boundaries

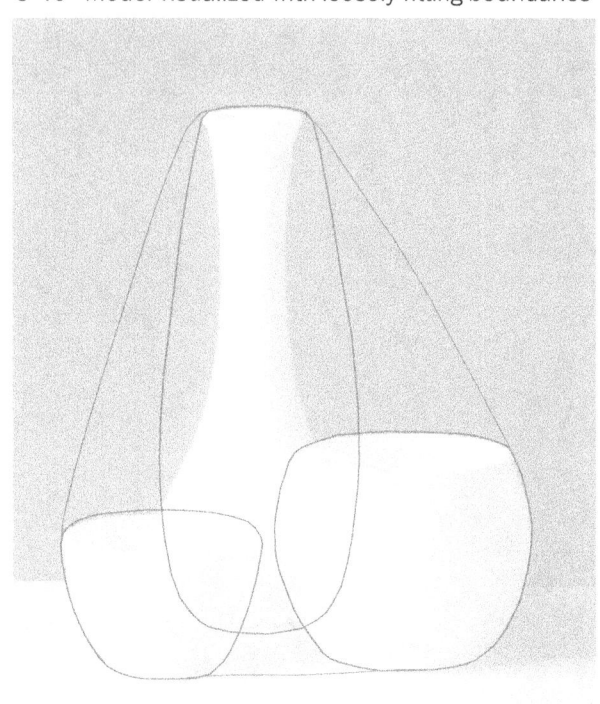

5-41 Squiggled example with innacurate proportions

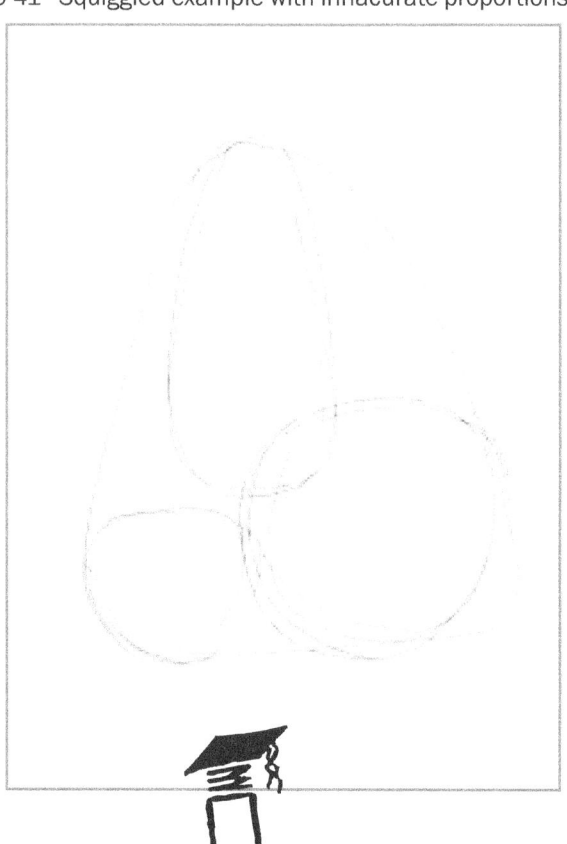

TIP This would be the time to make some basic adjustments. After all, one advantage of the squiggle method is that you can draw rapidly. Once something is down on paper, it's easier to see the areas that seem to be working and find those that don't. Then you can spot what parts need modifying more easily and you would attend to them. But you would still be working loosely. In other words your figures could still be flexible, allowing for futher modification, if desired.

Since you are not really drawing, pretend the adjustments have been done and let's continue.

Phase 5 At this point, you would look for divisions on the model. Notice all three figures have elliptical sub-sections. Plus, with x-ray eyes, you would see that the base of the figure on the left is another ellipse. In addition, the middle figure has a concave mid-section that flares (extends outward) toward the bottom. With relative proportion in mind, you would rapidly squiggle the ellipses, the same way you did in Chapter 1 (page 5). Your result would be a facsimile of illustration 5-43. Next, you would doodle the taper in the middle figure. Then your drawing would progress to resemble illustration 5-44.

5-42 There are four elliptical sub-sections and middle figure has a concave mid--section

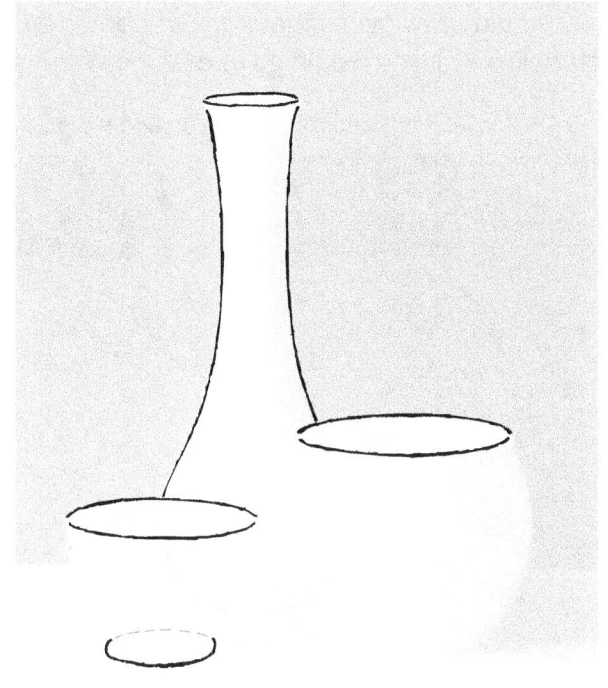

5-43 Squiggled ellipses

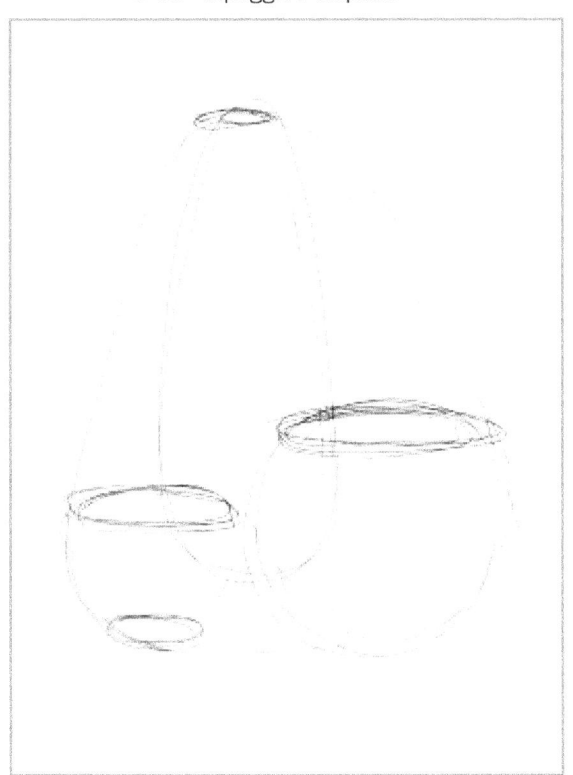

5-44 Squiggled middle figure's neck and shoulders

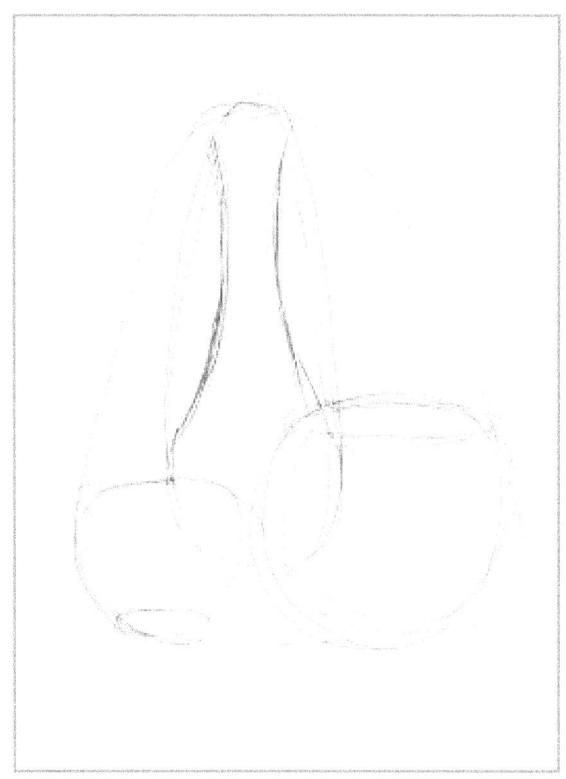

TIP When squiggling, your eyes and hand work in unison. What your eyes observe, your hand draws simultaneously (at the same time).

Phase 6 If you were drawing, you would dab your lines with your eraser to make them barely visible. Then, while looking at the ellipses on the model again (5-45), you would draw over your figure's opening *ellipses* to refine (5-46). Next, while referring to the model (5-47), you would go in or out of your lines, as needed, to refine the other edges (5-48).

5-45 Model with visualized outline around ellipses

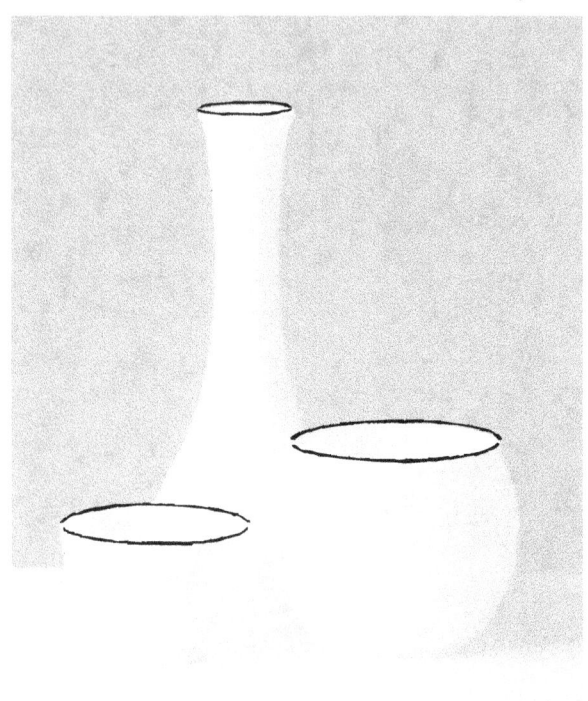

5-46 Squiggle ellipses refined

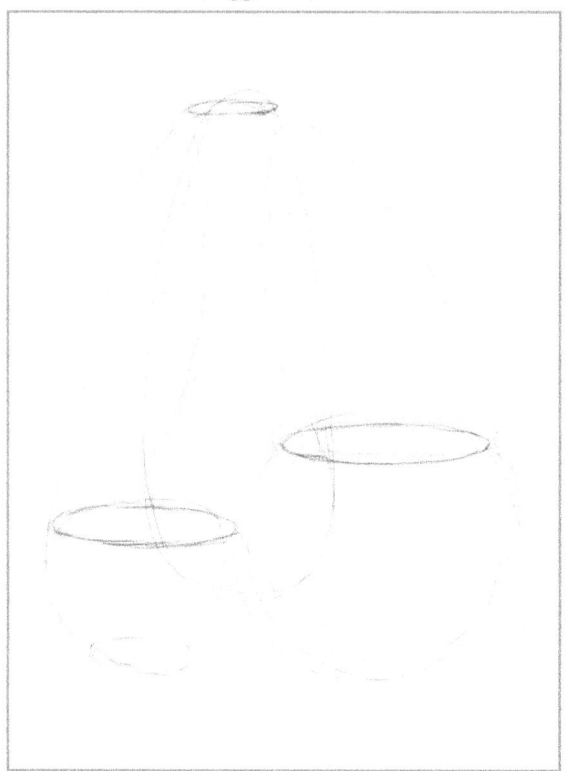

5-47 Model with visualized edges outlined

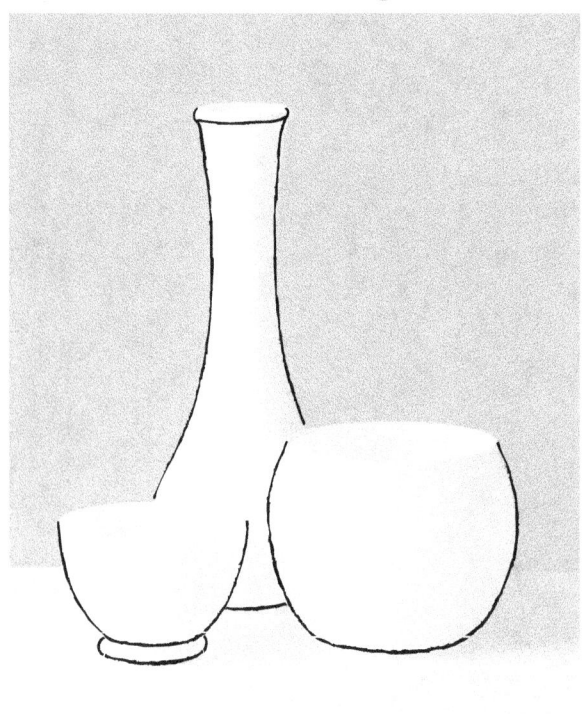

5-48 Squiggle edges refined

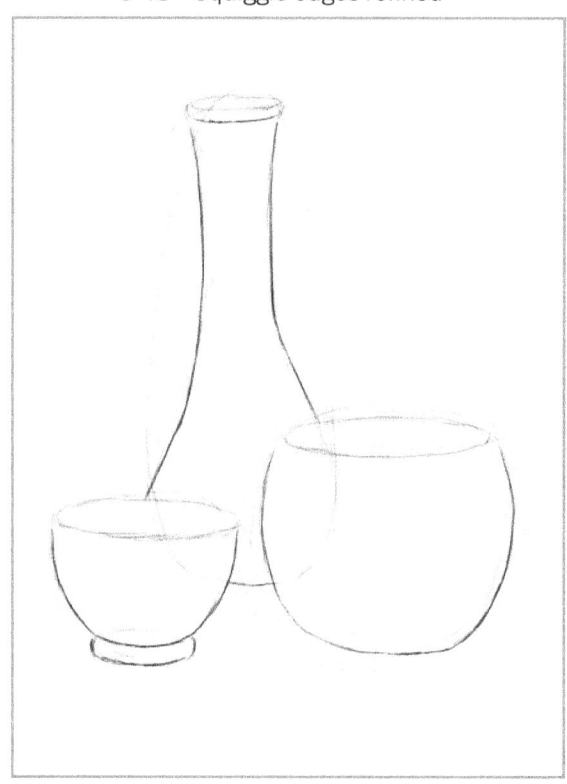

Phase 7 Excess lines would now be erased and a status check would be conducted to verify results. As example 5-49 illustrates, some things may pop out. For instance, the middle figure's shoulder on the right needs to be moved in, and the base should be lowered a bit. The line that represents the table back would also need to be included. With these improvements, and a few extra touches, the completed outline/contour drawing would eventually appear much like example (5-50). Observe that it resembles those fashioned by the other two approaches we had previously examined. As I mentioned at the outset, they all can do the job. Which method is best, you ask? The choice is yours. Perhaps you found one method more to your fancy than another. Maybe you liked some aspects of one and some of another. That's OK. You are free to pick, choose, combine them in whatever way feels comfortable to you and makes sense.

5-49 Erased excess squiggle lines reveal areas requiring adjustment and addition

5-50 Squiggled drawing after adjustments and finishing touches

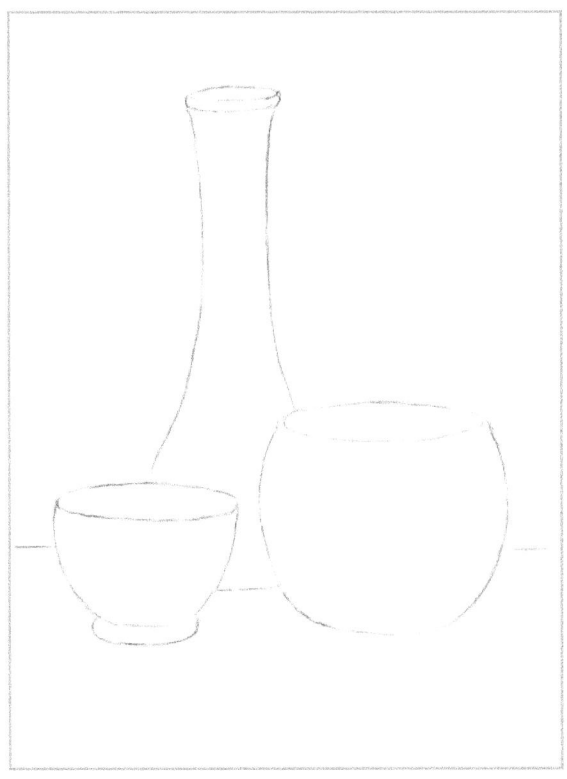

GRAB YOUR PENCIL. IT'S TIME TO DRAW THE STILL LIFE. Choose the method(s) you like.

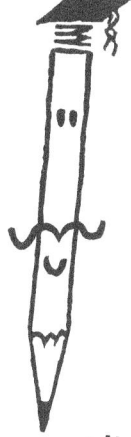

After your outline/contour drawing is fairly accurate, put in the tones as you learned in Chapters 2 & 4. Then stand back, enjoy your accomplishment and be sure to read the follow-up.

Chapter 5
FOLLOW-UP

Drawing methods are like tools, aren't they?   Each has it benefits.   For instance, when selecting the *overall method,* you can foresee how much space you will need. This can be a confidence booster because you would be able to tell whether or not your figures would fit on your paper in the size and position you desire.

If you were to choose the *crisscross method*, you would divide the overall area into four parts. This kind of segmenting would help pinpoint where figures would be located. In addition, the *streamline method* could be harnessed to simplify the forms, before the curves go in.

Another pair of tools to choose from are the *random and attach methods*. You could begin anywhere, pick any figure, and any part of it for a starting point, then add figures the same way, one by one.   The overall, crisscross and the streamline methods could also be employed by *visualizing* their guide lines.   Throughout the process, you would also be able to rely on the TRUSTY 7 structural components to help you plan, organize and layout your drawing.

In the event your selection is the *squiggle method*, many of the other methods, including the TRUSTY 7 would come into play, but in a subordinate role, especially in the early stages. Mainly, you would allow your instincts to guide you. Starting very flexible, you would quickly doodle an *overall* area that loosely surrounds the subject matter.   Then you would *randomly* squiggle one figure at a time. You could even begin that way, without the overall area.   After a brief status check, you would doodle the sub-sections, followed by another progress evaluation. At this stage, the TRUSTY 7 would take the lead to help you make adjustments.   With your figures firmly in place, and using your basic shapes as a reference comparison to your model, you could refine as much as you want.

With all these available options, now I suspect you are wondering, how do you choose the appropriate method?   It's not as difficult as you might think. Pick one procedure, or a set of procedures, that appeals to you. If things don't seem to work well, simply switch to Plan B.   Different situations require different tactics. So try to adapt accordingly and please keep an open mind.

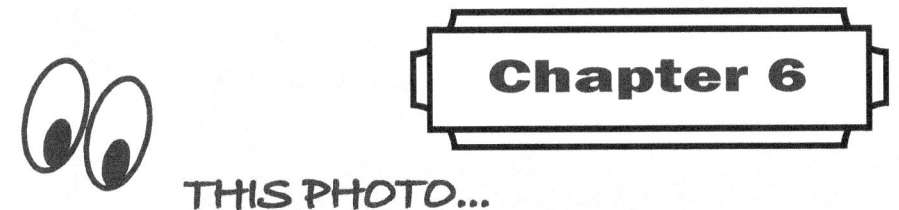

THIS PHOTO...

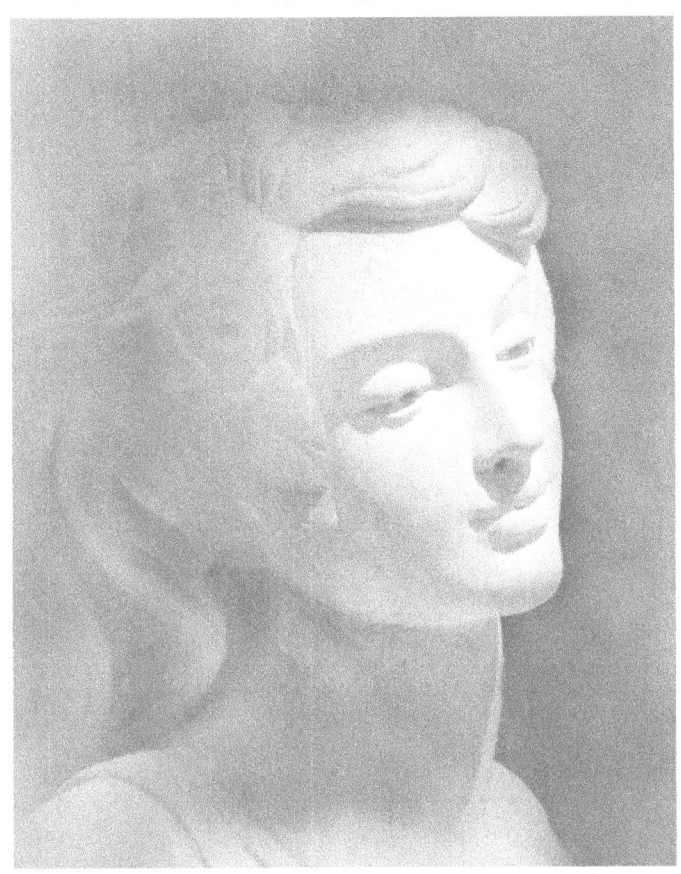

...INSPIRED
THIS DRAWING

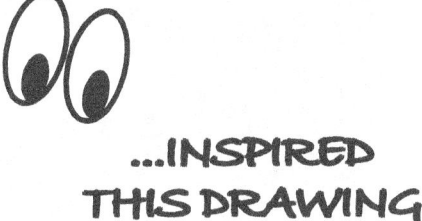

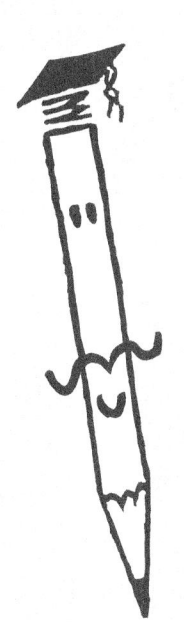

How was the sketch created? Keep going to find out.

Guess what? Faces can be streamlined too!

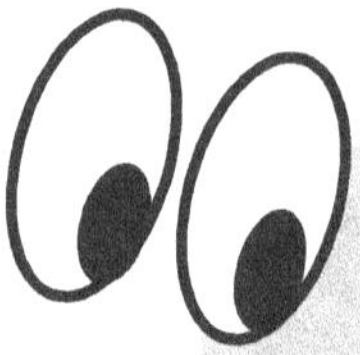

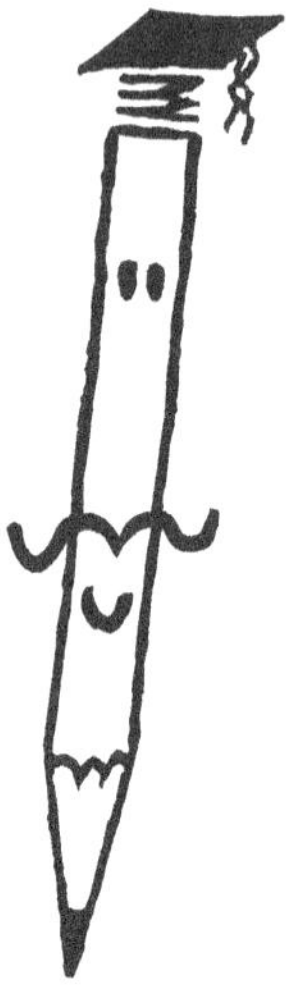

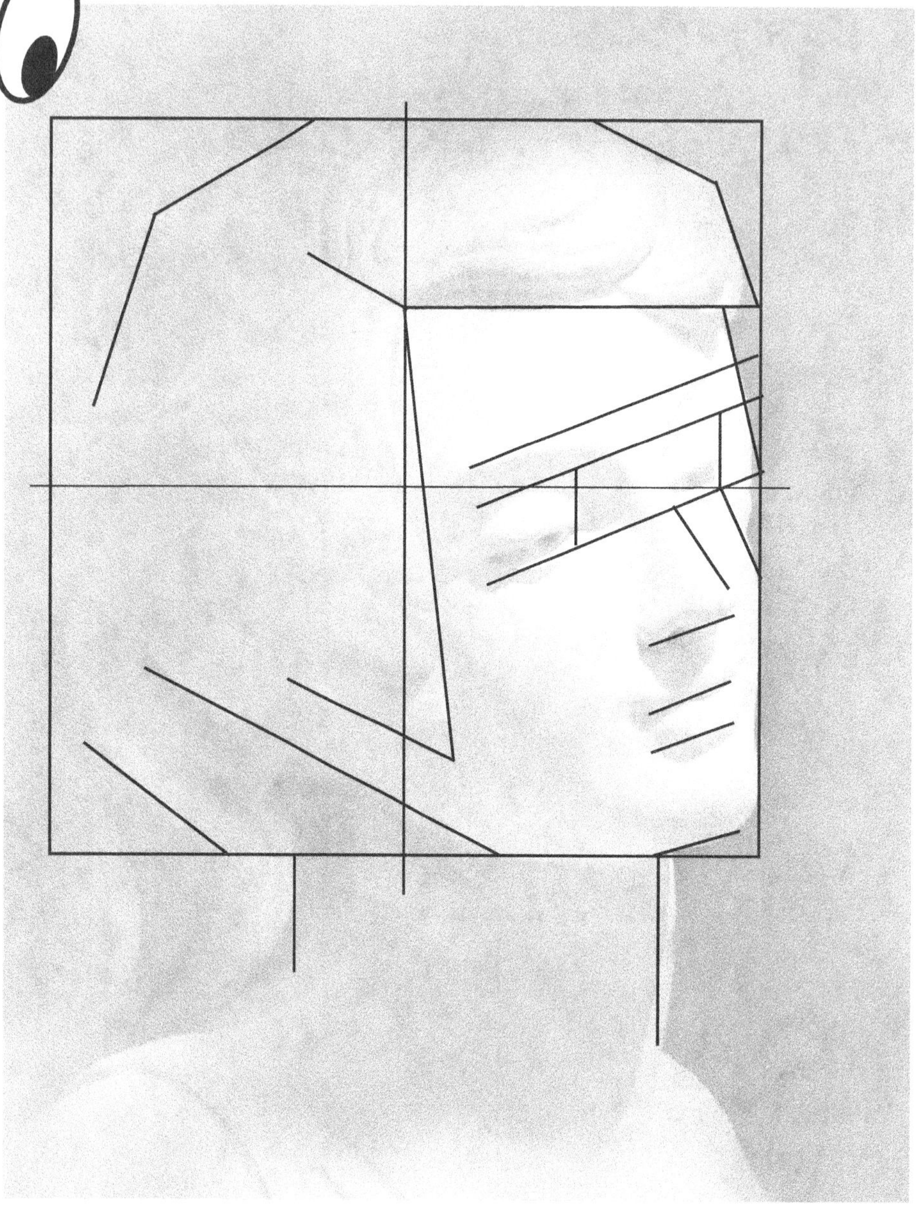

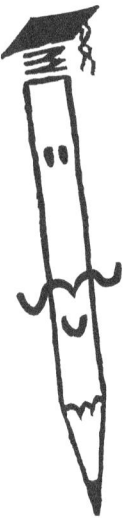

Visualize the main features on the model, simplified
with straight lines, along with an overall square that
surrounds the head. Then make believe a crisscross
bisects the square and presto! You have a reliable
foundation and a way to draw the figure in two stages.

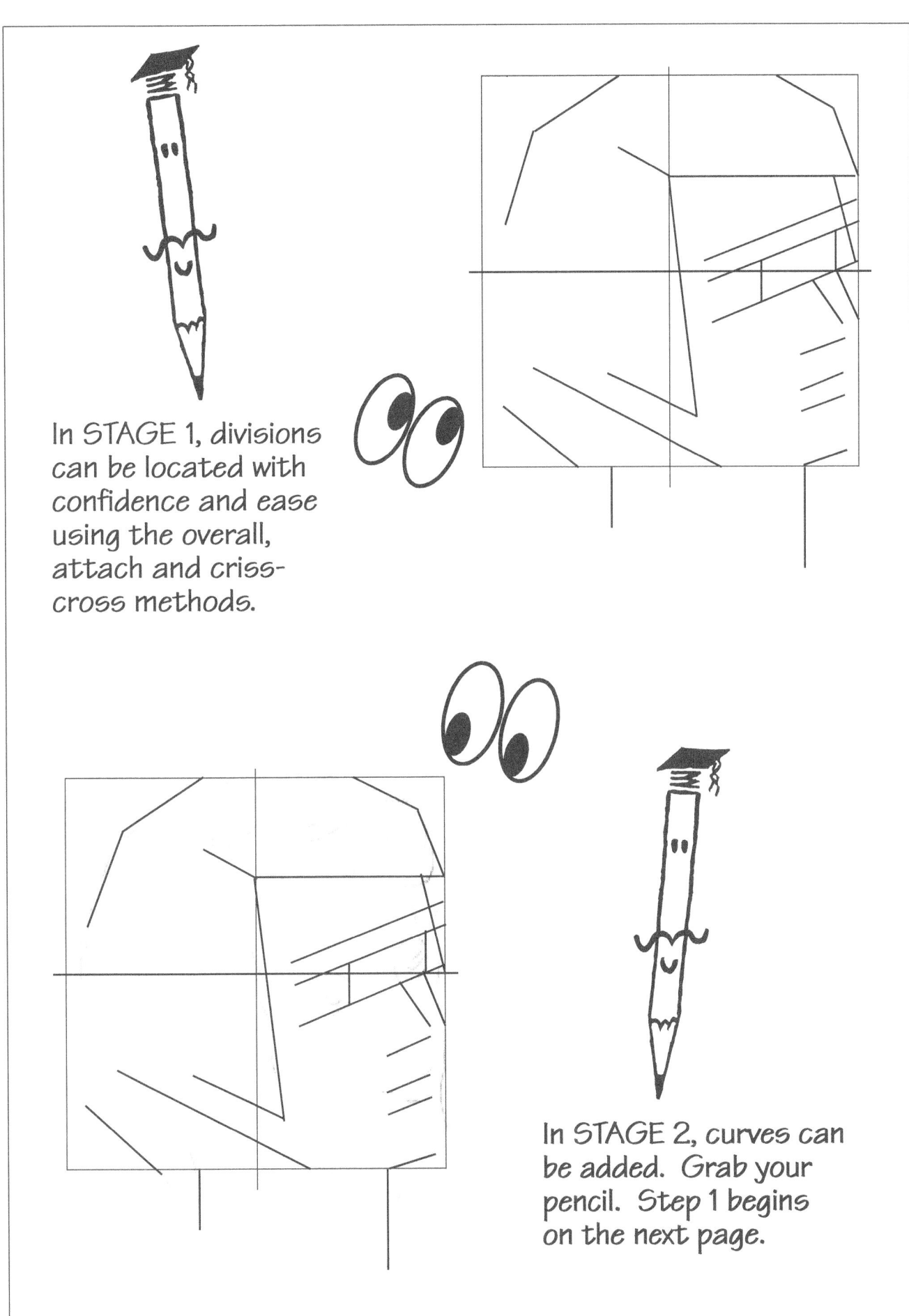

In STAGE 1, divisions can be located with confidence and ease using the overall, attach and criss-cross methods.

In STAGE 2, curves can be added. Grab your pencil. Step 1 begins on the next page.

STAGE 1 - THE STREAMLINES

STEP 1 Since the overall method would be an effective way to draw the head and face, let's isolate the area with a *square*. As shown in illustration 6-1, the main facial features extend from the top of the hair (a) to the bottom of the chin (b). In view of this, it's sensible to use that span for the height of the head. Then, from cheek side (c) the same dimension would locate the opposite end, at the back of the head (d). To insure that you will have room to attach the neck, *lightly* position your square a little above and to the left of center on your paper (6-2). Next, since we are also applying the crisscross method, *lightly* bisect your square horizontally and vertically (6-3).

TIP **Faintly visible lines are easier to erase.**

6-1 Visualize a square bordering the head

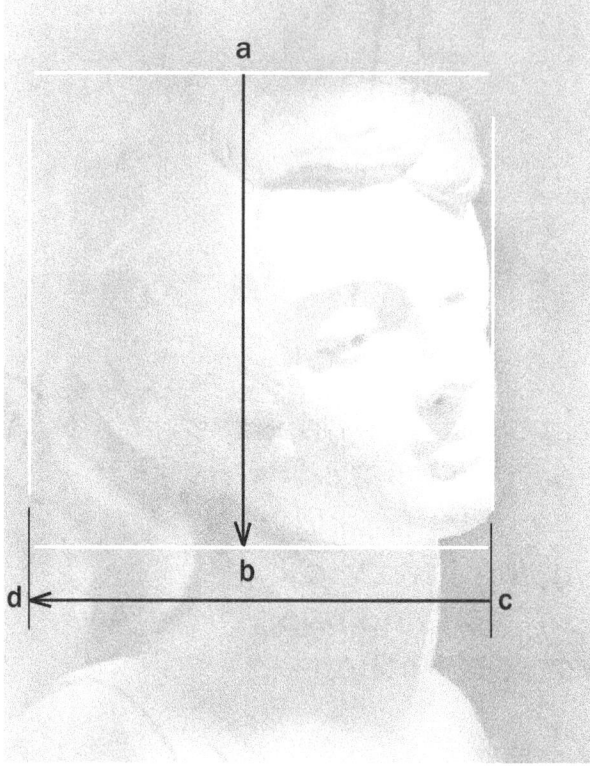

6-2 Lightly draw a square

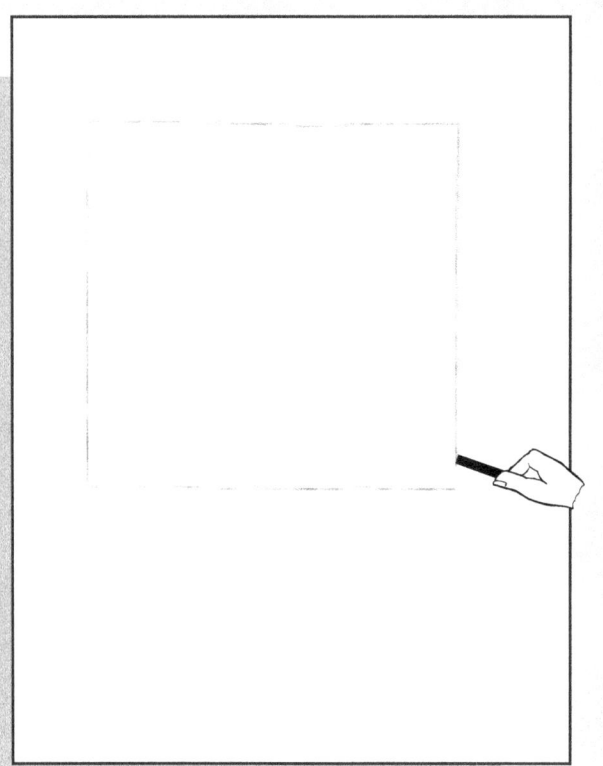

6-3 Lightly crisscross your square

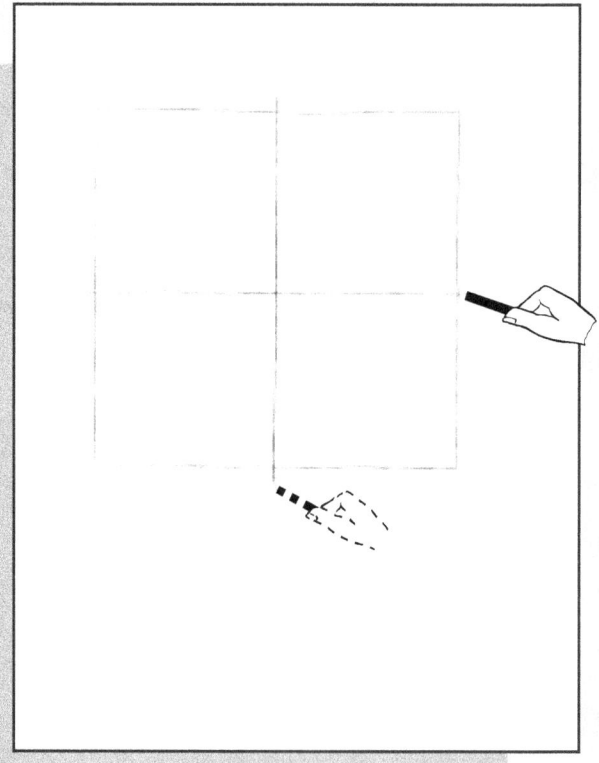

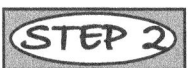 **STEP 2** With the aid of the crisscross method, the division lines can now be applied in any sequence. However, I suggest we concentrate on the model's hair first. This will help distinguish the face from the rest of the head. For instance, observe that on model illustration 6-4, the forehead hairline is level at reference point (a). The distance is a little less than half way down from the top of the square and the *horizontal* bisect. Hairline point (b), on the side of the face, angles inset to the right of the *vertical* bisect roughly an eighth of the way to the right side of the square. It ends about two thirds of the distance between the horizontal bisect and the bottom of the square. Using these coordinates, mark them proportionally on your drawing with dots. Then *lightly* connect *your* lines (6-5).

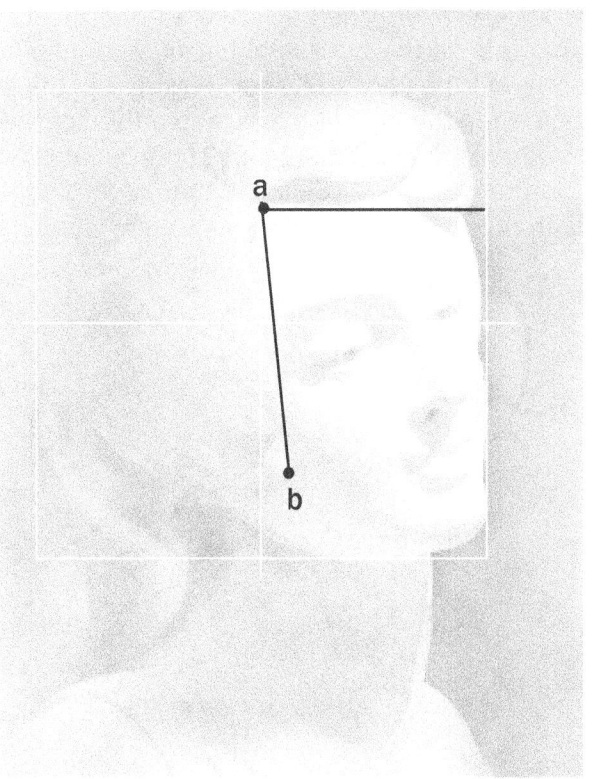

6-4 Lightly locate and draw face line divisions

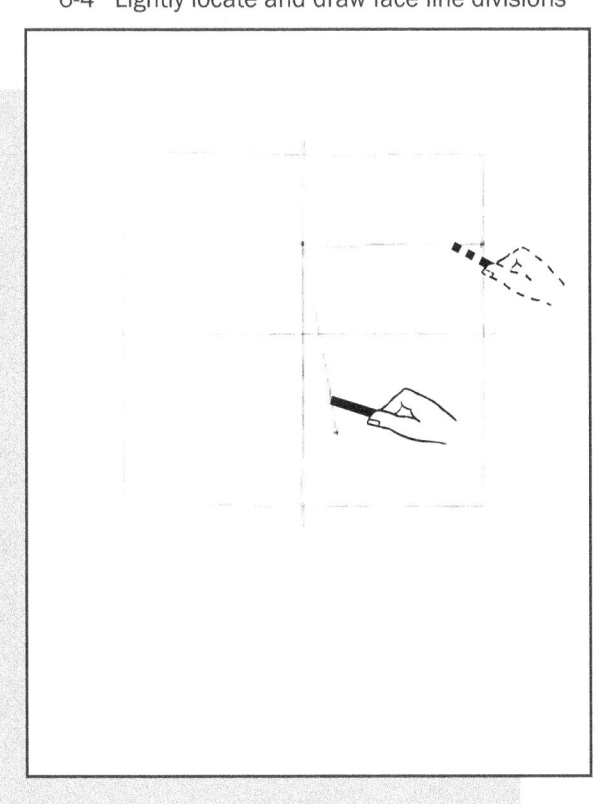

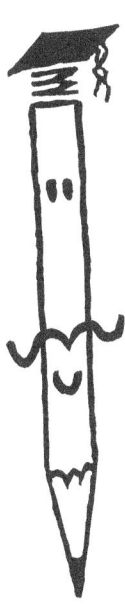

Now that you are quite experienced with locating reference points and lines, I'm going to condense the step-by-step instructions.

In the upper *left* quadrant, two straight lines visualized on the model locate the back of the head. Line (a) has a lower reference point roughly a quarter span above the horizontal bisect, and inset about one eighth of the way from the side of the squareto the vertical bisect. Further up, the second reference point lies about a third of the way *below* the top of the square, and a third of the distance from its side to the vertical bisect. Line (b) shares that point. The other one locates on top of the square, about a quarter distance left of the vertical bisect. Estimate these coordinates to scale on your drawing and mark the locations with dots. Then *lightly* connect them with lines.

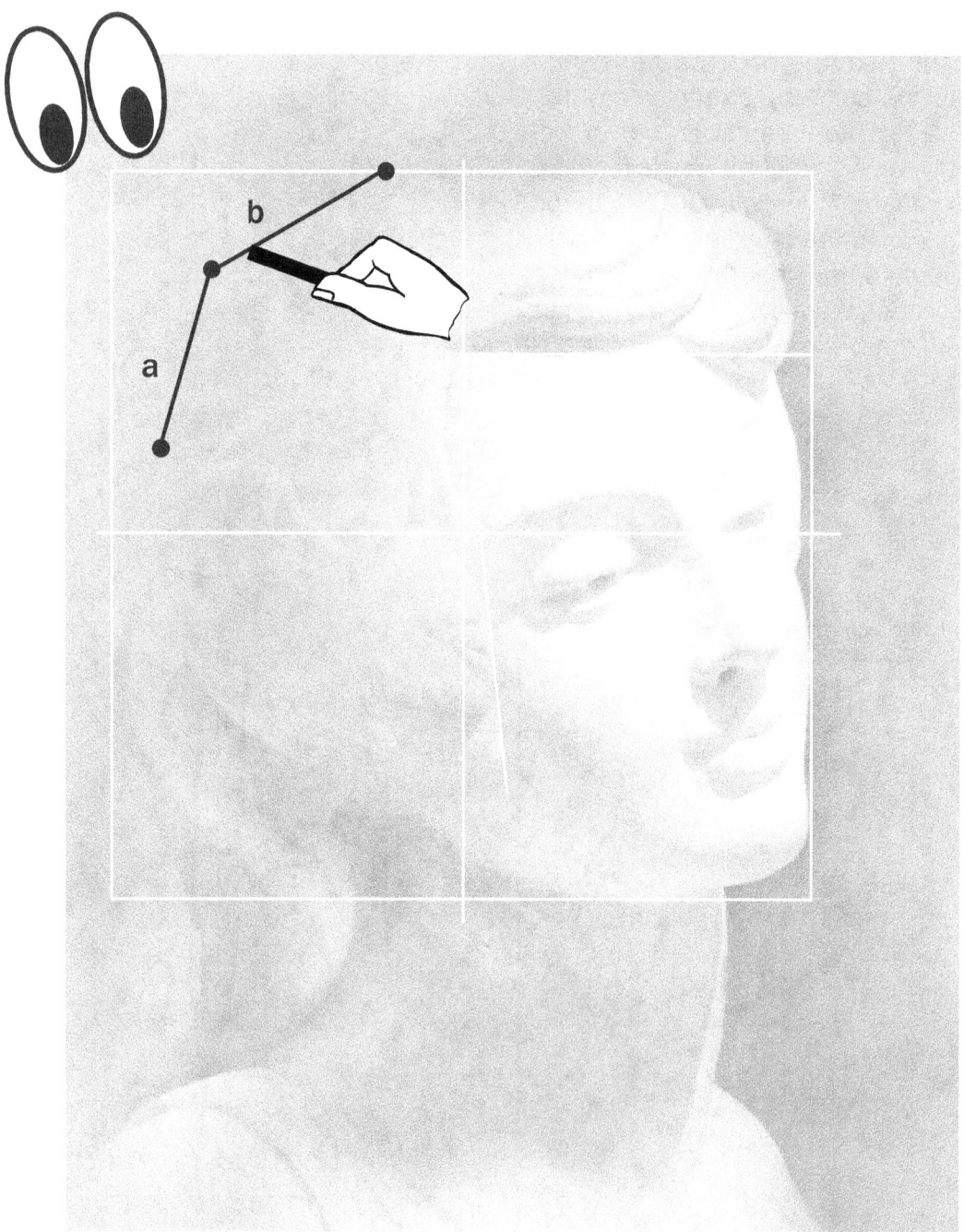

TIP A quadrant is a quarter section of a whole shape.

Let's locate some more hairlines. Observe that line (a) has a reference point on the top of the square's *right quadrant* near center. About a third of the way down to the horizontal hairline, and slightly in from the right *side* of the square, lies another reference point. Line (b) angles down from there, striking directly on the horizontal hairline where the right side of the square and the horizontal hairline meet. Line (c) starts on the horizontal *hairline*, vertically aligned with the closest point above. Tilting downward, it ends directly on the horizontal *bisect*. Find these coordinates on your drawing and lightly connect them with lines.

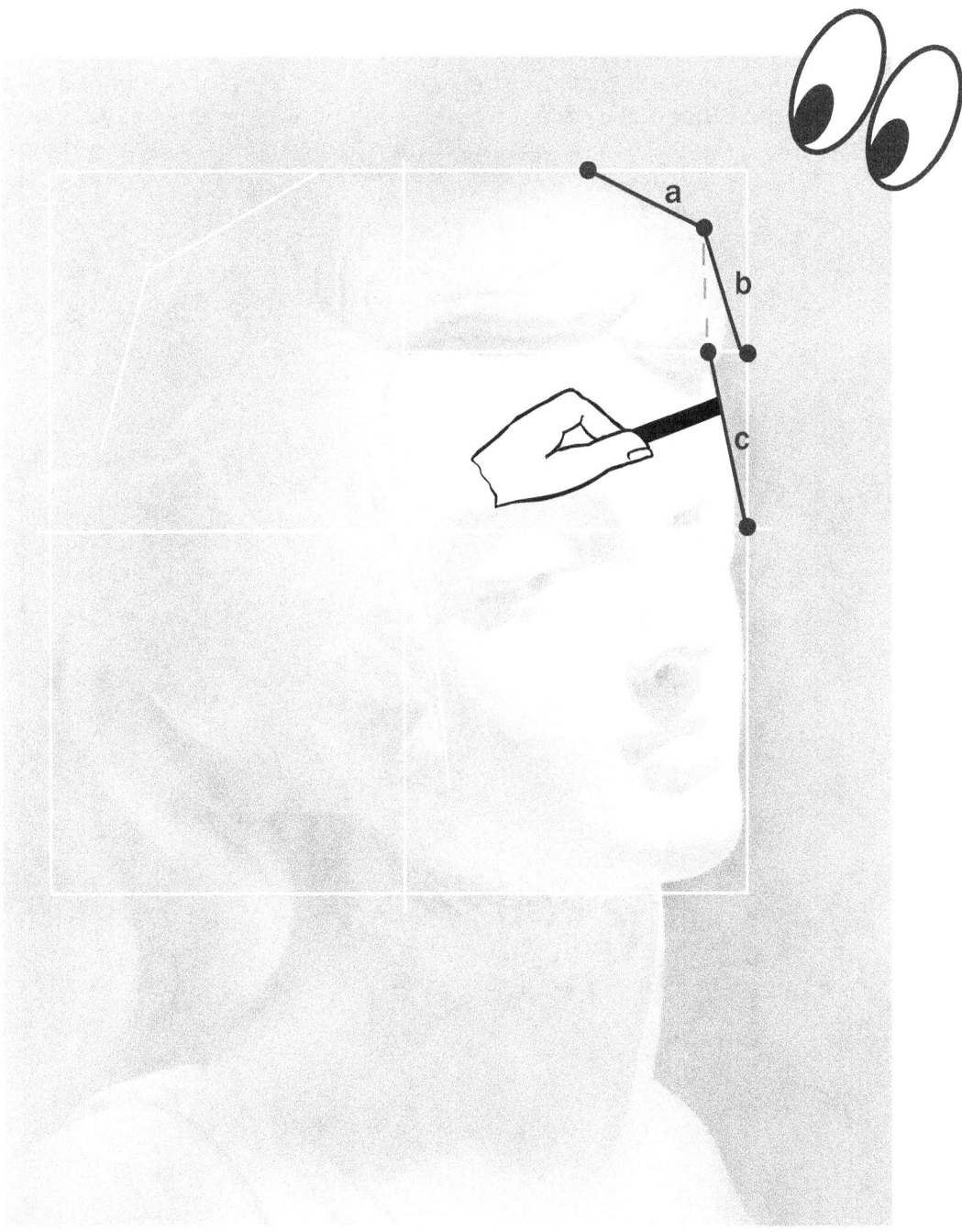

TIP A verbal description of reference point locations is a lot like a detailed explanation of how to tie your shoe laces. The task sounds complicated, but it really isn't. The coordinates are specified for you, but you can estimate them yourself.

As you can tell, line (a) parts the hair by tilting upward from the horizontal hairline at the vertical bisect. The stopping point is about a quarter of the way left from the vertical bisect, and a third of the way down from the top of the square. Hairline (b) attaches from the hairline that separates the side of the face. Tilting to the left and up, it reaches about half way between the horizontal bisect and the bottom of the square. The distance from the *vertical bisect* to the left side of the square is roughly a third of the way. Hairline (c) aligns with the chin. The upper reference point locates approximately a third span in from the left side of the square, midway between the bottom of the square and the horizontal bisect. The lower point sits in the right lower quadrant, directly on the bottom of the square, approximately a quarter span from the vertical bisect. Hairline (d) has one point that also strikes the bottom, but it is in the left lower quadrant, halfway between the left side of the square and the vertical bisect. The other end is about a third span up and slightly in from the left side. Locate these coordinates to scale on your drawing with dots. Then lightly connect them with lines.

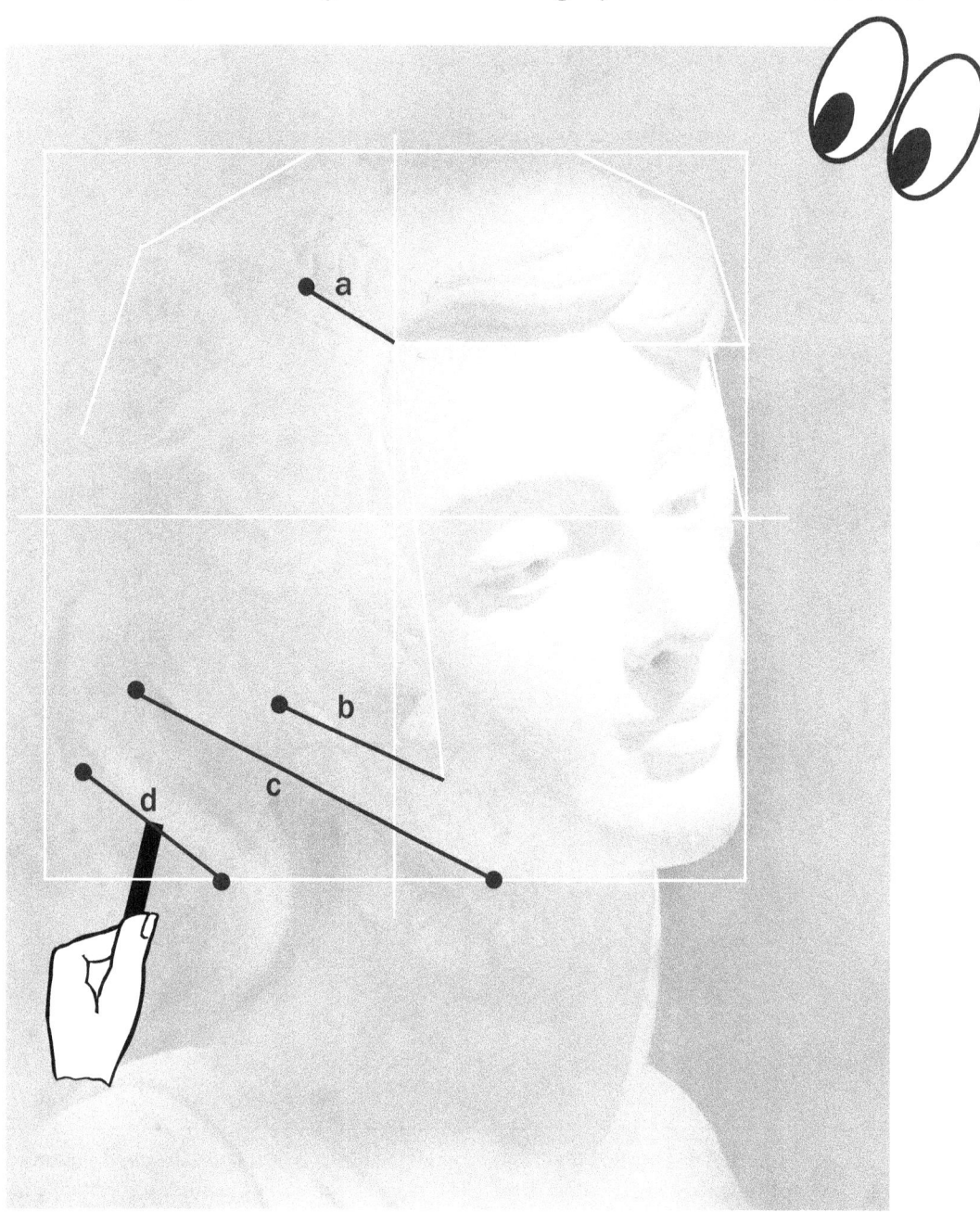

Lines (a), (b), and (c) have some things in common. They are parallel and of equal length. Each of the three lines has one reference point that locates on the right side of the square. Each line also has another reference point positioned about a quarter distance to the right of the *vertical* bisect. Eyebrow line (a) tilts downward toward the center of the square from about a quarter distance between the horizontal forehead line and the horizontal bisect line. Upper eyelid line (b) tilts down from a little above midway between the horizontal hairline and the bisect line. Lower eyelid line (c) angles parallel with lines (a) and (b) at a distance that is about twice the span between them. Lightly mark these coordinates to scale on your drawing with dots and lines.

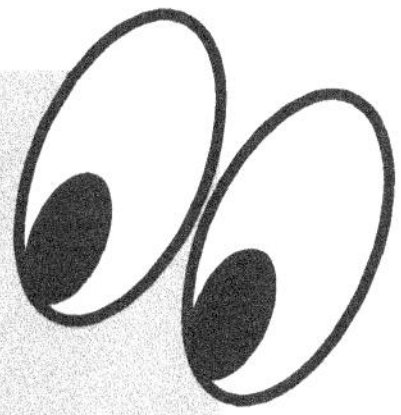

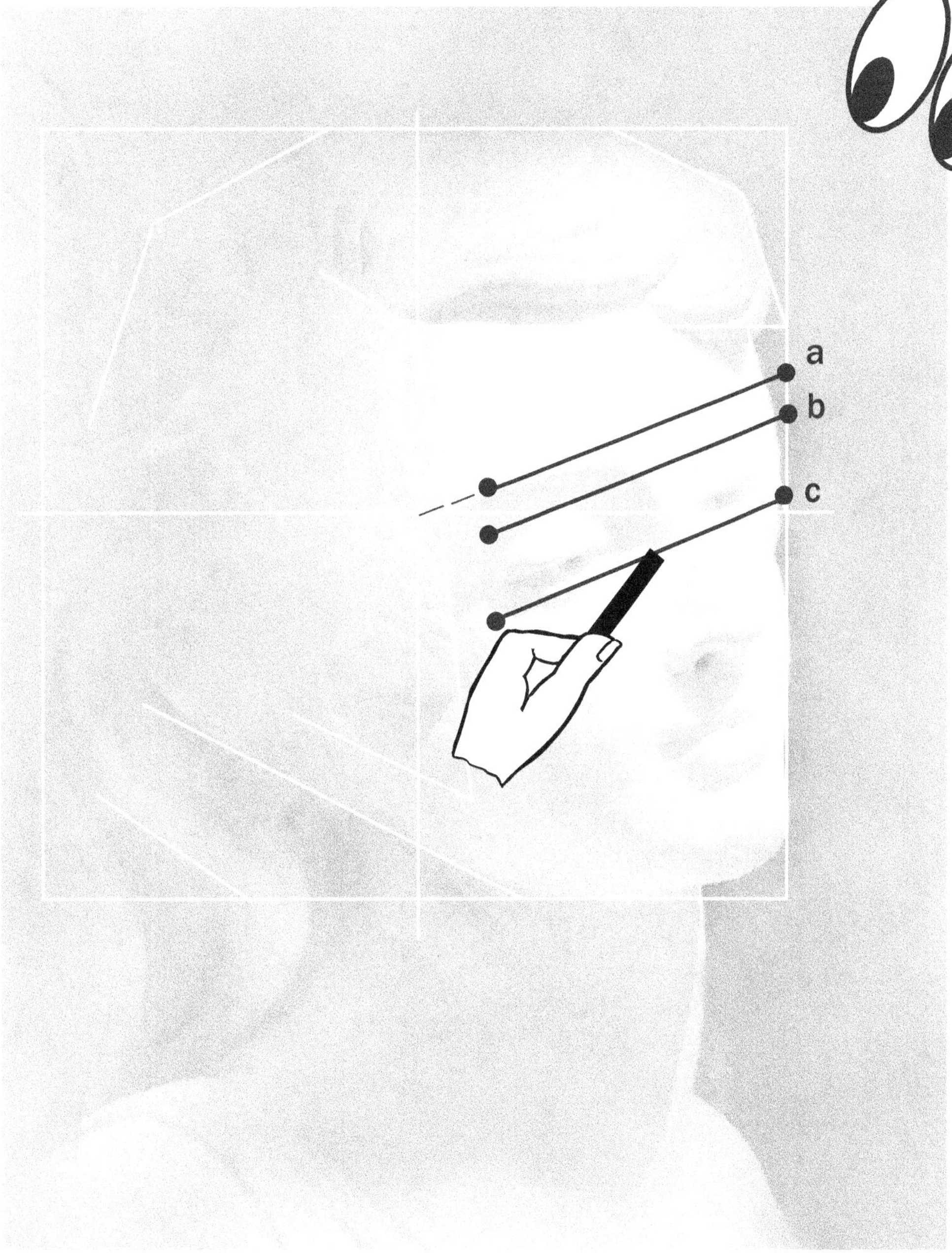

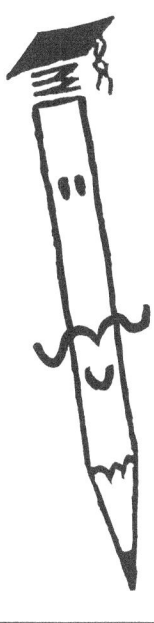

Are you drawing lightly? Barely visible
lines can be erased much more easily.

STEP 7 The *left* reference point of *nostril* line (a) locates at a distance somewhat less than a third span between the right end of the square and the vertical bisect. Checked vertically and downward, it lies less than midway between the horizontal bisect and the bottom of the square. Tilting upward, the nostril line ends at a point which is even with the angled hairline (see long dash line). Looking downward from reference point (a) approximately a third of the way to the bottom of the square (parallel to the nostril line), we find *mouth* opening line (b). Further down, *lower lip* line (c) runs parallel and even below lines (a) and (b) at a distance of about half the height between point (a) and the base of the square. *Chin* line (d) is a cinch to find, since it tilts upward from the bottom of the square and also runs parallel as well as even with the other three lines.

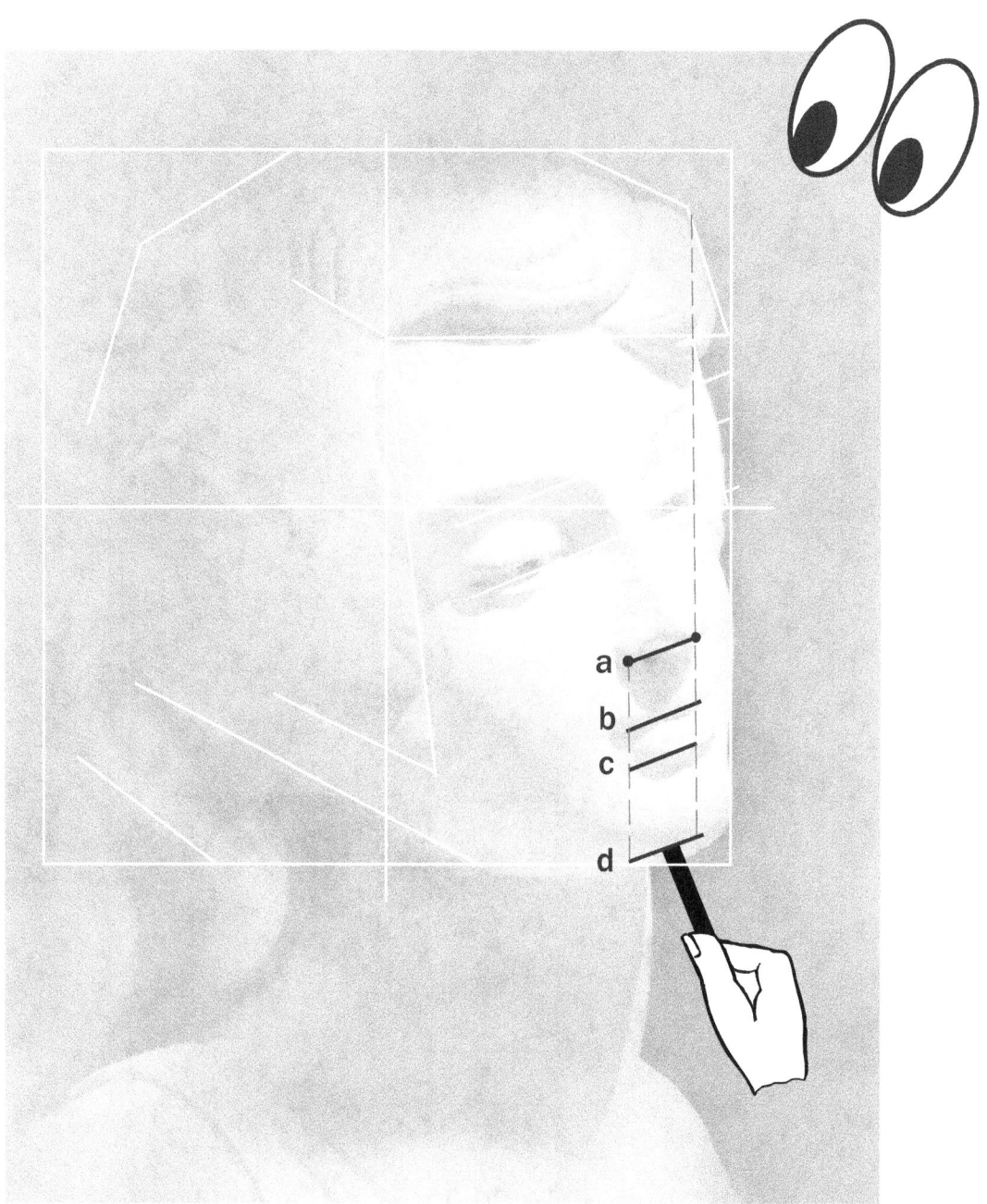

STEP 8 Vertical line (a) locates on the right side of the left eyelid, *nearly* midway between the vertical bisect and the right side of the square. It spans between the horizontal upper eyelid line and the lower eyelid line. The other eyelid (b) does the same thing, but it aligns with the angled hairline *indicated with dashes*. Cheek line (c) connects from the bottom of line (b) and tilts to a point about a quarter of the way down from the horizontal bisect, on the right side of square. Nose line (d) begins from the lower eyelid line, about two thirds of the distance between vertical line (a) and (b), then stops *horizontally* aligned with the bottom of cheek line (c). Neckline (e), doubling as a hairline, runs vertically from the bottom of the square, about a third of the way left of the vertical bisect. The length is roughly that same horizontal distance. Neck line (f) is approximately double that span and connects from the bottom of the square at the chin line (*vertically* aligned with the nose and mouth shown by dashes).

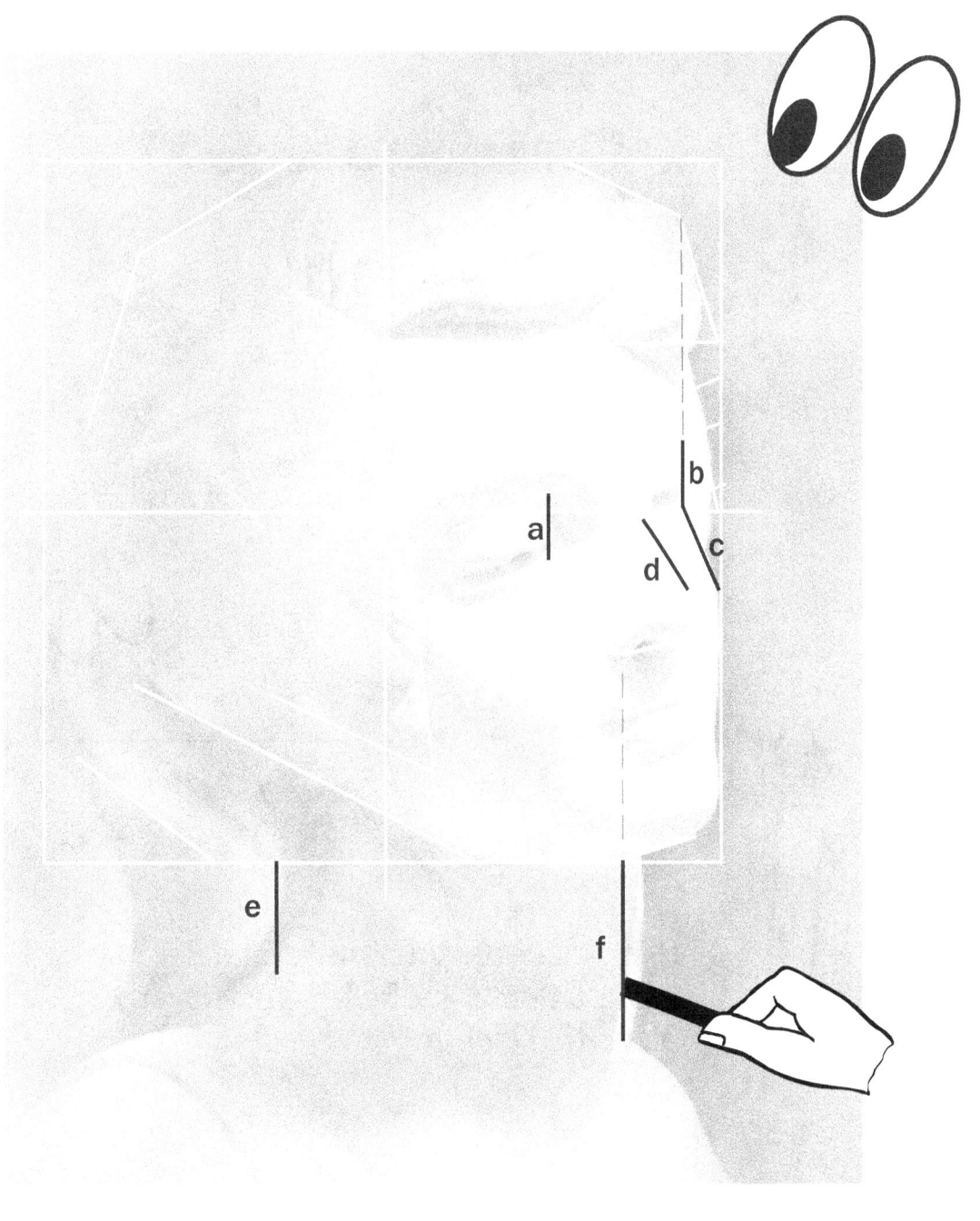

STEP 9 Time for a progress check. There seem to be enough divisions to see the basic format now. Too many guide lines, or not enough, can be confusing. The point is to be able to tell whether the main foundation, and the smaller ones within it, reasonably fit. This procedure helps to verify accuracy, before the curves go in. Study the following example. By comparing the nose, mouth and chin alignment between the drawing and the model, we discover that on the drawing they are too far to the left.

Model visualized with streamlines

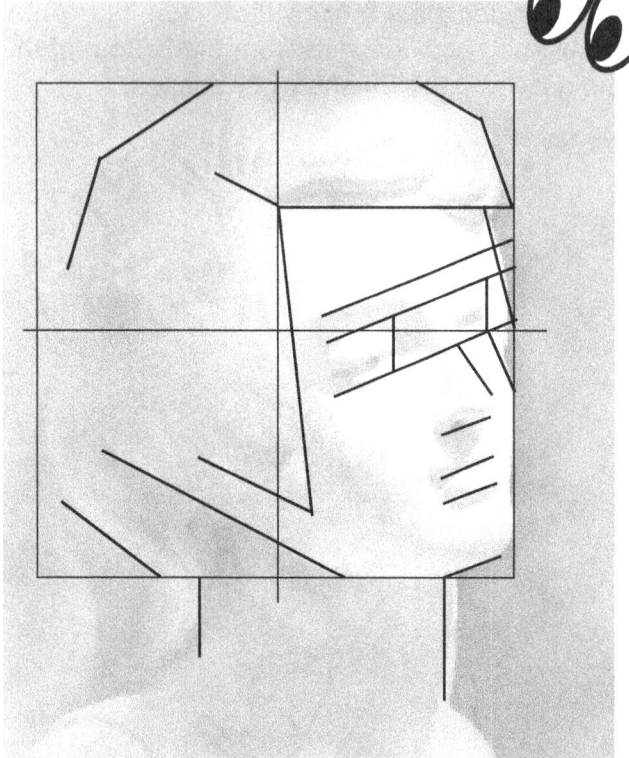

Comparison reveals the nose, mouth and chin lines on the drawing are too far left

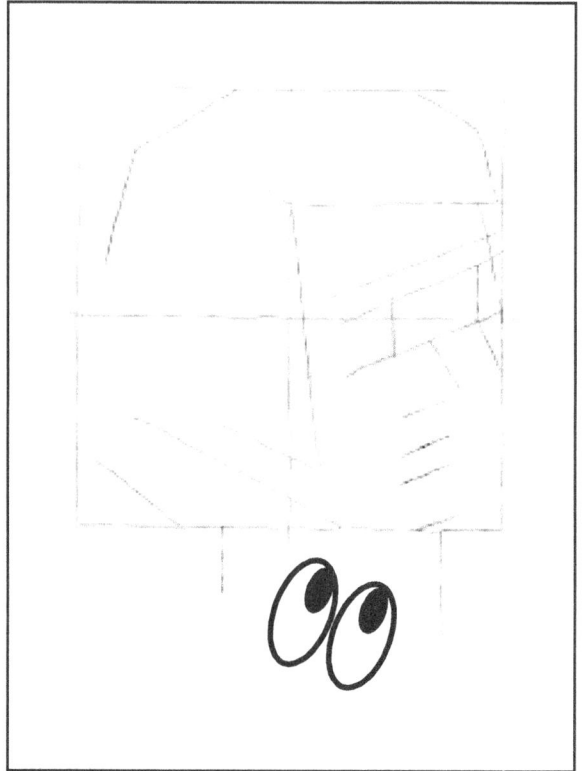

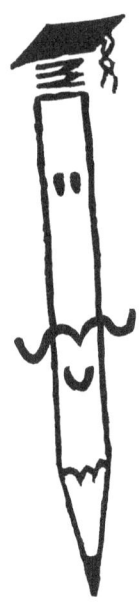

Is it necessary to make the adjustments BEFORE curves are added? Decide for yourself.

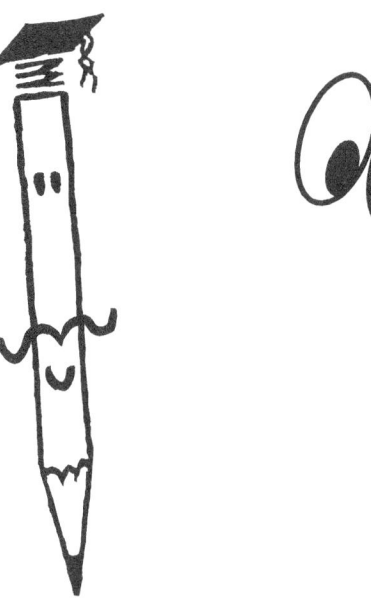

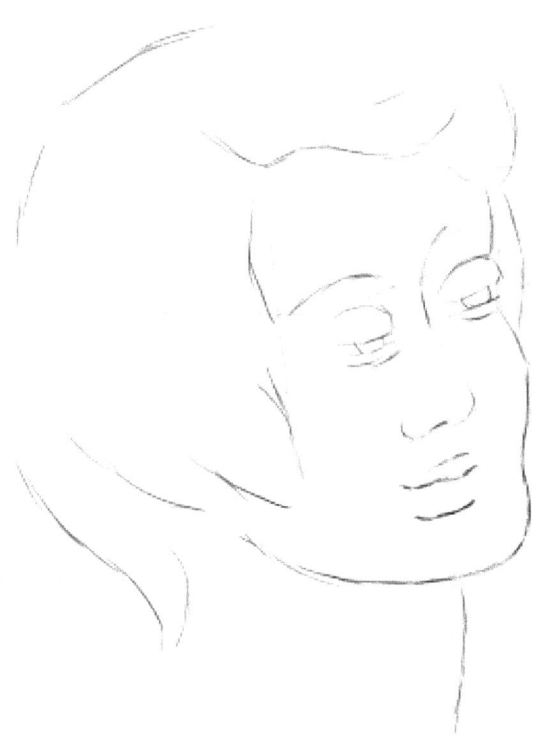

When curves were placed on the inacurate foundation, the distorted figure (above right) appeared. When adjustments were made, PRIOR to the curves, the result was the figure below.

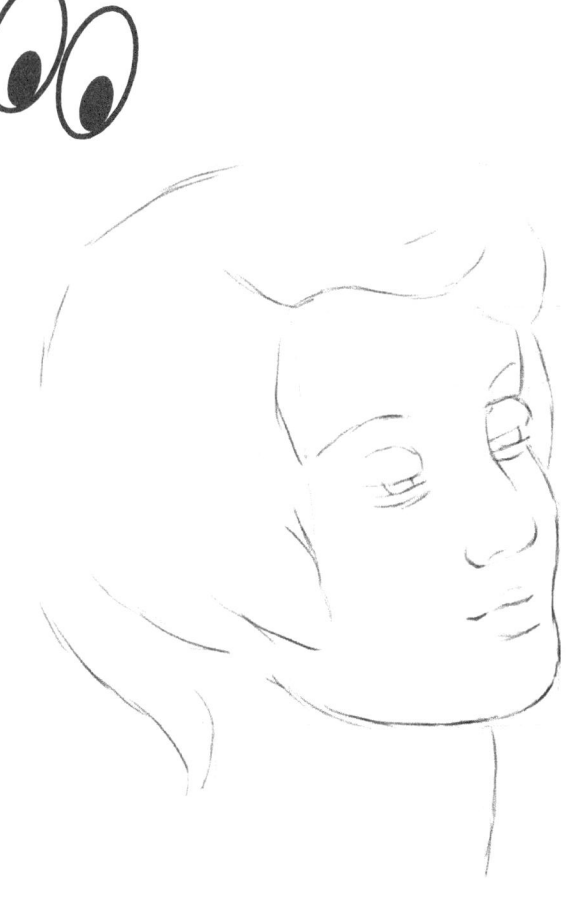

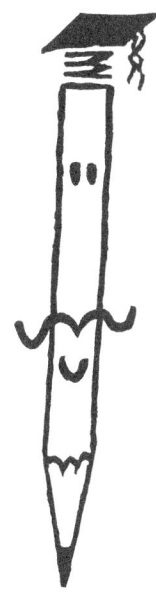

See the difference? Now, check your foundation for accuracy and modify as needed. Then continue.

It's nearly time to add the curves.
Here is how they might be visualized
on the model. What is your impression?

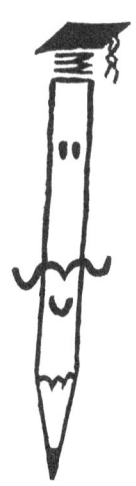

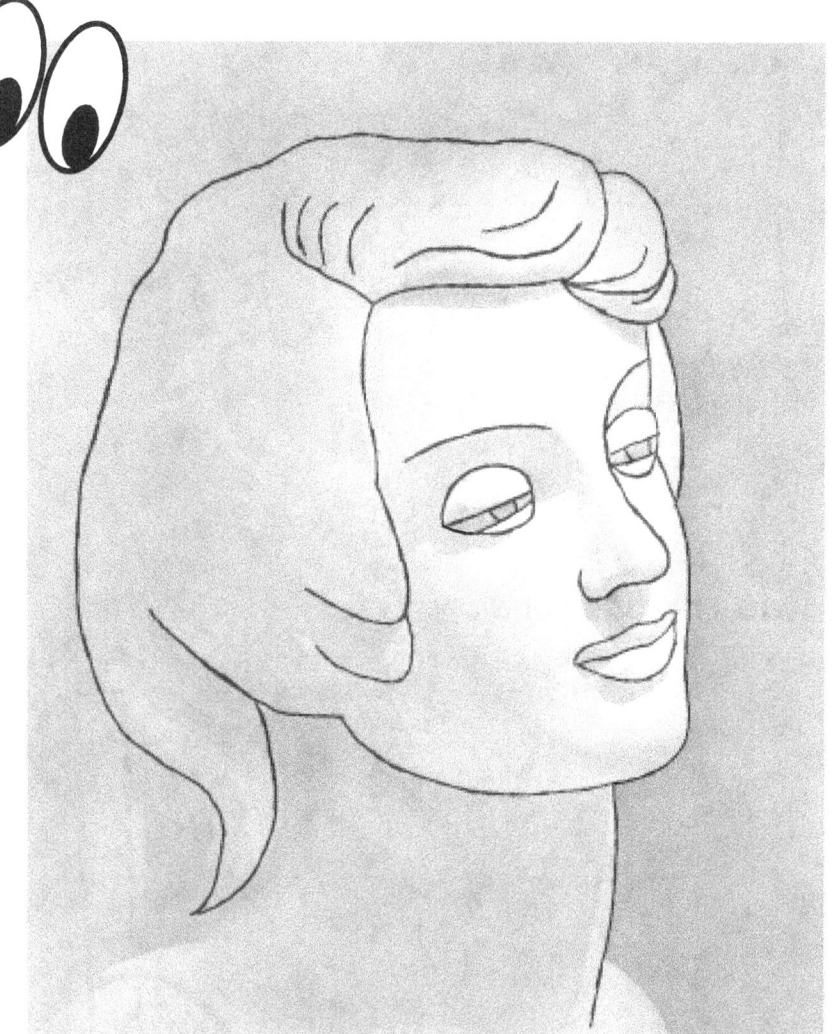

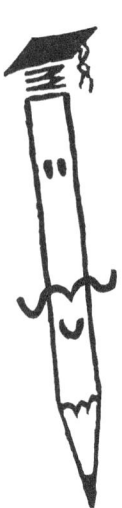

Do you find this look attractive? As you can
tell, people's features made with just solid
outline and contour curve lines can spoil the
aesthetic appeal. The next page shows the
outcome and an alternative.

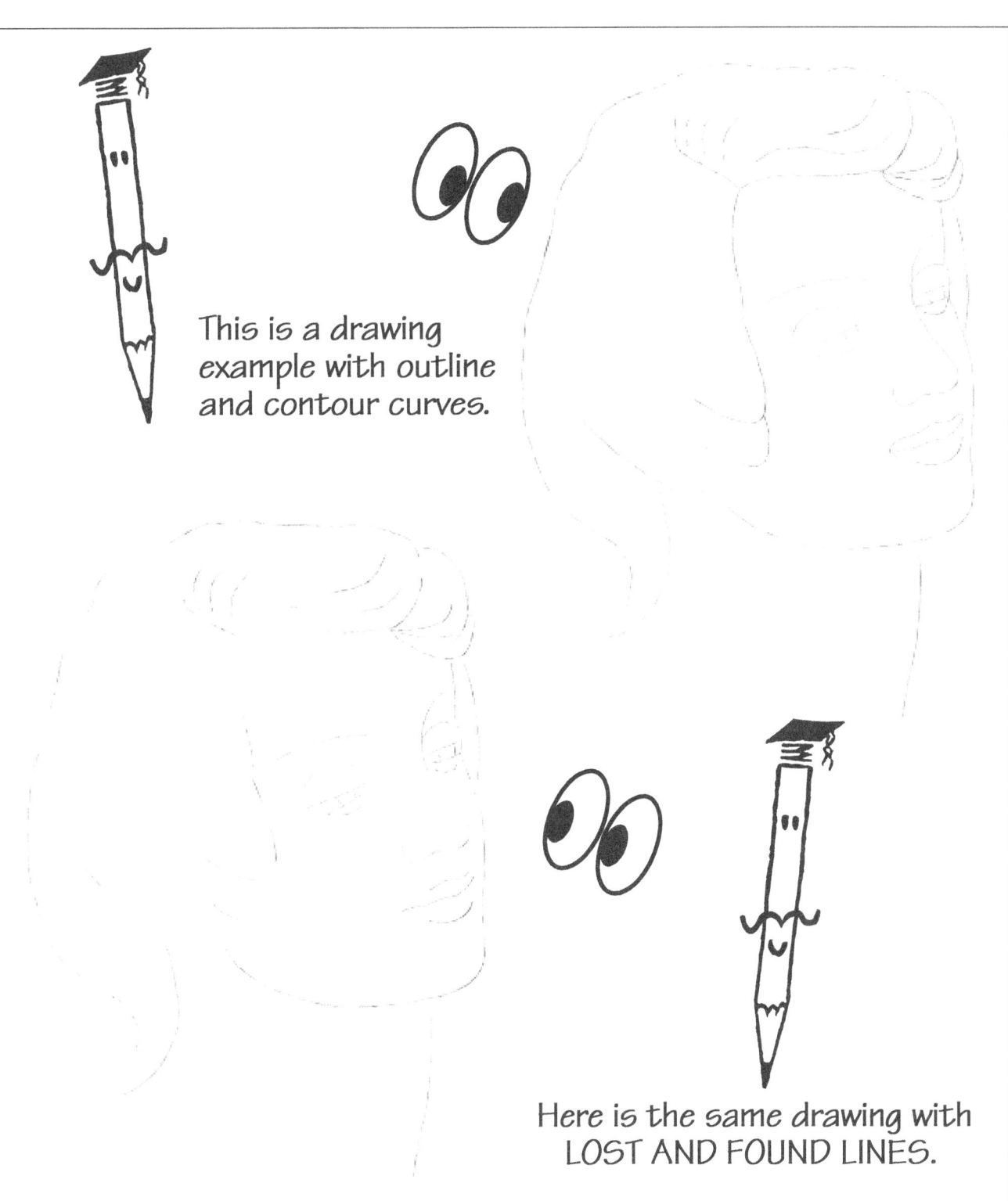

This is a drawing example with outline and contour curves.

Here is the same drawing with LOST AND FOUND LINES.

What are LOST AND FOUND LINES? They are edges with gaps. The effect helps to increase the impression of depth and motion. Compare the two drawings. The upper one seems stiff and motionless, wouldn't you agree? Now that you appreciate the distinction, prepare to include curves with your streamlined figure, using the lost and found line technique.

STAGE 2 - THE CURVES
YOU CHOOSE THE SEQUENCE OF STEPS

DIRECTIONS: Pick a curve at random in the figure below and compare it to the picture on the next page to determine where it locates with respect to the nearest guide lines. Find that area on *your* foundation and lightly duplicate the curve proportionally. Repeat the process by forming the rest of the curves in scale. Although many are connected, do them *one by one*. As you proceed, check your results and don't assume all your guide lines are accurate. Move those as necessary, and/or your curves, to compensate for any inaccuracy. Even though you are drawing the image of a face, remember the model is a statue made of simple shapes and curves. Keep this in mind, not only during the present exercise, but also when drawing real people. By seeing the features merely as forms, you will be less likely to unknowingly exaggerate them.

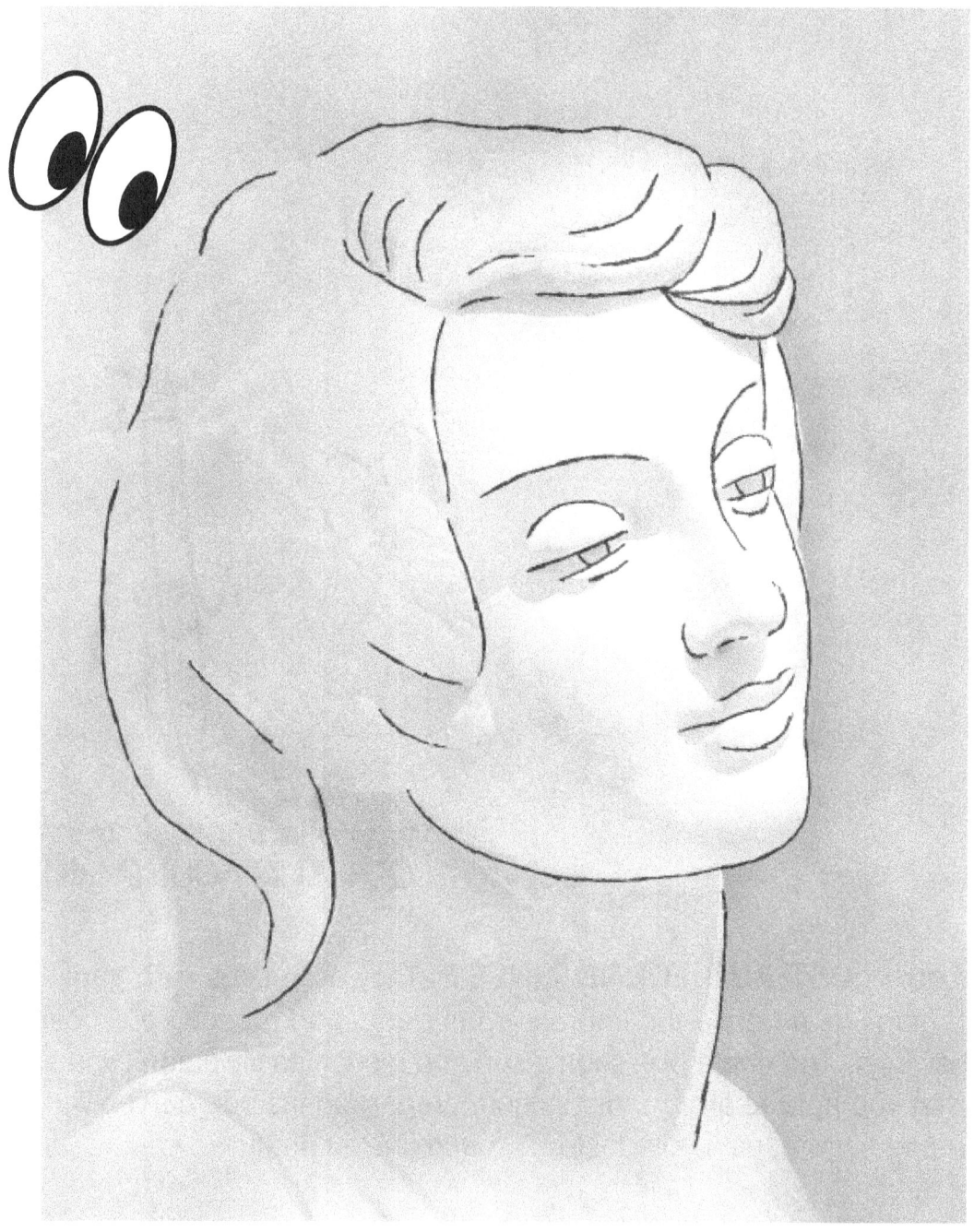

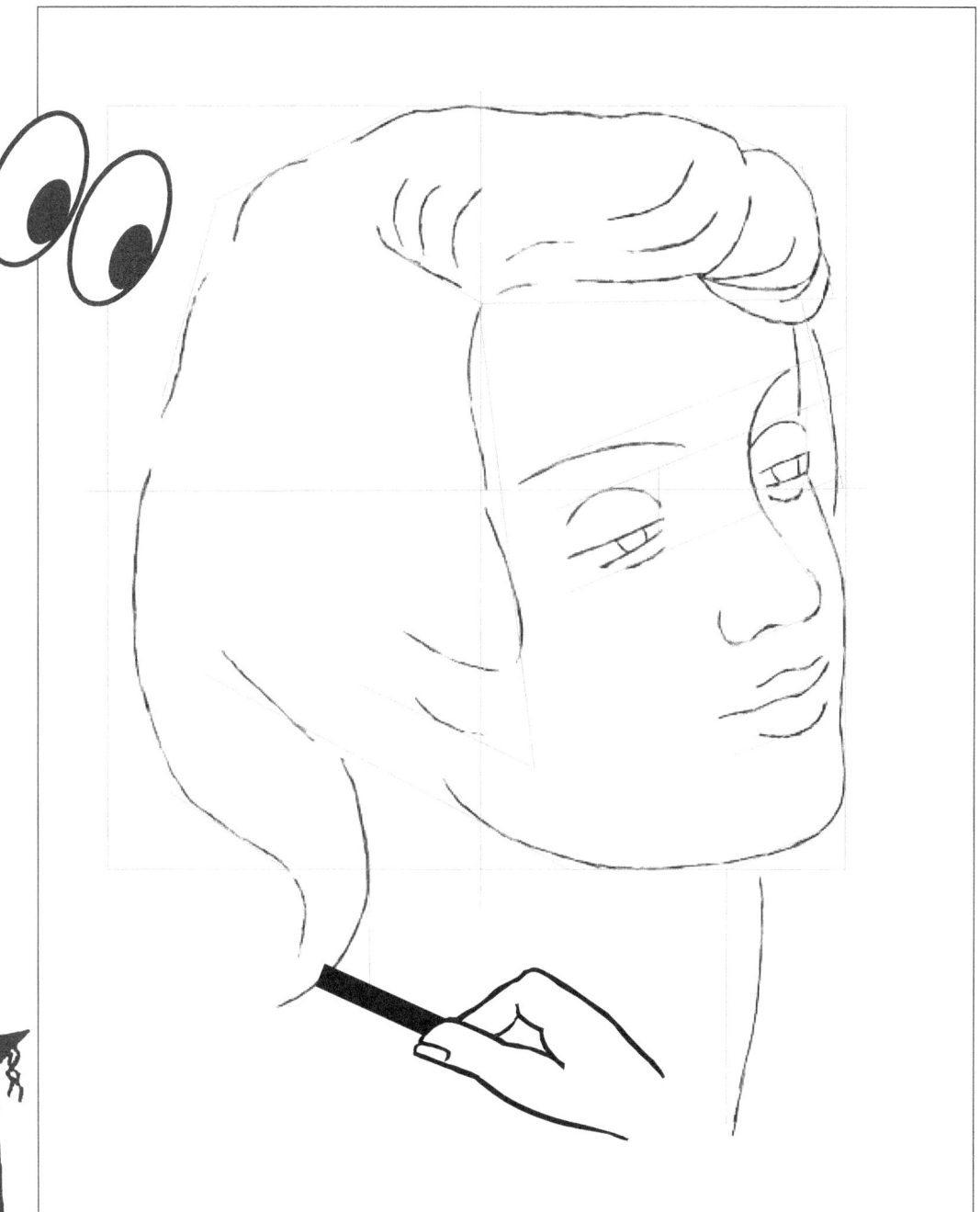

Having finished adding curves to your foundation, prop it up beside the illustration shown above. Stand back a few paces. Compare your work and adjust as needed. Next, erase your guide lines and replenish any curves you might accidentally remove. Then turn the page to continue.

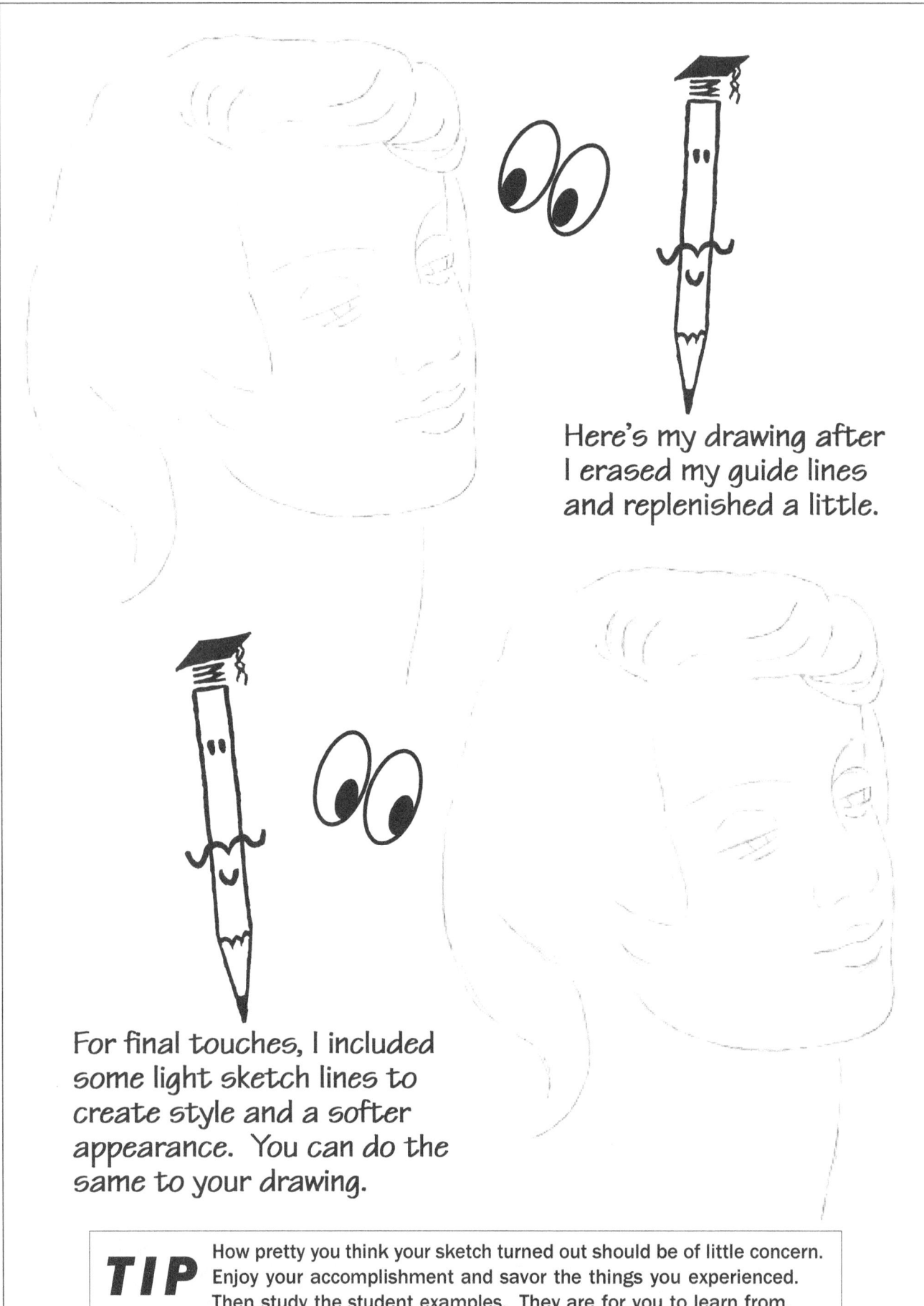

Here's my drawing after I erased my guide lines and replenished a little.

For final touches, I included some light sketch lines to create style and a softer appearance. You can do the same to your drawing.

STUDENT SAMPLES

Example A

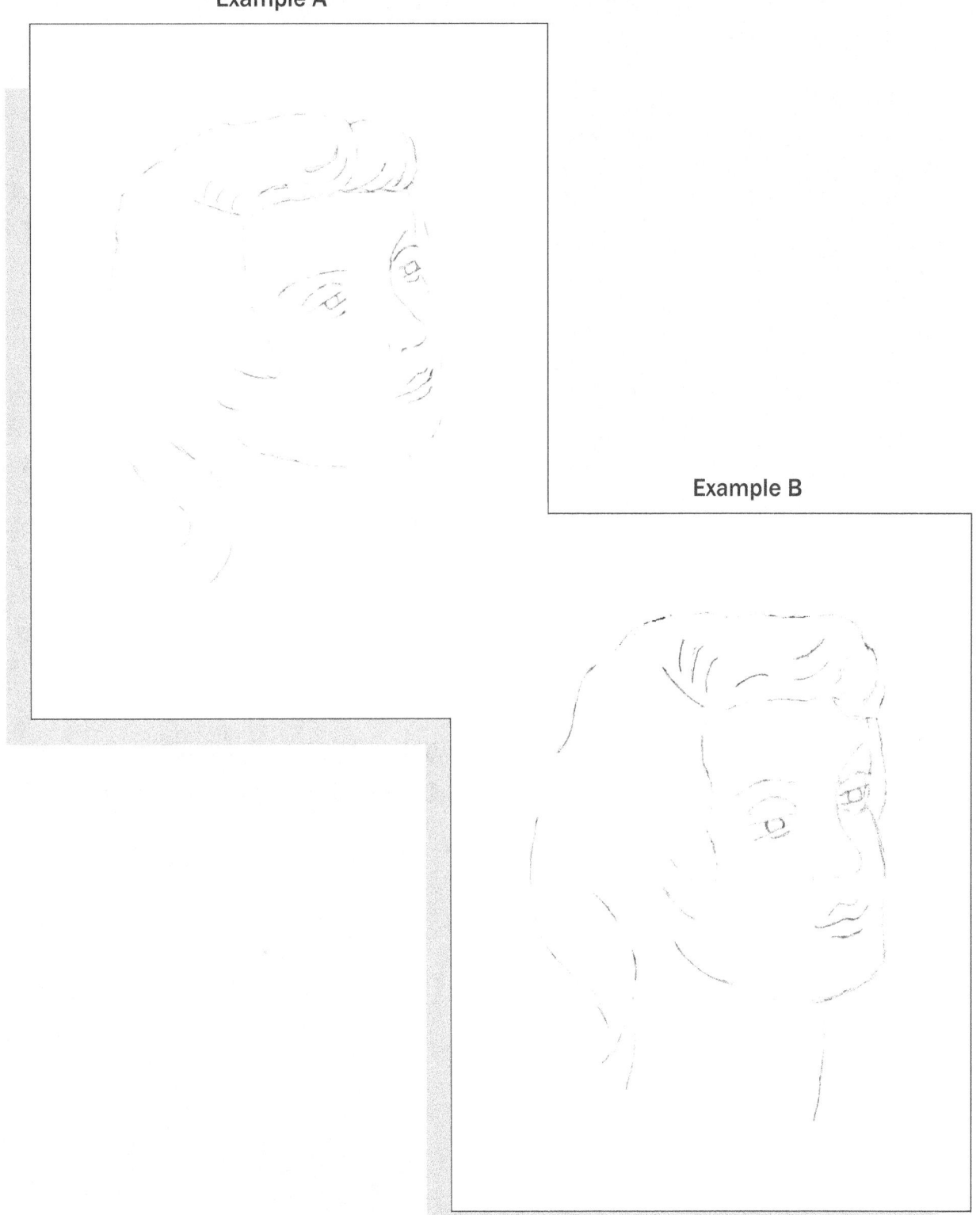

Example B

Chapter 6
FOLLOW-UP

Wow! Isn't it terrific to discover you can also streamline faces? The overall and crisscross methods make it easy. For that matter, the random and attach methods, the squiggled approach, or any combination you select, would work just as well. Come to think of it, when you stop to consider, essentially faces and their features are shapes. Seeing them not as eyes, nose and mouth, but rather as just *forms*, can make a big difference. Why? Because you are apt to look closer in search of unique characteristics and therefore likely to draw your lines more accurately.

While we're on the subject of lines, now I will let you in on something else. Lines do not really exist in nature. Lines are a man made invention, used to separate boundaries. When it comes to drawing, lines can distinguish figures from ground and background. Apart from that, as you have discovered, lines do not have to always connect. Much like the closure principle (where you fill in the gaps mentally), lines that start, stop and start again become *lost and found lines*, also called *lost and found edges*. These usually add style and momentum to a picture, especially with sketch lines.

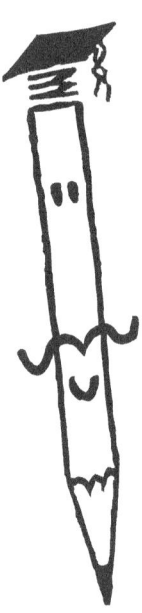

In the next chapter, we will take streamlines, sketch lines, and edges to even greater heights.

Chapter 7

DOES THIS LANDSCAPE SEEM DIFFICULT TO DRAW? IT'S NOT.

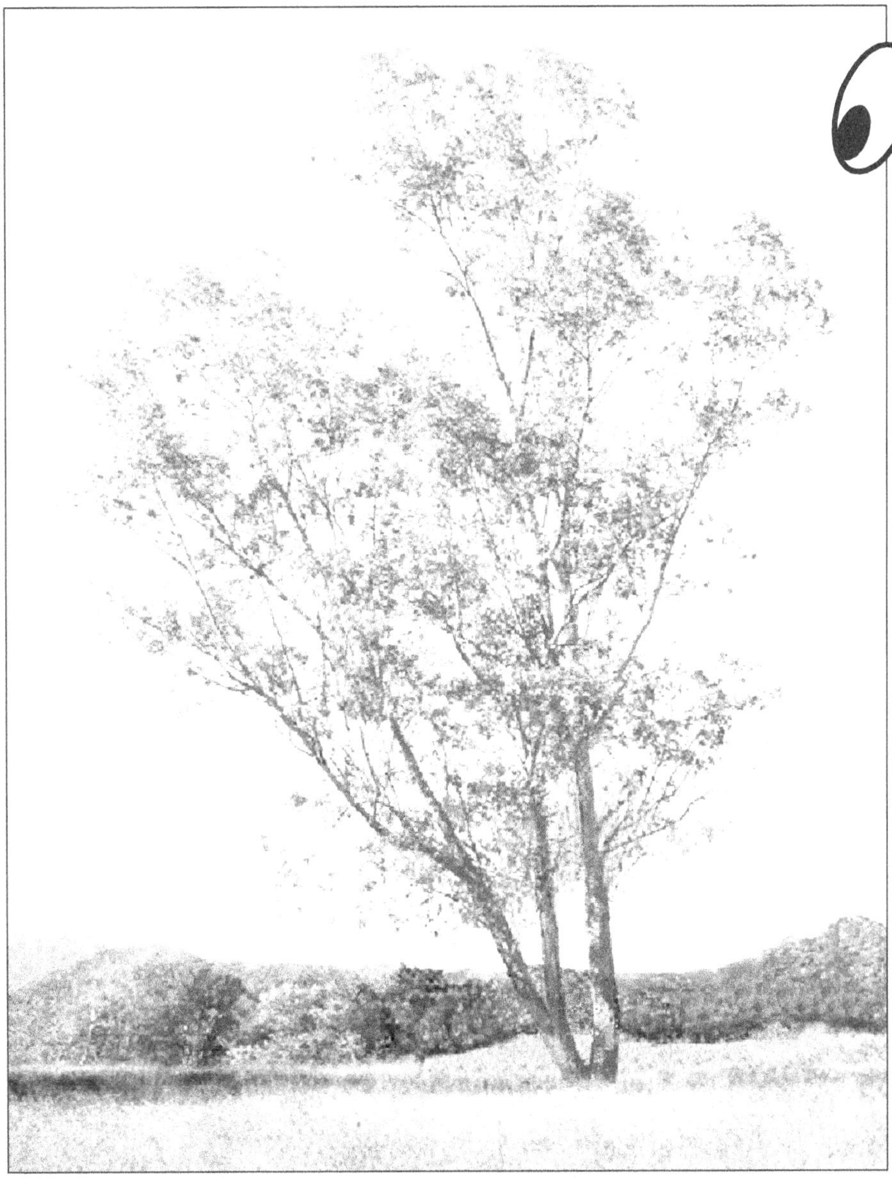

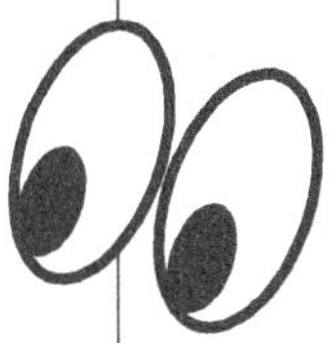

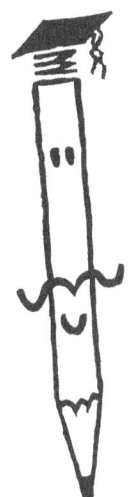

You just need to know what to look for.

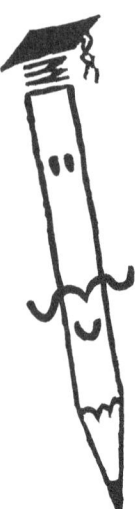

A few rectangles and triangles easily capture the general boundaries of this tranquil scene.

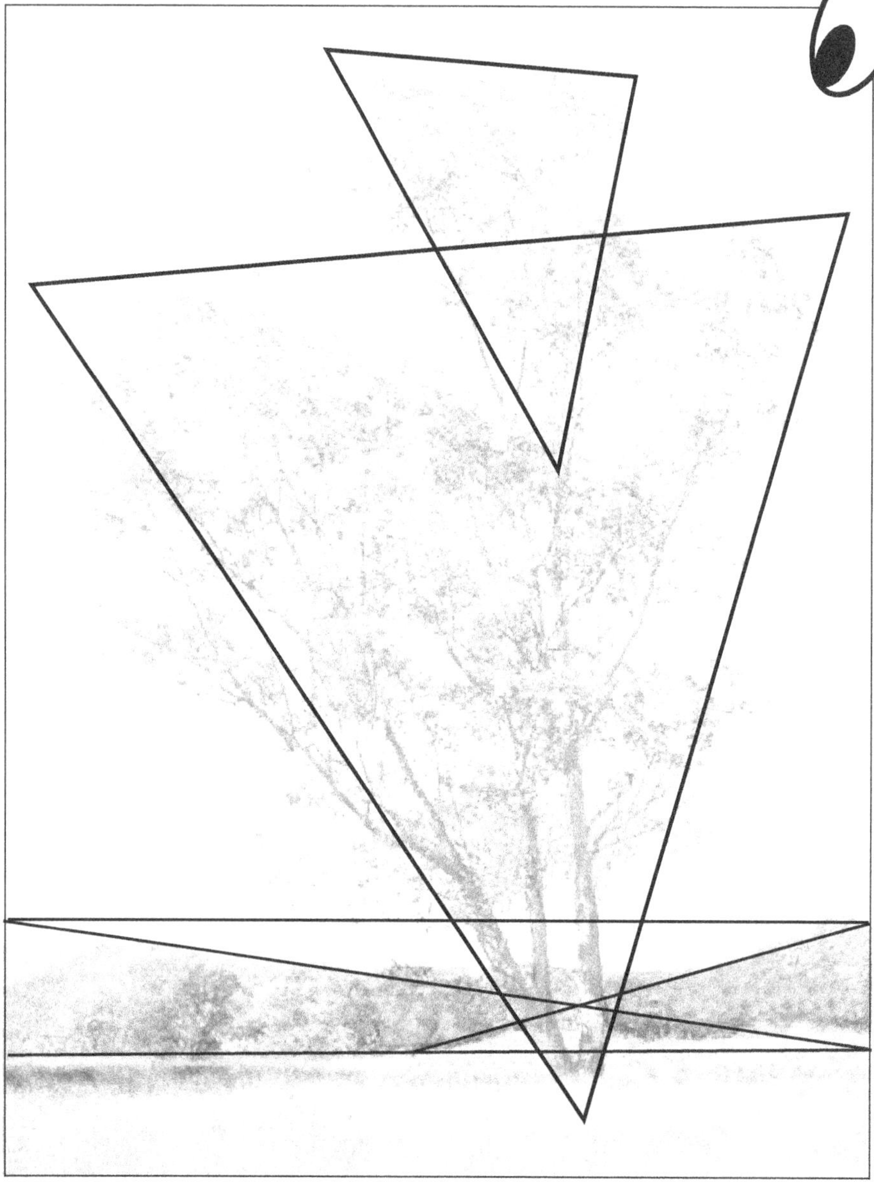

Here's the same scene
in its simplified form.

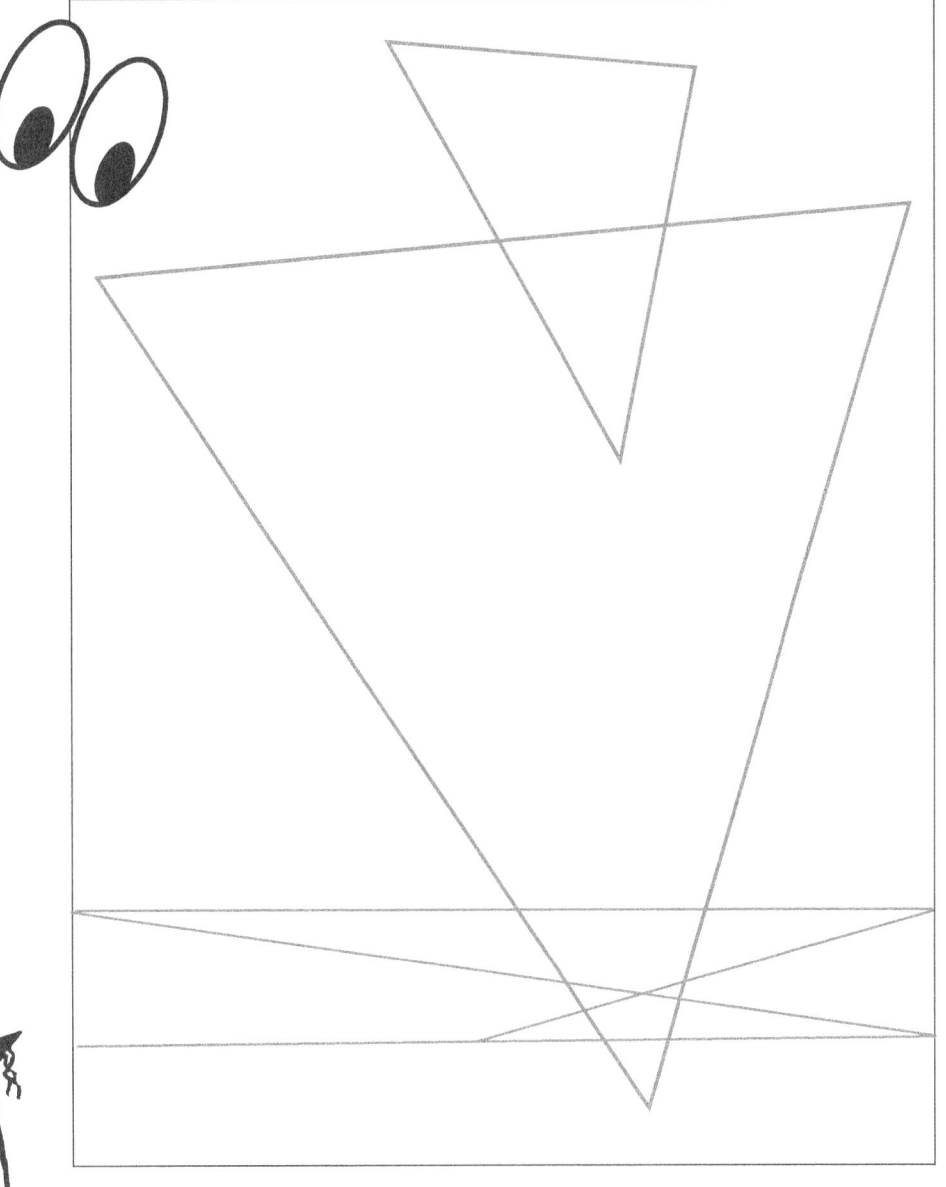

Having visualized the landscape
streamlined, we are ready to draw.

STEP 1 Observe that just two level lines, visualized with *x-ray vision* on the model, easily divide the ground and the background in the picture (7-1).   The sky and hills (both part of the background) are separated by line (a), which lies somewhat less than a quarter of the way between the bottom of the photo and the middle.   The ground division, also called the *horizon line* (b), locates approximately midway from the bottom of the photo to hill line/sky line (a). Lightly draw these proportionally on your paper *(without the use of a ruler or straight edge)*. Next, study illustration (7-2). As you can tell, hill line (c) tilts downward from the left end of the upper horizontal line and ends on the right side of the ground line.   Hill line (d) slopes from the right side of the upper horizontal line and ends just to the right of midway on the ground line. Locate and lightly include these respective angle lines in your drawing.

7-1 Locate and lightly fashion horizontal hill and ground
     line proportionally in your drawing, based on model

7-2 Locate & lightly add angled hill lines
     in your drawing, based on model

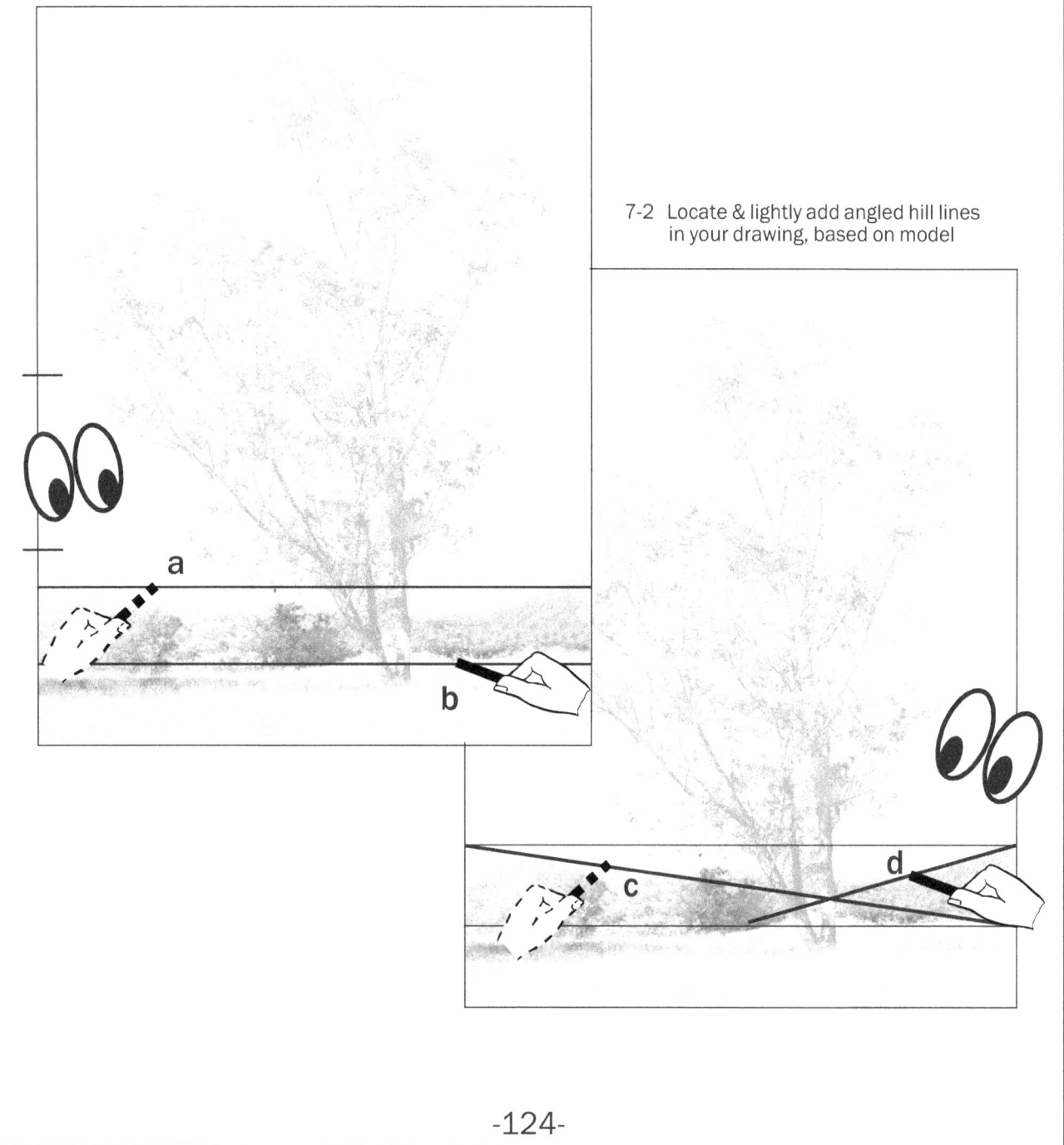

Concentrate on the lines that form the rolling hill and ground area. It's easier if you pretend you can see through the tree trunks. Then, with the help of your guide lines and illustration 7-3 for reference, *lightly* draw similar wavy lines on your drawing. They are indicated as (a), (b) and (c), but you can separate them into more sections. This will enable you to form the curves more easily. Afterward, erase all of your guide lines, except the bottom horizontal line. Drawing example 7-4 shows the outcome.

TIP My wavy lines do not exactly match those in the photo. Your lines do not have to be exact either. The important thing is to create natural looking, uneven shapes.

7-3   Using the model for reference, lightly draw the curves to form the wavy shapes

7-4   Drawing example-current stage

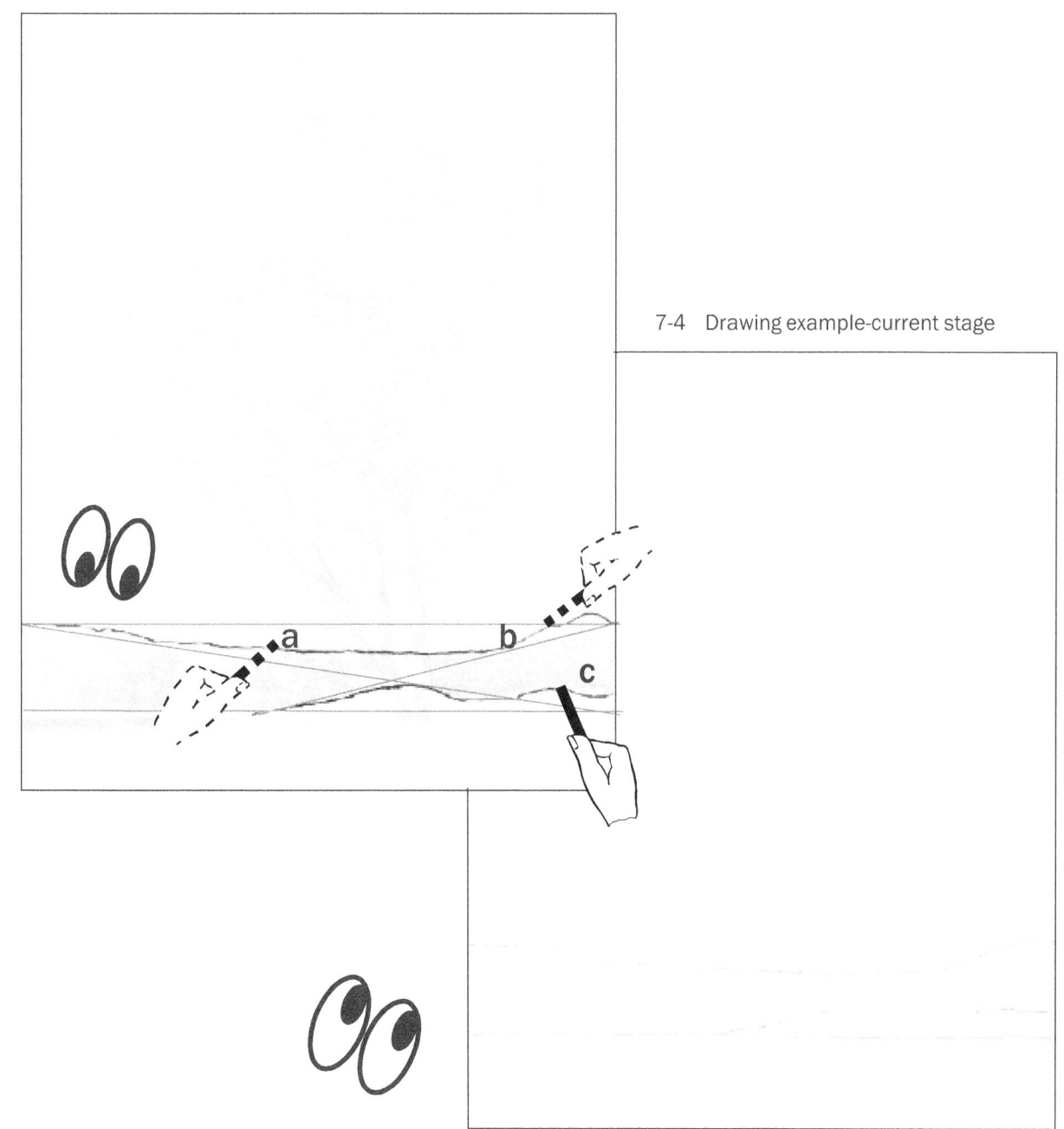

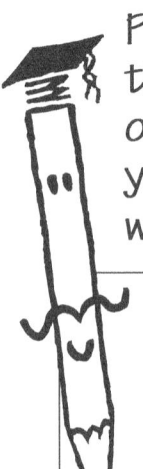

Please set your pencil down to just observe for now. In this chapter we will disregard the tree to concentrate on the ground areas. The framed sections below help you see the different shapes, edges, values and textures within the background, midground and foreground.

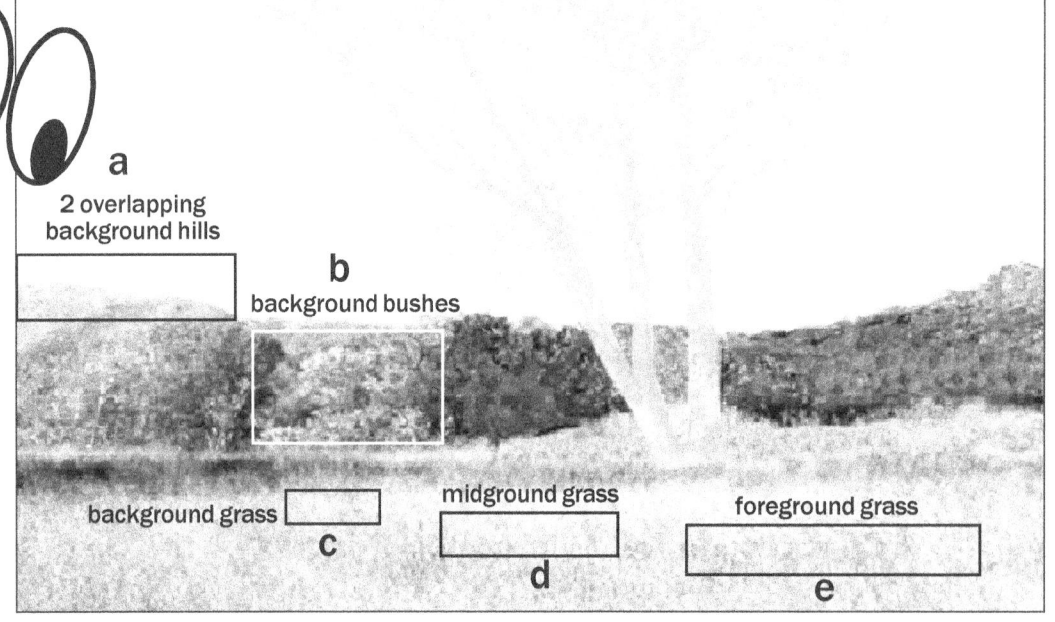

a
2 overlapping
background hills

b
background bushes

background grass
c

midground grass
d

foreground grass
e

TIP Start with the ground areas first, because it's harder to work along the edges of a figure (tree) that's already rendered.

LINEAR and ATMOSPHERIC **PERSPECTIVE** also play a role. They indicate whether things are near or far.

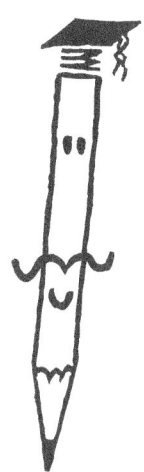

The word PERSPECTIVE may sound complicated, but it is simply a point of view.

LINEAR **PERSPECTIVE** refers to the visual phenomenon (observable event) that things look smaller than they really are when they are far from our point of view. The closer they are, the larger they appear.

ATMOSPHERIC **PERSPECTIVE** gives us the visual impression that things appear slightly blurry and less distinct when they are far from our point of view. The closer they are, the more sharp, clear and detailed they become.

How do linear perspective and atmospheric perspective contribute to a landscape? Study the photo on the *previous page*. Focus on the hills (a). The shapes seem quite small, vague and practically blend into the sky, especially at the edges, right? That's because the hills are far and there is air (haze, or atmosphere) between us and the hills. Notice that one hill (the lighter value) is behind, *overlapped* by another that is darker. Yet, both hills are dwarfed by the bushes (b) which are also in the background. Being closer, their overall size is proportionally larger by comparison to the hills, plus the *textures* and *edges* in the bushes are more distinct (visible). Next, observe the distant grass section (c). It appears to be very fuzzy. Linear and atmospheric perspective are at work there, too. So much so, you could be in for a shock if you expect the textures of grass up close to appear like the textures of grass far away.

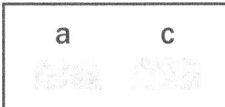

To illustrate, I cut a piece of light gray texture from the photo of the hills (a). Then I did the same from a portion of grass (c). Had I not marked them here on the left, could you tell which texture belonged to the hill and which belonged to the grass? Usually, it's the various textures, edges and forms with respect to other such features in their proximity (location) that reveal what we are seeing, and whether we are viewing from near or far. As we scan to the midground (d), then to the foreground (e), we also observe increasing size, tone intensity and clarity. Although we are not yet near enough to see individual blades of grass, we experience the impression of space and depth. Illustration (7-5) demonstrates the concept with gradually smaller vertical lines, diminishing value intensities and overlapping forms. For the full effect, stand back and take a look at the examples from a couple of paces. Assimilation (visual mixing) will be especially apparent.

7-5 Decreasing size A, decreasing tone intensity B and overlapping C help create the illusion of depth

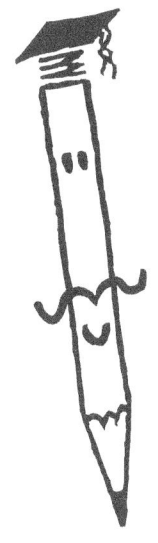

A

B

C

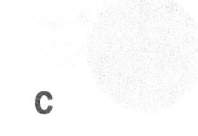

With linear and atmospheric perspective in mind, we are ready to explore several exciting texture and edge techniques.

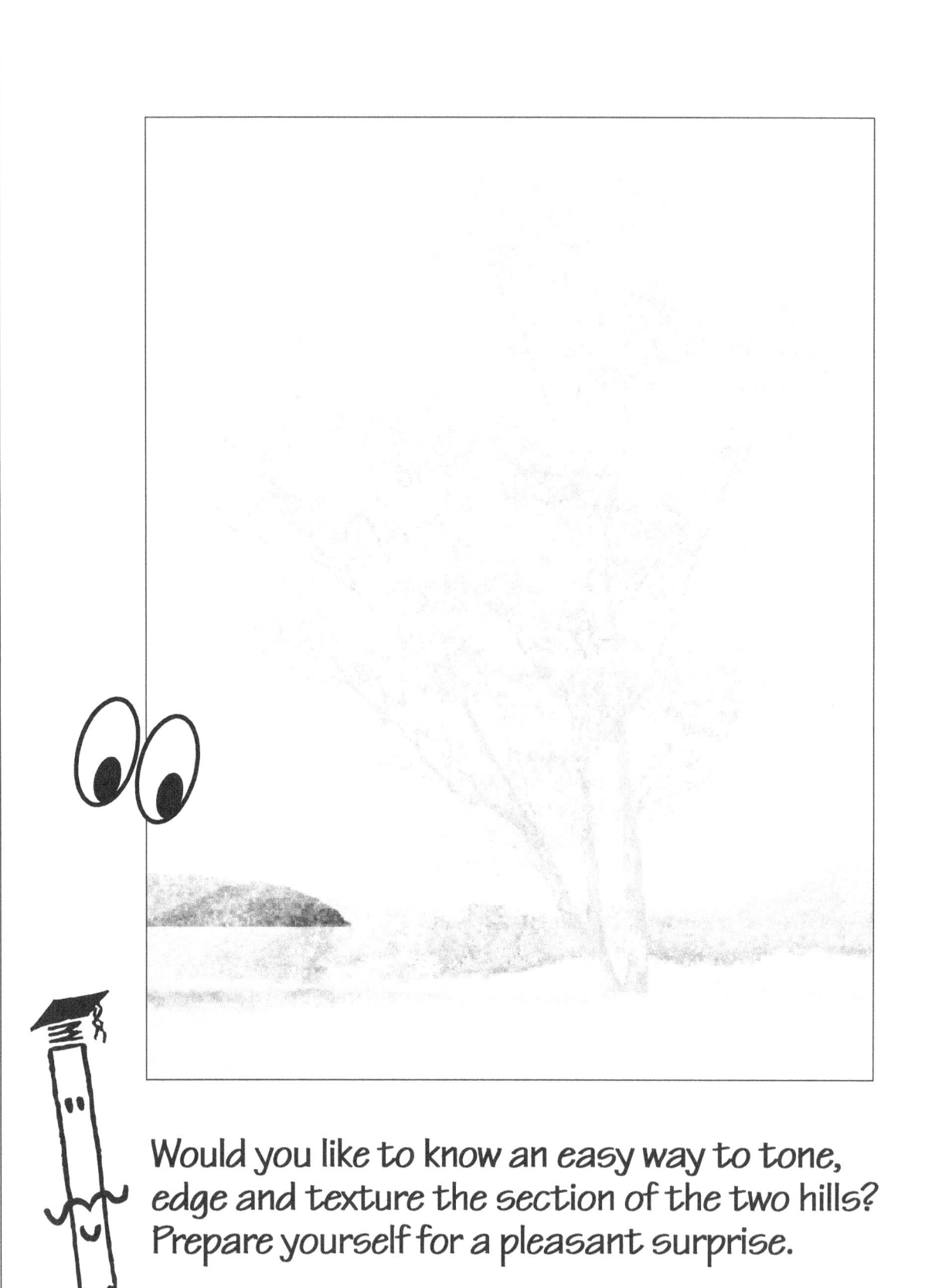

Would you like to know an easy way to tone, edge and texture the section of the two hills? Prepare yourself for a pleasant surprise.

BLOTCHES CAN BE USEFUL

You may recall in Chapters 2 and 4, you encountered *blotches*. These are spots of uneven light and dark values, brought on by inconsistent pressure during toning. On the still life subjects you drew, spotting seemed out of place. In this chapter, you will see that they are actually helpful, especially when combined with the principles of atmospheric and linear perspective. Take a look at the two hills on the previous page again. One is larger, darker, more distinct and overlaps the other. Such clues indicate which figure is in front and closer. In order to imitate the appearance, I began with the very soft tone for the far away hill, but formed the shape of both hills (A). The task was simple because the paper also has a slightly rough surface (or tooth as it is called). By only skimming the top, using the side of my pencil lead and vertical strokes, a light texture with vague edges was easy to achieve.

For the closer hill in front (B), I added another layer into the first tone with the same method, but increased the pressure. Next, as shown in example (C), I darkened the right end (shade side) of the front hill to further the illusion that it has a third dimension (depth). I then feathered in another layer of tone along the border separating the two forms. The higher contrast intensified the impression of distance between the two figures and caused the push-pull effect. You already learned about this in Chapter 2 (page 33). To demonstrate the concept here, I toned two pairs of spheres (D & E) below. Although identical in proportion, set (D) seems to have more space between the spheres, while in set (E), the orbs (another word for spheres) seem to be closer together. Why? Set (E) has *low contrast*, especially at the boundary between the two forms. As you can see, a little contrast or a lot makes a big difference.

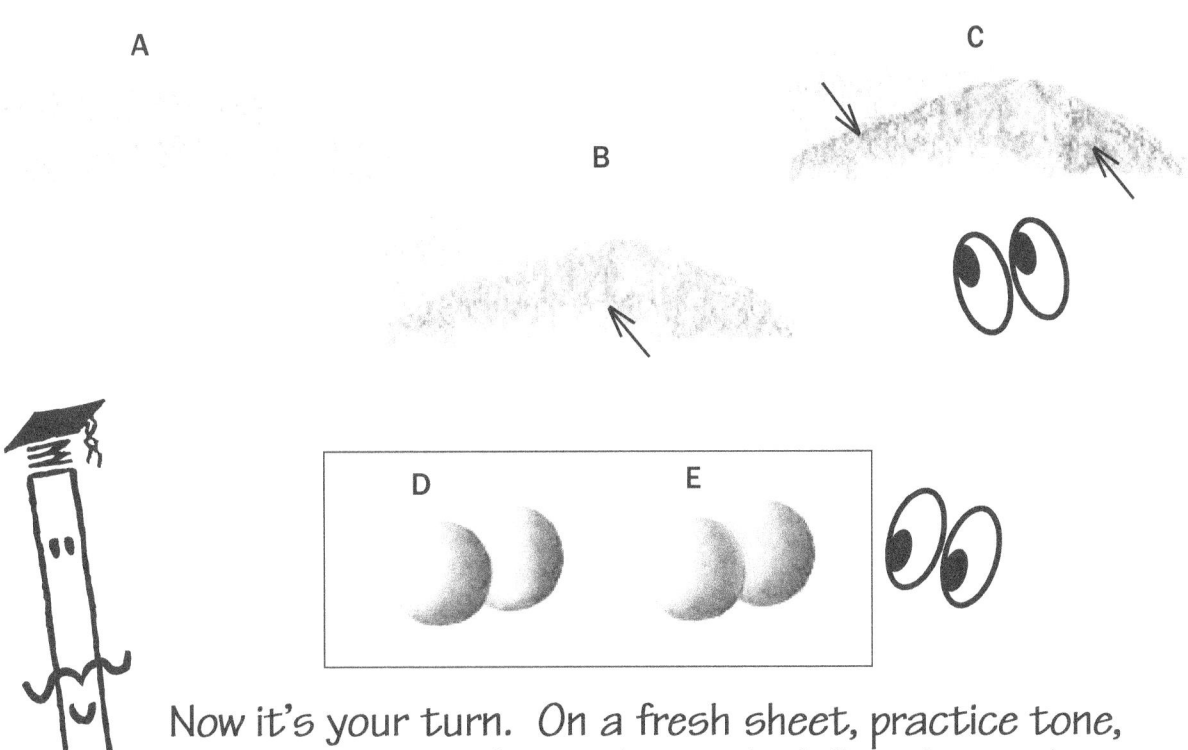

Now it's your turn. On a fresh sheet, practice tone, edge and texture by rendering the hill peaks similar to the way I did until you've got the hang of it.

TIP Your version should not be an exact duplicate of mine. Yours should have *your* marks, textures and unique characteristics.

How would you produce textures and edges to create the impression there are clusters of bushes in the distance?

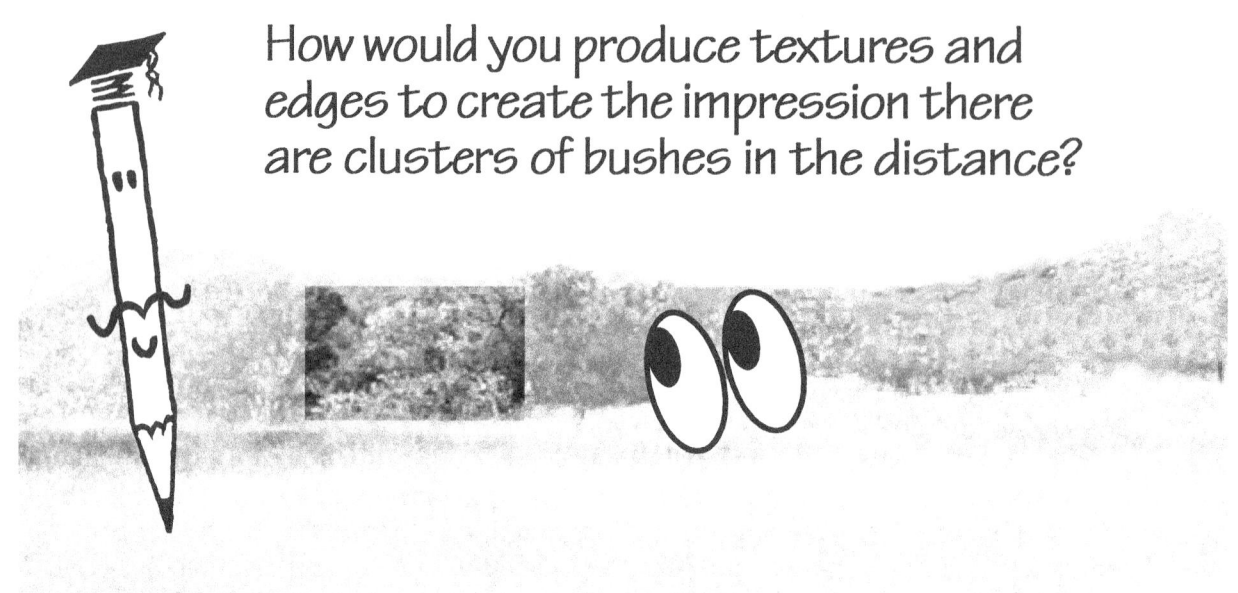

I replicated the likeness of bushes in several stages. The next page shows how I did it. Initially, I laid down a very light gray tone, using soft upward and downward strokes (A). In phase (B), I began forming the darker shade area bordering the upper and lower row of bushes. Glancing back and forth between the model and my work, I *lightly* drew the shape with small dashes, because continuous lines would get in the way of the stroke quality and the irregular saw-tooth edges I sought. In phase (C), I applied long and short upward and downward strokes. By increasing the pressure inconsistently, this enable me not only to fill the area with uneven tones, but also create the rough, natural appearance. Next, I produced the same type of effect for the left side and top portion by repeating the procedure (D.) I continued with the method for the bottom and right side as well (E). The lighter shapes appeared *indirectly*, much the way negative space forms positive space. While doing all this, I made certain *not* to go dark quickly. After all, effective toning and texturing is performed *gradually*. Had I made my values too strong at the outset, it would have been more challenging to develop the overlapping effects and other nuances later.

To produce the subtle (barely visible) variations in the next phases, I gently began including small zigzag strokes (F & G). Moving from one part to another, scribbling on purpose, I also included a stipple (dot) technique. Combined, this allowed me not only to create the bristle-like textures and edges, but also to control the contrasts that were being affected due to the ongoing *assimilation* process. In other words, as marks were being added, the scene kept changing. All along, I made sure my additions improved the overall developing effect by frequently comparing my work to the model. That way, I didn't get carried away or lose sight of my goal to create an *interpretation* of the bushes, not an exact copy (H).

Even though I only showed you eight stages, many layers were actually applied, especially in the latter phases. I'd like to also point out that none of the phases were difficult. *They all just needed a little more time, a little more effort, and a little more patience. The end result was well worth it. Quality shouldn't be rushed.*

TIP For a review on the effects of assimilation, please refer to page 127.

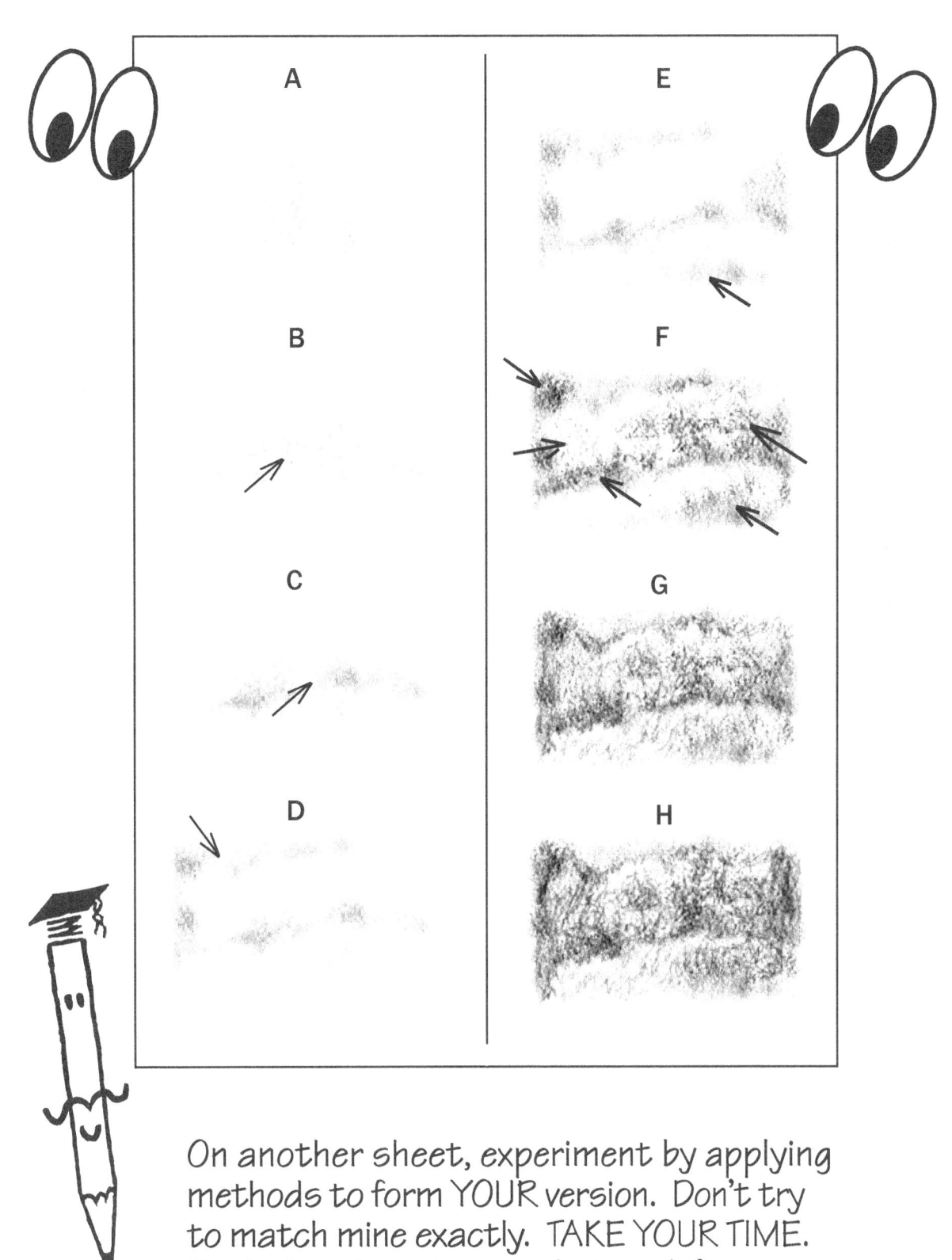

On another sheet, experiment by applying methods to form YOUR version. Don't try to match mine exactly. TAKE YOUR TIME. Be daring. Invent ways that work for you.

TIP Be sure to refer to the photo along with my examples. Avoid using your eraser as much as possible. If an area gets dark too fast, *do not start over*. Dab lightly with your eraser and continue. Also please remember, in this case the bushes are supposed to appear as though they are far away. Overworking can spoil the impression.

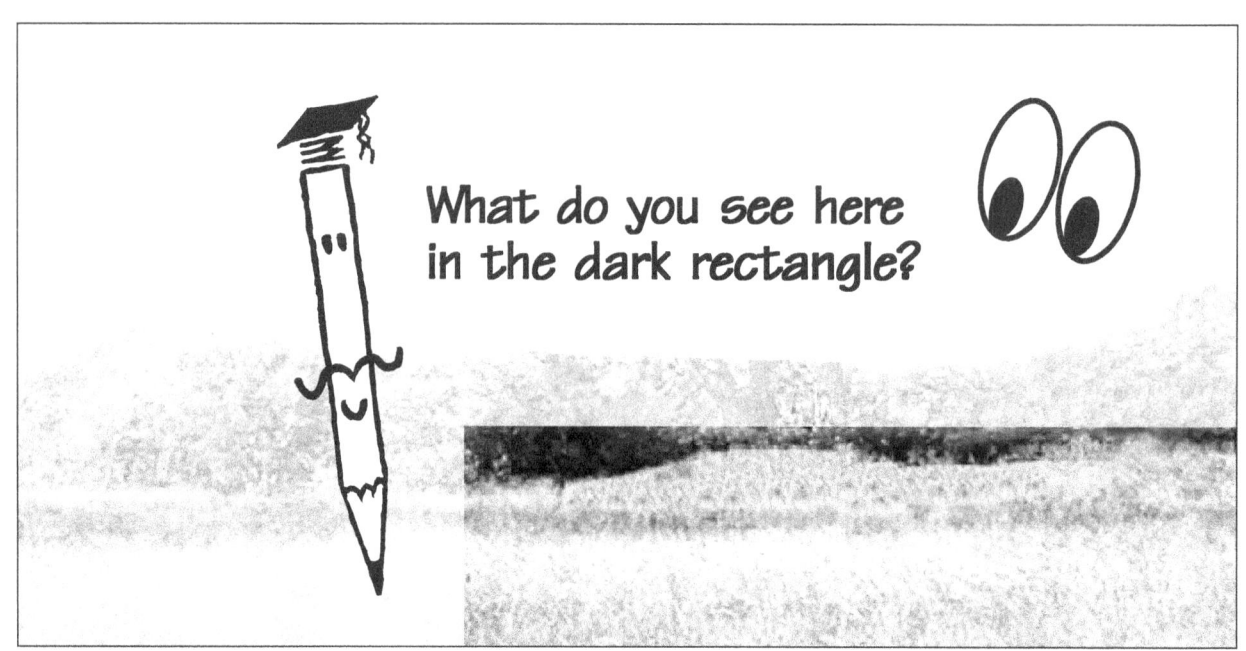

What do you see here in the dark rectangle?

Would you say it's just part of the landscape? Well yes, that's right, but there is more. Essentially, you are also observing *shapes, tones, textures, edges, contrasts and values*. Together they tell you a grassy knoll (mound) lies in the distance, along with more grass in the midground and foreground. The next page illustrates how I achieved the likeness.

In phase (A), I applied a soft tone using upward and downward strokes. I didn't stop until a long, very light gray rectangular value appeared (in basic proportion to the photo). While glancing back and forth between my drawing and the photograph, I used the same kind of strokes to fashion the darker shape along the upper portion (B). This required varying the lengths and increasing the pressure intermittently (starting and stopping often). The contrasting value simultaneously formed the mounds below. Initially, I could have marked the divisions with dashes (the way I did for the bushes). However, in this case, I felt I could produce the natural appearance without first mapping out the shape.

> **TIP** Choosing to use dashes to layout the shapes doesn't mean you are less skilled. Exercise your options according to each situation.

For phase (C), I switched to many short, vertical up and down strokes at slight angles to establish uneven striped textures. Mostly, this was done quickly, as I made my way across from one end to the other, simulating the kind of spiked marks a seismograph makes while recording the rumblings of the earth. Moving a little lower, I did the same thing in phase (D). However, I *reduced* the pressure and eventually formed one long convex arc that extended from the left side to the *middle*. From there, I made similar strokes in the shape of a concave arc that reached the right side. Dropping down one more interval, I applied yet another layer (E). On this trip, I *increased* the pressure and the height of my strokes. Then I went back and put in some dotted textures in the mound. I also increased the value along the top edge for higher contrast (F). This heightened the impression of depth behind the mound and helped make it stand out. Compare the mound *before* (E) to the mound *after* (F). You can really see a difference.

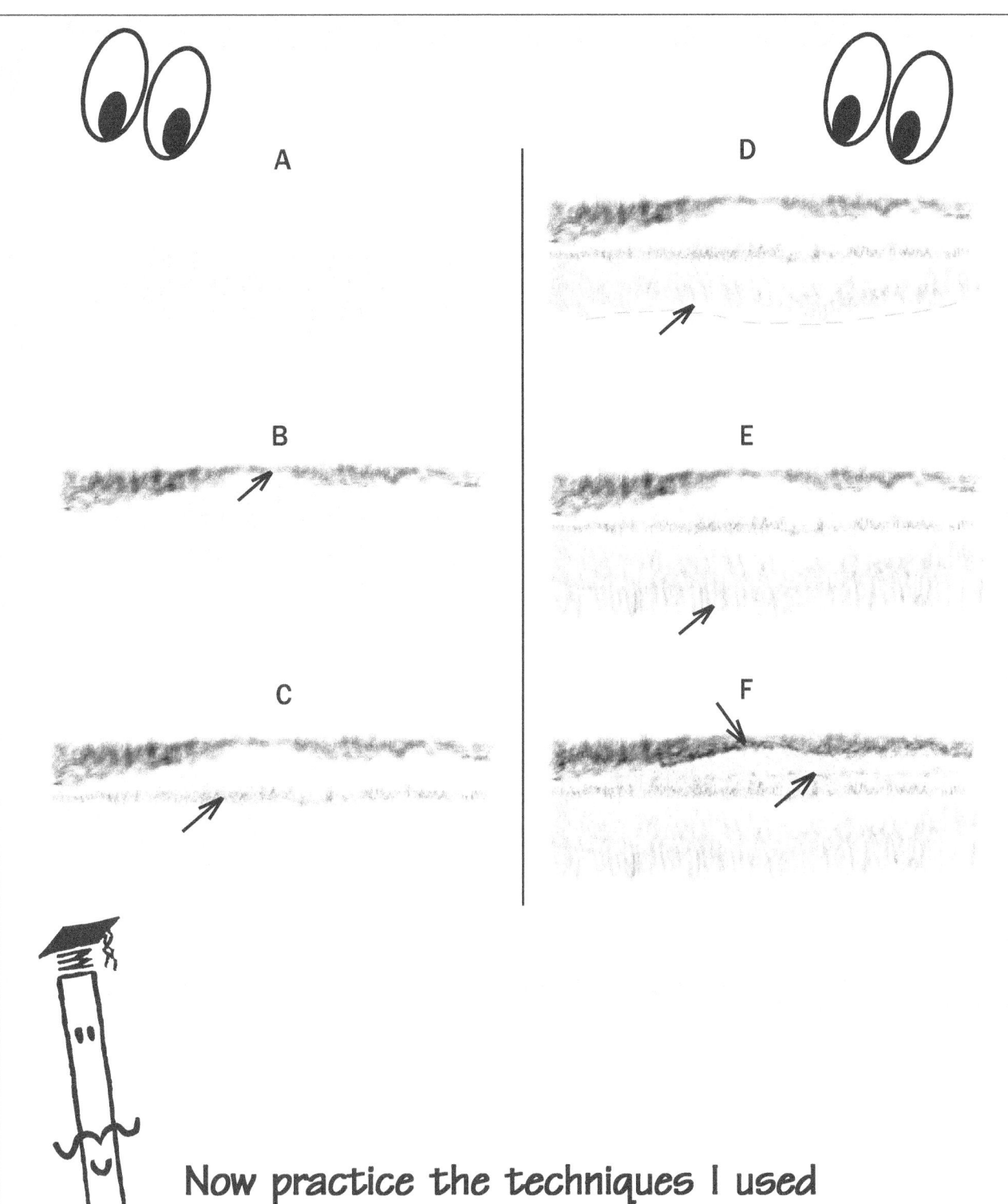

A

B

C

D

E

F

Now practice the techniques I used to get the desired effects. Also, ad-lib with variations of your own. The knowledge and experience will come in handy.

Having practiced some texture techniques you are ready to resume your drawing.

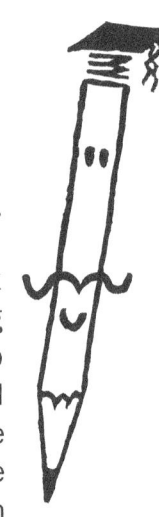

STEP 1 Visualize the ground shapes in outline format (7-6). Next, see them in your mind as values resembling puzzle pieces (7-7). By toning the forms in similar fashion (during the initial stages), this will enable you to establish secondary divisions. The method also creates a foundation (or *base*) you can work into, the way you practiced. However, on this occasion, being that you will be toning a much larger field, if you prefer you can stroke laterally (sideways) instead of up and down (7-8). Pick one direction or the other. Mixing them will cause an unwanted checkered appearance. Proceed from the left, at the furthest hill and advance across to the other end of your paper. Press very gently and consistently using the side of your pencil to fill the upper section. Then move to the lower portion representing the grass. When completed, the entire ground area should be covered with a fairly even spread of soft tone (7-9.

7-6 Visualize the ground area in outline format

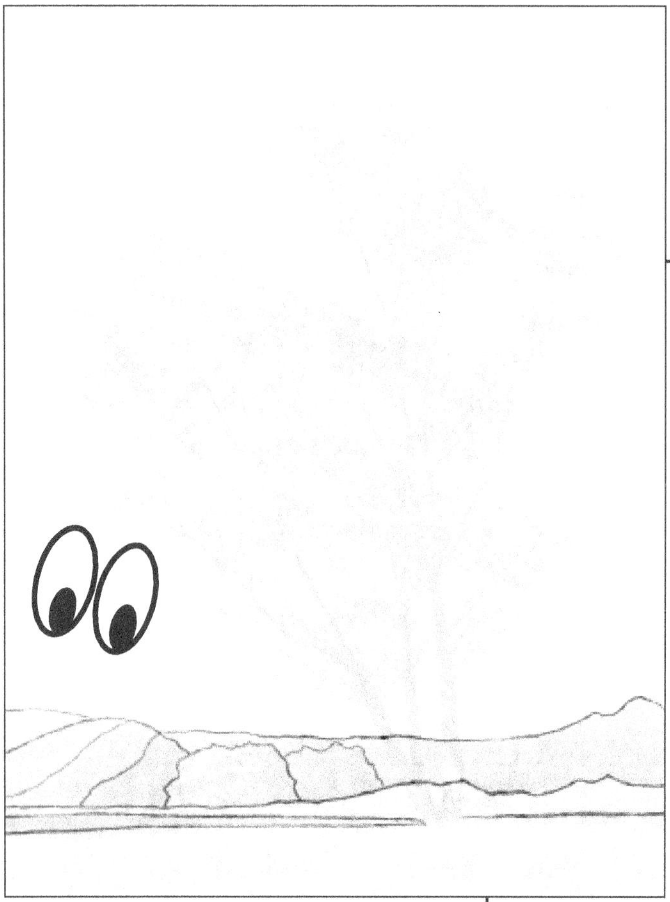

7-7 Pretend the sections are solid puzzle pieces made of tone values

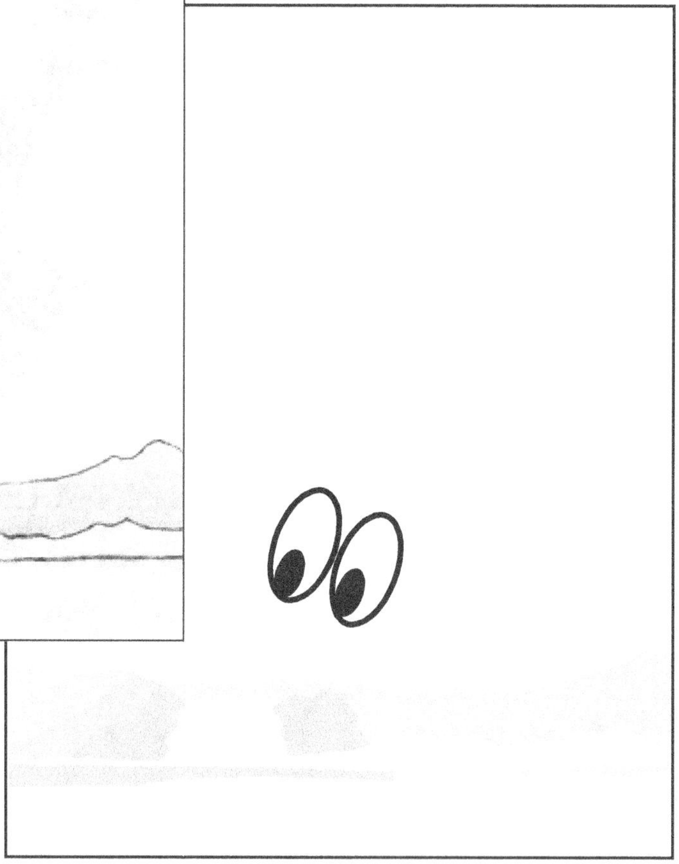

7-8 *Lightly* fill the upper part of your background areas with tone using gentle, consistent strokes

7-9 *Lightly* fill the lower part of your ground areas with gentle, consistent strokes

Toning and texturing is meant to be done in gradually developing layers.

Study the secondary divisions in the ground areas on the model. The main ones include the boundary between the two hills, the borders between the clumps of bushes, as well as the darker bushes to the right, and the long shadow in the grass. These are indicated with dash lines (7-10). Apply them likewise on your drawing, *LIGHTLY* (7-11).

7-10 Visualize the secondary divisions bordered with dash lines

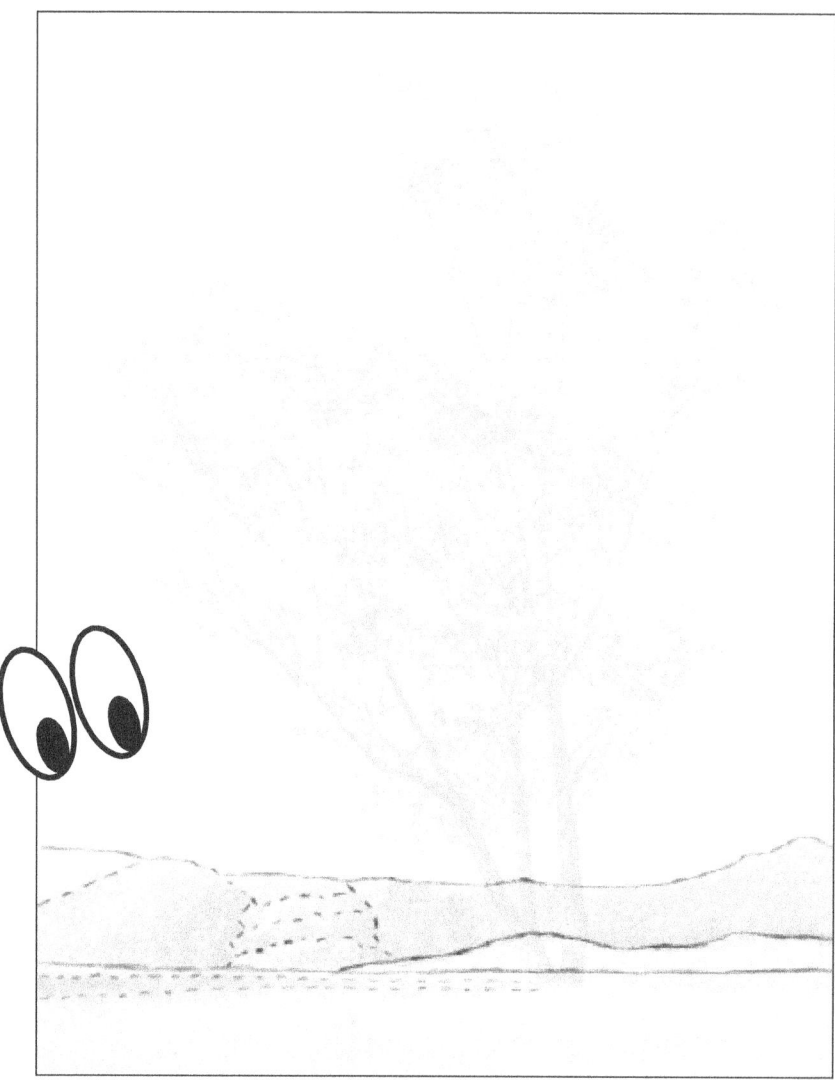

TIP Dash lines convert to ragged edges and textures more easily.

7-11 *Lightly* apply divisions with dash lines on your drawing
(even lighter than shown)

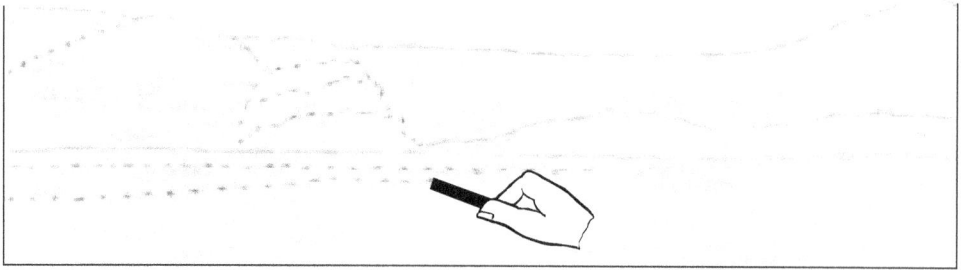

STEP 3 Observing model 7-12, we see that the lightest value is labeled (A). This is the value you currently have in the ground area of your picture. The next darker value is in the hill section designated (B). To the right, a slightly darker tone is indicated (C). Still further to the right, an even darker tone (D) exists (just to the left of the bushes). On the opposite side, a similar dark value covers a large section, and also lies in the grass on the left. These darkest segments are all marked (D). Since sections (B) and (C) are darker than (A), tone those respective parts with a slightly darker value than the intensity you used to cover your entire field (7-13). By doing so, you prepare your surface for the next phase - *textures*. Make the (D) value textures with (C) *value* to enable the darkest parts to be added later. As you work, be sure to use the model for reference. Apply uneven, random zigzag strokes for the patchy background, then switch to vertical motions when you get to the grass (7-14).

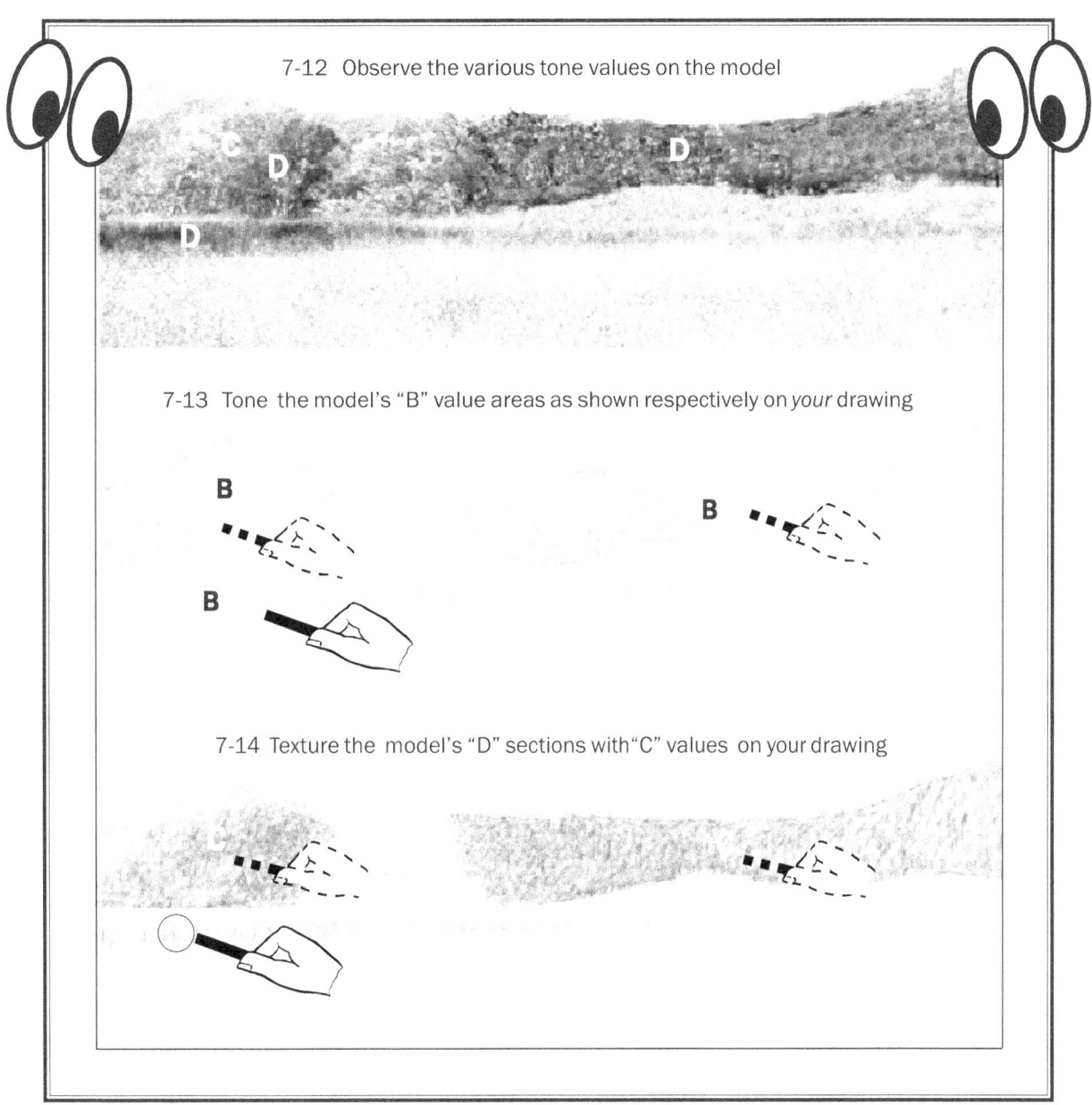

7-12 Observe the various tone values on the model

7-13 Tone the model's "B" value areas as shown respectively on *your* drawing

7-14 Texture the model's "D" sections with "C" values on your drawing

TIP The darkest tones should not be applied yet. They should be reserved for last It's easier to assess and balance contrasts after all the sections are semi-rendered.

STEP 4 Time for more details. The suggested sequence is numbered from the background forward Why? Because, as you are aware, things that are far away are usually more vague and are overlapped by things in front of them. Based on this, it's easier to draw something behind, then superimpose (overlap) another item over it. You already applied the principle in the previous step when you toned the lightest value for the furthest hill, then overlapped with a darker texture to suggest another hill in front of it. Next, while referring to the model (7-15), texture the bushes so they appear a little more forward as shown in illustration 7-16. Then proceed to the grassy mound (2) per illustration 7-17.

TIP If you did not practice texturing during pages 129 to 133, please do so now.

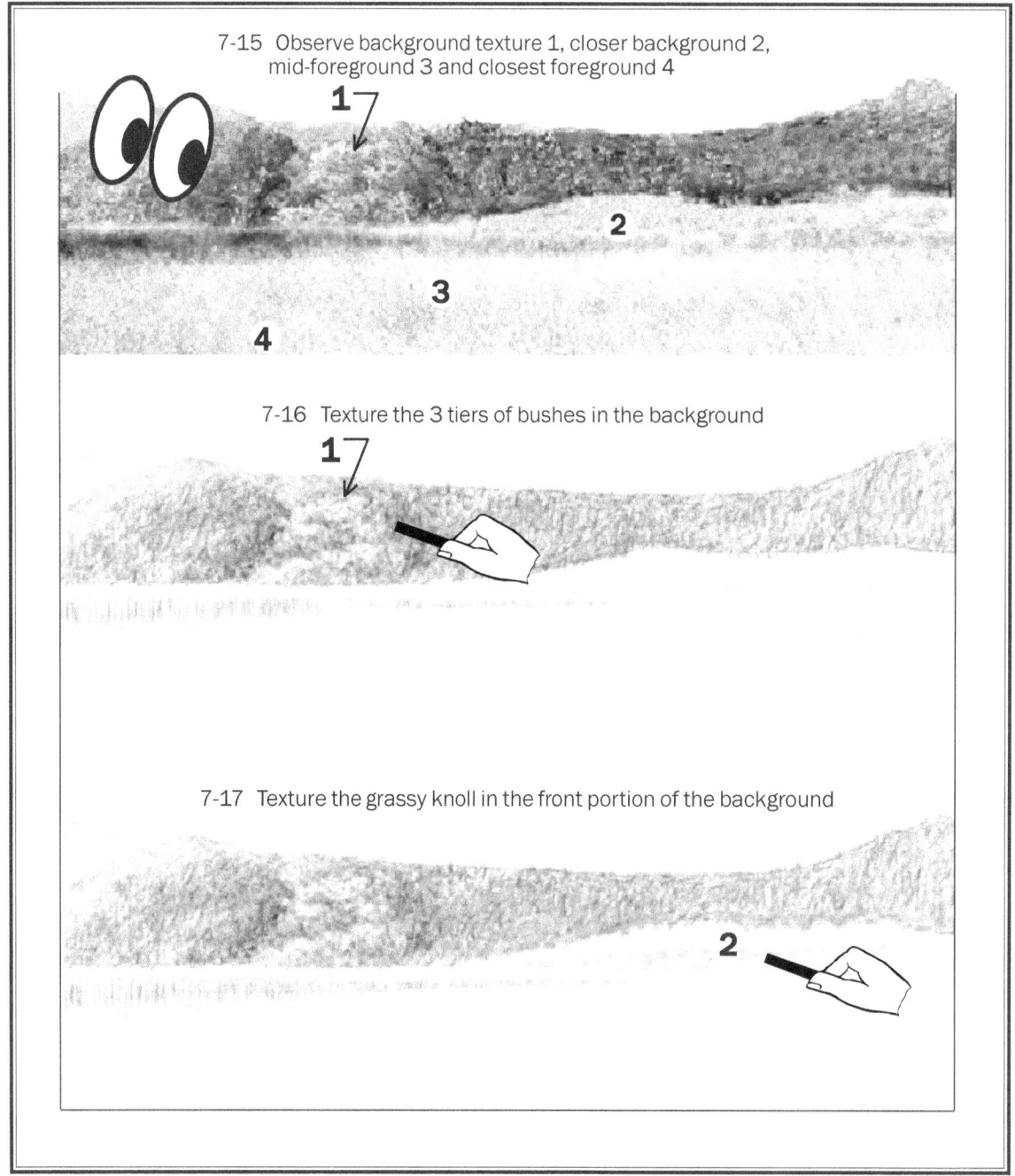

7-15   Observe background texture 1, closer background 2, mid-foreground 3 and closest foreground 4

7-16   Texture the 3 tiers of bushes in the background

7-17   Texture the grassy knoll in the front portion of the background

STEP 5 While referring to model 7-15 *(previous page)*, texture the grass. Apply gentle vertical strokes as you proceed laterally (sideways) from one side of your paper to the opposite end, along the mid-section. This area is designated (3) in illustration 7-18. With increasing pressure and higher vertical strokes (suggesting linear and atmospheric perspective), repeat the process by stacking two or three taller and taller rows, one under the other. Darken little by little as you make your way down, to simulate the foreground grass (4) per illustration 7-19. Eventually your marks should reach the bottom.

TIP Vary your strokes a little by tilting and wiggling them occasionally to bring about a more natural effect. After your grass strokes are finished, use your putty eraser to blot areas that appear too dark or patchy.

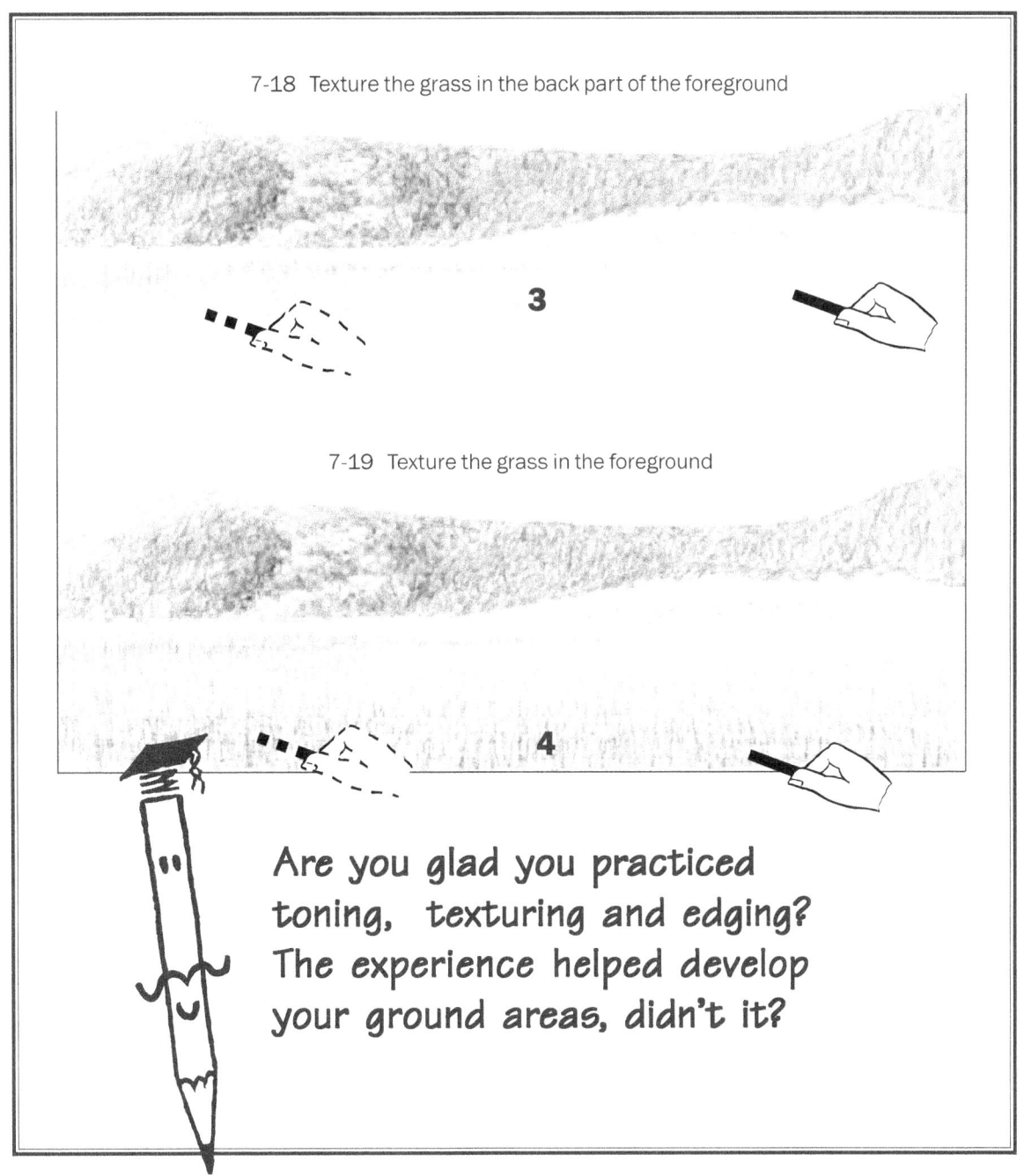

7-18 Texture the grass in the back part of the foreground

3

7-19 Texture the grass in the foreground

4

Are you glad you practiced toning, texturing and edging? The experience helped develop your ground areas, didn't it?

Chapter 7
FOLLOW-UP

In view of all you have experienced thus far, I'm sure you agree that a landscape is also made of shapes, values, textures, contrasts and edges. Speaking of *edges*, during previous chapters, you learned about *soft* and *hard* edges, as well as *lost and found* edges. In this chapter you discovered there are *spiked, wavy* and *serrated (saw-tooth) edges*, just to name a few more. And guess what? There are many others types, serving a variety of functions.

Fundamentally, edges help distinguish one shape from another. Coupled with stroke techniques (which can produce textures) even more possibilities emerge. For instance, when you include the principles of atmospheric perspective and linear perspective (a cousin to planes) you can create a convincing impression of greater distances and depth. Of course, such marvelous visual effects are achieved gradually in layers and developing stages. This means all parts of the picture should be in place before the darkest values are applied. Case in point, let's attend to the tree in the next chapter.

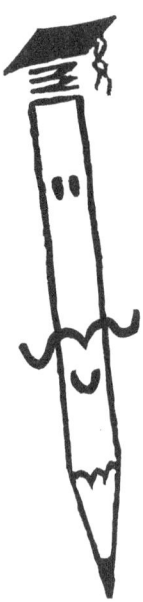

You are making excellent progress.
Take a break, then continue.

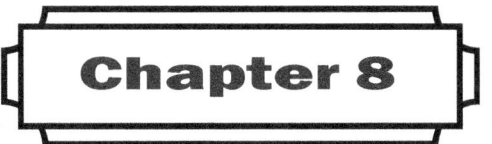

THE NEXT PHASE

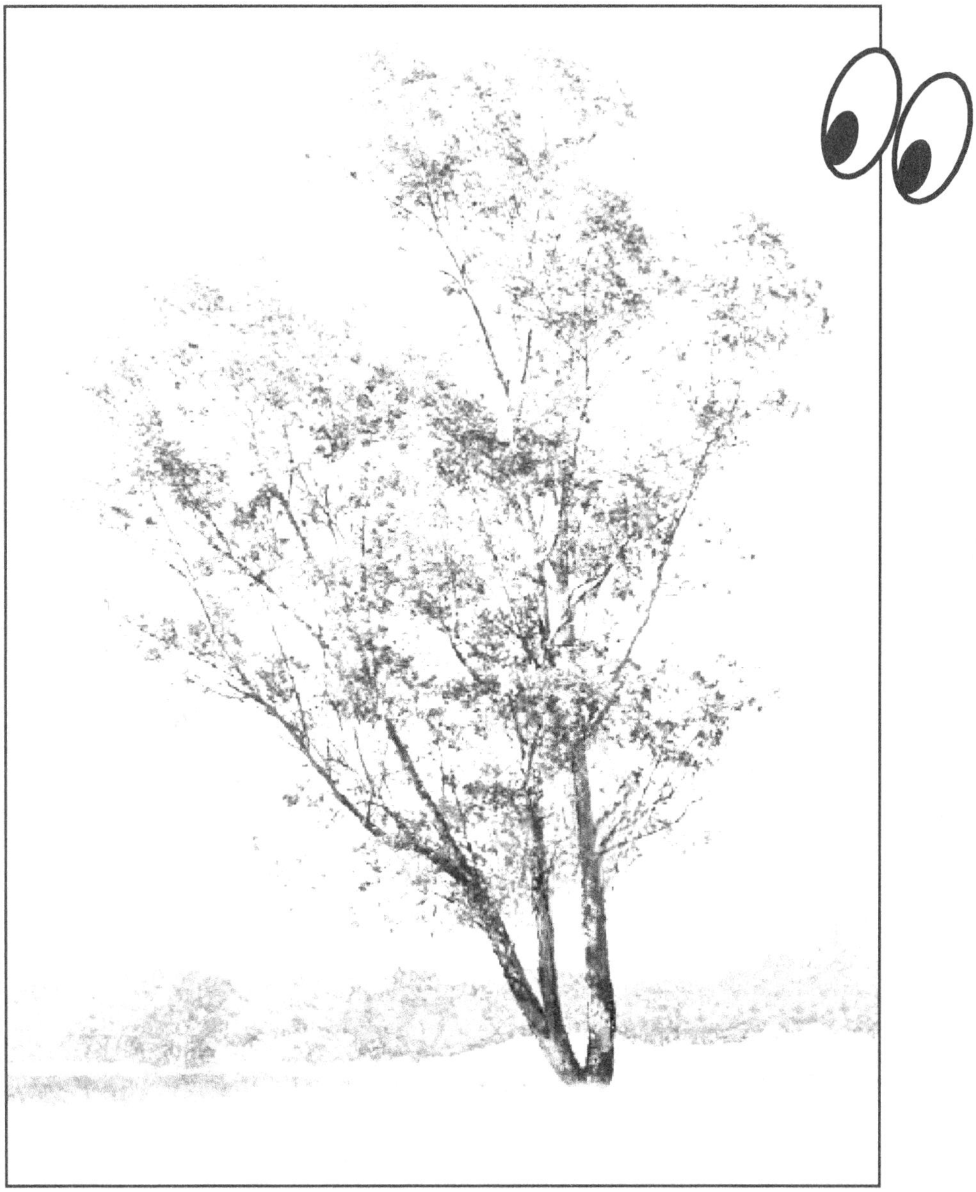

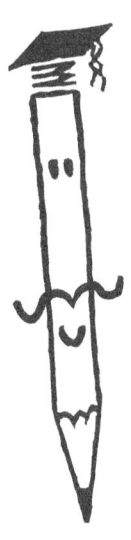

The tree is also easy to draw
when organized into stages.

STAGE 1 - THE TRUNK & BRANCHES

As you know, trees grow from the ground up. The trunk starts out thick, then bends, twists and narrows to become branches, followed by twigs, to which leaves attach. These various traits combine to display the unique character, personality and form of trees. And since trees also have shape, they too can be streamlined. The following example shows that our particular tree has trunks that form a triangle. This can serve as an ideal foundation, made with two main lines which converge (come together at a point).

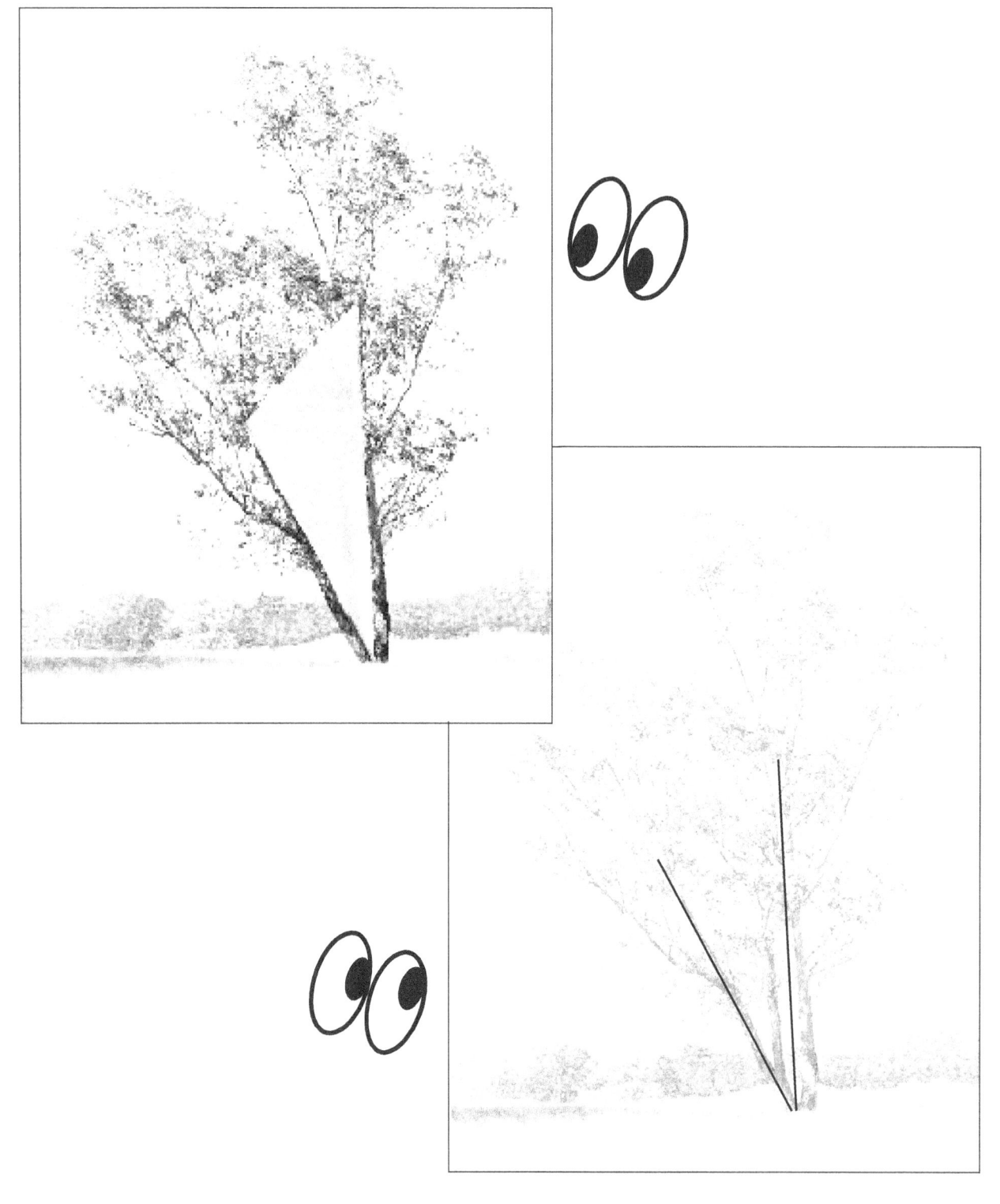

STEP 1 The triangular shape we discovered in the tree formation can be located with 3 reference points. Find those positions and *lightly* mark them on your drawing with dots (8-1). Then, while glancing at the photo on the previous page, use slightly curved and jerky lines to simulate the respective inside edges of the tree trunk (8-2). In this case, the photo and a typical eight-and-a-half by eleven inch sheet of paper are identical in proportion. That means, if your paper is the same standard size, the *sides* of your paper and the *sides* of the photo can be used as references. For instance, observe that the *lower* point lies conveniently on the shadow line, about one third of the distance between the right side of the photo and the left side. The *upper* point is vertically aligned a little bit above midway at a slight angle to the left of the lower point. The *third* point is somewhat below and just to the left of center.

TIP When your paper and the photo do *NOT match* in scale (or if you were on a real site), the method using the sides of your paper and the side of the photo to locate reference points does not apply.

8-1 *Lightly* mark dots to locate position of tree trunk

8-2 *Lightly* connect dots with lines resembling the V-shape proportion of the tree trunk

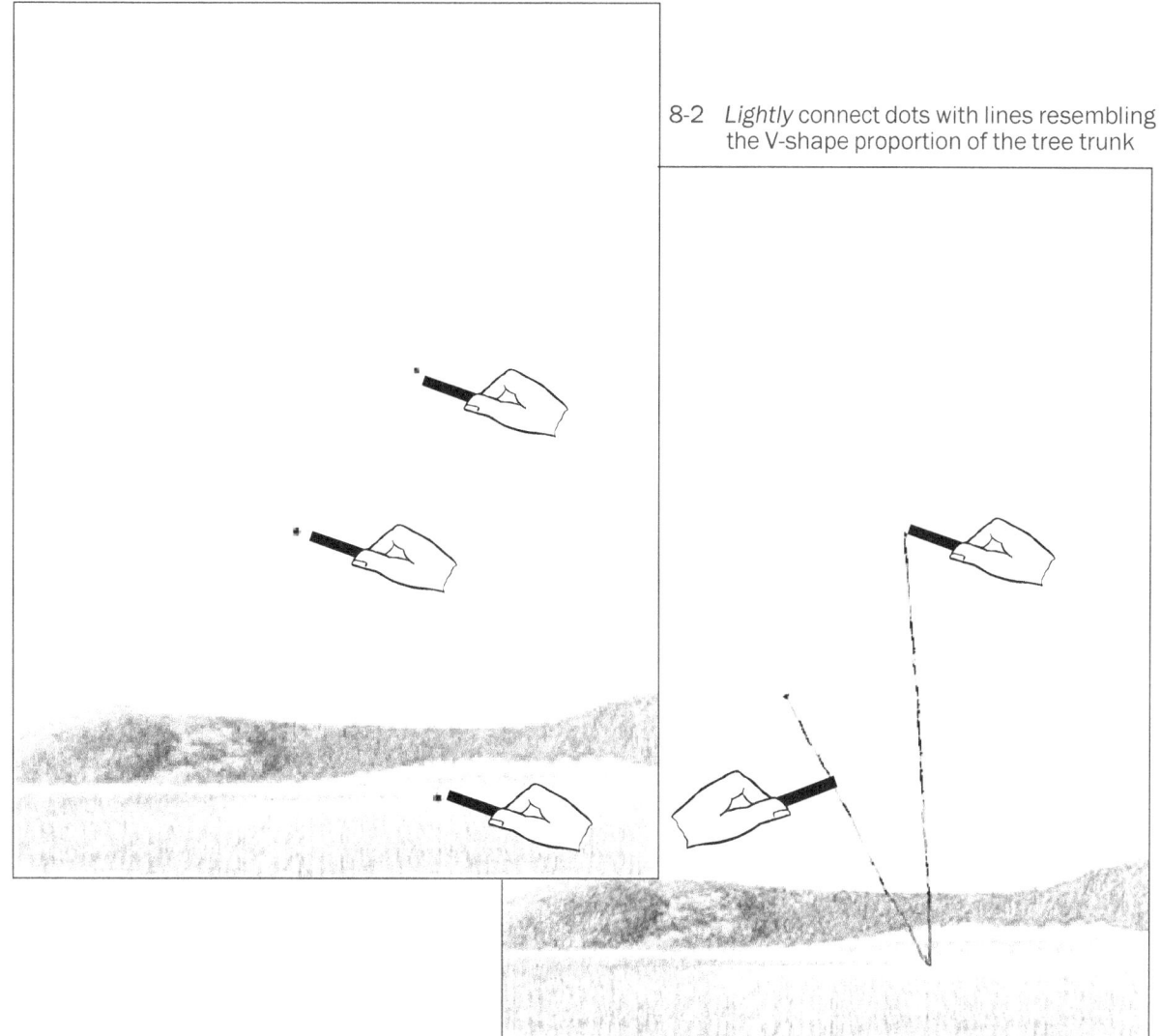

STEP 2 As shown in illustration 8-3, there is another section that grows between the V-shape, and there are more lines that are needed to form the trunk. Using the example for reference, *lightly* fashion the remaining four lines that establish the base of the tree (8-4). You do not have to match it exactly. Just make certain the figures you create are in relative proportion. Plus, be sure they have slightly irregular, natural looking forms that gradually taper (narrow) upward. My example is dark in order for you to see more easily, but your version should be much lighter.

8-3 Observe that there is an extra limb
within the V-shaped tree trunk

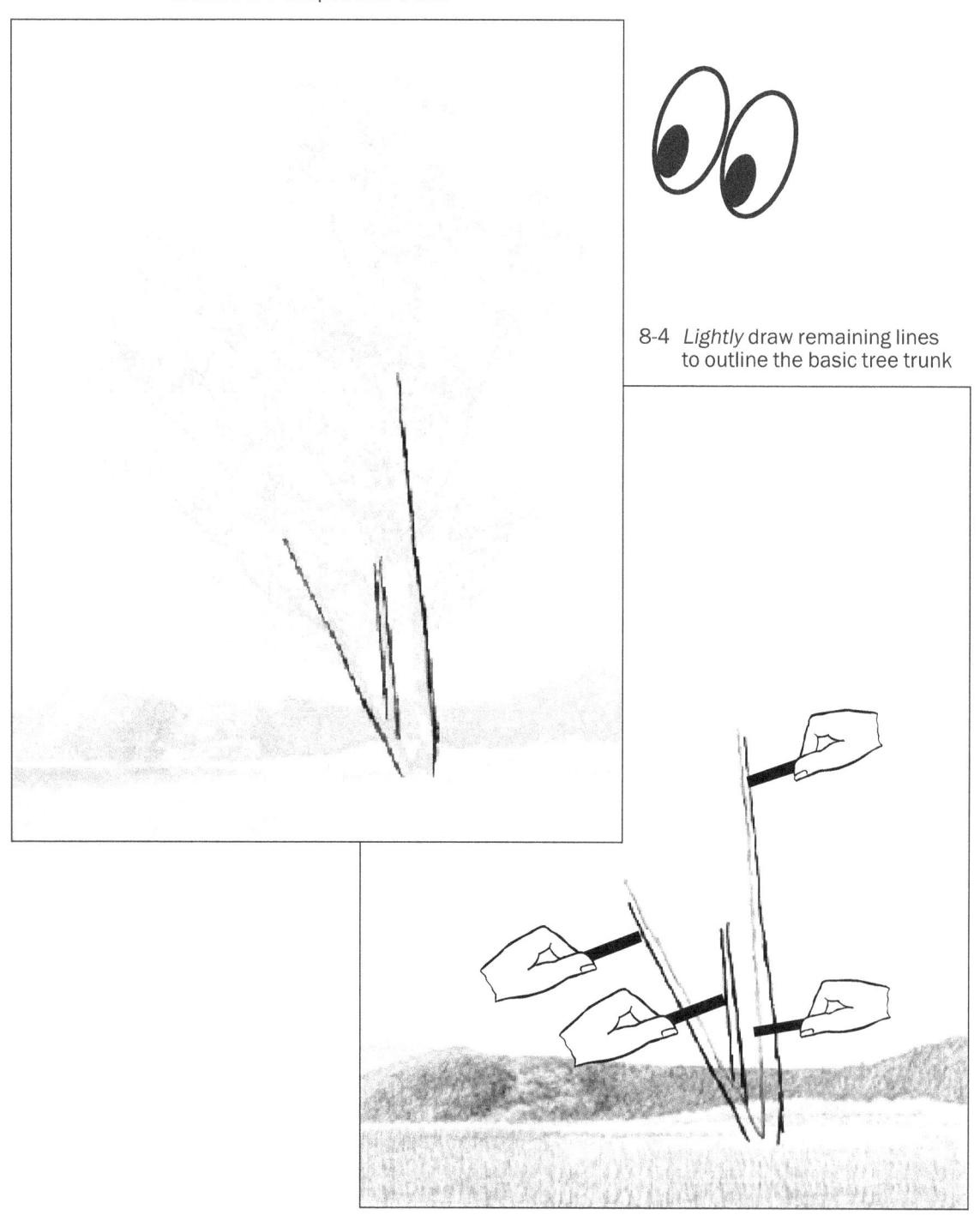

8-4 *Lightly* draw remaining lines
to outline the basic tree trunk

STEP 3 According to illustration 8-5, we see that there are 4 main branches extending from the tree trunks. *Lightly* mimic them on your drawing, one by one with wavy lines that follow in the general position, shape and proportion (8-6). My lines are dark for ease of visibility, but make yours much lighter.

TIP Holding your pencil gently, a few inches back from the point, start your lines from the trunk and draw upward, the way the tree grows. Use slightly jerky, continuous motions for each branch to create the natural effect. If this technique feels awkward, practice on a separate sheet until you get the hang of it.

8-5 Study the shape, scale and location of the 4 branches

8-6 *Lightly* draw the 4 branches one by one with wavy lines

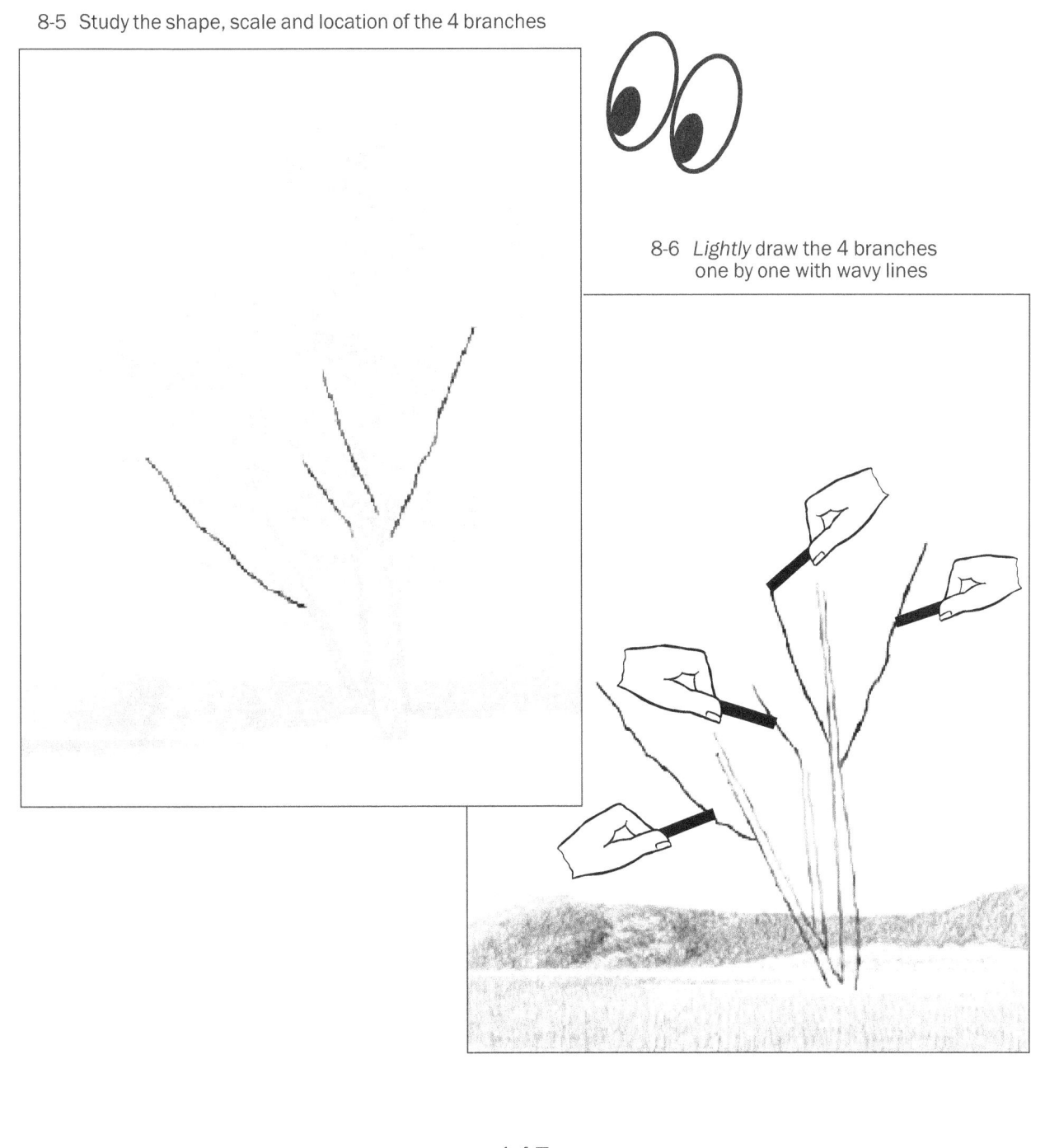

STEP 4 Illustration 8-7 shows us more branches extending upward. While referring to the model, fashion these lightly on your drawing as indicated in example (8-8). Remember, you do not have to match the lines exactly. Just try to stay in relative proportion and position to capture the unique character of the tree. By applying wiggly and jerky motions, you will find your effects are more convincing. Again, my lines are dark to make them easy for you to see. Your lines should be much lighter.

8-7 Study the shape, scale and location of the 4 branches

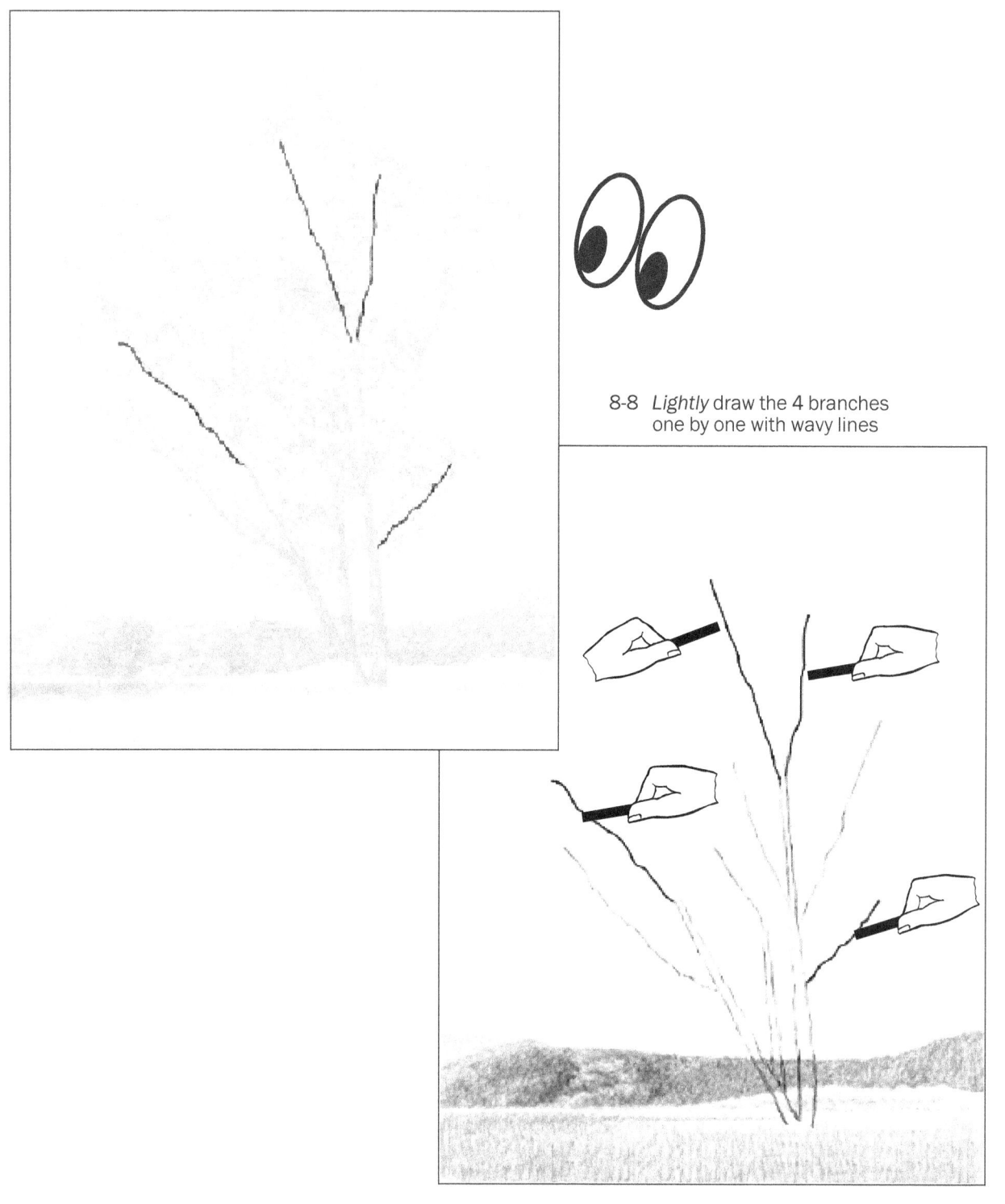

8-8 *Lightly* draw the 4 branches one by one with wavy lines

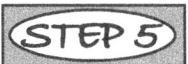 **STEP 5** Using illustration 8-9 for reference, *lightly* fill your replica of the tree trunk with uneven patches of tone to indicate bark textures (8-10).

TIP By keeping your values light for now, this will enable you to work into them later.

8-9 Study the patches of texture in the basic tree trunk

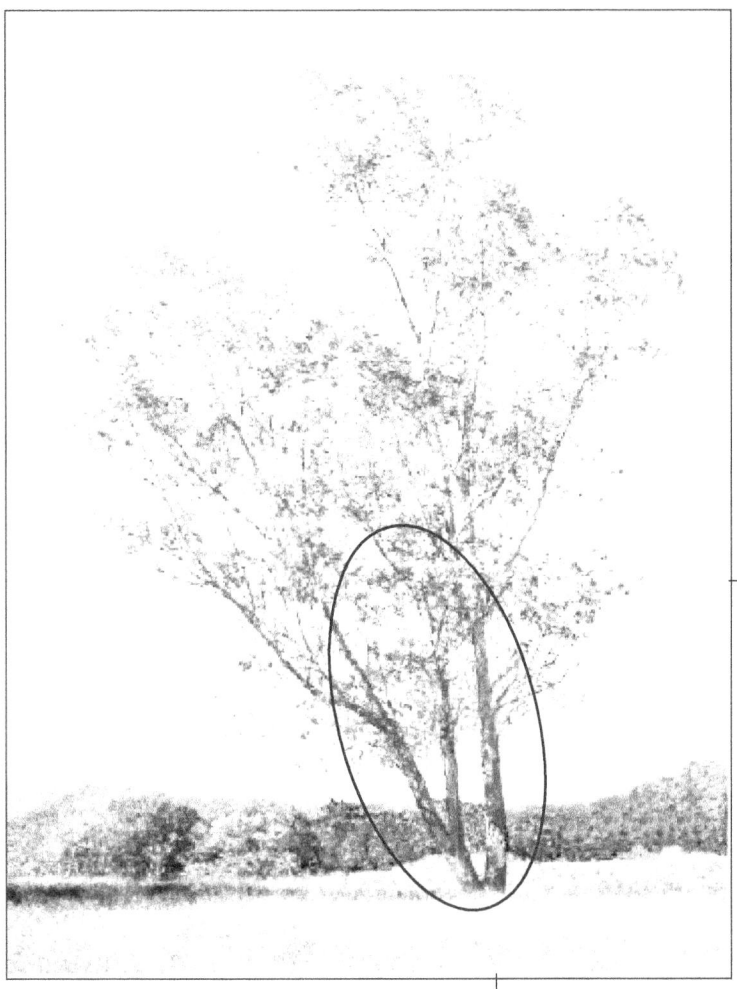

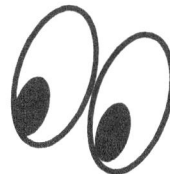

8-10 *Lightly* mimic the patches of texture of the tree trunk

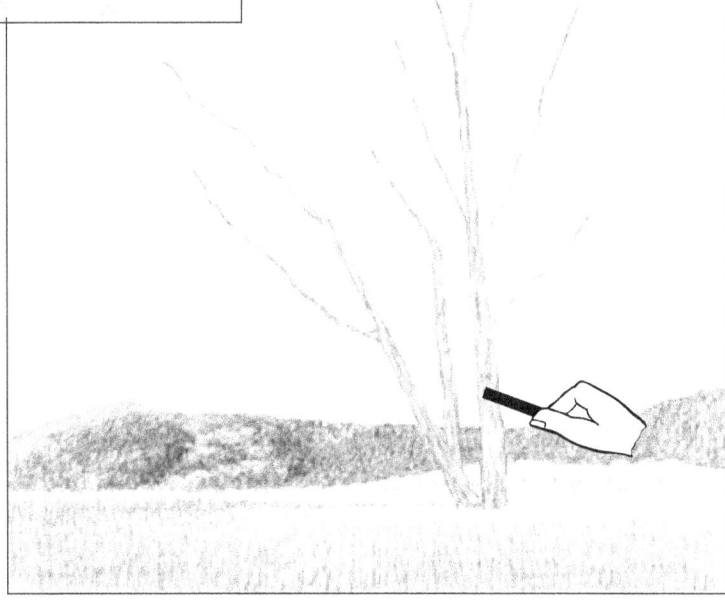

STAGE 2 - THE FOLIAGE

STEP 1 On page 122, you may recall, we found a triangular shape in the tree trunk. The same kind of streamlining procedure can also be applied to the foliage (clusters of leaves). Take a look at illustration 8-11. There are triangles there, too. I found some of the more obvious ones and outlined them with dash lines (8-12). Using these for reference, *lightly* locate the triangles proportionally on your drawing, one at a time with dots and connect with dash lines before moving to the next triangle. My dots are large and the lines are dark to make them easy for you to see (8-13). When completed, your triangles should be fashioned with smaller, lighter dots and dashes than example 8-14.

8-11 Can you see triangles in the clusters of leaves?

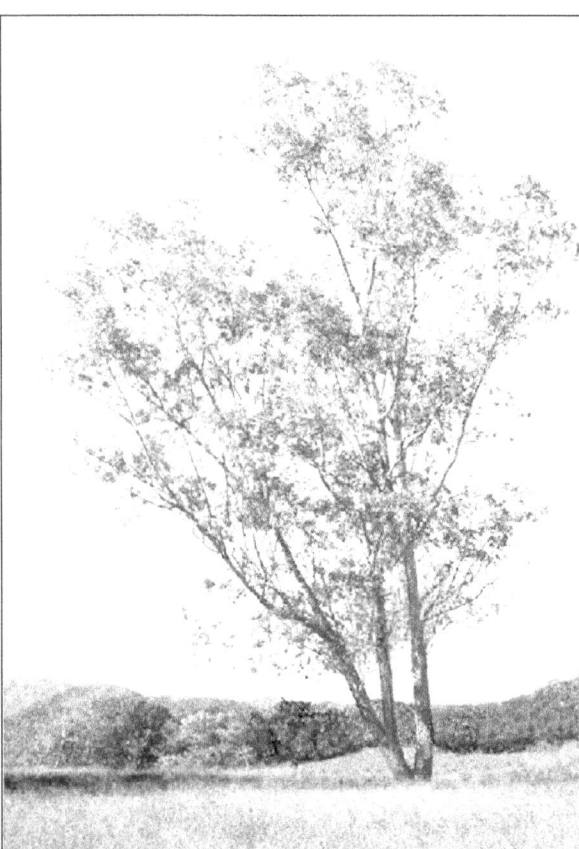

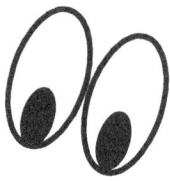

8-12 The triangles are more visible outlined with dash lines.

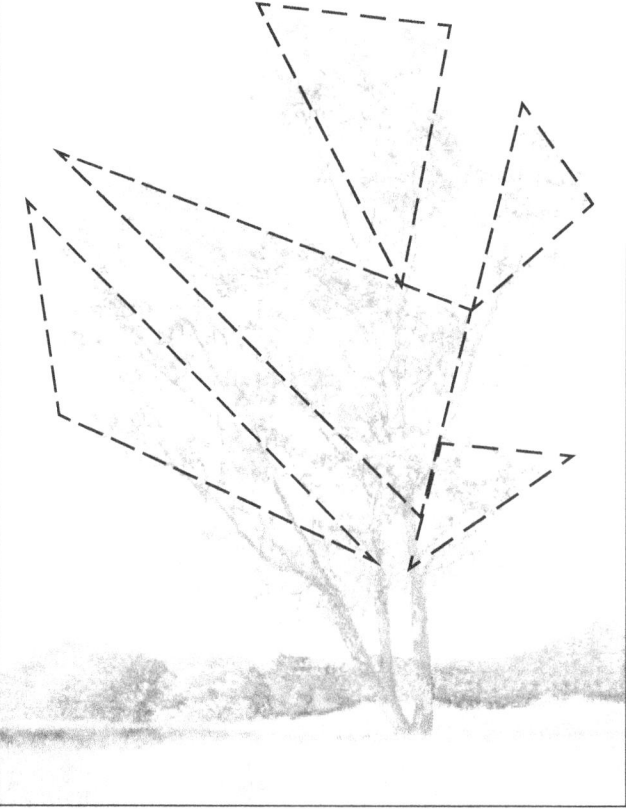

TIP I'm sure you see other triangles, and lots more. But these five are enough divisions. Too many streamlined shapes can be just as confusing as none at all.

8-13 *Lightly* locate a series of 3 dots and connect
dash lines to form triangles, *one set at a time*

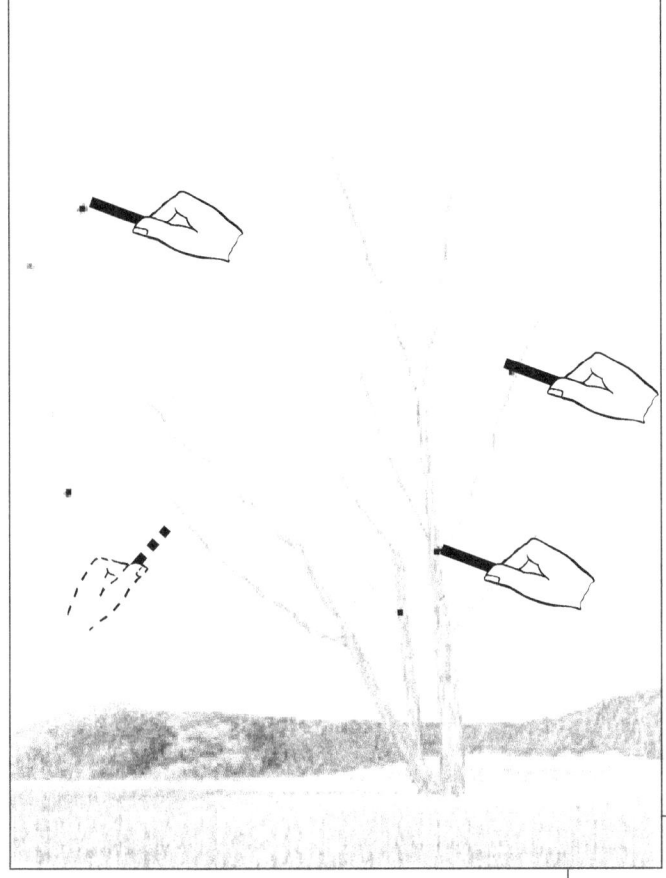

TIP Your triangles do not
have to match mine,
but make certain your shapes
reasonably capture the basic
character of the tree.

8-14 Example of dots and dash lines forming
5 triangles that form basic shape of tree

TIP Light dash lines are easier
to convert to leaf textures.

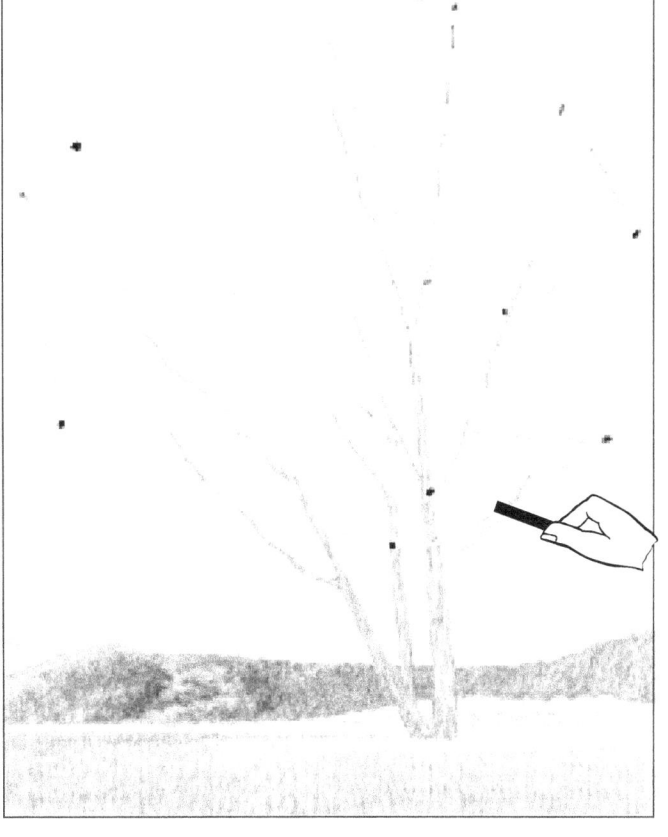

STEP 2 Pretend the foliage in the tree is nearly all in the lightest value range (8-15). Visualized as such, it is easier to see the larger overall shapes made by the smaller clumps (or groupings). Observe the uneven gaps within and around the asymmetric (uneven) forms. These reveal the natural, unique characteristics of the tree. On the next page, example 8-16 indicates some of the main reverse spaces accented in white. With the help of the illustrations, (including 8-17 showing the triangular streamline format), apply gentle pressure with the side of your pencil and use zigzag strokes to simulate a very light texture on *your* drawing. This procedure will provide a base to work into, similar to the way you textured your ground areas. Advance slowly, section by section, a little at a time, until the basic shapes and spaces appear as soft patchy tones (8-18).

8-15 All foliage visualized as very light texture

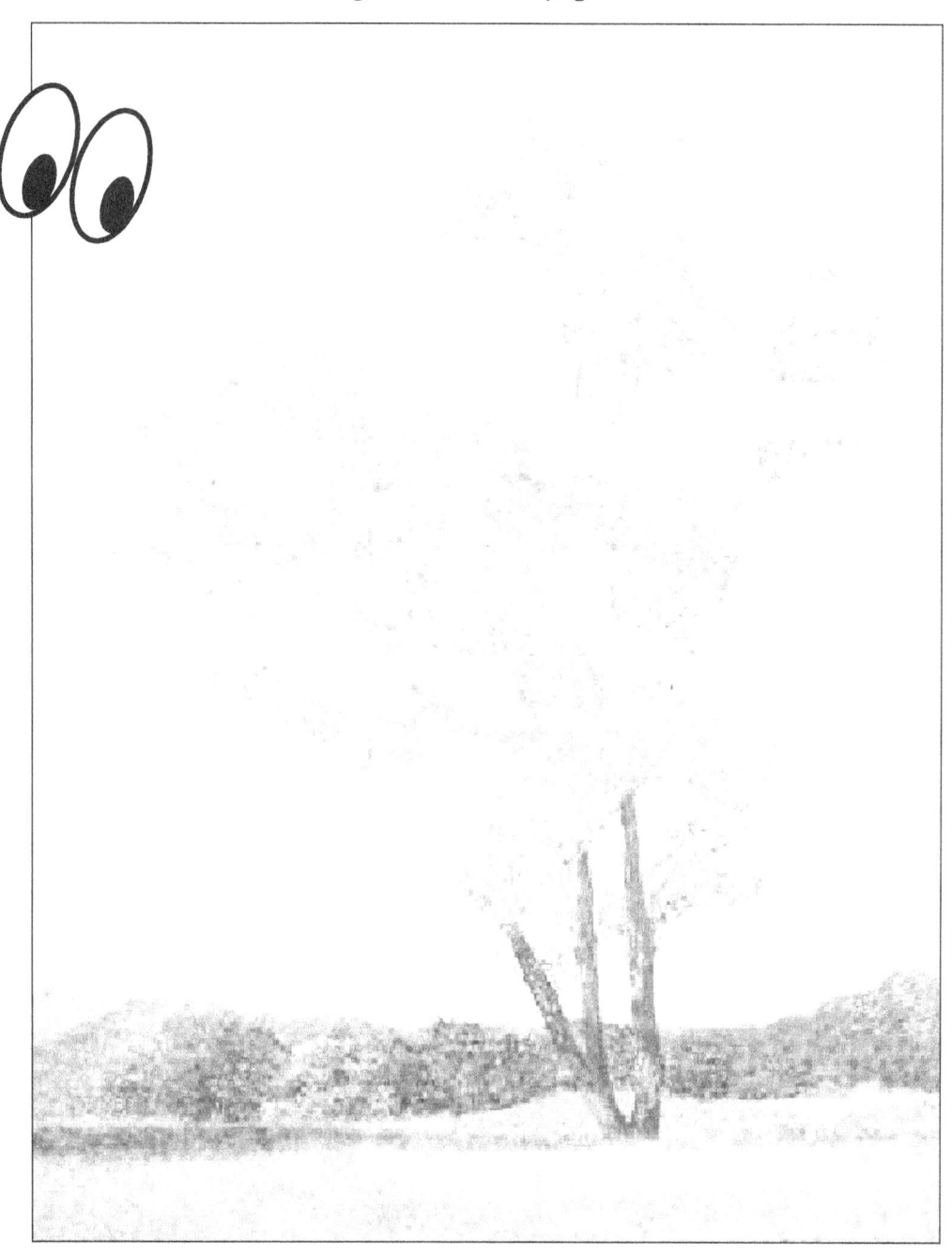

8-16 Observe the reverse spaces (white)

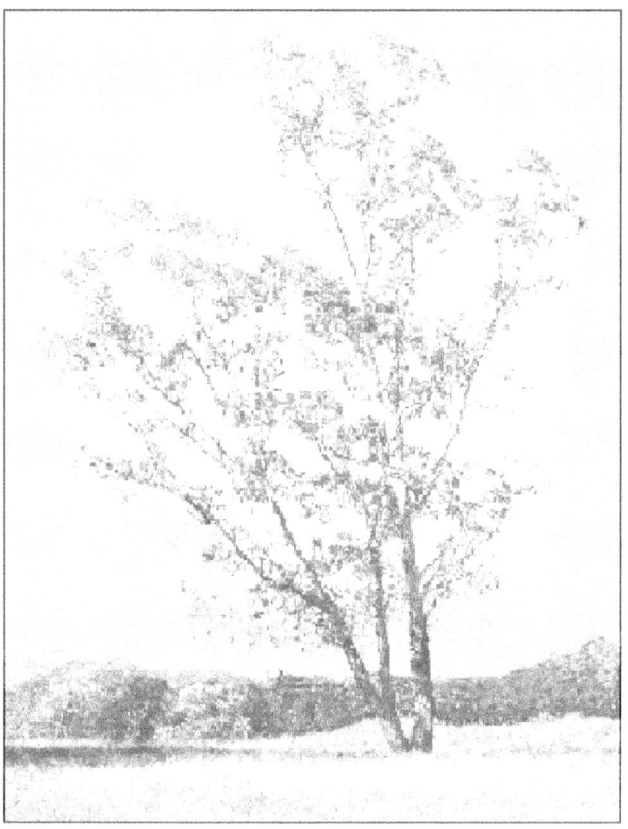

8-17 Observe foliage outlined with triangles

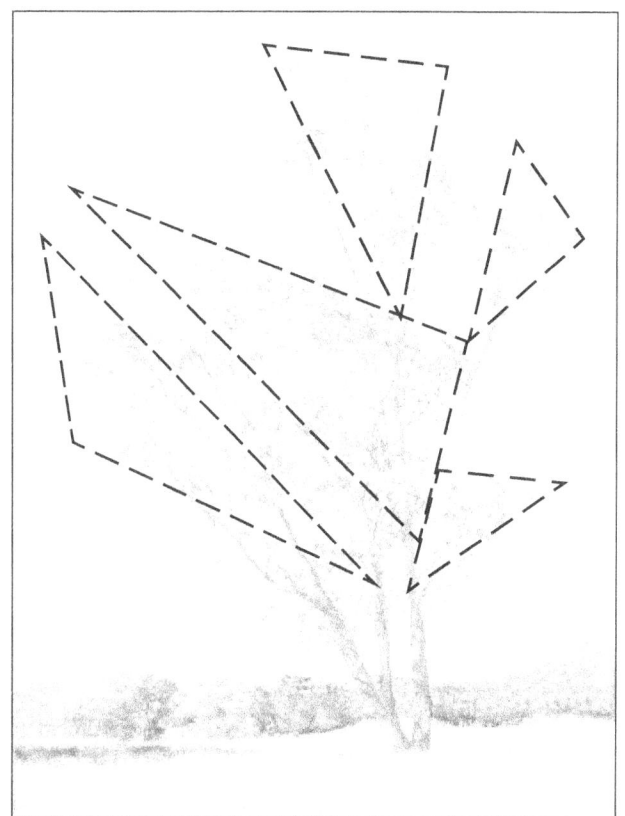

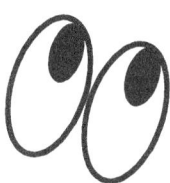

8-18 Layer texture to mimic the light tone foliage

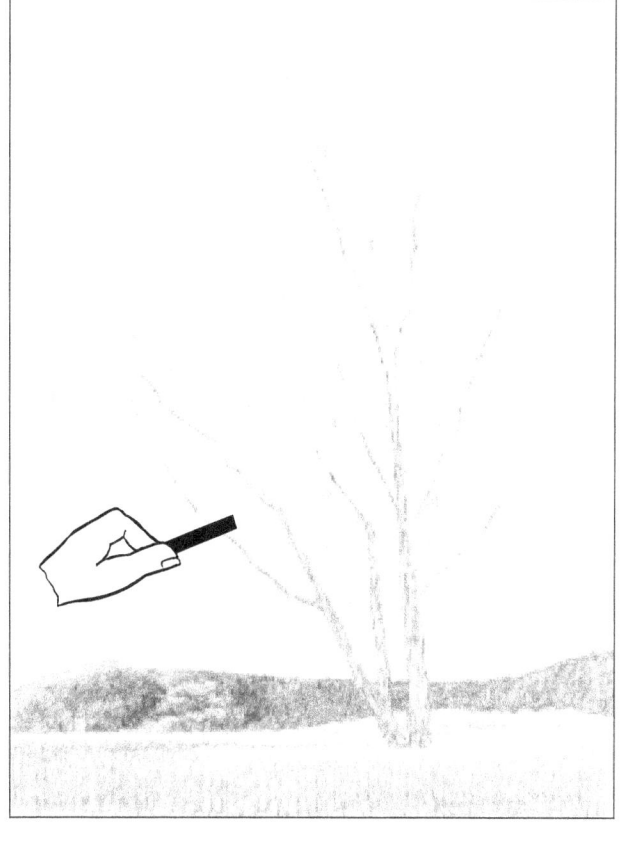

TIP Apply tone *randomly* by switching from one area to another and back, so as not to over work a segment. Use gentle jerky strokes. The spaces you leave are just as important as the forms you make. Together they reveal the individual character and personality of the tree. Your shapes do not have to match mine, nor the photo. The objective is to capture a fair likeness. In order to soften your textures, you can smudge the edges a little with a blender or with your finger.

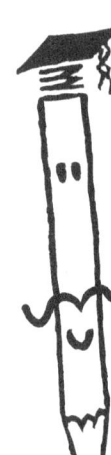

We are about to add more texture. Please take another glance at the tree below. The leaves look like one big jumble of spots, right? Now let your eyes scan. Then lock in on one area of foliage. Although the leaves still resemble blotches, you can see the clusters more clearly.

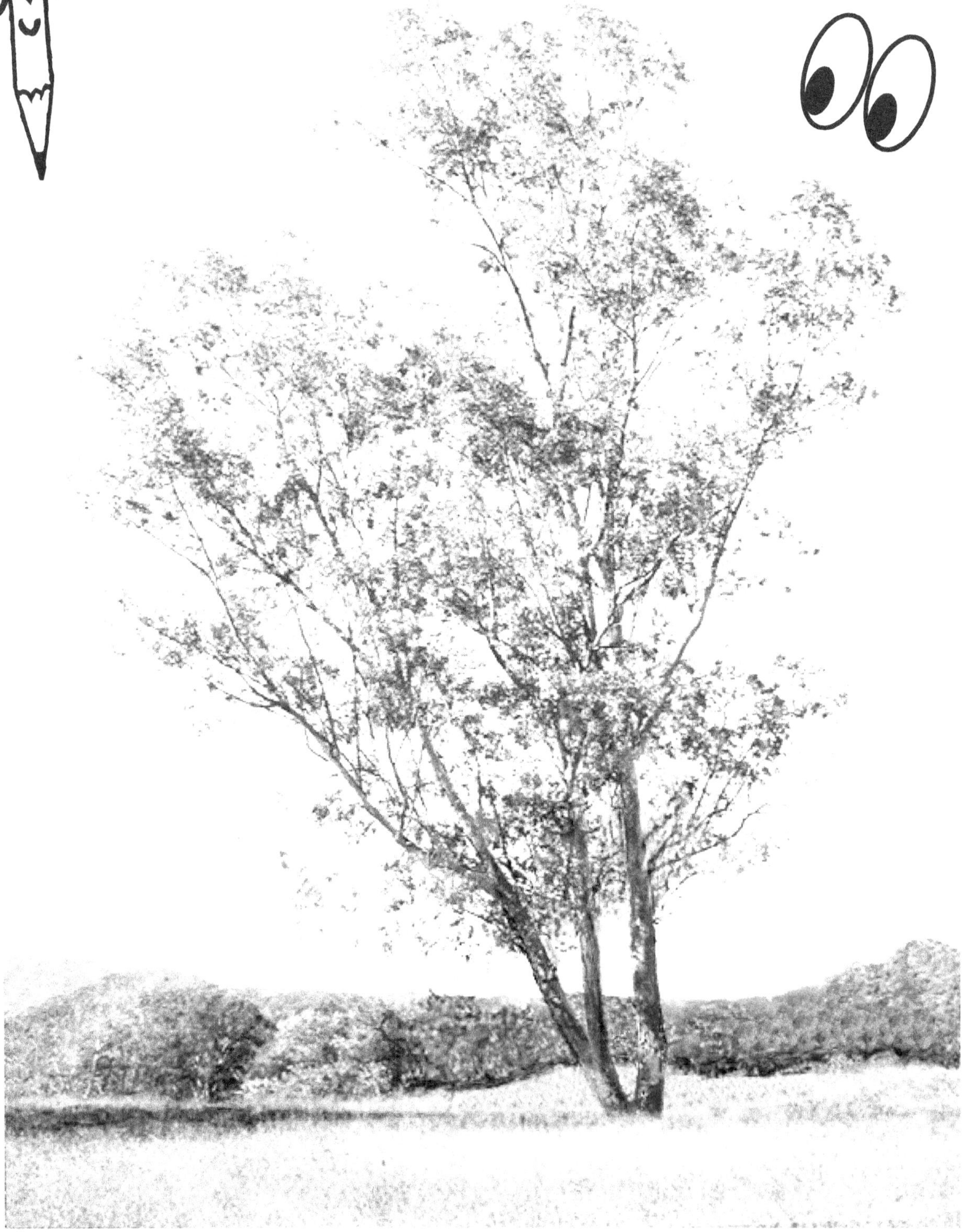

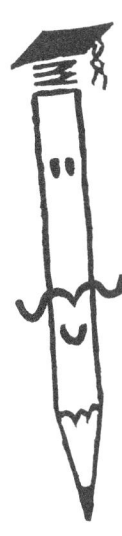

To observe even more features, a view finder comes in handy. It isolates sections and helps train your eyes to zoom in. Make a view finder from a piece of dark paper or thin cardboard by cutting out a rectangular opening about the same size as mine, then continue.

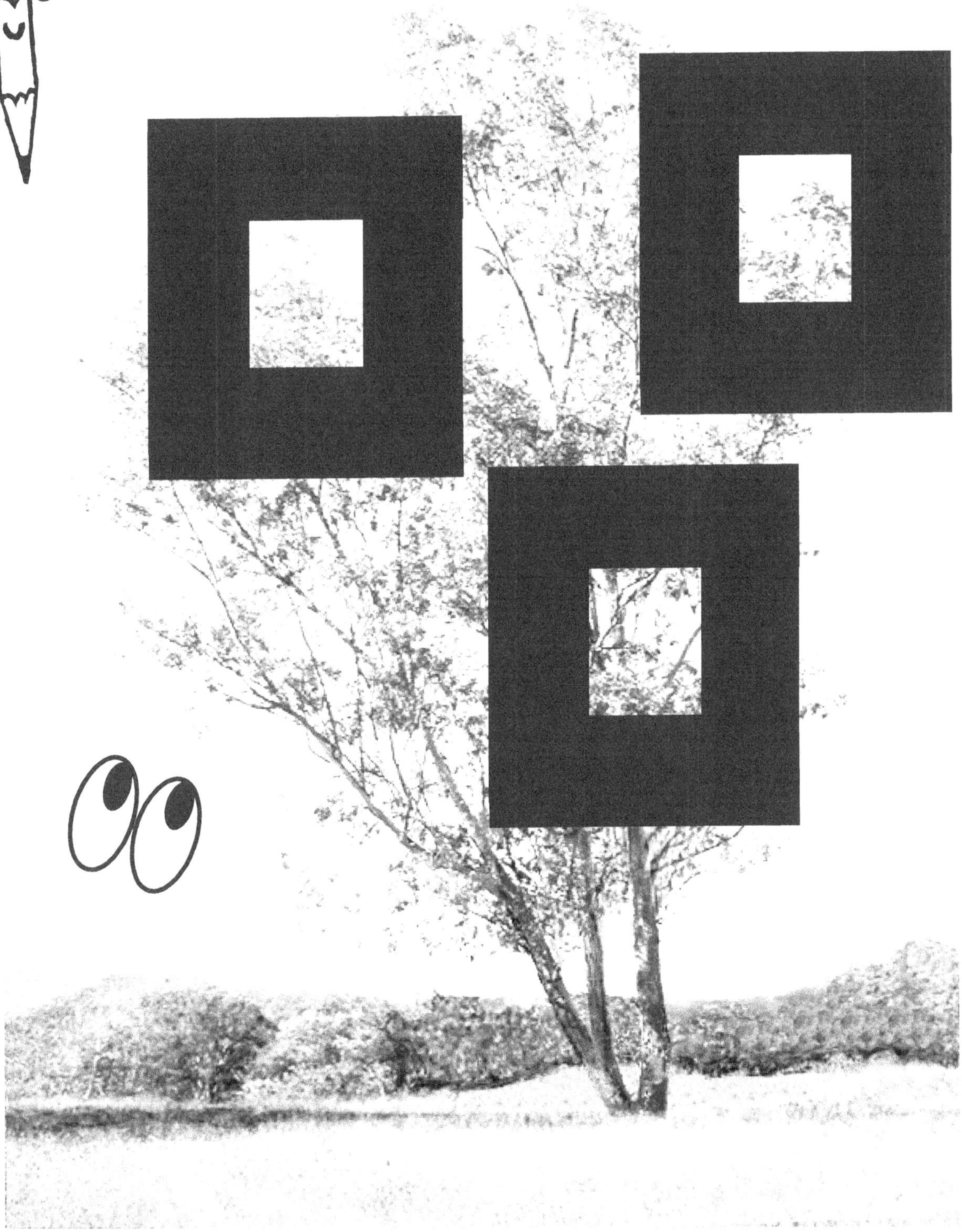

STEP 3 With the aid of the photo below for reference, add a layer of texture to your tree by applying small, jerky, zigzag strokes. These should be the *slightly* darke*r*, blotchy values you see in various sections of foliage. It's common to get confused in all the shapes when your eyes zoom in to study the smaller segments. Make a mental note as to which of the streamlined triangles you happen to be in. Then go to that respective part on your drawing and do some texturing, but do not stay for long. There is a natural urge to pattern the foliage evenly, depite the fact that leaves are usually *unevenly* distributed. By the same token, although the gaps and spaces within the clusters are generally random and asymmetric, you may find yourself overtaken by a nearly irresistible desire to neatly fill them in as well. To counter such tendencies and maintain the integrity (true likeness) of the tree, make a few marks that replicate a portion of texture and move on. This promotes variety and keeps freshness in your strokes. When you have visited throughout, go for another layer, this time with *gentle* dotted strokes to show the more dense parts. Include thin lines to depict twigs and use your view finder to see the details. *Save the darkest stage for later.* Drawings 8-19 and 8-20 are examples of the basic progression. Your drawing should not be identical. It should be *your* unique version.

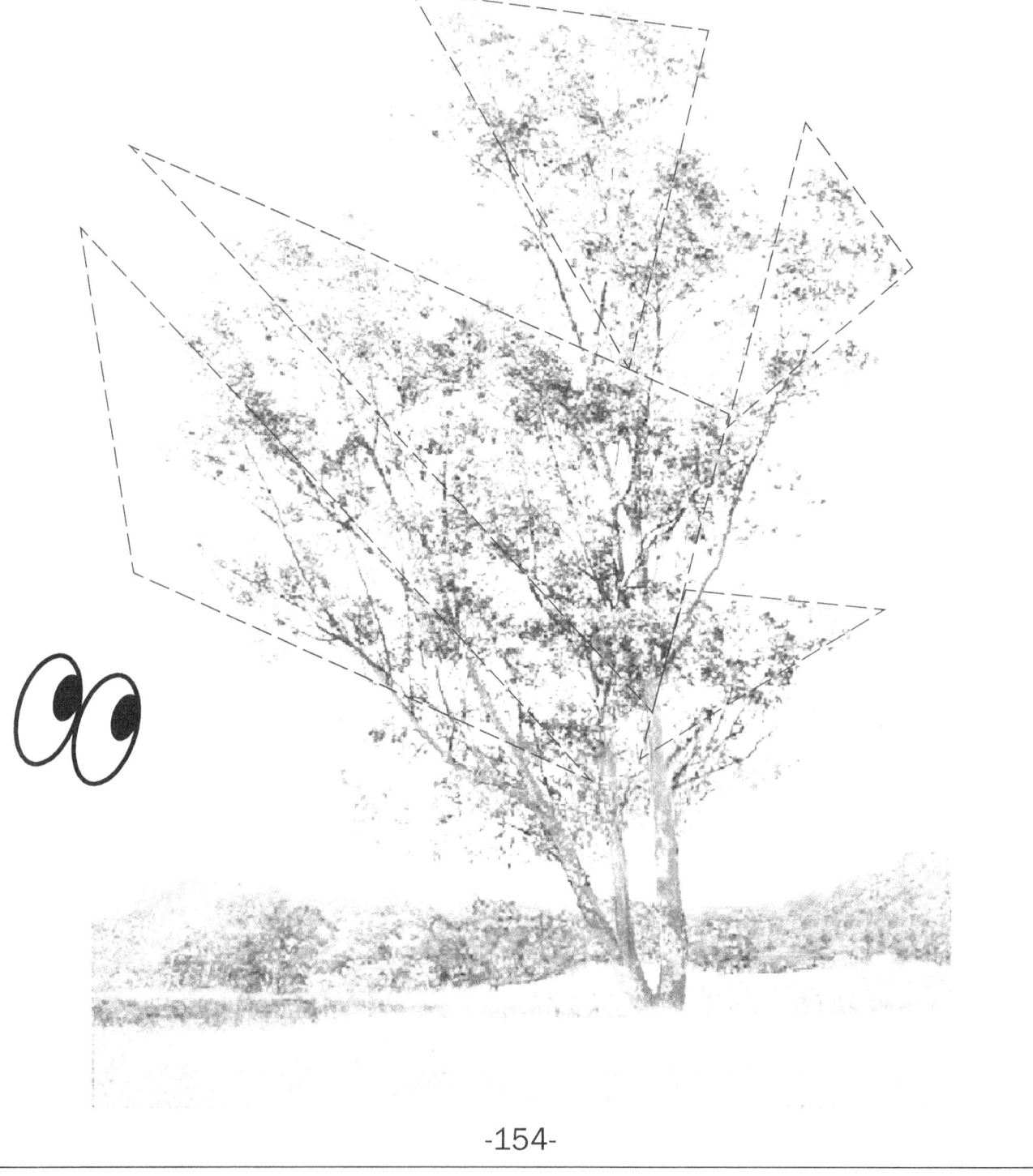

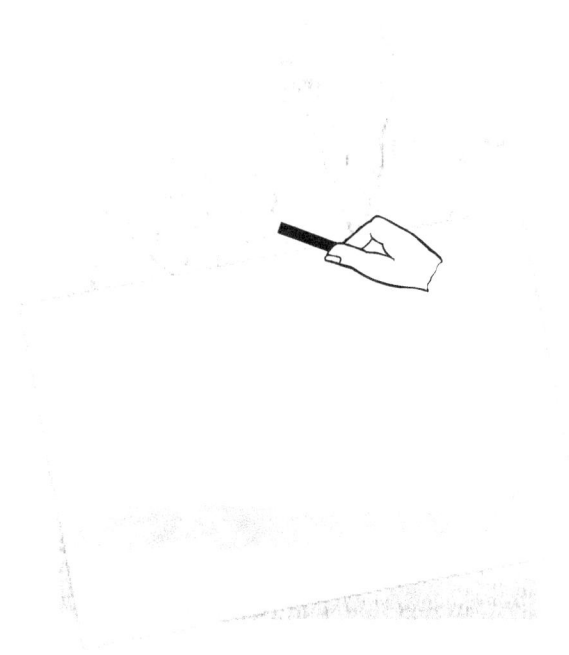

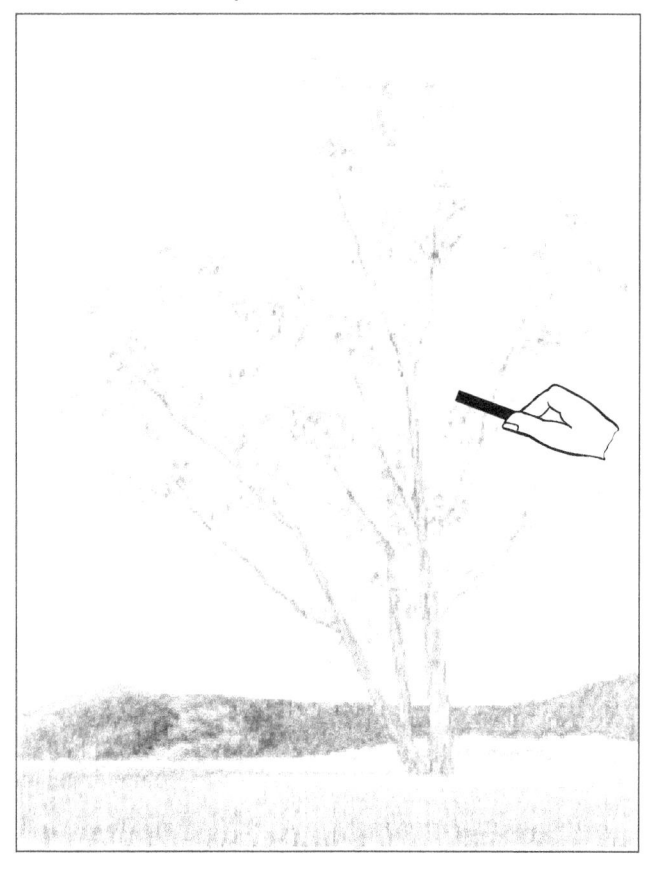

TIP To reduce smearing, cover the section not being worked on with wax paper or another sheet.

8-20 Layer the darker textures but not the darkest

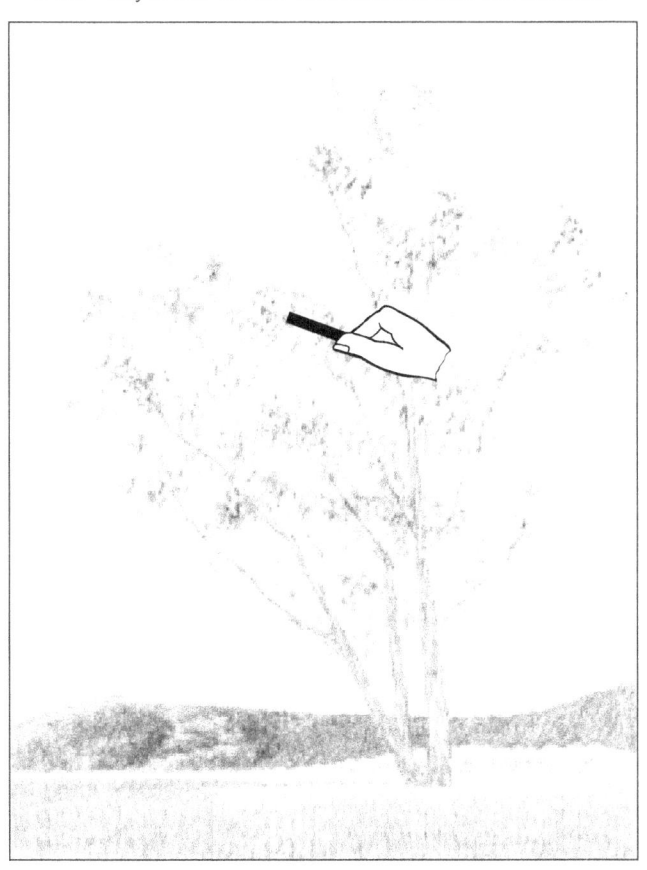

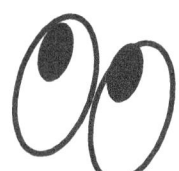

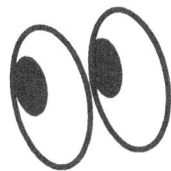

TIP The darker areas represent densely packed leaves. Since light usually penetrates more near the edges, your values should be *softer* and not as intense there. Remember: the darkest textures are yet to come. If you find it is necessary to lighten some parts, dab, don't rub with your eraser to prevent smudges.

STAGE 3 - THE FINISHING TOUCHES

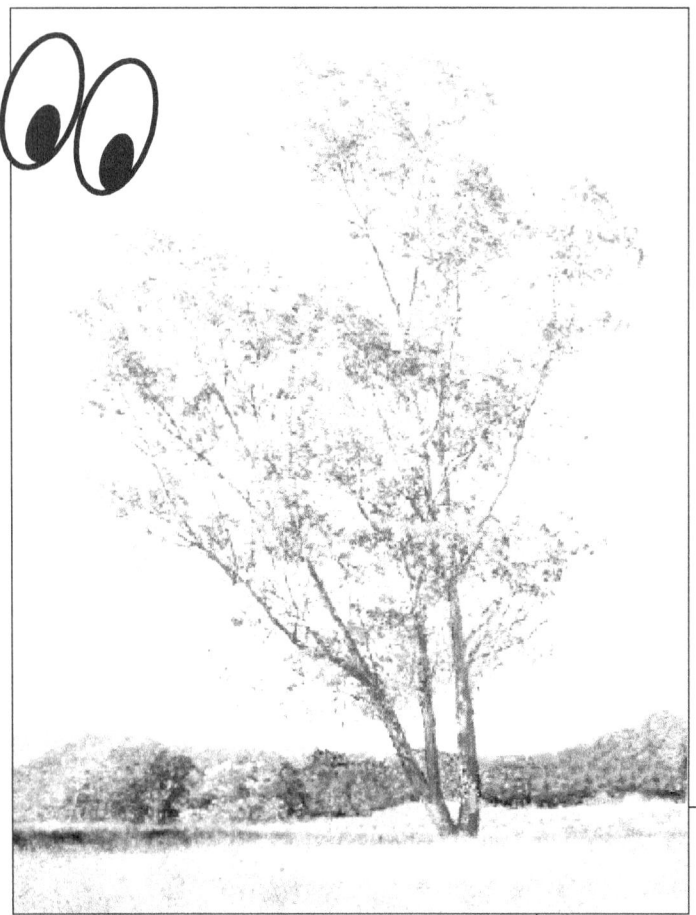

Since all parts have been semi-rendered in the picture (as shown below), it's time for a check-up. By comparing the results with the model, side-by-side from a slight distance, assimiliation (visual mixing) can help reveal telltale differences. For instance, in the photo we can see there are some dark values on both sides of the bushes. The contrast makes them stand out. Dark textures also exist along the rim, bordering the grassy mound. This tends to *push* the background area, as well as *pull* the knoll, thereby depicting bigger space in between. Currently, these factors are absent in my drawing. Did I goof? Not at all. The darkest values were saved for last, when they are easier to balance on the whole.

The photo also indicates there are darker patches in the foliage and in the tree trunk. Those features make them more prominent. Notice too, that the shadow in the grass is proportionally darker. Speaking of the grass, mine is darker in the foreground. For that matter, in my drawing, the lighter part of the shadow is missing on the right side of the tree. Does this imply a blunder? On the contrary. The goal was to create an interpretation, not an exact copy. Since we already have an entire picture, it's easier to decide what to leave alone and what to change. Examples 8-21 and 8-22 indicate the modifications I elected to include.

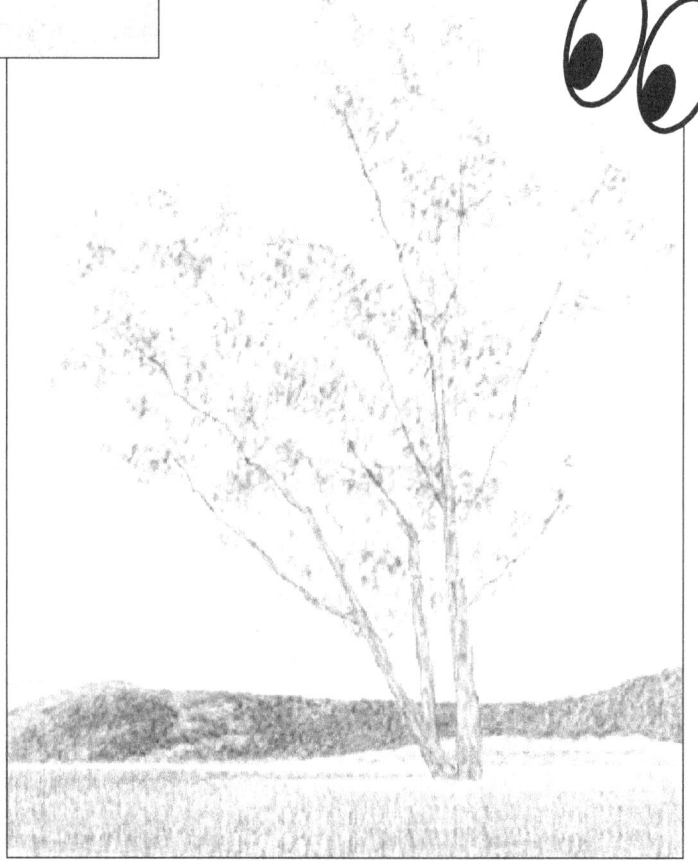

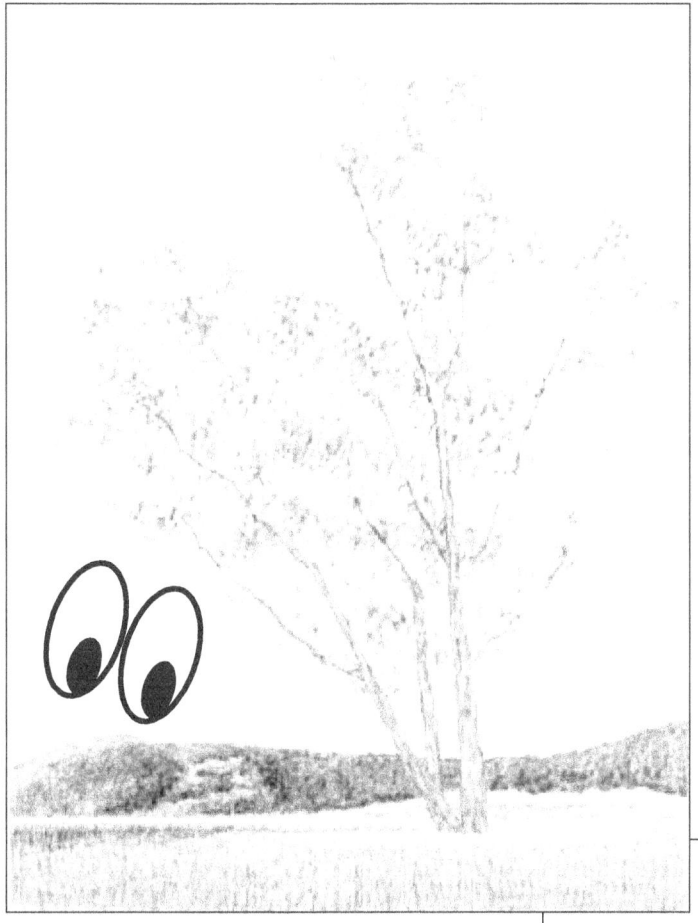

Drawing 8-21 shows the result after I increased the contrast on both sides of the bushes, causing a *push-pull effect*. This was achieved by *feathering* in darker values along the rim of the grassy knoll. I also darkened the shadow in the grass, *just a little*. Compare before (previous page) and after.

Next, as illustrated by drawing 8-22, the visible triangles (originally made with dash lines) have been erased. I also darkened select areas of the tree trunk and *carefully* increased a *little* of the subtle values in parts of the foliage. Compare the tree in drawing 8-21 to 8-22. Then compare drawing 8-22 to the drawing on the previous page (before changes). Both versions are fine. Which do you prefer?

8-22 Example after increasing tree trunk values

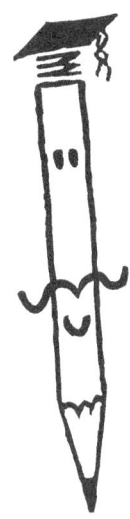

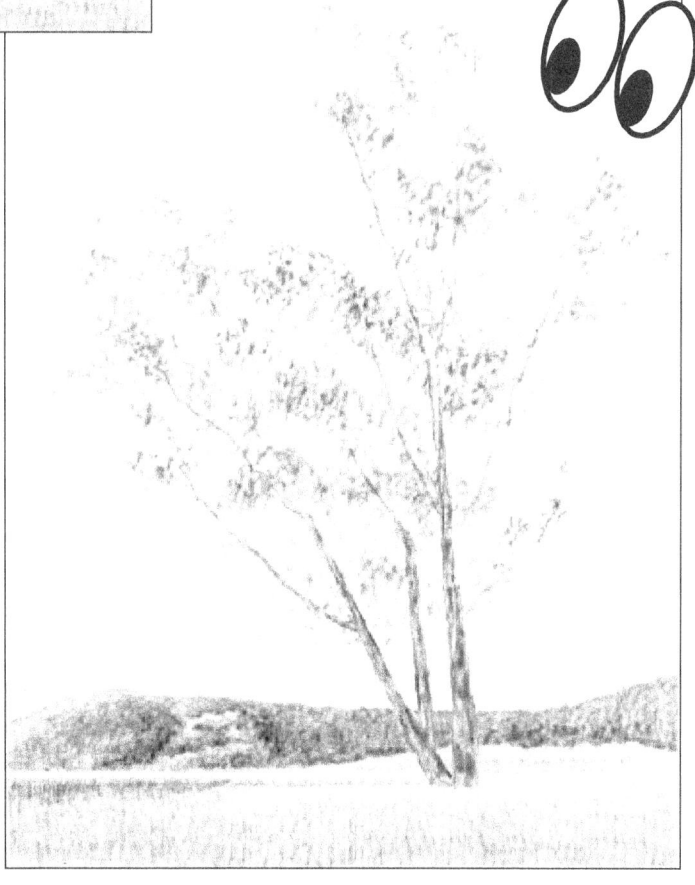

Now, compare your work from a distance, beside the model on p.152. Do YOUR finishing touches. Then, browse the student gallery (next page).

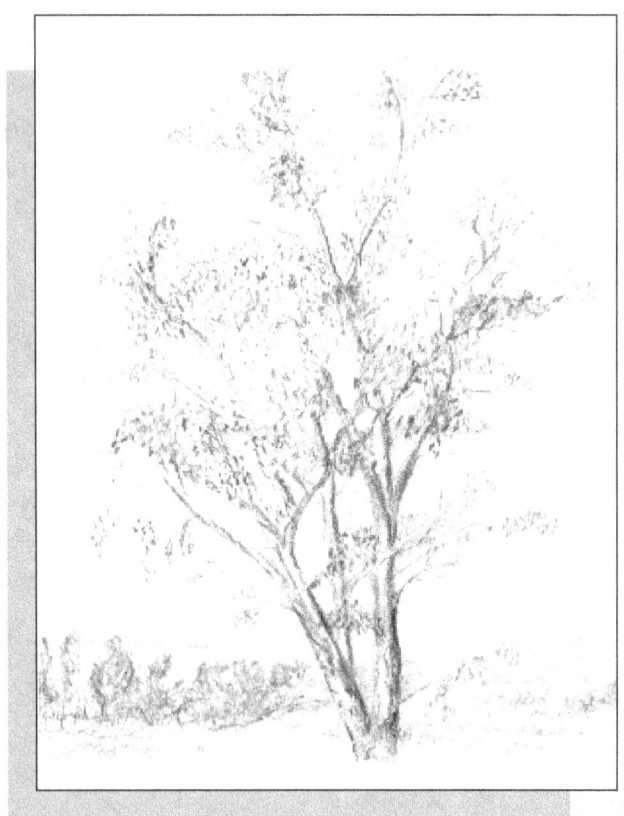

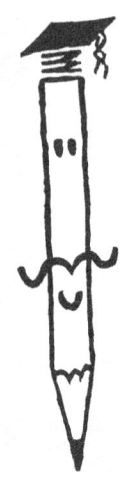

Remember that the goal was not to make an exact copy of the photo.

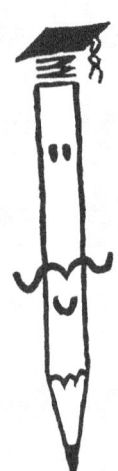

The objective was to create an interpretation of the landscape.

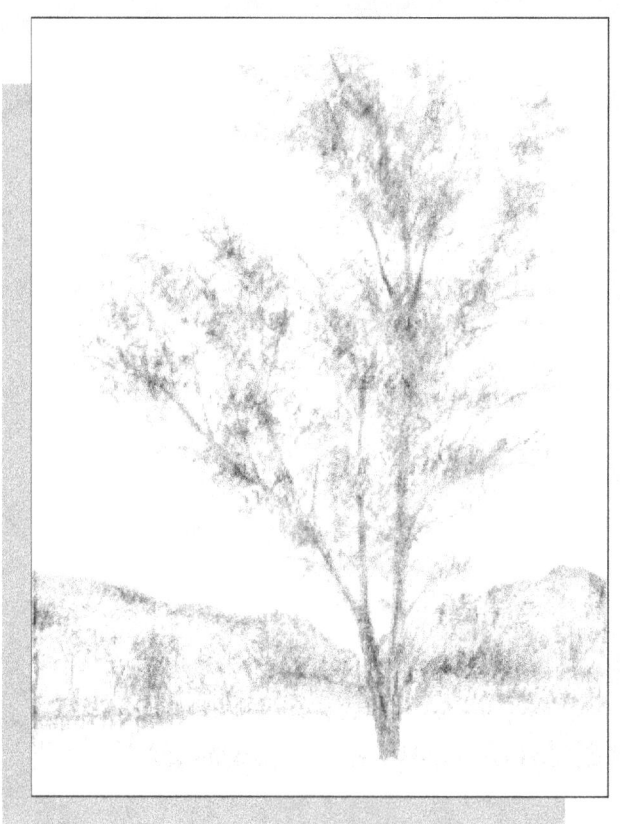

STUDENT GALLERY

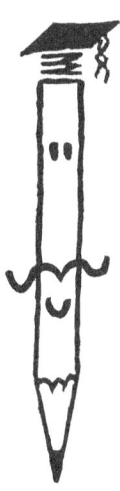

These are original, one of a kind renditions, conveying individual quality and style.

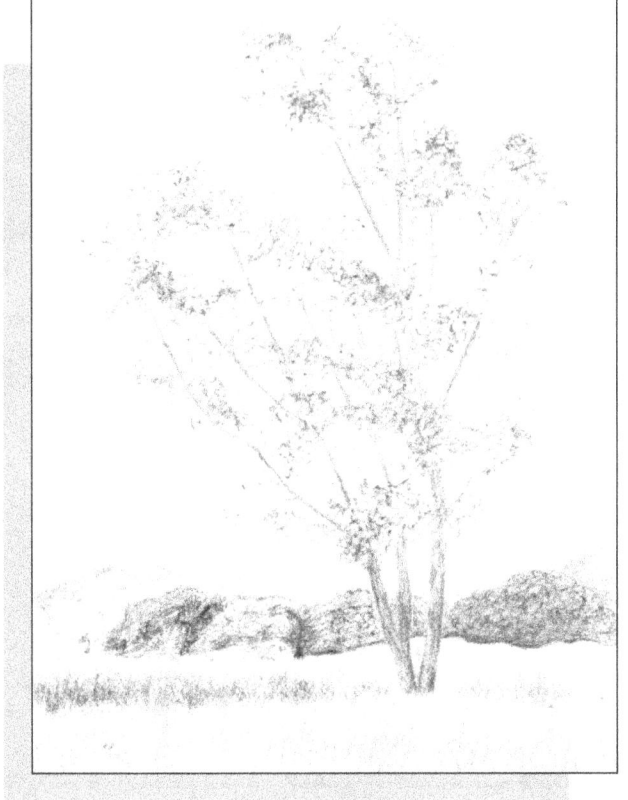

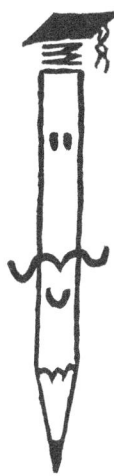

Isn't it great that each creation is a unique version of the scene? I'm sure yours is, too.

Chapter 8
FOLLOW-UP

   At times, you may have felt apprehensive about the prospect of drawing a complete landscape. As you have discovered, it's not really difficult when you divide the process into stages and gradually developing layers. Like everything, a scene with trees, rocks and hills for example, when simplified essentially consists of shapes, tones, textures, contrasts and edges. Sure, it may take time to include all of them, but not because the features are harder to replicate. There are just a lot of marvelous sights to see and render.

   Initially, even a single tree may appear like a maze of confusion, until you realize you can find shapes within it, much the way you can find forms in clouds. That means you can streamline even the seemingly complex parts of a tree, or an entire landscape for that matter, by simply turning it into your own personal road map. It only has to make sense to you, nobody else. After all, people really do observe things differently. This is one of the reasons why any given scene can be created in unlimited ways. This is also one of the countless wonders that makes drawing so exciting.

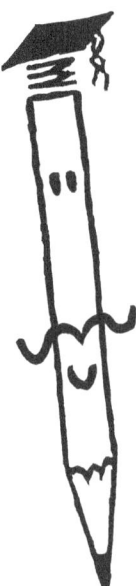

Next, you will *see* that the methods you have been using *to* draw still life, faces and landscapes also apply *to* yet another type of subject matter.

FIND THE BASIC SHAPES
It's easy, if you know where to look.

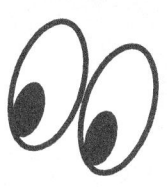

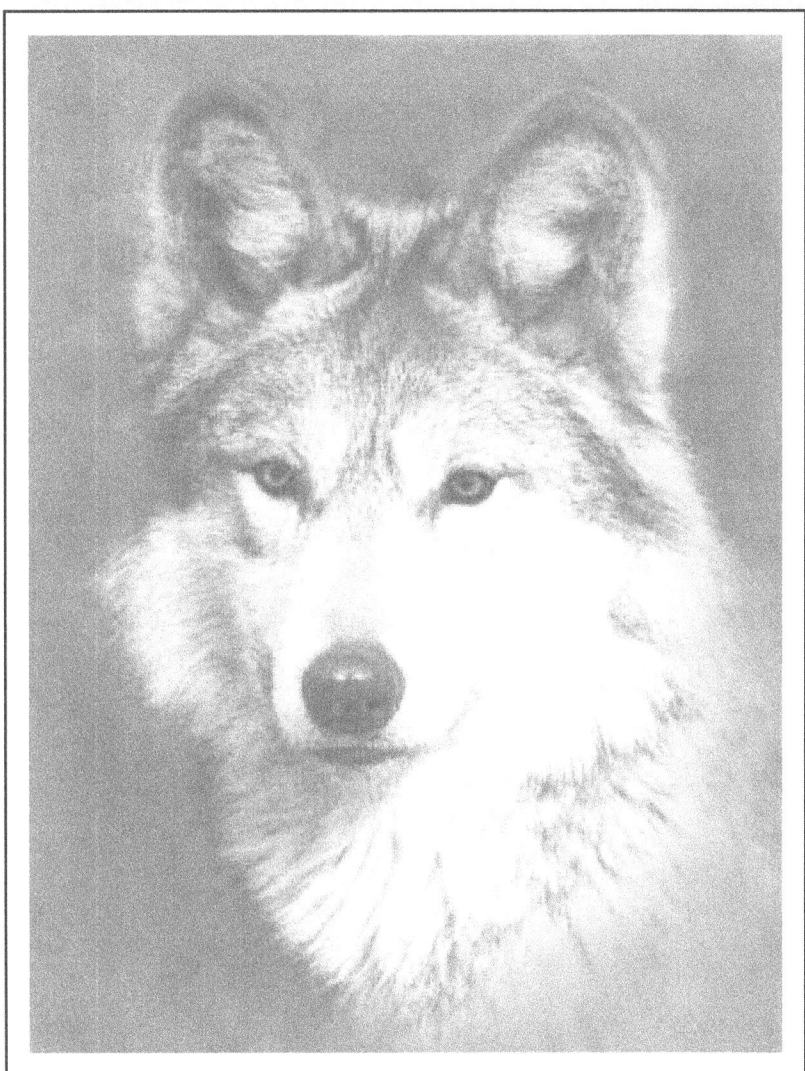

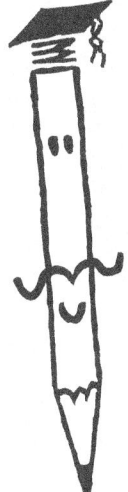

In this chapter we will outline and contour the figure. Tone and texture will be added in the next chapter.

STREAMLINING ALSO APPLIES TO WILDLIFE
THIS WOLF CONSISTS OF GEOMETRIC SHAPES

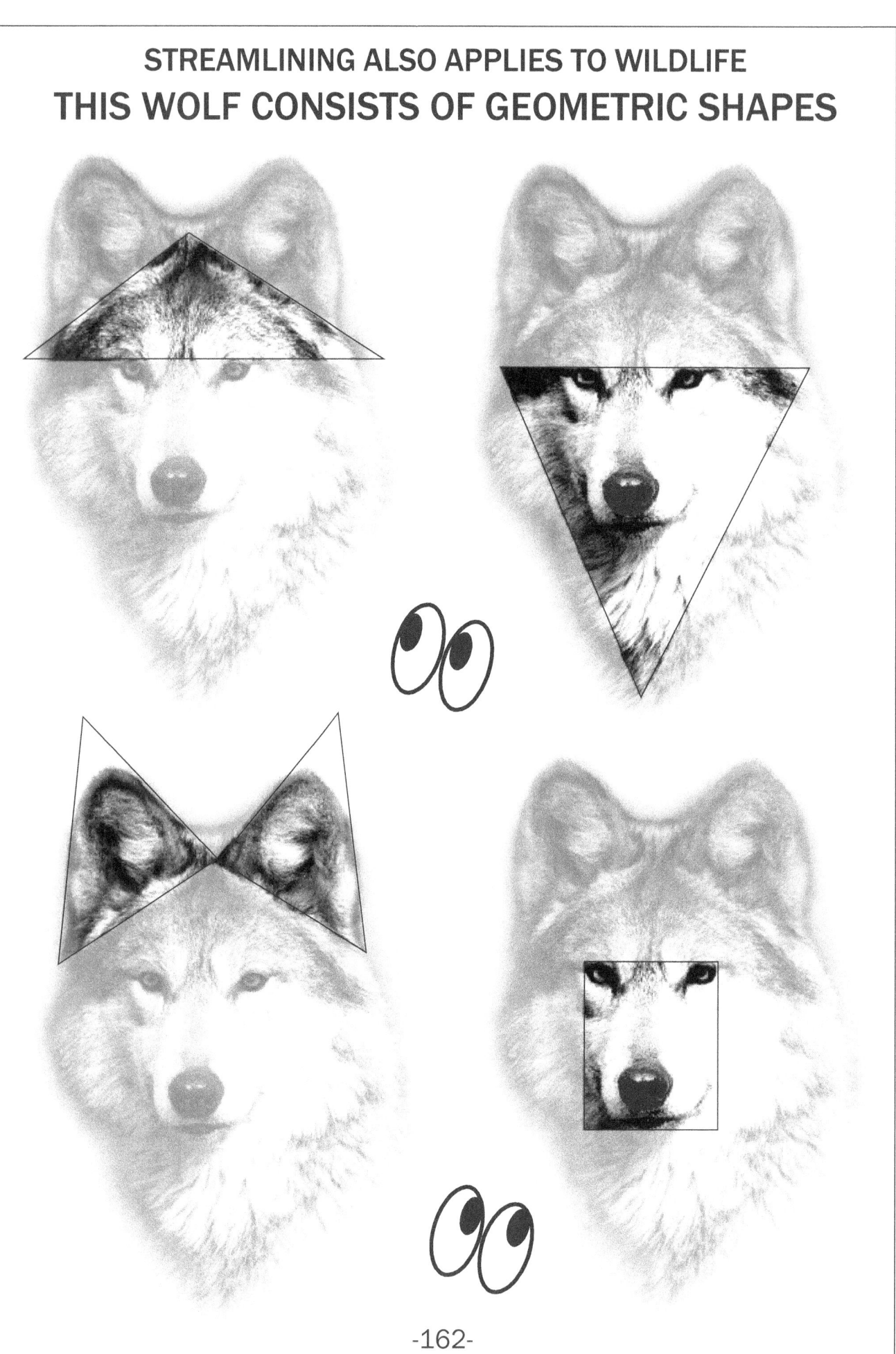

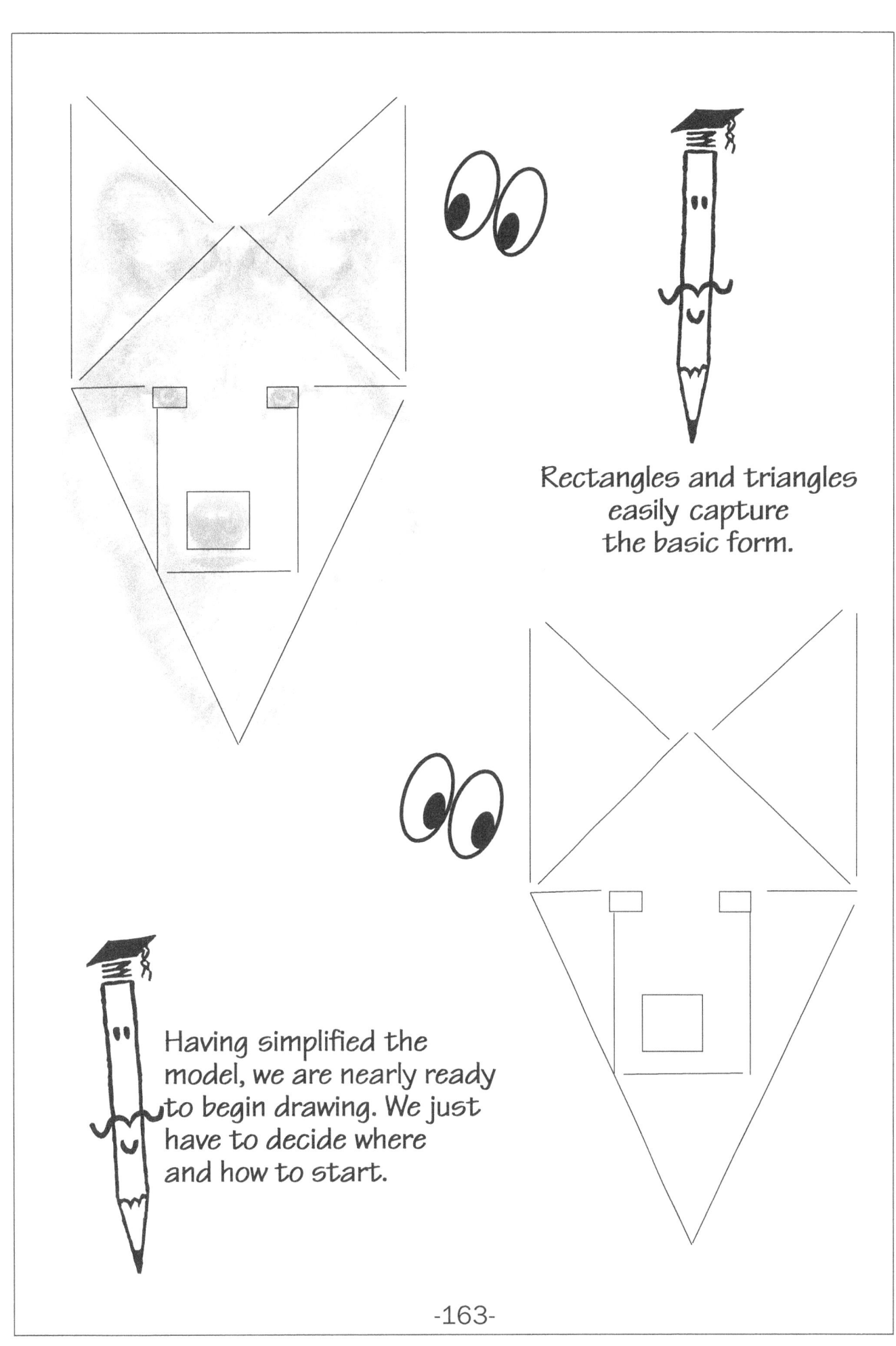

Rectangles and triangles
easily capture
the basic form.

Having simplified the
model, we are nearly ready
to begin drawing. We just
have to decide where
and how to start.

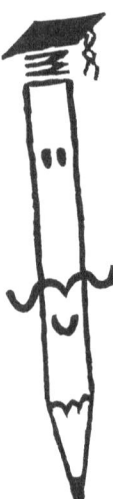

We're in luck! A closer look reveals that the rectangle bordering the figure's eyes, nose and mouth, combined with the triangle in the forehead, creates an ARROW proportional to a SQUARE. This makes for an ideal FOUNDATION for streamlining and a great way to begin.

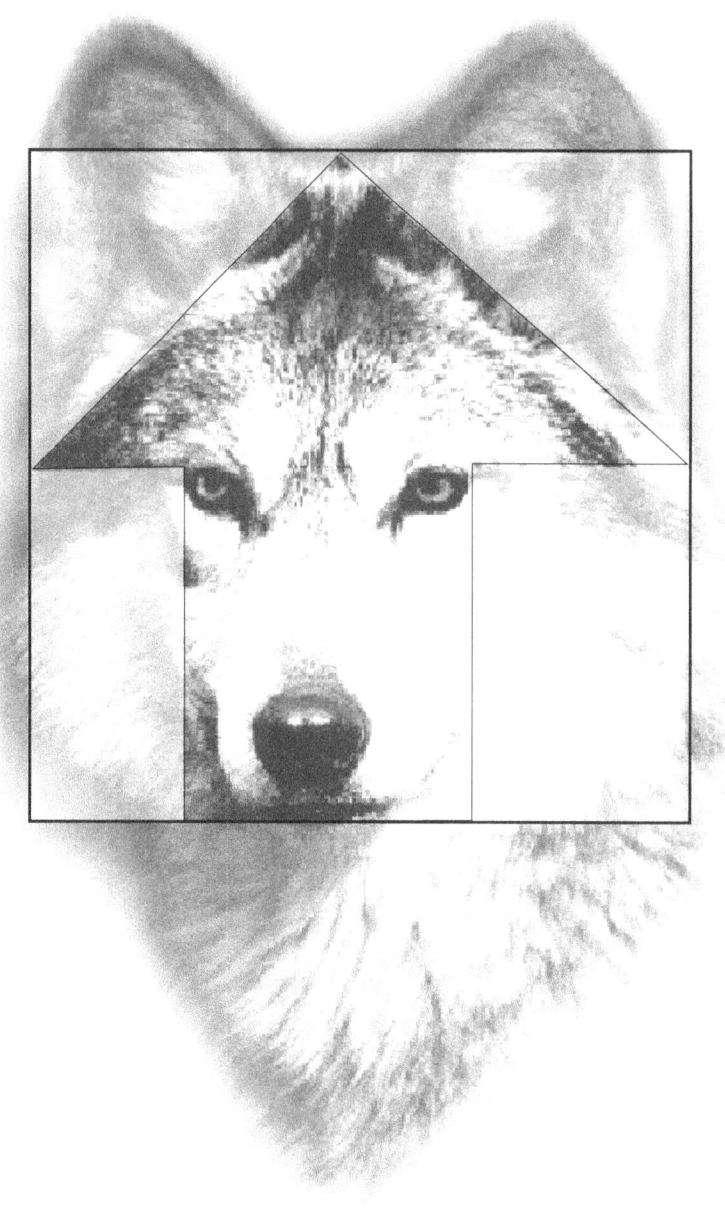
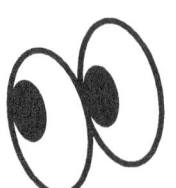

STAGE 1 - STRAIGHT LINES

STEP 1 Start with the square. Based on illustration 9-1, we can see that the wolf's face and part of the ears fit inside. However, more space is required in order to streamline the rest of the ears and neck. With this in mind, visualize the square in relative proportion to the *entire* figure as though its overall boundaries were already streamlined. Such forethought will help you decide a size and position that is feasible (will work). After you have made your decision, *lightly* fashion your square as shown in illustration 9-2.

9-1 Face fits within a square but space above and below is needed for other parts

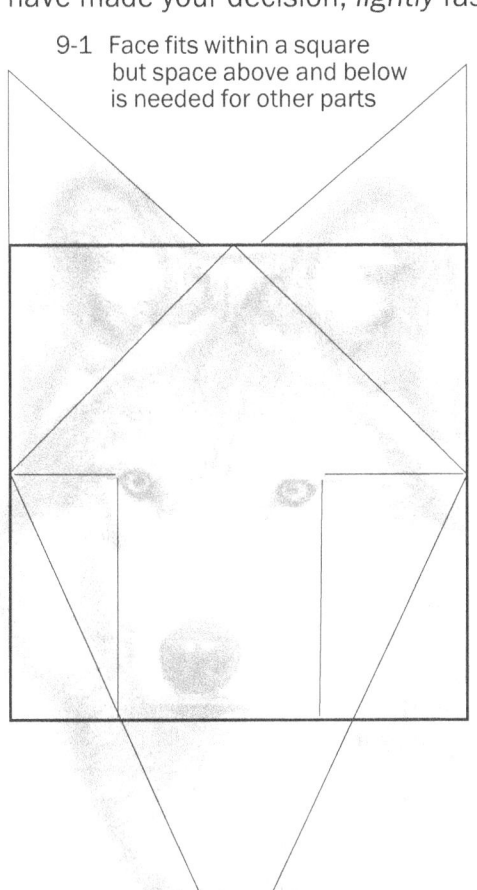

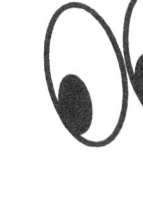

TIP *Lightly* form your square. Its lines and those to follow will create a basic format which will be erased eventually.

9-2 Draw a square with respect to the other parts to come

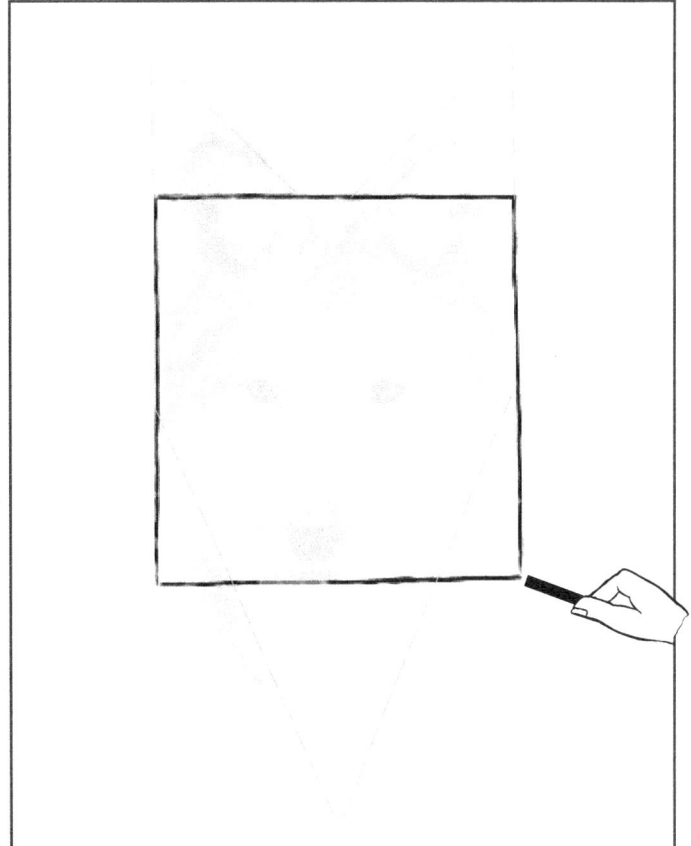

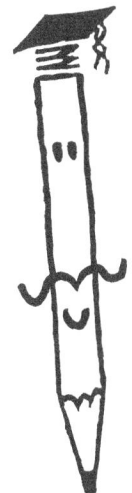

PLAN AHEAD.
Choose your square's size and placement wisely.

Illustration 9-3 indicates that the 3 points of the *triangle* in the *arrowhead* are located *midway* on the top and the two sides of the square. As for the *shaft,* the *left* edge is vertically aligned between the outer edge of the eye (on our left) at a point about *half way* from the left side of the square to the middle, along the bottom (a). The *right* edge of the *shaft* is vertically aligned with the other eye along the bottom of the square at roughly *one third* the distance from the *middle* to the *right side* (b). Based on these coordinates, find the reference points proportionally on your square, and mark the locations with dots. Then, lightly connect your dots with lines to form the arrow (9-4).

9-3 The triangle in forehead plus the
    rectangle surrounding eyes, nose
    and mouth form an uneven arrow

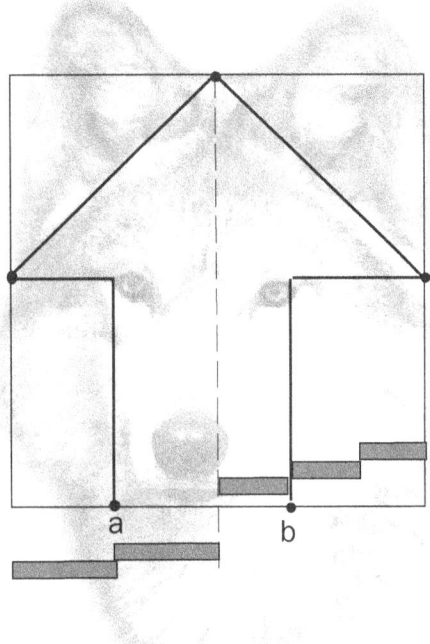

a   b

9-4 Lightly draw uneven shaped arrow
    proportionally within your square

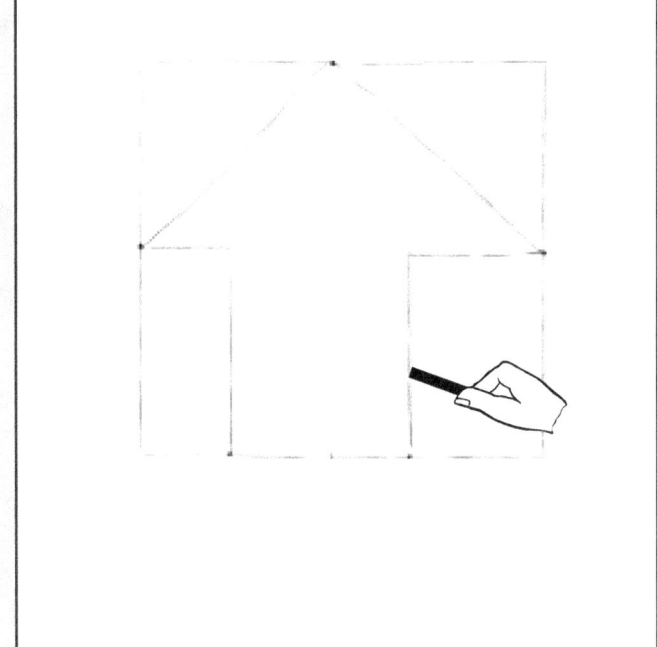

TIP *Do not use a ruler.* Drawing is meant to be achieved with visual estimates and freehand lines.

As shown in illustration 9-5, the eye sockets of the wolf are located inside the area of the arrow shaft, just below the arrowhead. The *length* of each socket appears to be roughly one fourth the *horizontal* distance of *the arrow shaft*. The *height* of each socket seems to be about *half* that span. Next, we see that the *muzzle* side, *on our left*, vertically aligns approximately with the midpoint of the respective eye. The *muzzle* side *on our right nearly* reaches the corresponding edge of the arrow shaft. Using these observations, lightly draw two rectangles, in scale, to establish the position for the eye spaces on *your* wolf. Then lightly place two short vertical lines, in proportion, for the two sides of the muzzle (9-6) .

9-5 Eyes locate along arrowshaft, but left side of mouth lines up with middle of eye, while right side of mouth lines up with edge of eye

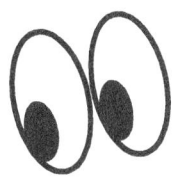

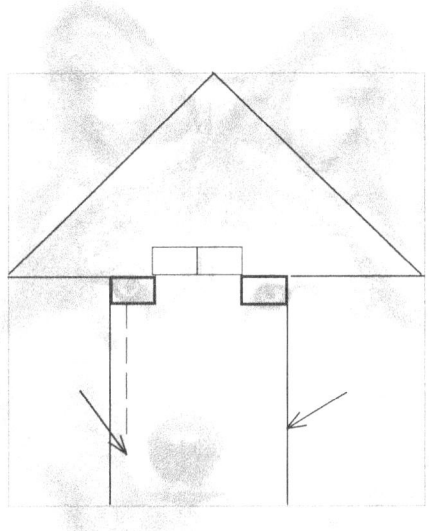

9-6 Lightly locate eye positions with two rectangles and align sides of mouth

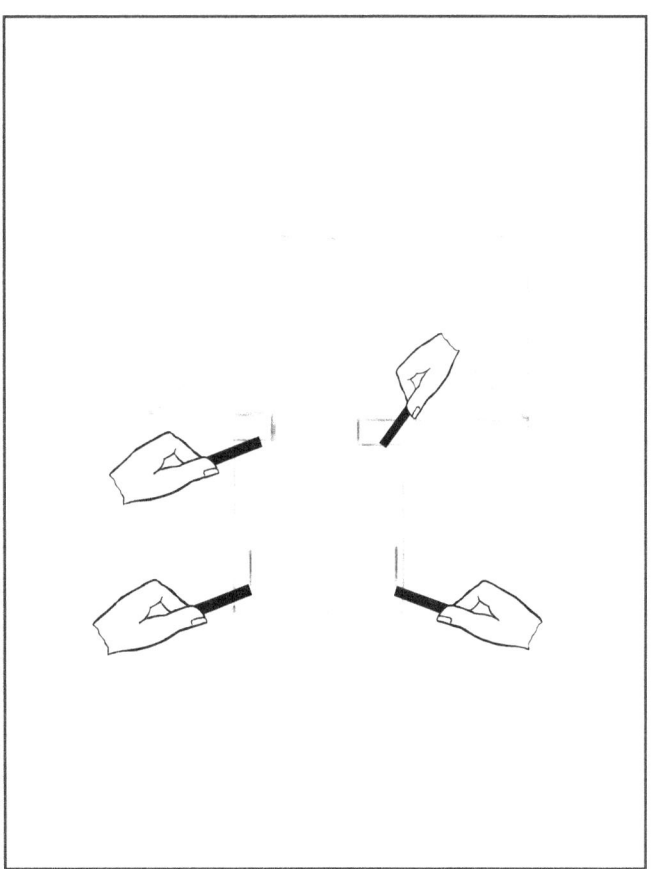

STEP 4 Illustration 9-7 shows us something very odd. Observe that the nose is situated slightly above the base of the arrow shaft. Its overall proportion is nearly a square, with a height which appears to be a little less than one third of the arrow shaft's height. That's not the strange part, though. The odd thing is that the end of the nose (on our left) is nearly vertically aligned flush (even) with the inside edge of the corresponding eye. However, the other side of the nose (on our right) vertically aligns to the left of that respective eye at a distance roughly equivalent to *half* the length of the eye. That means the nose is *not centered* between the eyes. How is this possible? The reason is that the wolf is slightly to the left of our line of sight. Since it is at an angle to us, we can see more of the mane and muzzle planes on one side than the other. With these factors in mind, draw a square in a size and position to fit the nose proportionally on your drawing (9-8)

9-7 Nose scale is nearly a square
Height less than 1/3 arrow shaft

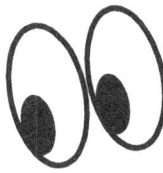

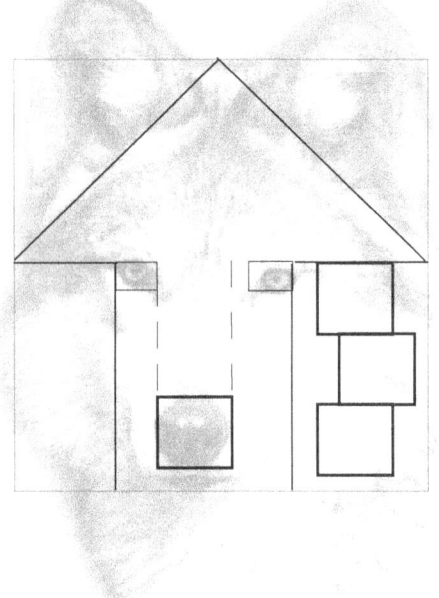

TIP We know that a nose is normally centered between the eyes. Because of that, there is an almost irresistible temptation to draw it that way, even though, in the present view, the wolf's nose is offset to the left. This is why the arrow and shaft do not line up symmetrically. Trust what you see, rather than what you *think* you *should* be seeing.

9-8 Lightly draw a proportional rectangle in position to locate nose

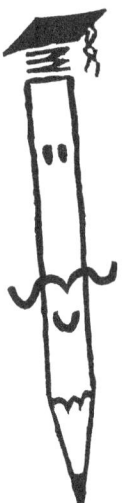

What we expect to see and what is really in our vision can be two different things. The key is to stay alert.

The base lines for the curves in the mane and neck apparently extend from the two side points of the arrow we found in the figure. They meet at a point centered below the square at a distance that is roughly the same as the span from the eyes to the mouth (9-9). Center a dot below your square proportionally, then connect the respective points with two lines (9-10).

9-9 Mane bottom is centered below the square at a distance
equal to half the height of the square, and from there, lines
diverge to arrow corners to form base lines for curves

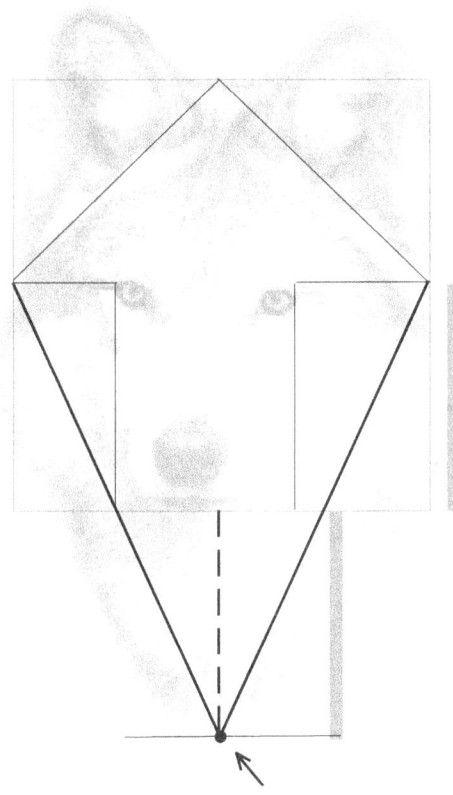

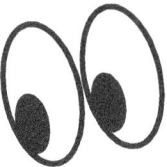

9-10 Locate mane bottom point to scale and
draw lines to respective positions shown

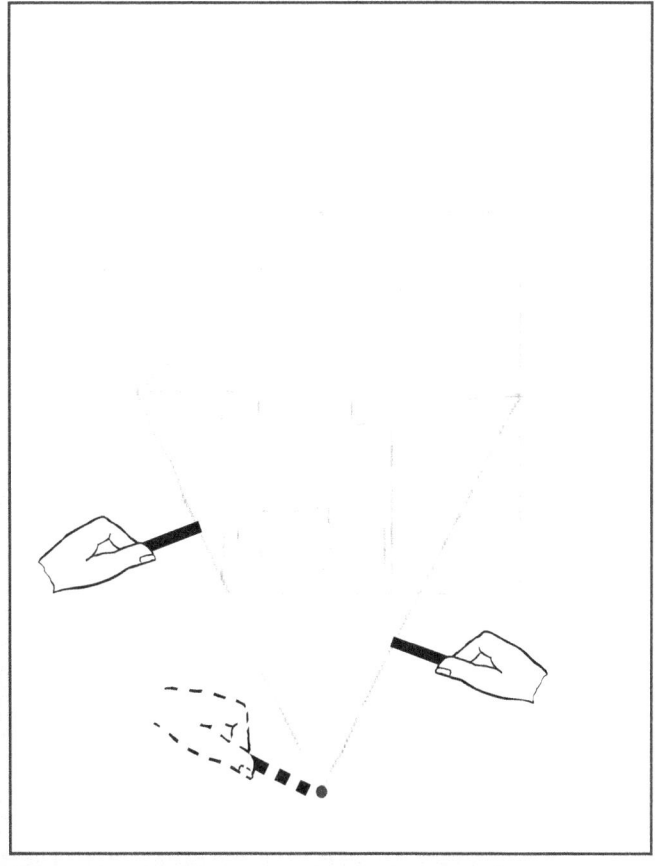

STEP 6 In illustration 9-11, we see that the ears extend above the sides of the square to a pair of reference points (a & (b). The distance appears to be somewhat less than *half* the height of the square. Two other reference points (c & d), horizontally diverge (separate in opposite directions) along the top of the square, a little past center. Estimate these coordinates to scale on your drawing and mark them with dots. Then lightly connect the dots with lines (9-12).

9-11 Streamlined ear points diverge laterally
      past center on square top & extend above
      less than half distance of square

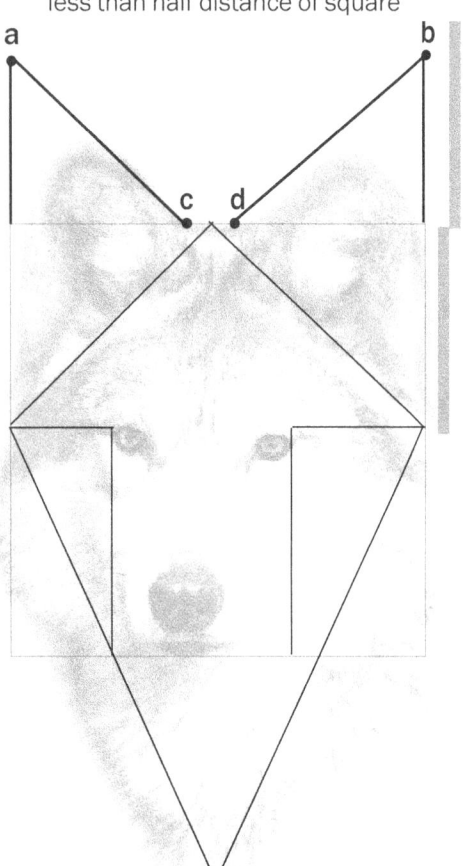
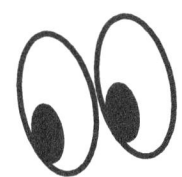

9-12 Find respective reference points
      in scale and connect with light lines

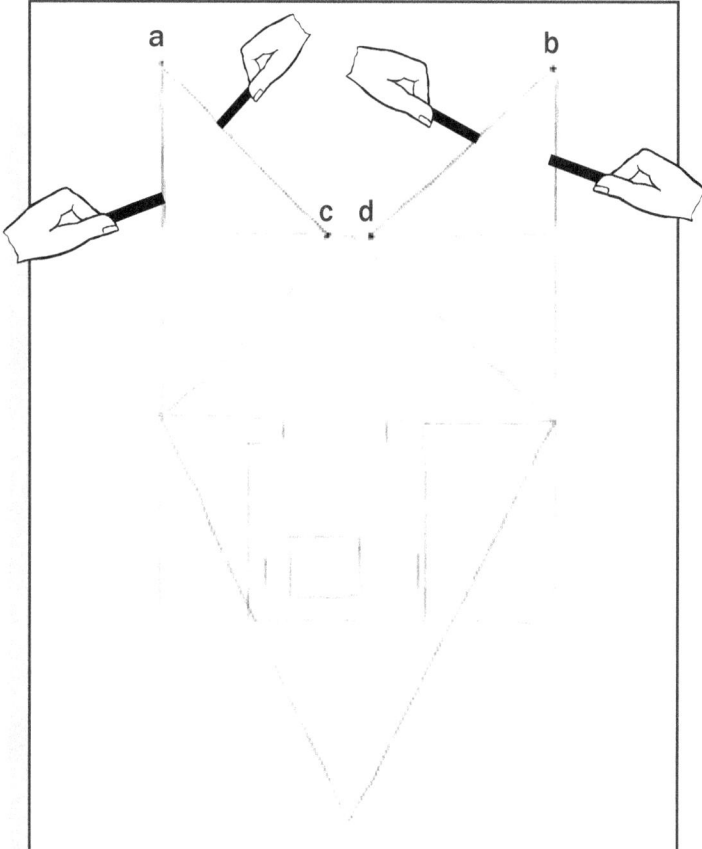

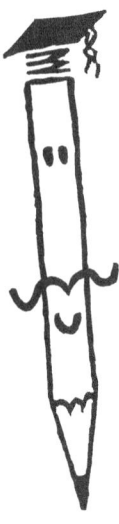

So far, you have been drawing straight lines which have now come together to produce a preliminary foundation. Before advancing to the next stage, check for accuracy by comparing your overall results to the format in illustration 9-12.

STAGE 2 - CURVES

STEP 1 While referring to illustration 9-13, lightly draw curves to form the ears and the right side of the mane to scale on your foundation. Example 9-14 demonstrates. I opted for two curves in each area during this phase. You can choose the sequence and number of curves you prefer to use. While my curves are shown dark to make them easier to see, your curves should be much lighter.

TIP Using more curves doesn't mean you are less skilled. Adapt according to each situation. Apply as many, or as few as you need to form shapes accurately.

9-13 Streamlines serve as guide lines to help see position and size of ears and mane curves

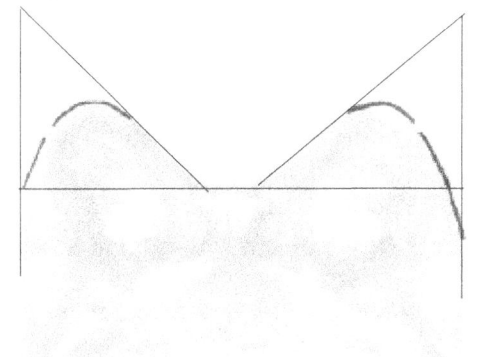

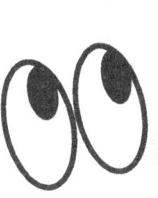

9-14 Lightly draw ear tops and mane with several smaller curves using streamlines for reference

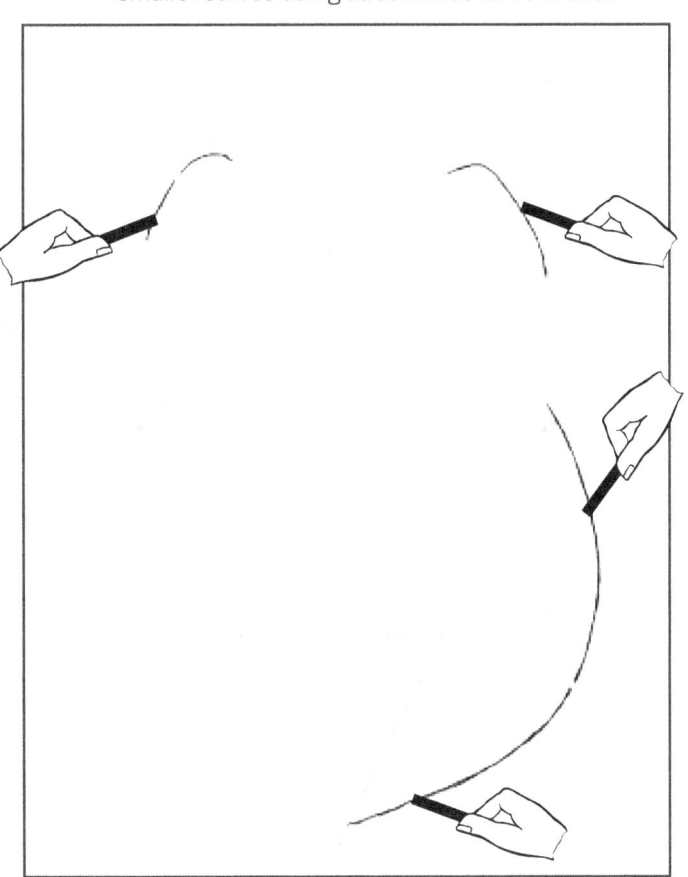

Take your time.
There's no rush.

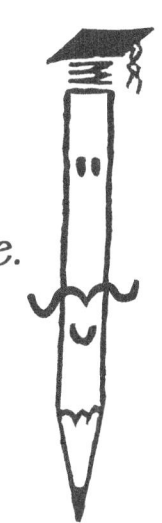

STEP 2 Illustration 9-15 shows us that each of the four curves forming the nose is a little different in size, shape and position. Lightly draw your curves one at time, proportionally. Then do the same to form the curves for the left side of the mane (9-16). Again, my curves are shown dark to make them more visible. Your curves should be much lighter.

TIP Notice the triangular reverse shapes created by the straight lines and curves in the nose rectangle. The arrow points to one of these shapes. Use it and the others as references to help you form your curves accurately.

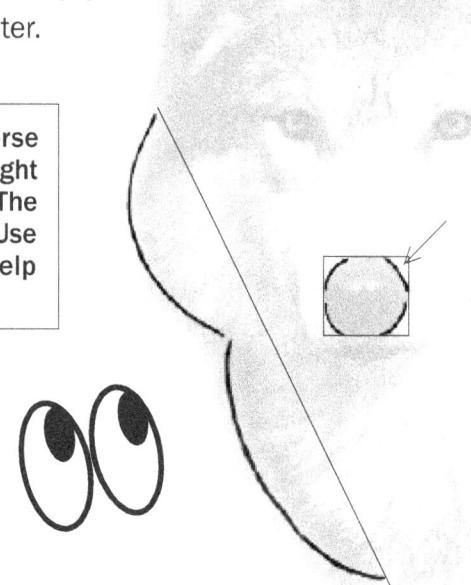

9-16   Lightly form nose and mane curves to scale

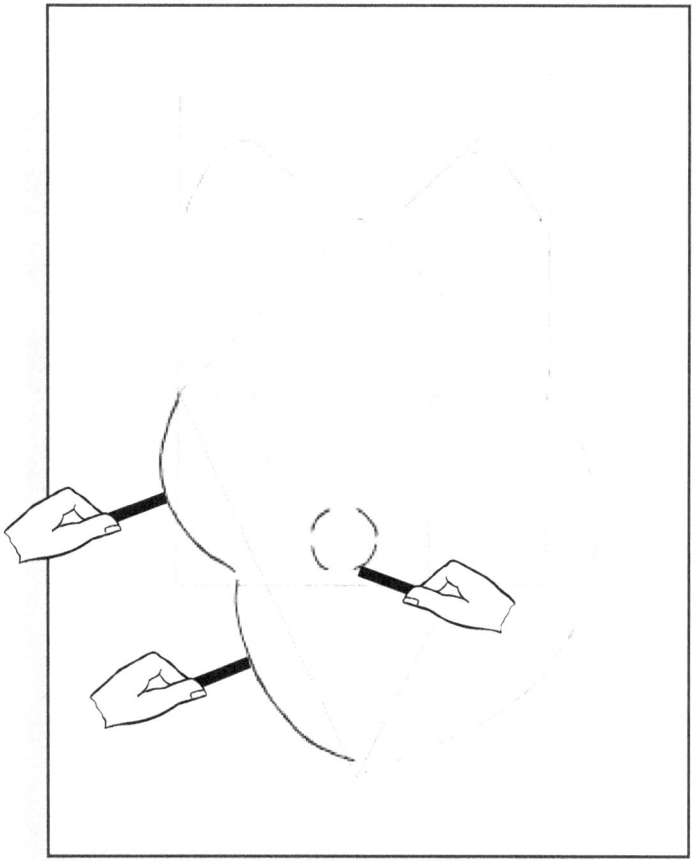

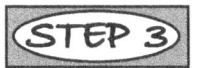

STEP 3 In illustration 9-17, we can see the curves that form the upper shape of the eye sockets. Notice that they exceed the border of the basic box which locates the general position of the sockets. Also, observe the angles and dissimilarity between one set of curves and the other. They are not mirror images. One socket shape is quite different from the other. The same holds true for the form of the mouth. The left curve is not the same as the right curve. Using these observations, lightly draw the curves respectively and in scale to fit your drawing (9-18).

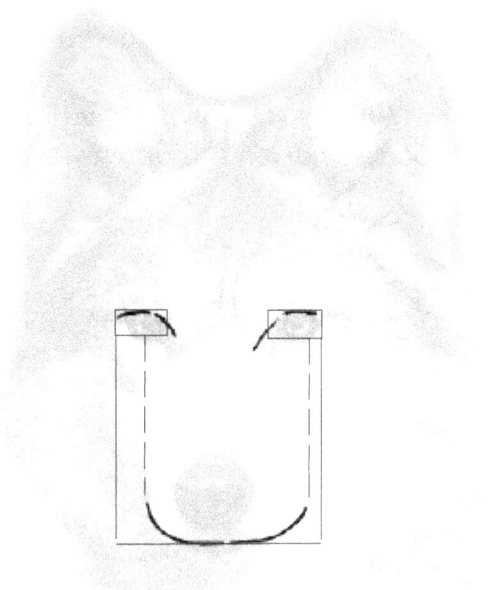

9-17 Streamlines serve as guide lines to help see position and size of upper eyelid and mouth

TIP You may have the urge to draw eyes, noses and mouths symmetrically, but they are actually asymmetrical. This applies to most living things. In fact, you may be interested to know, the left side of your facial features are a little different from your right side. Keep this in mind and look for subtle details. In turn, you will tend to become increasingly more observant.

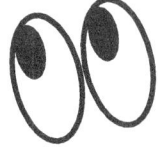

9-18 Lightly draw upper eye edges and mouth to scale

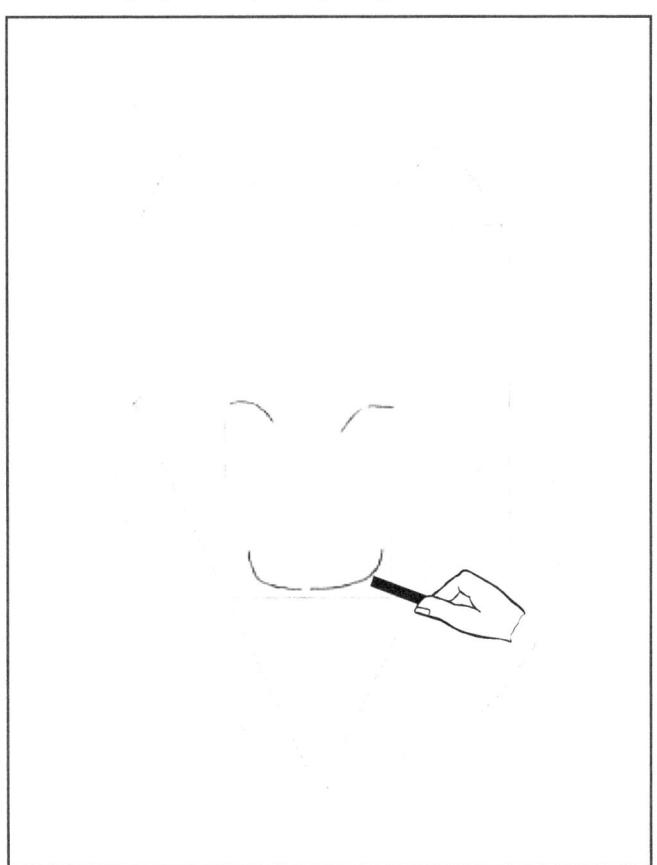

STEP 4 Illustration 9-19 indicates the curves that form the eyebrows as well as the lower shape of the eye sockets. As you can tell, the left set is a little different from the right. Lightly position and replicate these respective curves in your drawing (9-20).

TIP Draw each curve carefully. Small curves are just as important as larger curves. They all contribute equally to the whole.

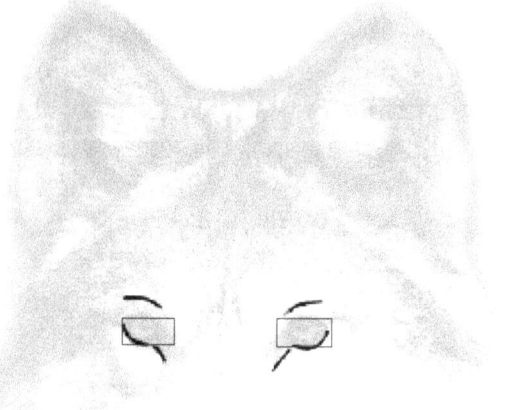

9-19 Streamlines serve as guide lines to help see position and size of eye lid and eye brow curves

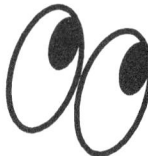

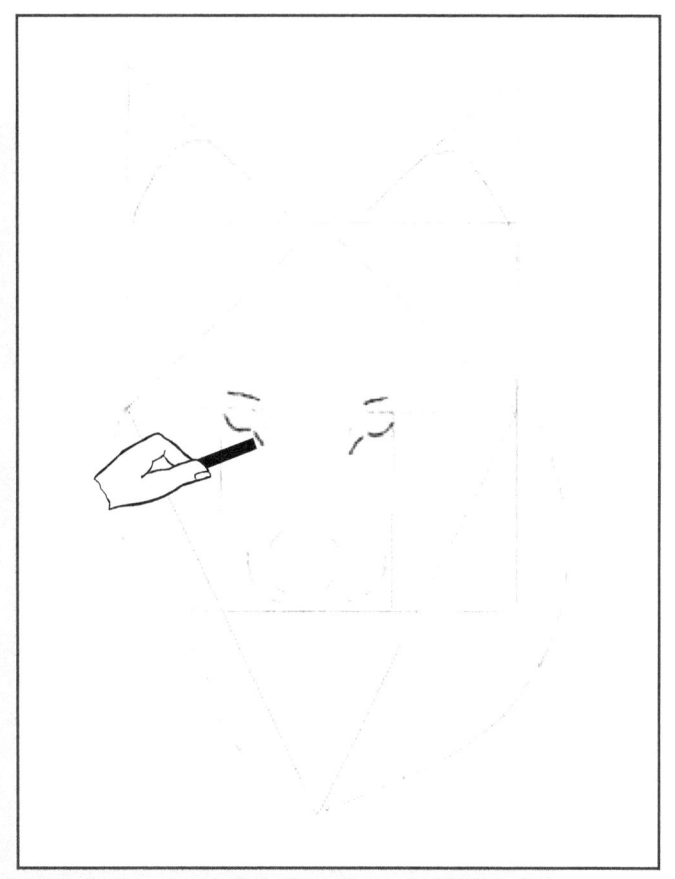

9-20 Lightly draw lower eye curves and eyebrows proportionally

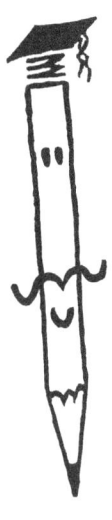

Can you see the image of the wolf developing?

In illustration 9-21 we observe that the eyes do not appear to be circular. They are oval shaped. Also, notice that they are not centered within the boxes that locate the eye sockets. Instead, they are slightly to the left, indicating the wolf is not looking directly forward. Next, let's look at the curves forming the wrinkles on the forehead above the bridge of the nose. Obviously, they are not mirror images. One curve is shorter than the other. With these observations in mind, lightly form the respective curves for the lower part of the eyes and brow wrinkles to scale and position on your drawing (9-22).

TIP Keep reminding yourself that you are drawing shapes made with curves which will eventually resemble features. By doing this, you will likely capture the unique traits more accurately.

9-21 Streamlines serve as guide lines to help see position and size of eye and wrinkle curves

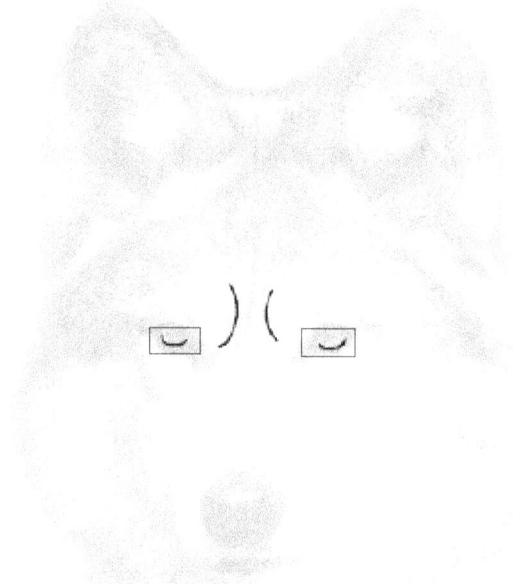

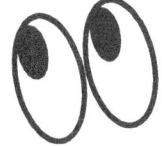

9-22 Lightly draw eye curve & forehead wrinkles to scale as indicated

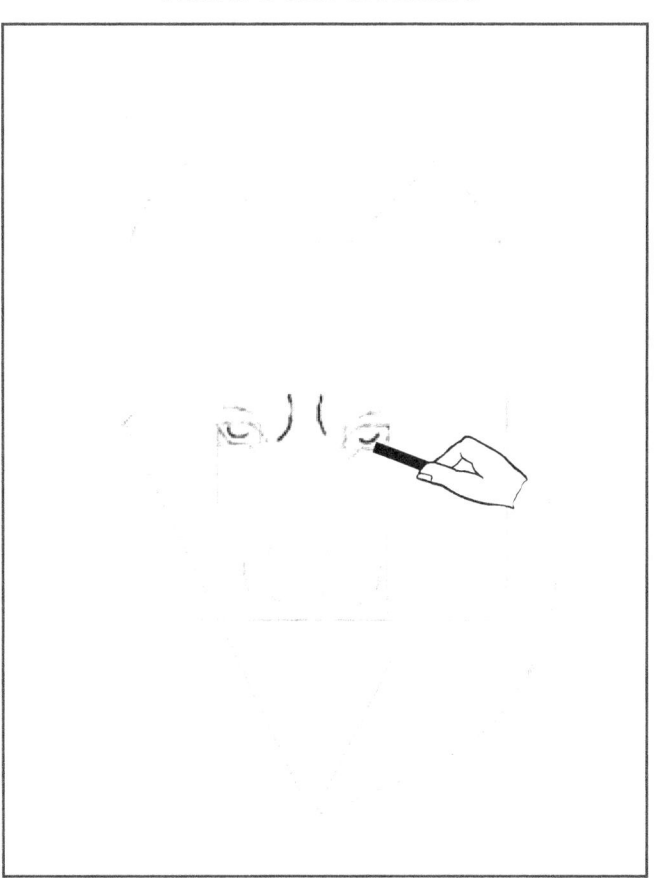

STEP 6 It's time to start focusing on the major separations in the fur. These are easy to spot because they are visible boundaries between light and dark sections. Using illustration 9-23, lightly locate and replicate the same divisions proportionally on your drawing (9-24).

TIP The light and dark patches of fur also indicate the character of the wolf. Although you do not need to be as careful with these areas as you were with the eyes, nose and mouth, you should still try to capture the distinctive markings with reasonable accuracy.

9-23 Streamlines serve as guide lines to help see position and size of fur divisions

9-24 Lightly draw fur divisions to scale as shown

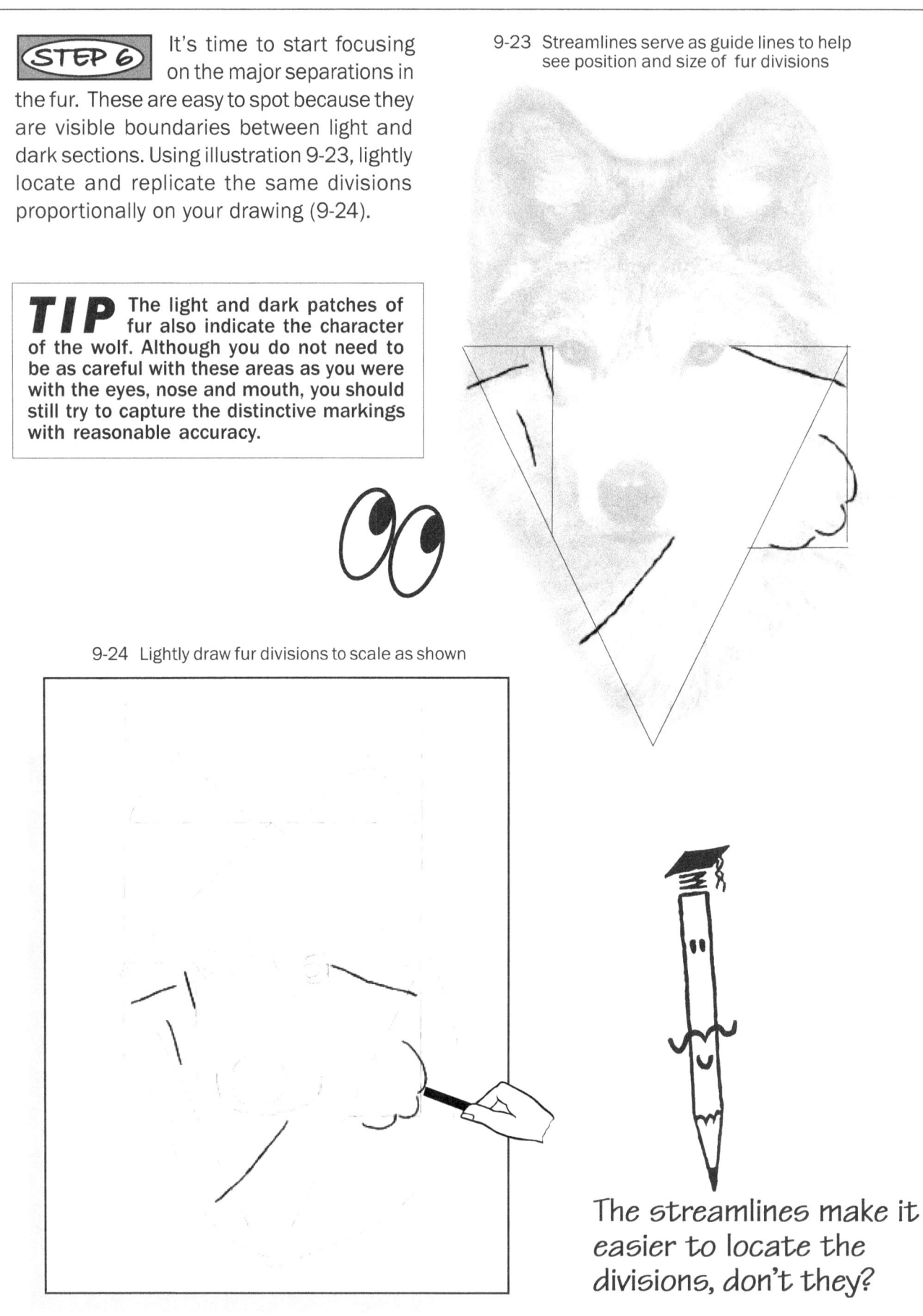

The streamlines make it easier to locate the divisions, don't they?

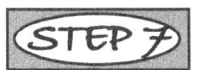 As shown in illustration 9-25, the forehead of the wolf also has light and dark markings. With the help of the triangular shape and the illustration, find these on your drawing and lightly include them proportionally (9-26).

9-25 Streamlines serve as guide lines to help see position and size of fur divisions on forehead

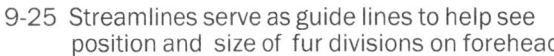

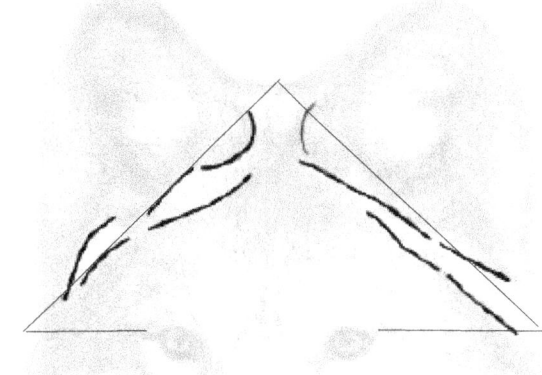

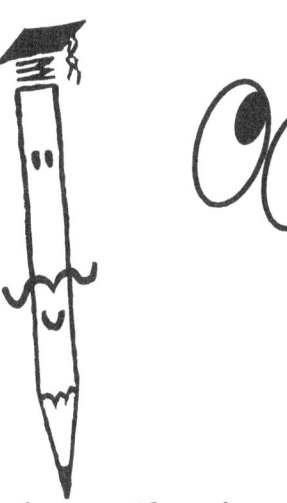

Hang in there. Fur divisons are also just shapes.

9-26 Lightly draw indicated fur divisions proportionally

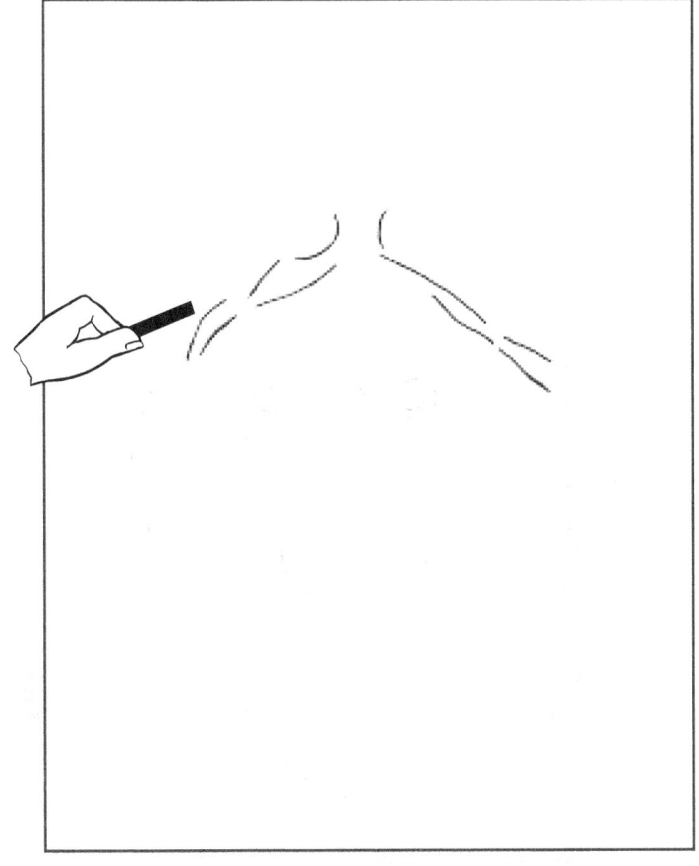

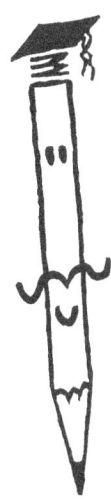

Since there are a lot of nifty things to draw, they take a little more time. Please be patient.

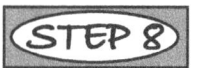 Illustration 9-27 points out the light and dark sections in the ears, as well as their sides connecting to the head. These divisions are also easier to locate with the streamlines. Find them on your drawing and lightly fashion the curves to scale as indicated by drawing example (9-28). Remember that I made my curves dark to make them more visible. Your curves should be much lighter than shown.

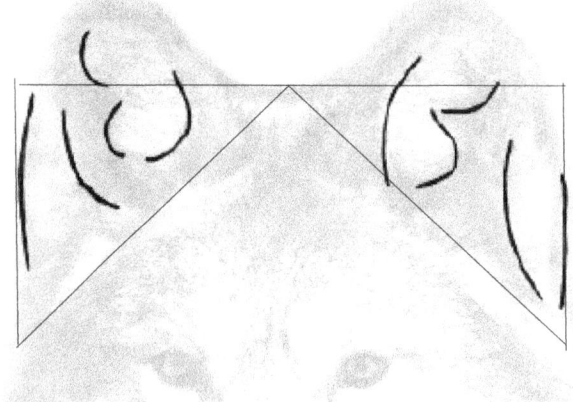

9-27 Streamlines serve as guide lines to help see position and size of fur curve divisions in ears

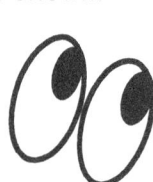

TIP Mimicking fur with dark, hard lines is much more difficult to change into the look of soft uneven edges.

9-28 Lightly form curve divisions proportionally in ears

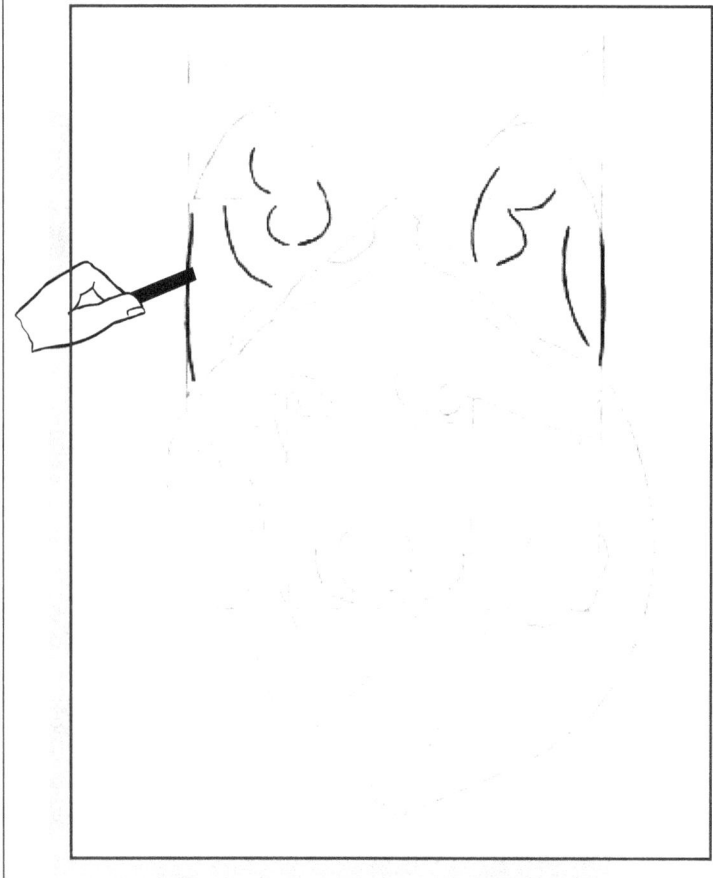

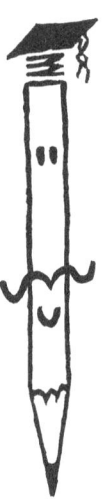

Advance slowly. Enjoy the drawing process. The doing is just as rewarding as the end result.

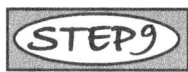 **STEP 9**

There are also markings in the neck area (9-29). Locate these on your drawing and fashion them lightly in scale (9-30).

9-29 Streamlines serve as guide lines to help see position and size of fur divisions in neck mane

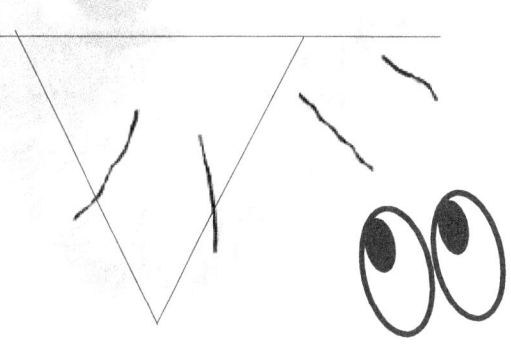

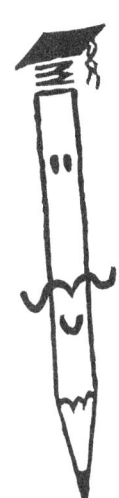

Finding divisions and drawing them one by one is quite effective, don't you think?

9-30 Lightly draw respective fur divisions to scale as shown

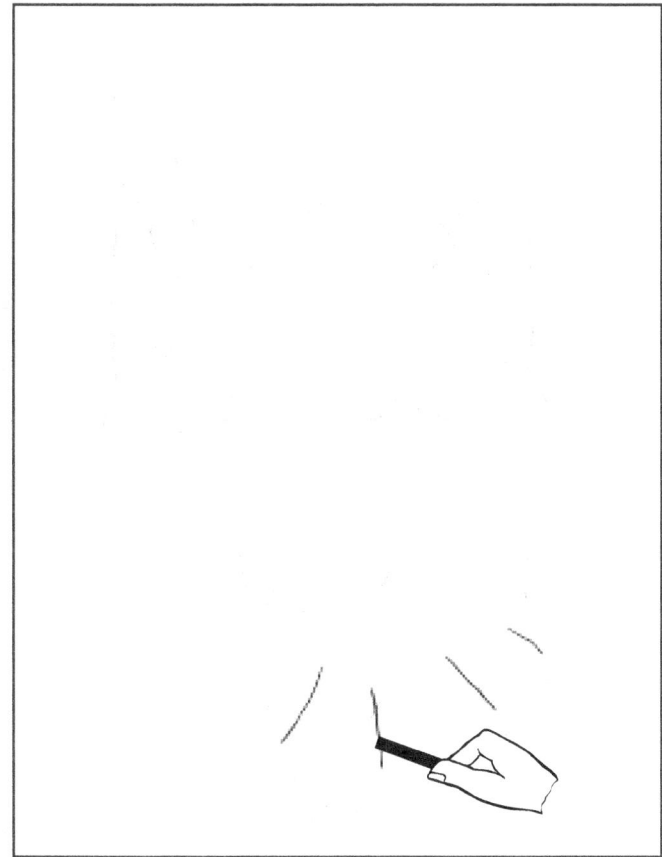

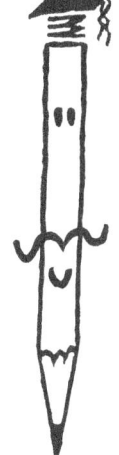

When you perform each phase carefully, you are likely to achieve a successful outcome.

STEP 10 Continuing with the mane area in the neck, locate those divisions on your drawing with the help of illustration 9-31. Lightly draw your lines one by one. At this point, you will have enough divisions to capture the basic markings of the wolf (9-32).

TIP Although, there are plenty of other light and dark values in the fur, too many lines that represent the divisions can be confusing. The rest can be applied during the tone and texture phase.

9-31 Streamlines serve as guide lines to help see size and position of more fur divisions in neck mane

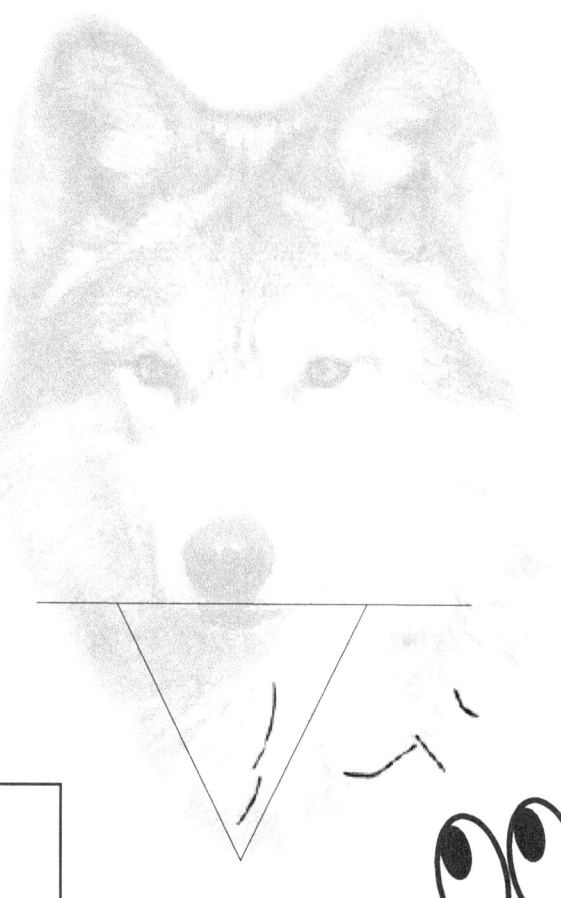

9-32 Lightly draw respective fur divisions to scale as shown

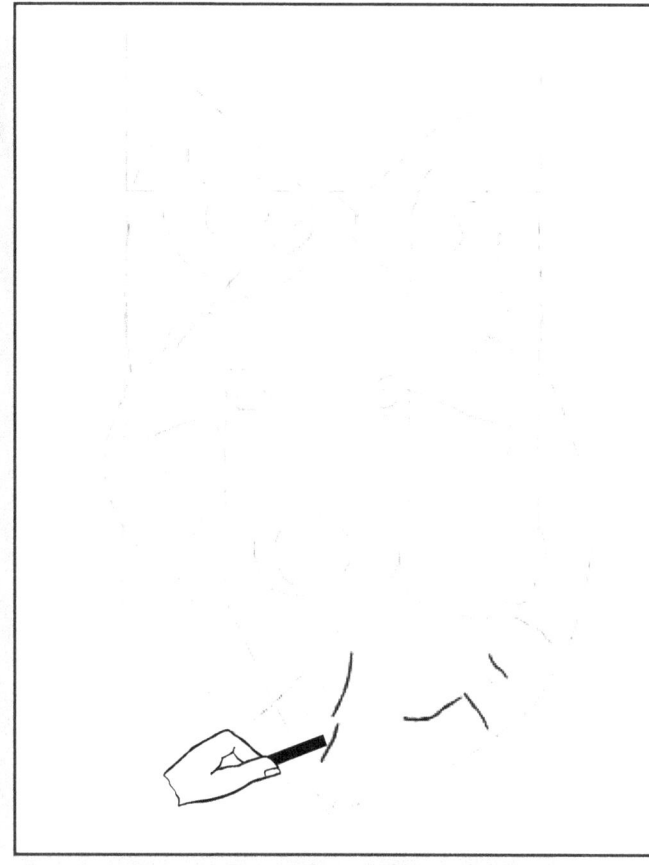

With practice, you will know when there are just the right amount of lines you can follow without getting lost in them.

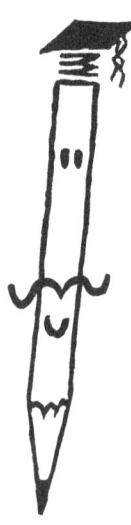

TIME FOR A PROGRESS CHECK

By now, your work has undergone many steps and procedures. Since drawing is based on visual estimates, it helps to verify your results by applying the 7 structural components. If you recall, these are reference points, proportions, reverse space, angles, curves, straight lines and alignments. Speaking of alignments, they go hand in hand with reference points, and generally just two are required. What you may not know, however, is that you can also line up more than two reference points. Take a look at model 9-33, alignment (a). I found it by lining up the bottom of the nose at center, through the eye, and up to a division in the corresponding ear. Compare that alignment in drawing 9-34. The features align closely similar, so accuracy is verified, wouldn't you agree? Next, as alignment (b) indicates, I also visualized a lineup in the model along the right side of the nose, to the left side of the other eye and continued to a division in that corresponding ear. When I did the same procedure in the drawing, I discovered the eye needs to be moved a little to the right. See how easy it is to notice dissimilarities with the aid of some random visualized alignments?

9-33 Visualized alignments in model
show where various points line up

9-34 Visualized alignment (b) comparison in
drawing shows eye should move to right

a

b

a

b

OK. It's your turn. Give your work a once
over before advancing to the next phase.

Most of your original foundation (made with straight lines), can now be erased. They are dark in illustration 9-35 to make them easy for you to see. When you have finished erasing your lines, except the small horizontal portion centered between the ears, your drawing should resemble example 9-36.

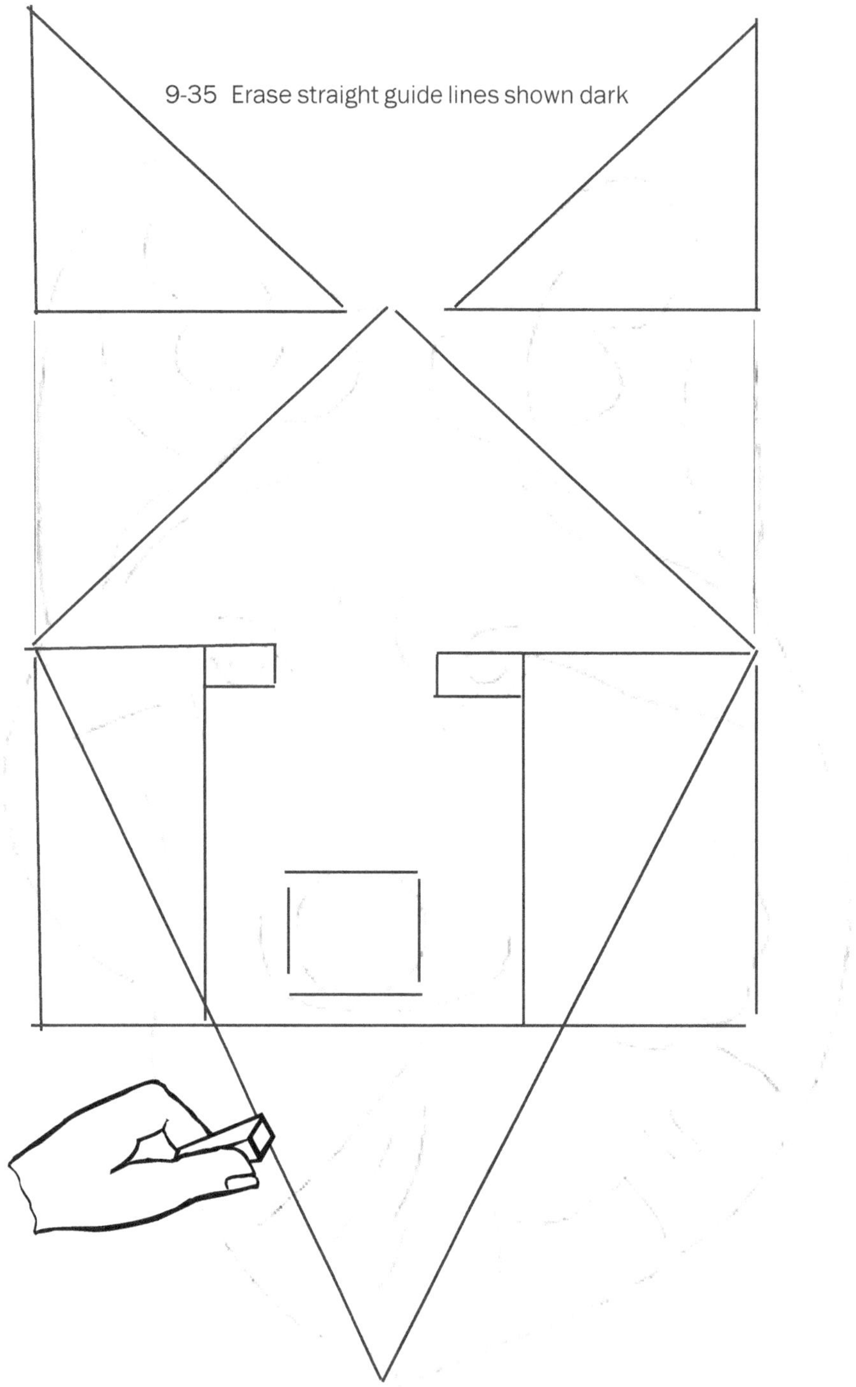

9-35 Erase straight guide lines shown dark

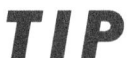

TIP You do not need to erase your straight lines completely. Just make them faintly visible. The toning phase will usually cover the remainder. If you have accidentally removed parts of your curves, simply draw them back in.

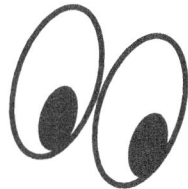

9-36 Drawing example after guide lines erased

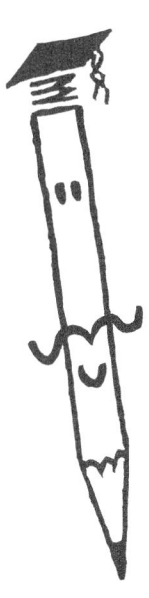

Aren't you glad you drew lightly? If you didn't, do not worry. You have options.

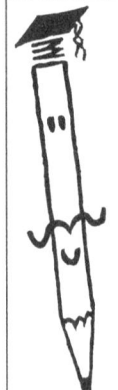

In the event your guide lines did not erase well, or you are not satisfied with where your figure is located on your paper, I have good news. You can transfer your drawing to a new sheet.

TRANSFER METHOD

DIRECTIONS: Affix your drawing *backwards* to a window with adhesive tape. *Be sure the side you drew FACES THE GLASS.* During daylight, you will be able to see a reverse image of the wolf. Applying the underhand method, tone your lines, preferrably using a *soft* lead pencil as shown in illustration (9-37). Next, tape a fresh sheet of paper on a board or table. Position your drawing (*now face up*) to the desired location on top of your new paper. Fasten it with two strips of adhesive tape along the upper portion. Then trace your drawing with dash lines (9-38). A colored pencil or a colored pen is recommended. This will enable you to see which lines have transferred and which ones are still needed. From time to time, lift your upper sheet and verify your progress (9-39). That way, you will be able to see how much pressure is too much and how much is just right. When you have finished, carefully remove your tape strips. Your duplicate drawing will appear similar to example 9-40. Although my marks are shown dark to help make them more visible, yours should be much lighter.

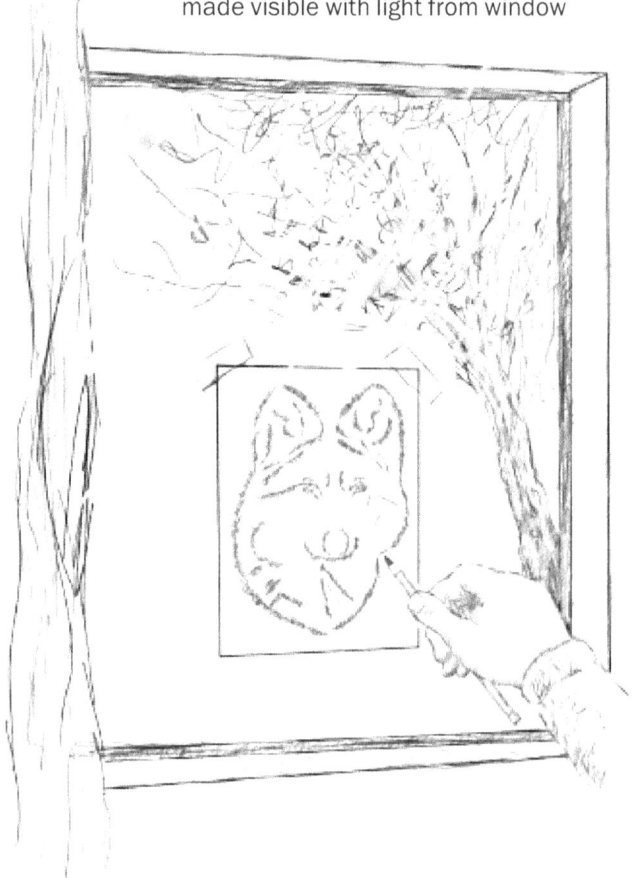

9-37 Add tone to back of your drawing made visible with light from window

---

TIP If you have run out of daylight and you happen to have a glass door between one room and another, you can attach your drawing to the glass door. Then, turn the light on in the room facing you.

9-38 Position & tape your drawing over another sheet and trace with dash lines

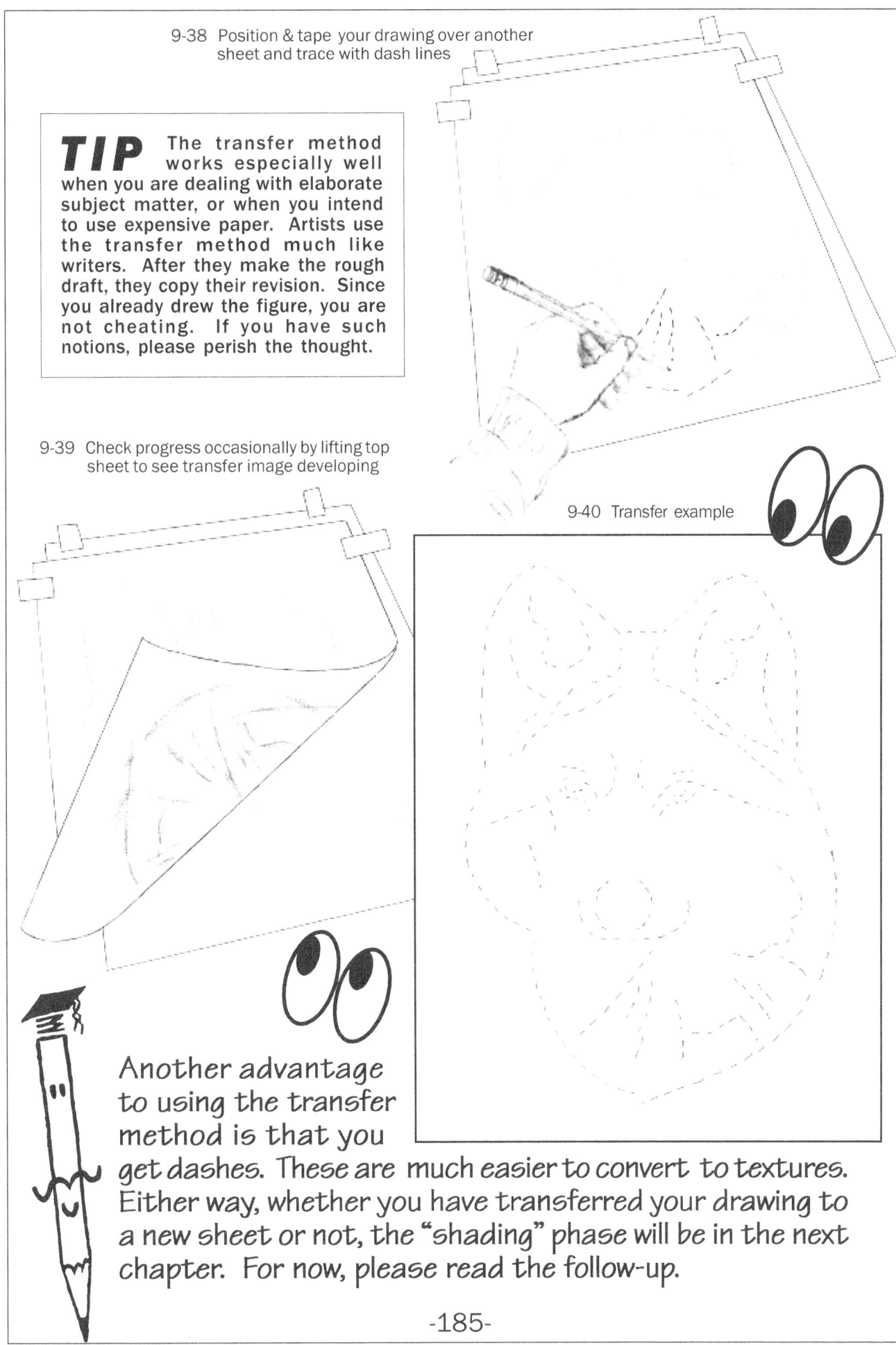

TIP The transfer method works especially well when you are dealing with elaborate subject matter, or when you intend to use expensive paper. Artists use the transfer method much like writers. After they make the rough draft, they copy their revision. Since you already drew the figure, you are not cheating. If you have such notions, please perish the thought.

9-39 Check progress occasionally by lifting top sheet to see transfer image developing

9-40 Transfer example

Another advantage to using the transfer method is that you get dashes. These are much easier to convert to textures. Either way, whether you have transferred your drawing to a new sheet or not, the "shading" phase will be in the next chapter. For now, please read the follow-up.

Chapter 9
FOLLOW-UP

Generally speaking, the wolf is like any other subject matter made of shapes, wouldn't you agree? Because of this, you can reduce the figure to simple geometric forms, then streamline it using straight lines, followed by curves.

During these early stages, it's important to see distinguishing features (like the eyes, nose and mouth) also as just shapes. When you observe this way, you are more likely to draw what is really there, not what you think should be there. In other words, the process enables you to be more objective and therefore able to spot distinctive characteristics. As a result, you are apt to capture an accurate likeness in outline and contour format.

More often than not, this is just the initial phase. If something should go wrong, you can always transfer your work to a fresh sheet of paper, instead of starting over. The advantage is that all your "trial and error roughs" can be done before the refined version is transferred to a new sheet.

The "second chance" method, as I like to call it, is especially handy when working with intricate subject matter and when erasing is not practical. For instance, perhaps the type of paper being used is too fragile, or maybe you will eventually want to switch to an indelible (non erasable) medium, such as ink. Then, with your choice of drawing implement, other traits such as fur textures can be added. The task may sound challenging, but it's actually quite easy, when you learn some basic techniques and ways to apply them.

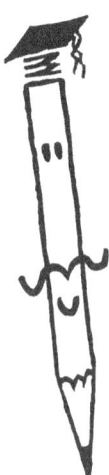

After a break, get ready to tone and texture your drawing of the wolf. We will continue using pencil.

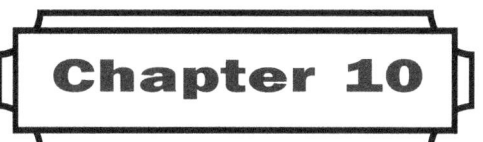

Chapter 10

FROM THIS

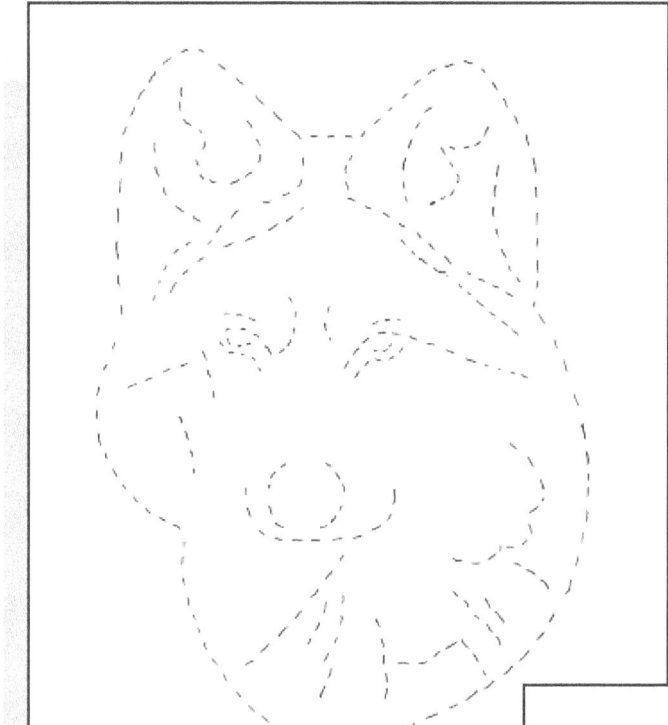

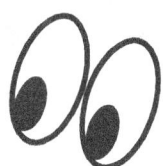

TO THIS

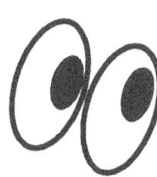

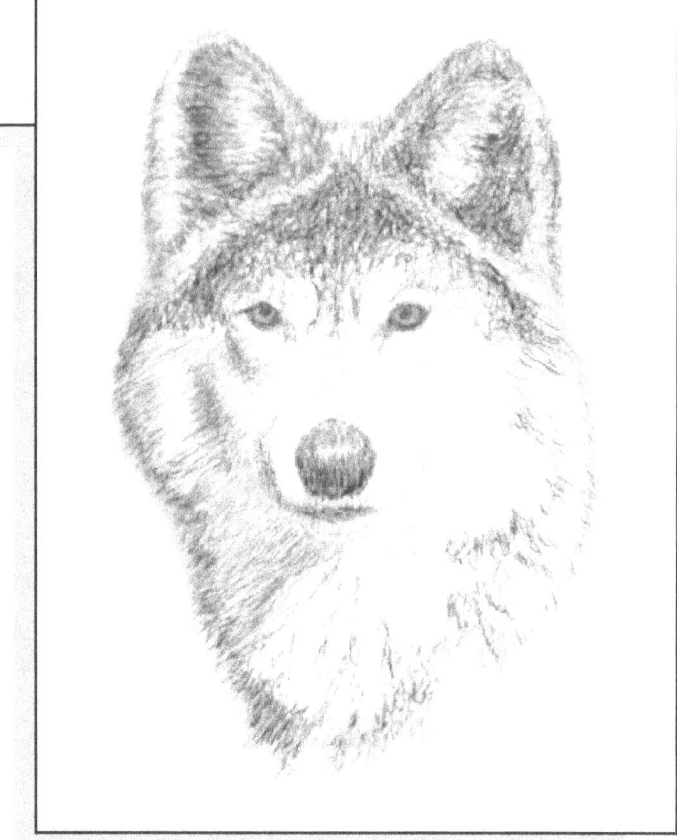

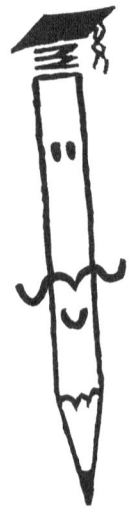

Where shall we start? I suggest the eyes.

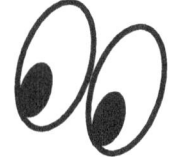

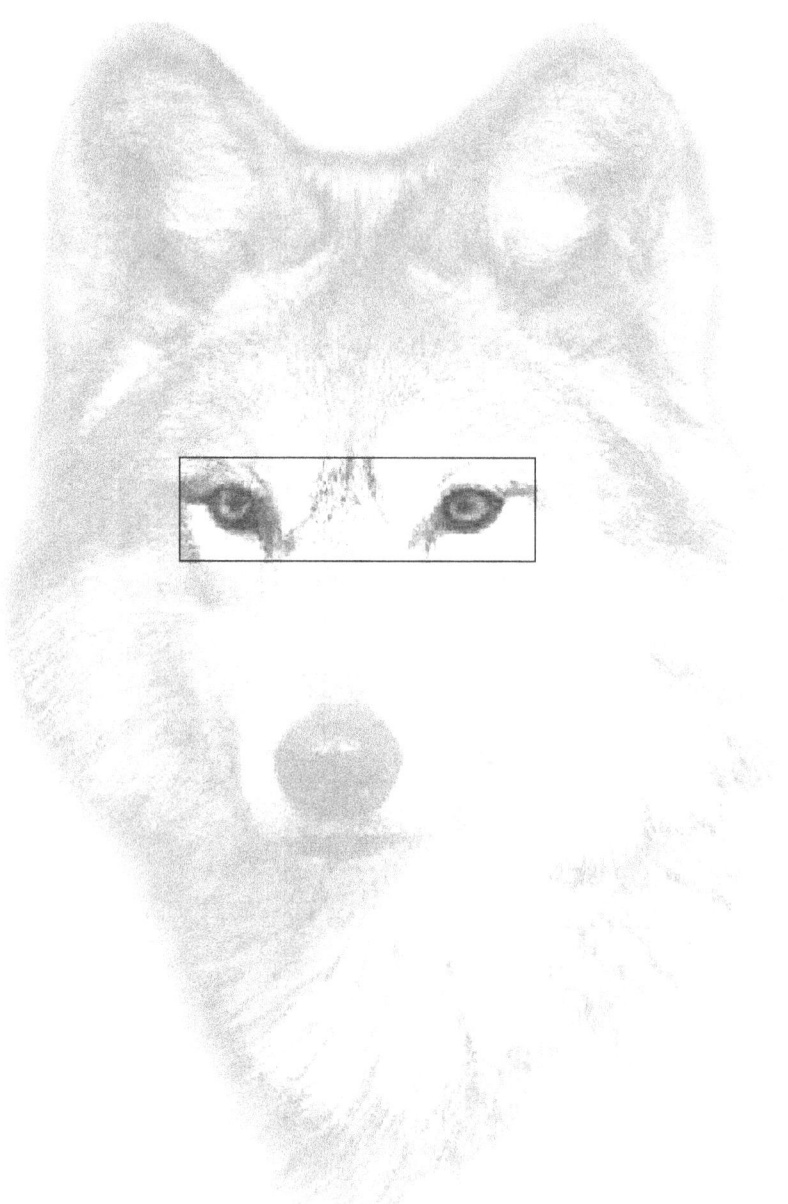

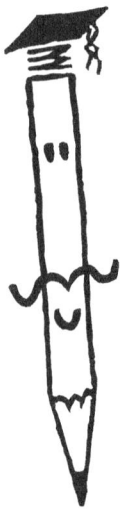

Why begin with the eyes? One reason is that they are set deep, so it's easier to render them from inside out. Besides, the eyes are captivating, don't you think? They reveal the intense gaze of the animal and help set the mood of the picture.

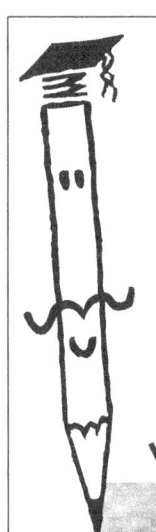

Before we tone and texture the eyes and nearby region, please study the following illustration. I have zoomed in to show you some interesting things.

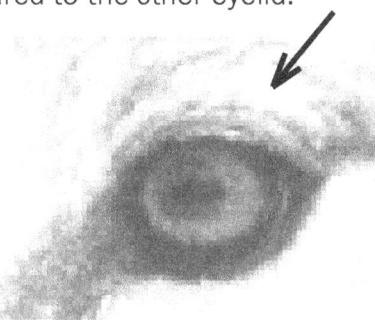

A. Look closely and carefully. As you can tell, the eyelid on your left appears to be a little darker and more textured, compared to the other eyelid.

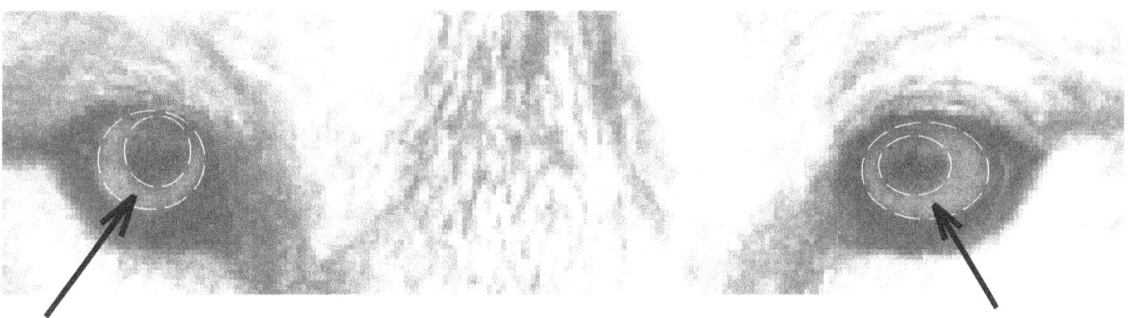

B. Notice on the left, the eye has an uneven circular dark portion surrounded by an uneven circular gray section, whereas the opposite set is elliptical. Furthermore, the dark portion is not centered within the gray shape in either eye.

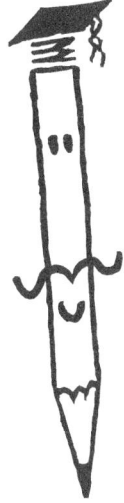

TIP In order to tone and texture the eyes accurately, look for the dissimilarities in textures, tones and shapes. If you do not search for the variations, you might give in to the urge to draw one eye and make a mirror image of it for the other eye.

Now that you realize there are several distinct differences between one eye and the other, let's handle them individually.

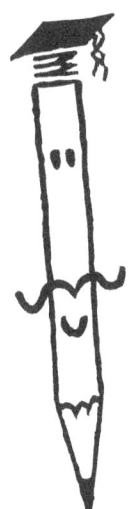

Follow along with me and learn an easy way to replicate the tones and textures of this eye in your contour drawing.

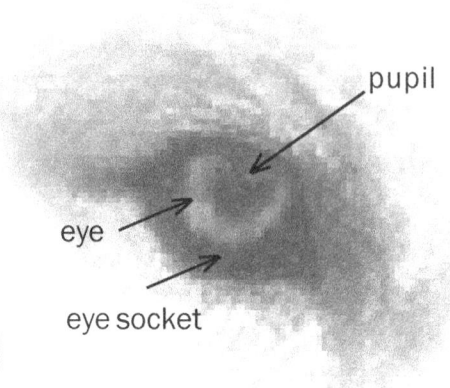

pupil

eye

eye socket

First, locate the respective eye in *your* contour drawing. If it has been transferred to a new sheet, you will have dashes, like example (A) on the next page. Either way, lightly fill your section with tone (B). In phase (C), proceed to develop the eye and nearby areas. With the model for reference, begin by forming the eye *socket* with *strokes of tone rather than by outlining,* and use the *reverse method.* That way, the *eye* shape will appear automatically and be less likely to look flat because it will have a *soft edge.* Next, tone the pupil inside the eye with a darker value (D). Chances are, this will cause the gray circular shape of the eye to change to a lighter value due to the *visual assimilation process.* To compensate, add tone until the contrast is decreased between the eye and the pupil (E). After that, include texture around the eye socket using short, uneven strokes. Be sure to decrease pressure near the outer perimeters. The procedure will enable you to gently fade your marks into the white of your paper (F). Also, soften the edge between the eye and the socket by blending, or by including a tone that is between the eye value and the eye socket value (G). Illustration 10-1 is an example of an outline/contour drawing at the conclusion of this stage, with the eye just semi-rendered. The final touches would be applied once all the features of the *entire figure* are brought to a nearly completed state. Then it's easier to effectively assess what may still be needed.

TIP A medium gray tone on a white surface will appear to be fairly dark until a darker value is placed beside it, or around it. That means, the appearance of your picture will be changing during development in more ways than you may realize. That's why it's important to check your progress as you draw. Then, do an overall evaluation to determine the effectiveness of your contrasts, tones and textures, after *all* the parts in the picture are nearly completed.

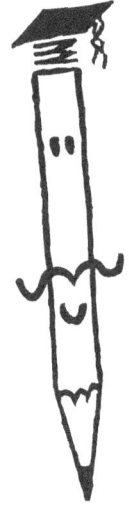

Texture and tone techniques are simple but they require care and patience. Take your time. As your drawing progresses, verify your results often by comparing them to the model.

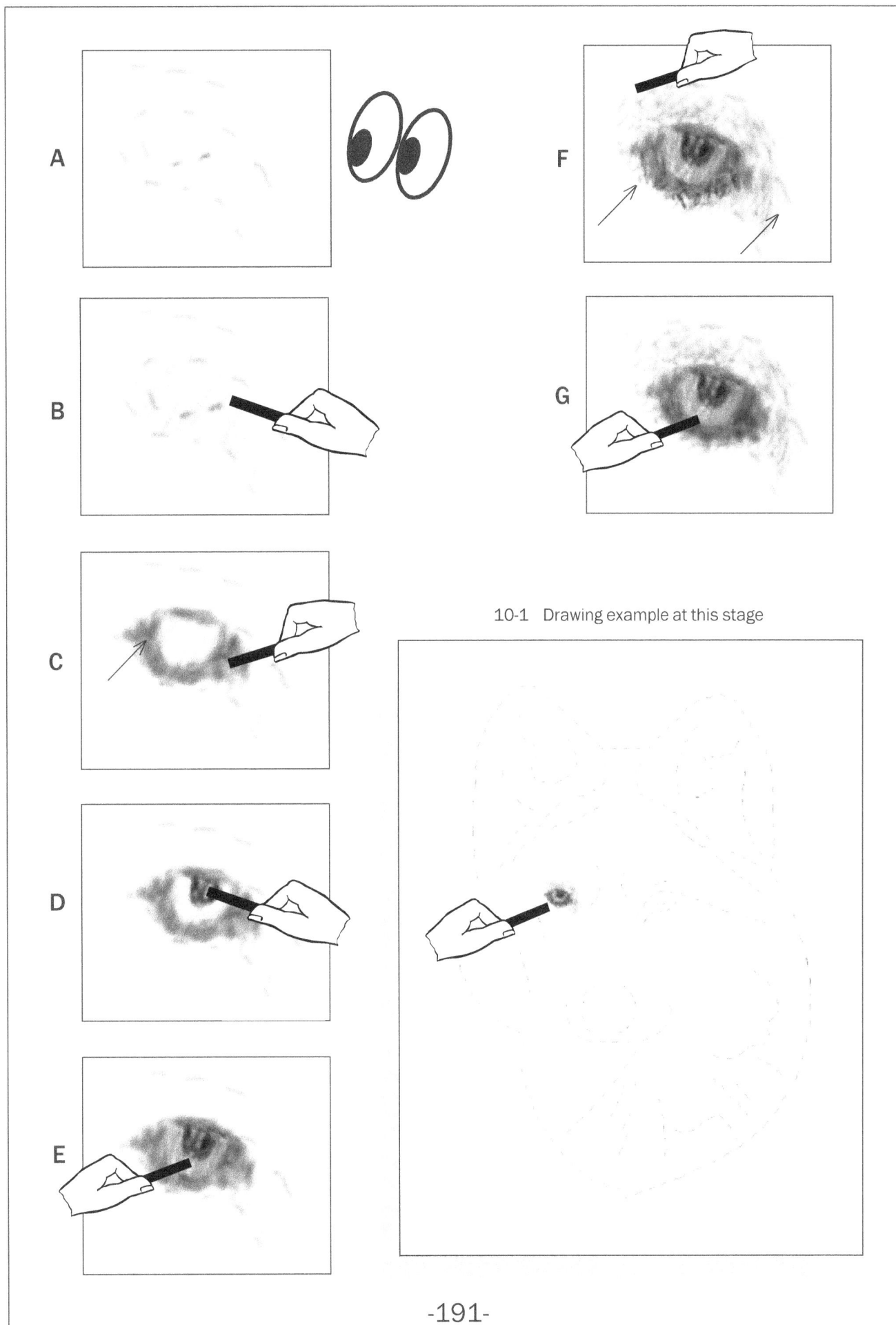

A

B

C

D

E

F

G

10-1   Drawing example at this stage

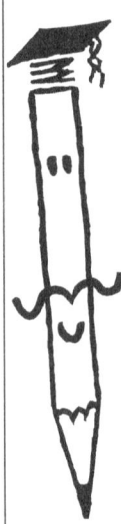

Now, I will explain the basic steps needed to shade the other eye. Sure, I could merely suggest that you repeat the process you used for the previous eye, but that would imply they match. On page 189 we saw that this is not the case.

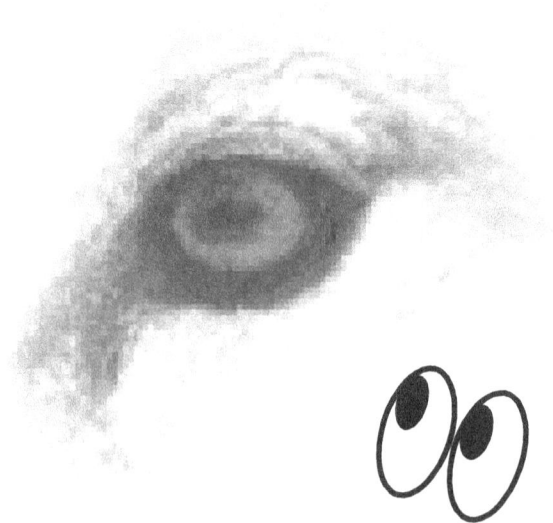

To be an effective artist, you should handle each phase as an important part of the whole, and treat the sections with equal attention. With this in mind, find the corresponding eye being addressed in your drawing (A). Lightly fill the section with tone (B). Next, while referring to the model, proceed to develop the details of the eye and nearby areas. Begin by shaping the socket and the eye using short, up and down as well as angle zigzag strokes (C). The result will be a *soft edge* (slightly uneven and fuzzy). The method brings about the desirable effect because the eye socket is deep set in shade and surrounded by fur. Plus, the eye socket gently *curves* inward from the cheek and forehead. While we are on the subject, *curvature* is also a factor when it comes to the eye itself. As you tone the pupil with a darker value (similar to the way you did the other eye), bear in mind that the eye is a ball. That means the tones *gradually fade from light to dark*. Ultimately, this means you should *not outline* the shape first, then tone. Form and tone the pupil with many small strokes, thereby darkening and shaping at the same time (D). In phase (E), do the same procedure to form and reduce the contrast between the eye and the pupil. In phase (F), include texture around the eye socket with short, random, uneven strokes. The technique will enable you to gently fade your marks into the white of your paper. At this stage, your drawing would contain two semi-shaded eyes (10-2). Later, when the entire picture has been nearly completed, it will be easier to balance the contrasts during the final phase.

TIP Be careful not to make the eye circular. It is elliptical. In the event you have outlined the eye shapes, the result will likely resemble example (G). While you may prefer the crisp appearance, please remember that linear perspective and atmospheric perspective are at work. Since our view of the wolf is not up close, we would not see clear, sharp details. If your lines turned out stiff and hard edged, flatten your putty eraser and dab gently. After lifting much of the graphite, you can make adjustments.

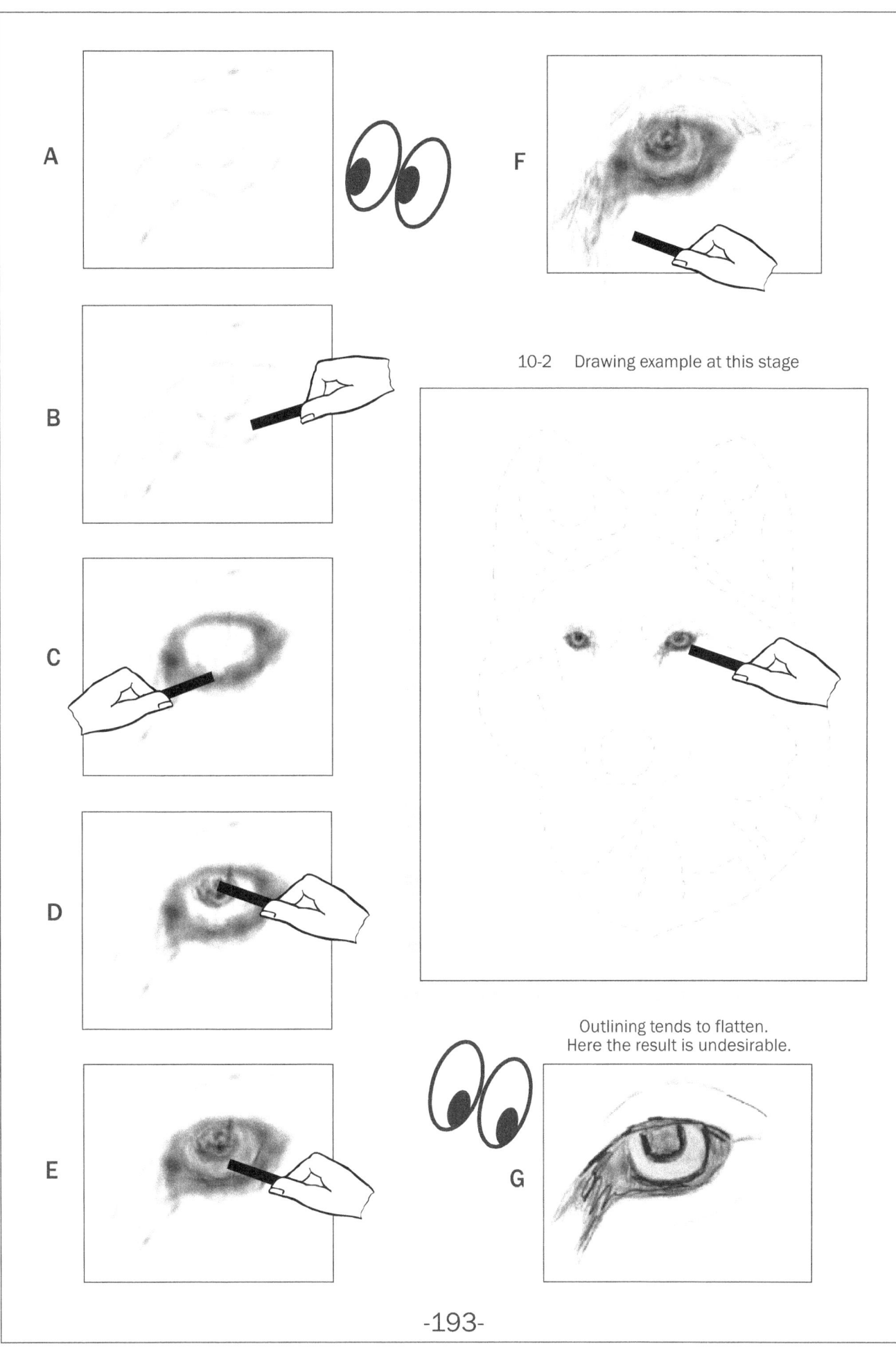

A

B

C

D

E

F

10-2   Drawing example at this stage

Outlining tends to flatten.
Here the result is undesirable.

G

-193-

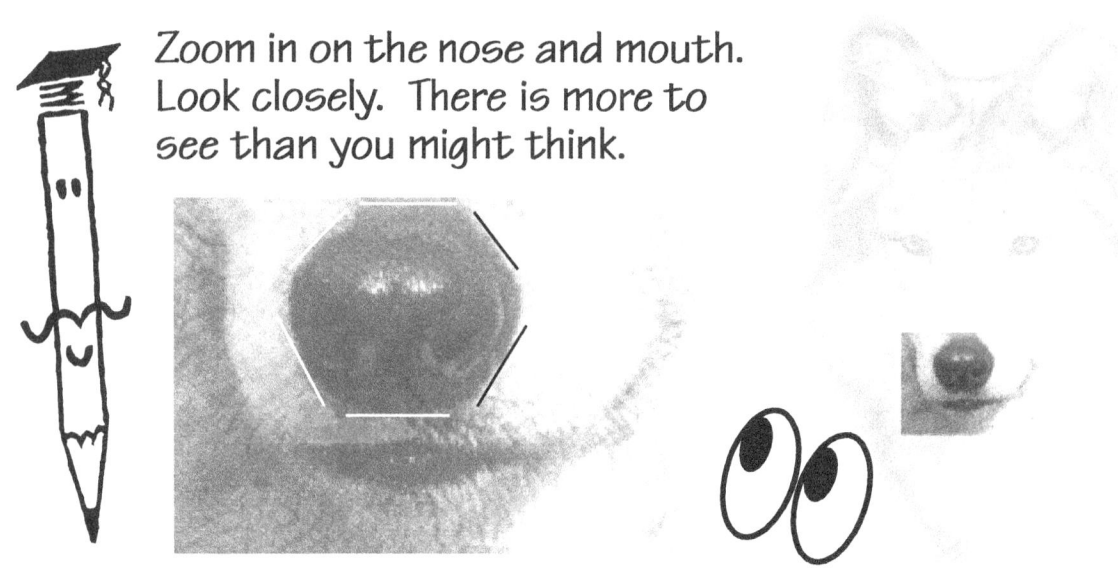

Zoom in on the nose and mouth. Look closely. There is more to see than you might think.

At first glance, the nose in the *small* photo above right appears to be just a flat, dark circle with two white dots. Since our view is from some distance, the nostrils are barely visible. However, we must not be too hasty. On second take, we notice this wolf happens to have a nose which is slightly hexagonal. The close-up makes it evident, especially with the six illustrated lines. Next, we see that the light source is coming from the upper right direction, as evidenced by the shadow cast from the muzzle. Because of that, the top one third of the spherical shape is lighter than the bottom two thirds, which gradually darkens as it goes increasingly into shade. At the tip are two highlights with *soft edges*. Why two? Apparently, our wolf has a little dip (or indentation).

Now, let's turn our gaze to the mouth and jaw. These are part of a cylindrical shape called the *muzzle*. On our right, we observe a portion ending with a curve, like a smile. Under the nose, part of the lips are visible with a shape that is nearly straight on top and curved on the bottom. Since the wolf is at an angle to us, we cannot see the end of the jaw on the left. We see only the edge of the muzzle, as it comes out toward us into the light. That's why that portion appears lighter and contrasts against the cheek, which is also cast in shadow. And as you can tell, since our model is furry, all the edges are soft and slightly ragged.

With the help of these observations, toning and texturing is a cinch. First, locate the respective area on your drawing (A). Fill the nose shape with a light value, using vertical strokes and the side of your lead (B). Repeat the process for the bottom two thirds of the nose, but this time use less pressure at the top of your strokes and more at the bottom. This will suggest that the curvature turns increasingly into shade (C). In phase (D) return to the upper one third portion by gradually darkening the tone until it is only slightly lighter than the lower two thirds segment. In phase (E), switch to the lower portion again for more darkening, and be sure to leave a little section of white in between the upper and lower parts for the highlight. Next, as illustration (F) indicates, apply short angular strokes to lightly texture the edge along the muzzle on your left. Work from top down and when you reach the lower section, use short vertical strokes to lightly form the bottom boundary of the jaw. As you make your way along, start leveling your strokes in order to texture the mouth on your right. Then, per illustration (G), add light texture for the shade area under the nose. Continue with short, lighter vertical strokes for the jaw as well (G). Follow through by shaping the darker front part of the lips (H). Example 10-3 shows the current stage of development. Remember, at this point tones and textures should only be semi-completed. The finishing touches will be easier to handle when *all* the features have been addressed.

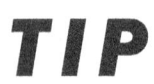

TIP *Create your own version. Do not try to match the book.* **Advance slowly. Build your tones and textures** *gradually* **from light to dark. This enables you to control the intensity and subtle variations more easily.**

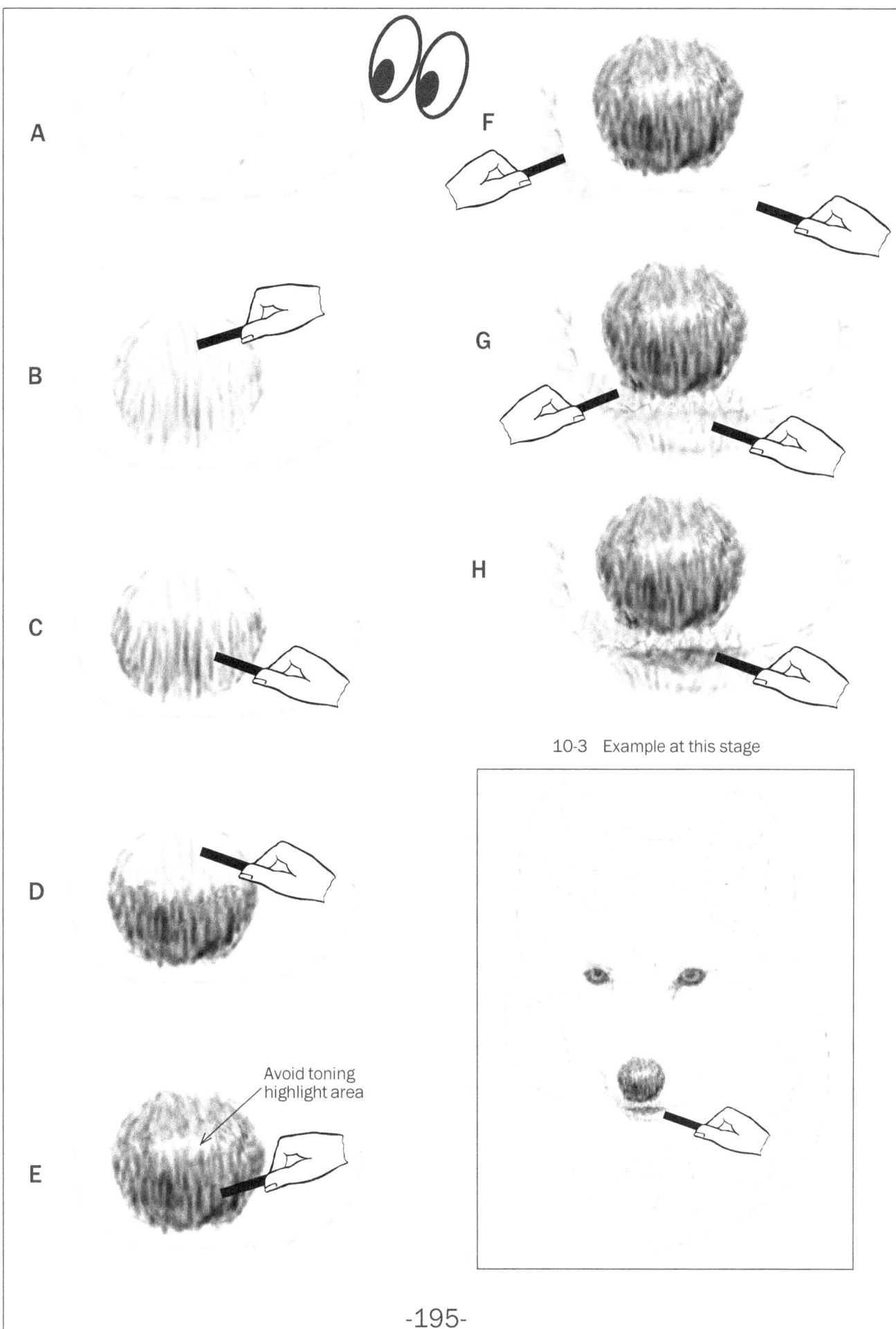

A

B

C

D

E

Avoid toning
highlight area

F

G

H

10-3   Example at this stage

Next, let's study the fur. It has many different kinds of textures, doesn't it?

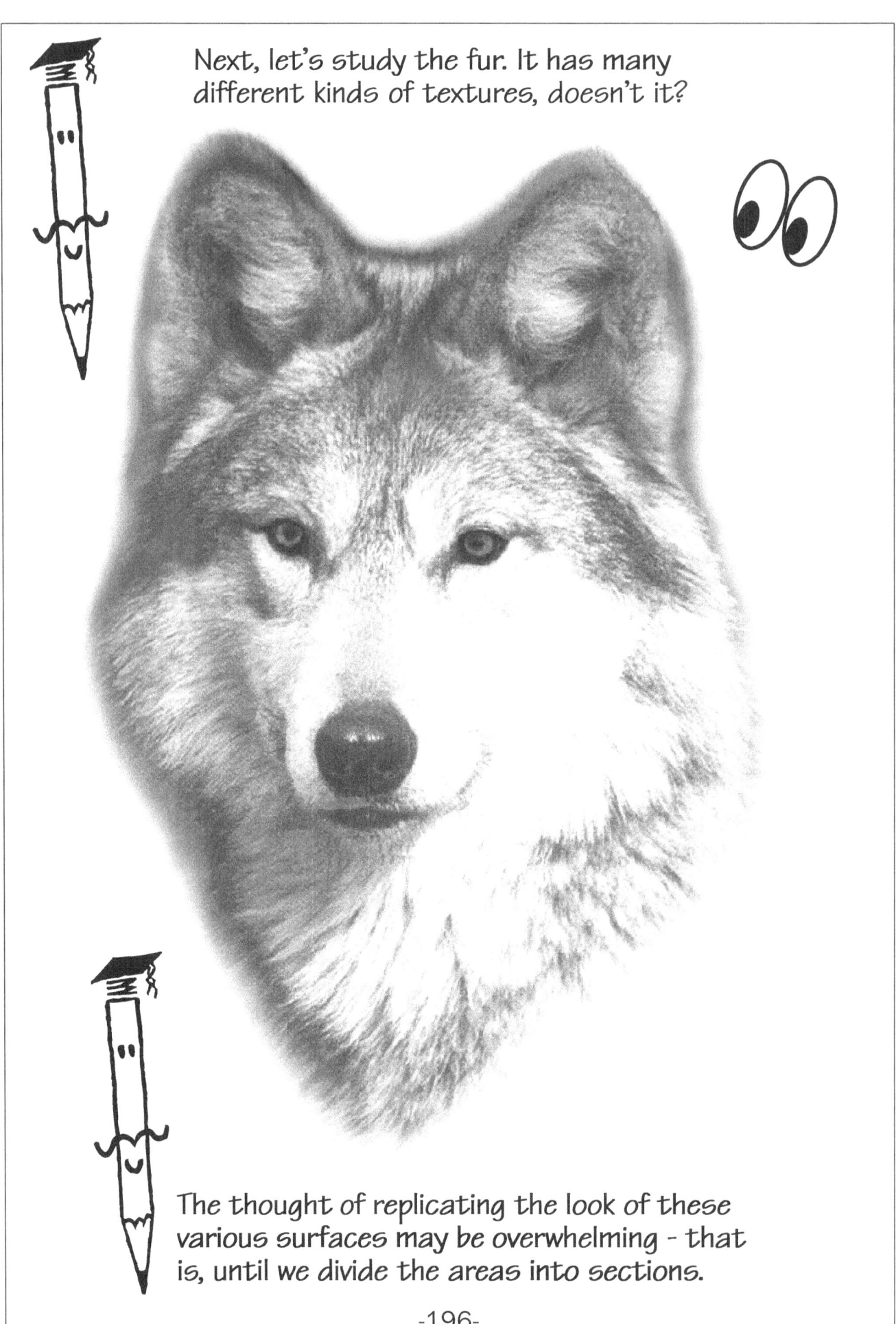

The thought of replicating the look of these various surfaces may be overwhelming - that is, until we divide the areas into sections.

The same method used to spot details in the tree foliage in Chapter 7 can also be applied here. The subtle variations in the fur are more visible with the aid of the view finder.

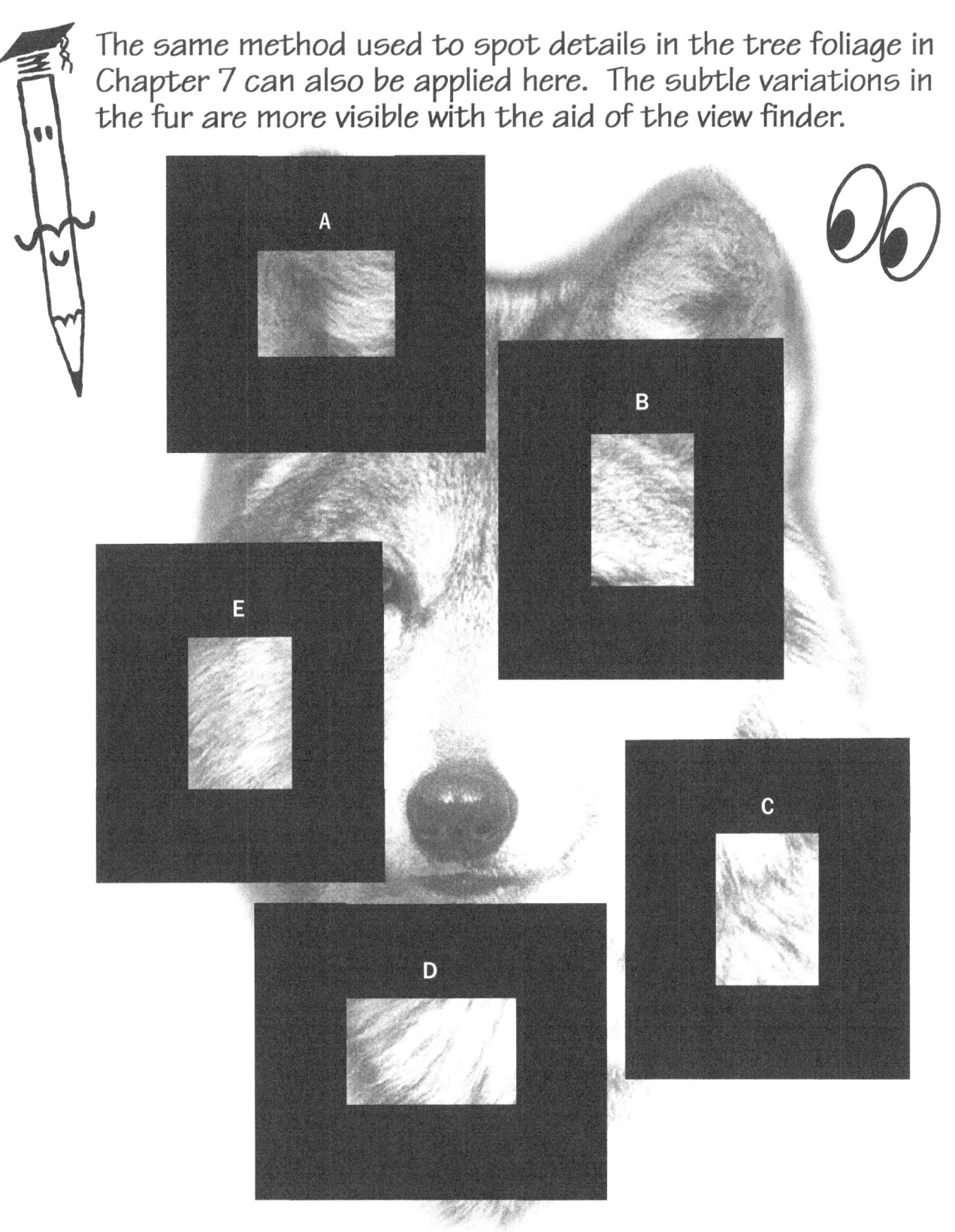

Section (A) appears soft, unlike the coarse, dotted texture in section (B) and the dense zigzag strokes of section (C), don't you think? As for section (D), its texture is yet another version, reminiscent of strands in a whisk broom. And take a gander at section (E). Doesn't it look like the side of a hay stack? Or maybe it reminds you of some other kind of texture. Get the hint? Since we are about to replicate a variety of fur textures, it's helpful to see the features simply as tones, values, shapes and edges.

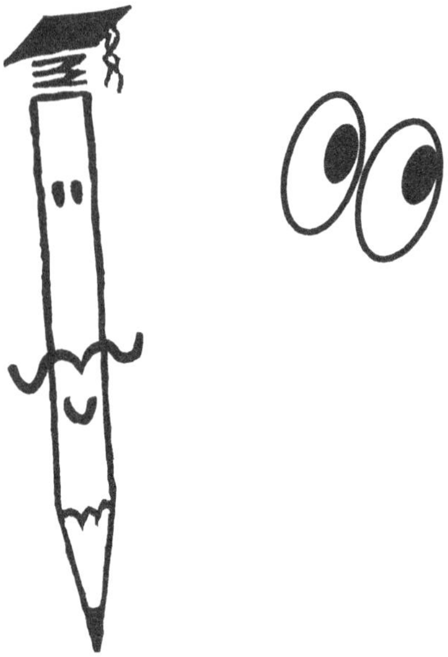

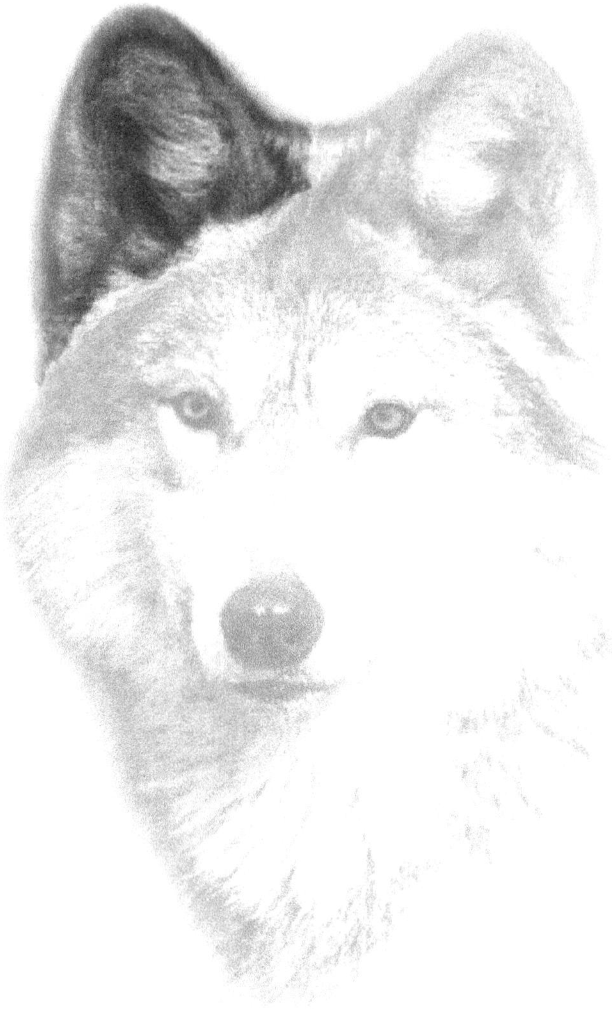

Working randomly, we
can begin by texturing
an ear. Let's start with
the one on our left.

The lightest value in our model appears to be the highlight located on the tip of the nose. The next very light value is the portions of cheek and muzzle on our right. Compared to these values, even the lightest part of the ear is darker. Based on the distinction, I proceeded to texture the ear. Follow along with me. First, I located the respective ear in my drawing. If you applied the transfer method, your shape would resemble a dash line pattern like mine (A). In any event, I began toning by using gentle *horizontal* strokes to fill an uneven layer of *light* tone. Why did I choose to go horizontal instead of vertical? As you can see in the illustration above, the fur mainly flows laterally. During phase (B), while referring to the model, I began to apply short, uneven strokes in appropriate angles. The change enabled me to mimic not only the darker values representing the deeper parts of the ear (in shade), but also the various directions of the surface contours (C). For the next step, I repeated the method. By applying additional layers, I was able to achieve a *gradual* darkening effect where needed (D). Then, for even more density, I went through one more time (E). In phase (F), I applied the blender to bring about the softer appearance. Although I show only six stages, many layers were actually produced. Example 10-4 indicates the result. It also shows my use of a wax paper covering. The method helped me avoid smearing the eyes while I worked on the ears. Currently, they are not necessarily finished. That is to be decided when *all* the parts have been semi-rendered. Now it's your turn. Using the texture techniques I described, create *your* version. Advance slowly. Build your tones and textures little by little.

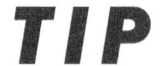 To see details more clearly, refer to the larger model on page 196.
For even closer study, use your view finder as shown on page 197.

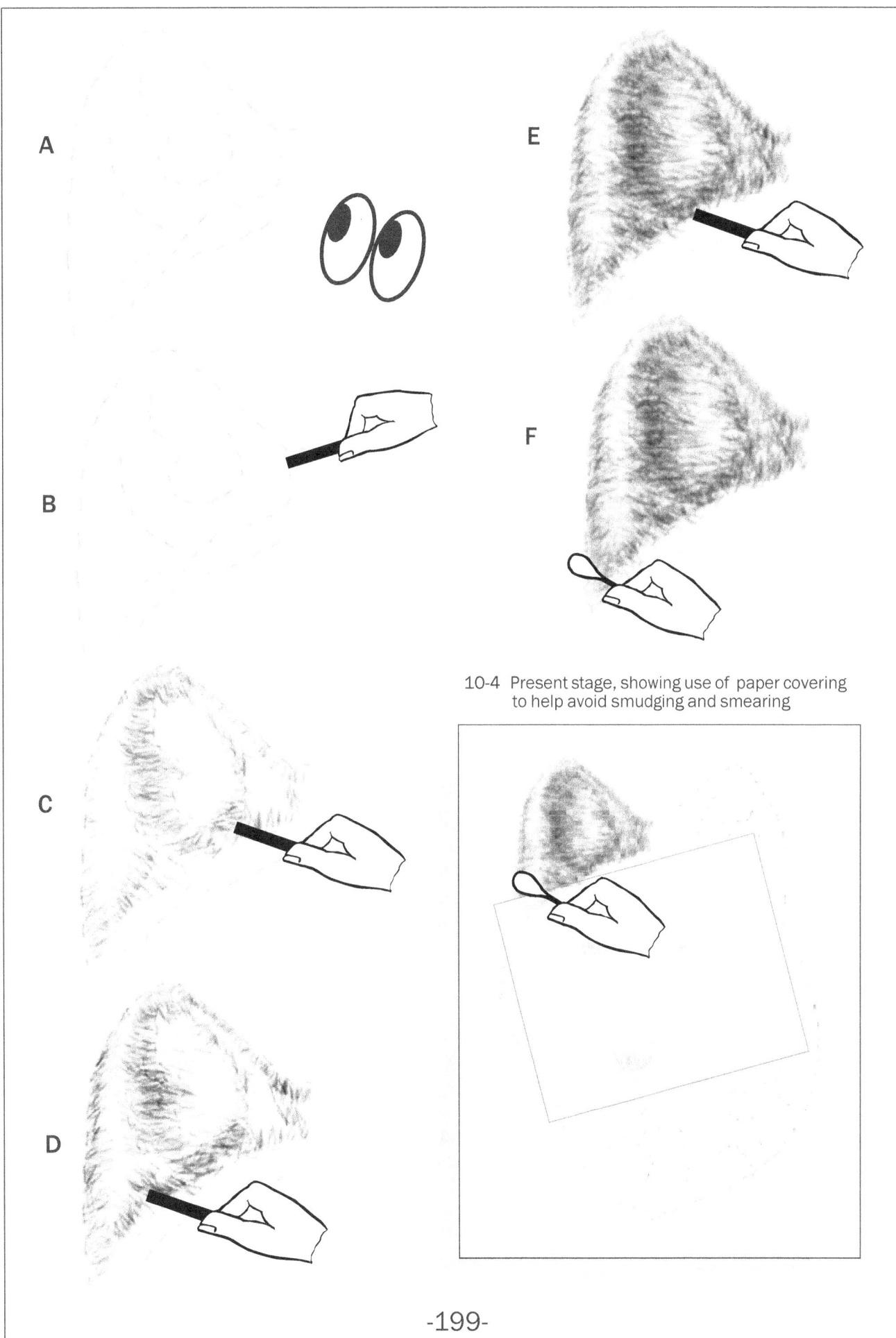

A

B

C

D

E

F

10-4 Present stage, showing use of paper covering to help avoid smudging and smearing

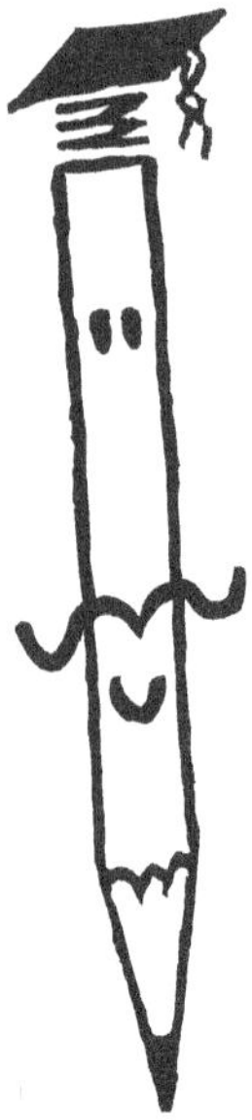

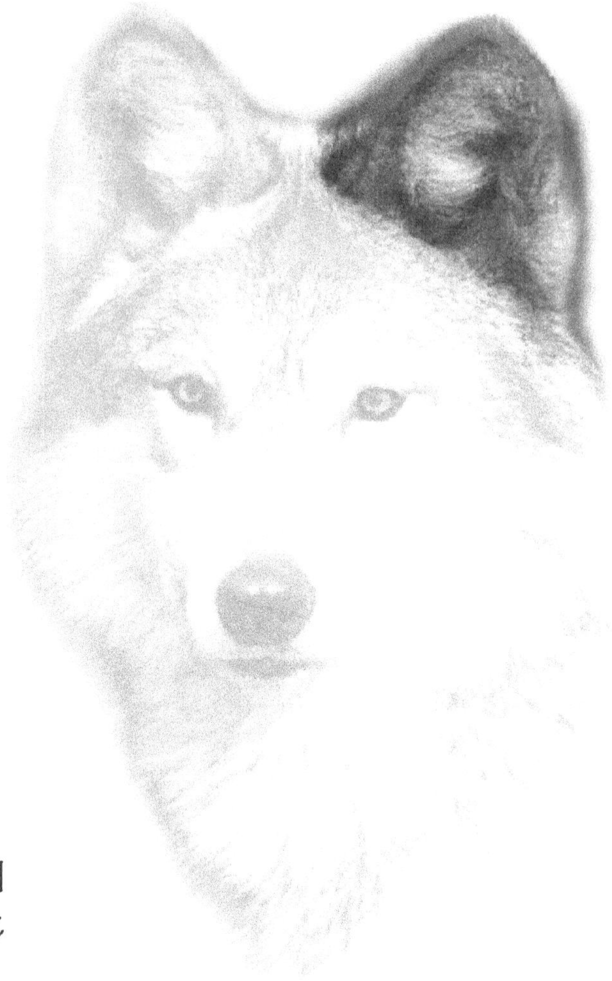

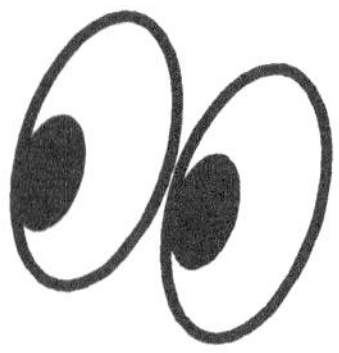

Now, texture the other ear similar to the way I did. Again, I have explained the steps in detail as a reminder to treat each phase with equal care. The ears are not mirror images.

Starting with example (A), we see the contour shape made with dash lines. In step (B), I began developing the form by applying gentle lateral strokes that follow the horizontal flow of the fur. This allowed me to have a base to work into. In step (C) however, I began switching to uneven strokes in appropriate angles to replicate the subtle changes in fur direction based on the model. The procedure also enabled me to start replicating the gradually darker values representing the deeper parts of the ear (in shade). Next, I applied the same process to bring about the softer inside edges, as well as additional details (D). Then, in stage (E), I went around again in select areas, to achieve more density. For the soft outside edges, the blender was also employed (F). As you proceed to texture the second ear on *your* drawing, please keep in mind that although only five texturing stages are shown, many gradual layers were actually applied in each stage. Build your layers a little at a time, and cover areas you are not working on to help prevent smearing (10-5). Be sure you refer to the larger model on page 196. In addition, remember that the final stage should be saved until all the features have been textured. Then, with the aid of the *assimilation process*, you will be able to see which areas may need additional attention. In turn, this will enable you to bring about more effective tone values and convincing details.

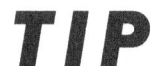 **TIP** Do not stay strictly within your original boundaries. Give yourself the option to modify as needed. Adjustment is part of the process.

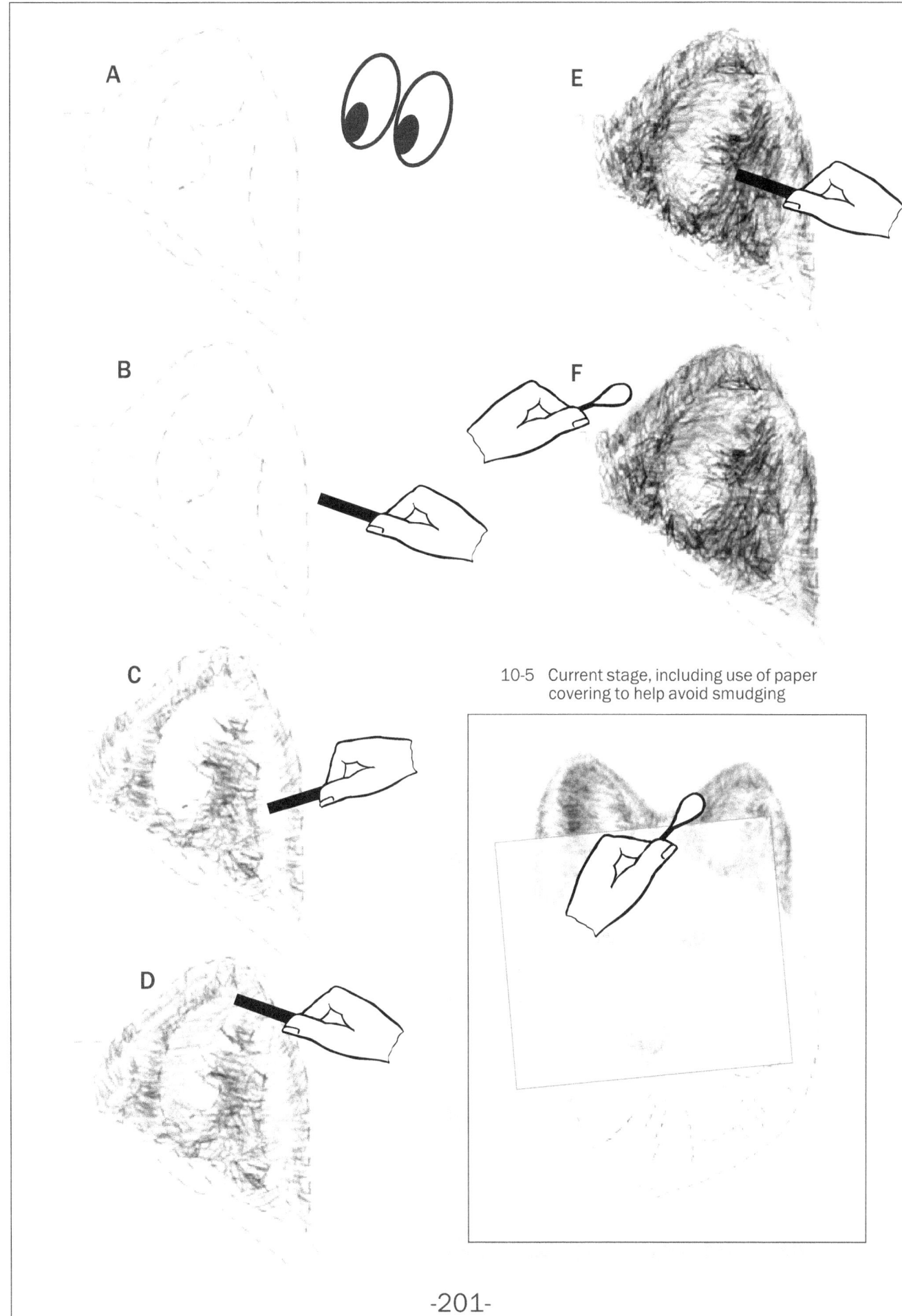

A

B

C

D

E

F

10-5 Current stage, including use of paper covering to help avoid smudging

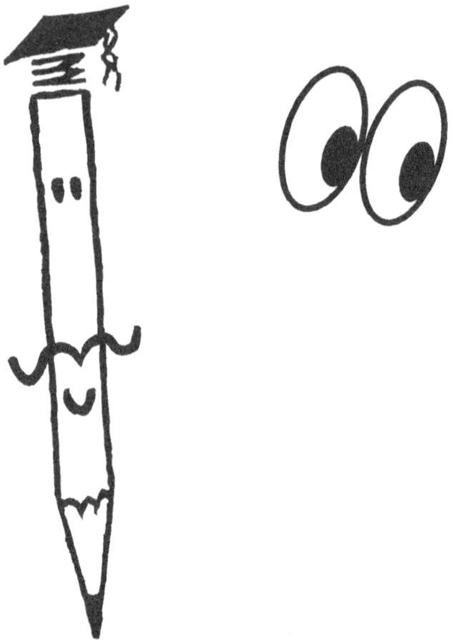

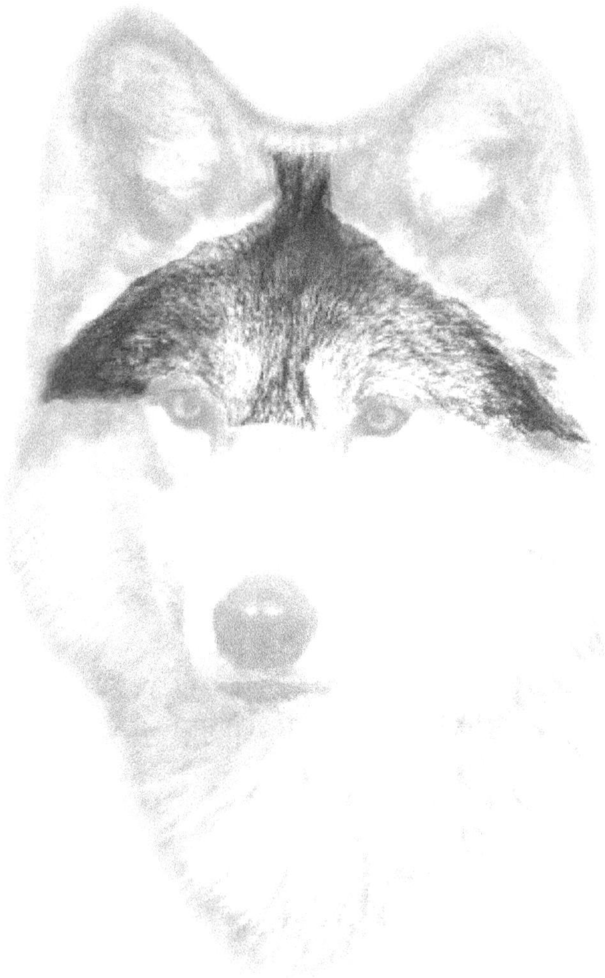

To minimize the chance of smearing, proceed from the ears down by texturing the forehead.

Example (A) shows my rendition before I began adding texture to the forehead. Next, while referring to the model, slowly and carefully I began lightly covering the appropriate areas with short dotted strokes (B). I then applied the same procedure in step (C) using very little pressure to increase the darker values as needed. Where the fur appeared to be more dense however, I used additional strokes and placed them closer together. I also made sure my marks followed the contour and direction according to the flow of the fur. For instance, in some places the hairs ran vertical, while in other areas they were angled, and still other areas they laid horizontally. Continuing in step (D), I repeated the techniques for even more density, where applicable. Plus, I included some lines at an angle to replicate the soft hairs connecting the forehead with the ears. Then, mimicking the light and dark patches, I filled-in some spots as needed (E). When my textures were brought to a semi-finished state, my drawing appeared as shown in illustration 10-6. As you proceed with your version, you can use the techniques I described, but I encourage you to invent some of your own combinations and methods. *Remember to refer often to the model above, and to the larger photo on page 196. Be patient. Work slowly. Build your layers gradually.* If you accidentally darken too much within a section, flatten your putty eraser and dab. Do not rub, as this will blend and smear the soft bristle-like appearance.

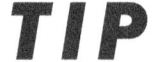

TIP To help avoid smudges, remember to place a separate sheet, or a piece of wax paper over the area you are not working on.

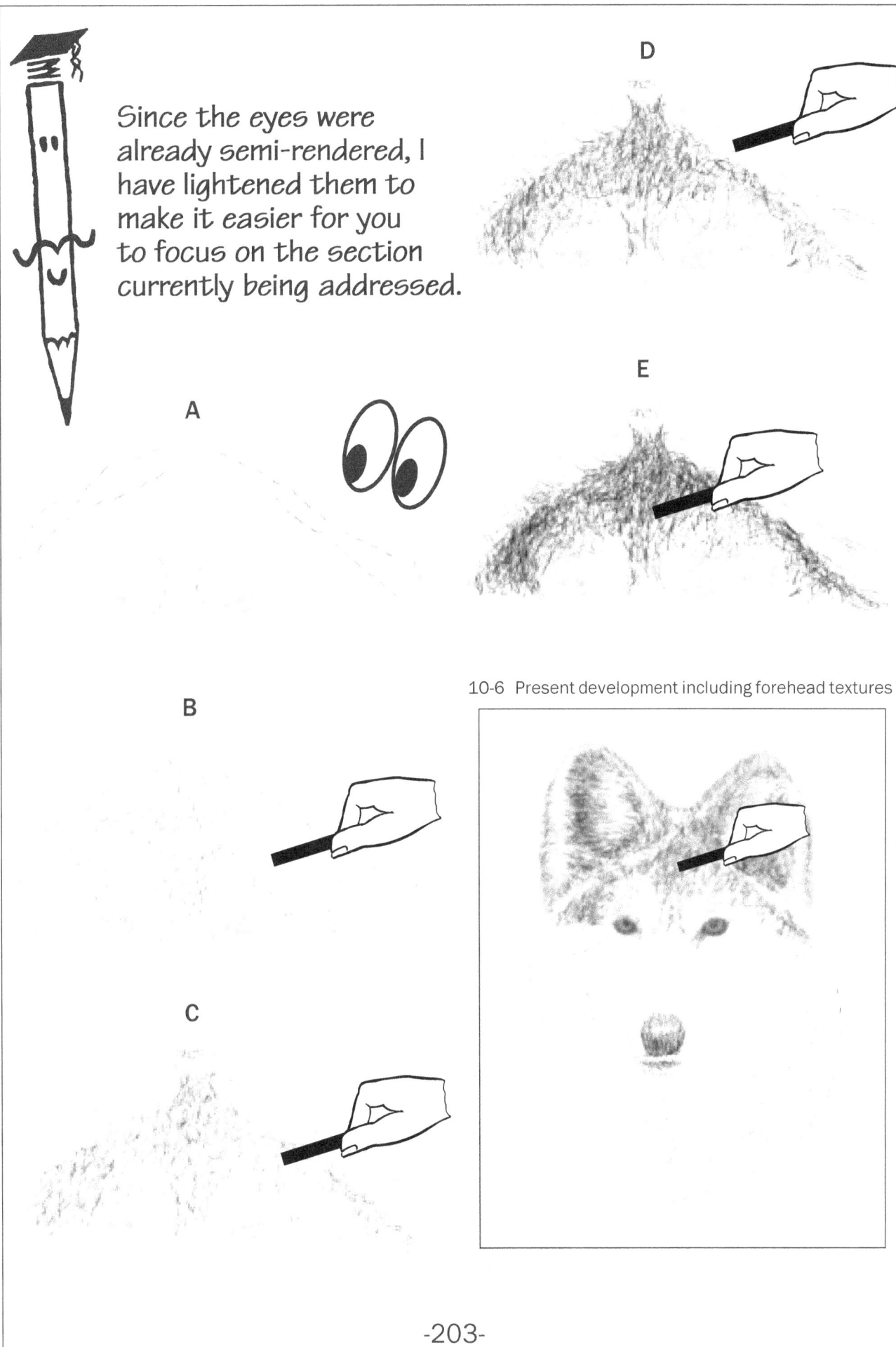

Since the eyes were already semi-rendered, I have lightened them to make it easier for you to focus on the section currently being addressed.

A

B

C

D

E

10-6 Present development including forehead textures

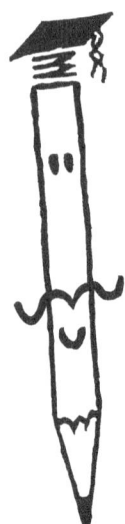

Let's texture the section of mane to our left and the cheek beside it.

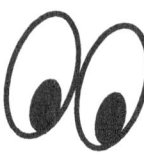

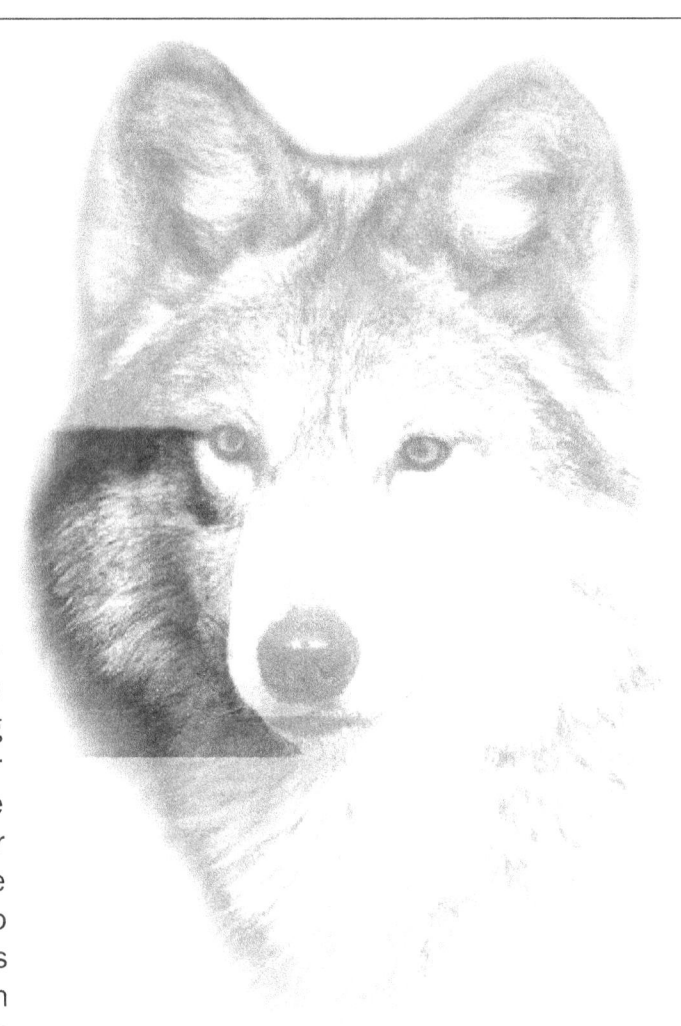

Observing the model, we see that in the photo, the muzzle is lighter than the mane on our left. In the present drawing state (A), that corresponding area is paper white. So I darkened the *mane* value slightly with thin, intermittent angular lines (B). This not only helped mimic the flow of the fur but also provided a base to work into. Continuing the angular process in stage (C), I glanced back and forth between the model and my drawing, while adding sporadic (occasional) lines along the outer perimeter (or boundary). The technique enhanced the illusion of density and brought about a more natural, uneven appearance. Since there is a dip in the cheek and shade there, I then placed my lines closer together for a gradually darkening effect. In stage (D) I repeated the procedure by adding more uneven angular lines where needed. The technique increased the look of density, while preventing hard edges. Switching to shorter, more erratic (inconsistent) angular strokes, some harder, others not as hard, in stage (E), the change enabled me to replicate and develop the coarse (rough) parts of the fur. In the process, a negative impact occured, however. The edges along the boundary of the mane seemed to go flat and stiff. To soften the appearance and create a suggestion that the mane turns toward the background, I gently used my blender. Again there were pitfalls. Several lines that should have remained crisp (hard, clear edge) became blurry. For a remedy, I lightly re-clarified the parts that became vague by adding back the lines (F). Illustration 10-7 shows the semi-rendered outcome. As you texture the respective portion in your drawing, apply the techniques I used as you see fit, and invent some of your own. Details are much more visible in the large version of the model (page 196). Use your view finder. Proceed slowly and carefully.

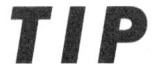 **TIP** Don't stay in any one part of a section for long. Move about often. This enables you to gradually develop all portions as a whole segment.

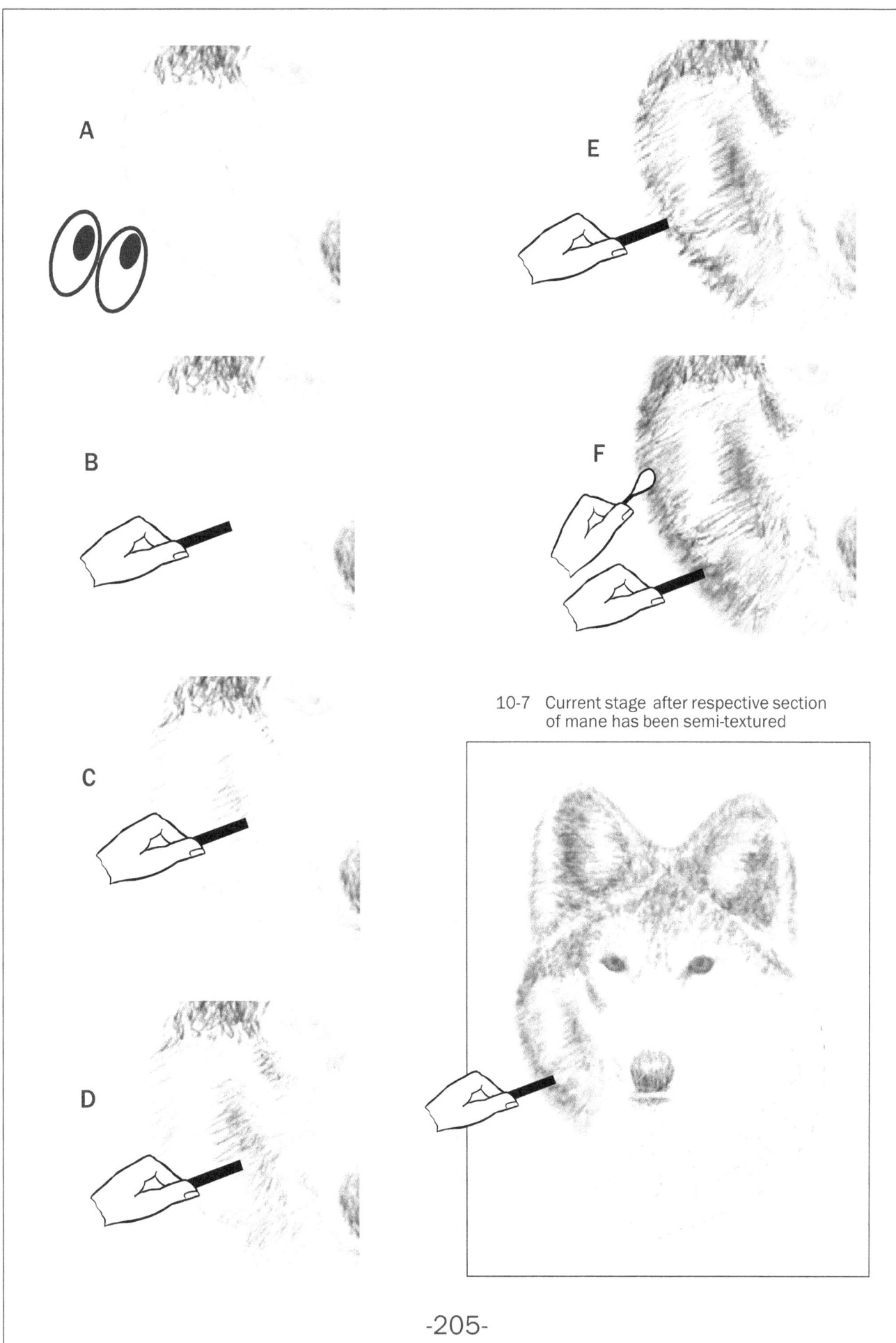

A

B

C

D

E

F

10-7 Current stage after respective section of mane has been semi-textured

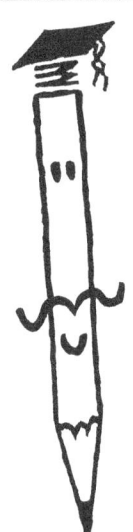

Now we are ready for the neck area.

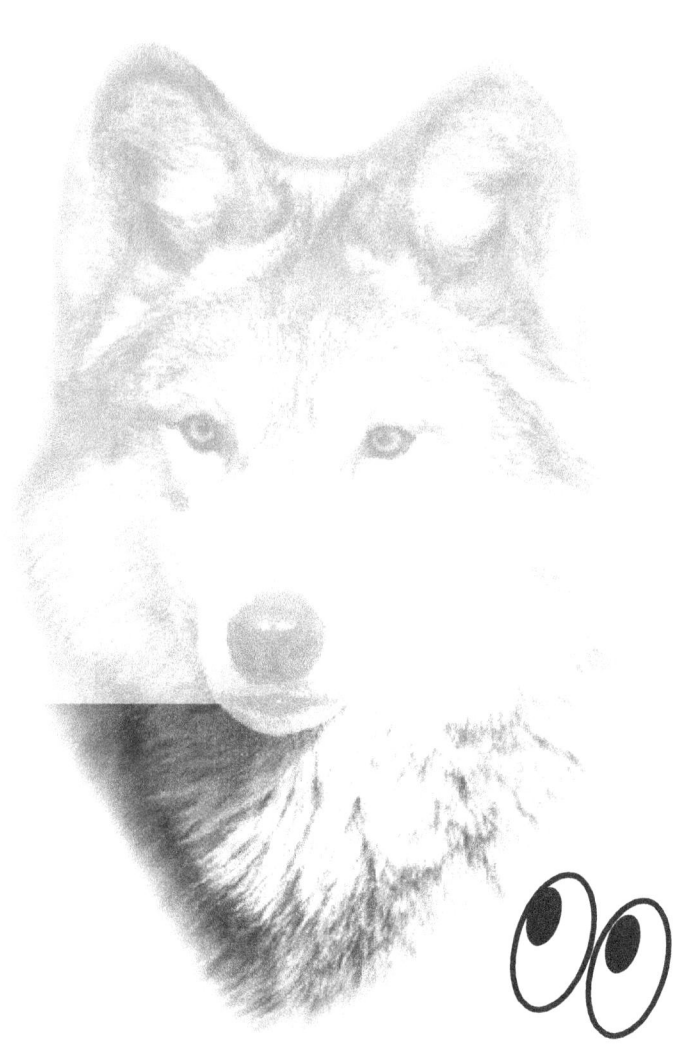

In our view, the figure has a cast shadow caused by the muzzle which is struck by light from the upper right. As a result, most of the neck and fur on the right is also bathed in light. That means much of the corresponding area in the drawing could remain white as the paper (A). However, for the folds in the fur (where less light penetrates), I added gentle, random strokes at an angle. These began from the upper right and tilted down and left. Of course, while placing them, I made sure to often refer to the model. This enabled me to replicate the shapes and reasonably follow the surface of the fur (B). Next, in phase (C), I lightly textured the shadow area with similar angle strokes. Why? Because they were darker versions of that area. I also included shorter strokes along the outer edges, on my left. They brought about the look of irregular strands which reminded me of uneven fringes. On the opposite side of the figure, the fur appeared thicker and matted, like tufts that angled toward the right. I adapted accordingly, changing stroke direction, size and type. This time, I used random, short choppy movements. In stage (D) I switched again. Applying very little pressure, I replicated what looked like wavy fur in the lighter portions by using thin lines. At that point, *visual assimilation* began to take hold. I could see that the shadow needed to be darkened. In response, I added another layer of angled strokes (E). Then I also increased the value of the outer boundaries, by using short, random strokes where appropriate. To keep the look of light coming from the right, I was careful to make the side on my left darker and the edge to my right lighter (F). Ultimately, in stage (G), I employed my blender a little for the softer edges. When texturing your drawing, using the techniques I described, be sure to refer to page 196, as I'm sure you have been doing. It has a larger version which comes in handy. Also, please remember that although I show 7 stages, each one was slowly and meticulously (very carefully) developed. Illustration 10-8 shows the semi-rendered outcome. Take your time, be patient and work diligently. Your extra attention will pay off.

TIP By drawing the dark, irregular serrated shapes, you also create lighter, *opposite* irregular serrated shapes.

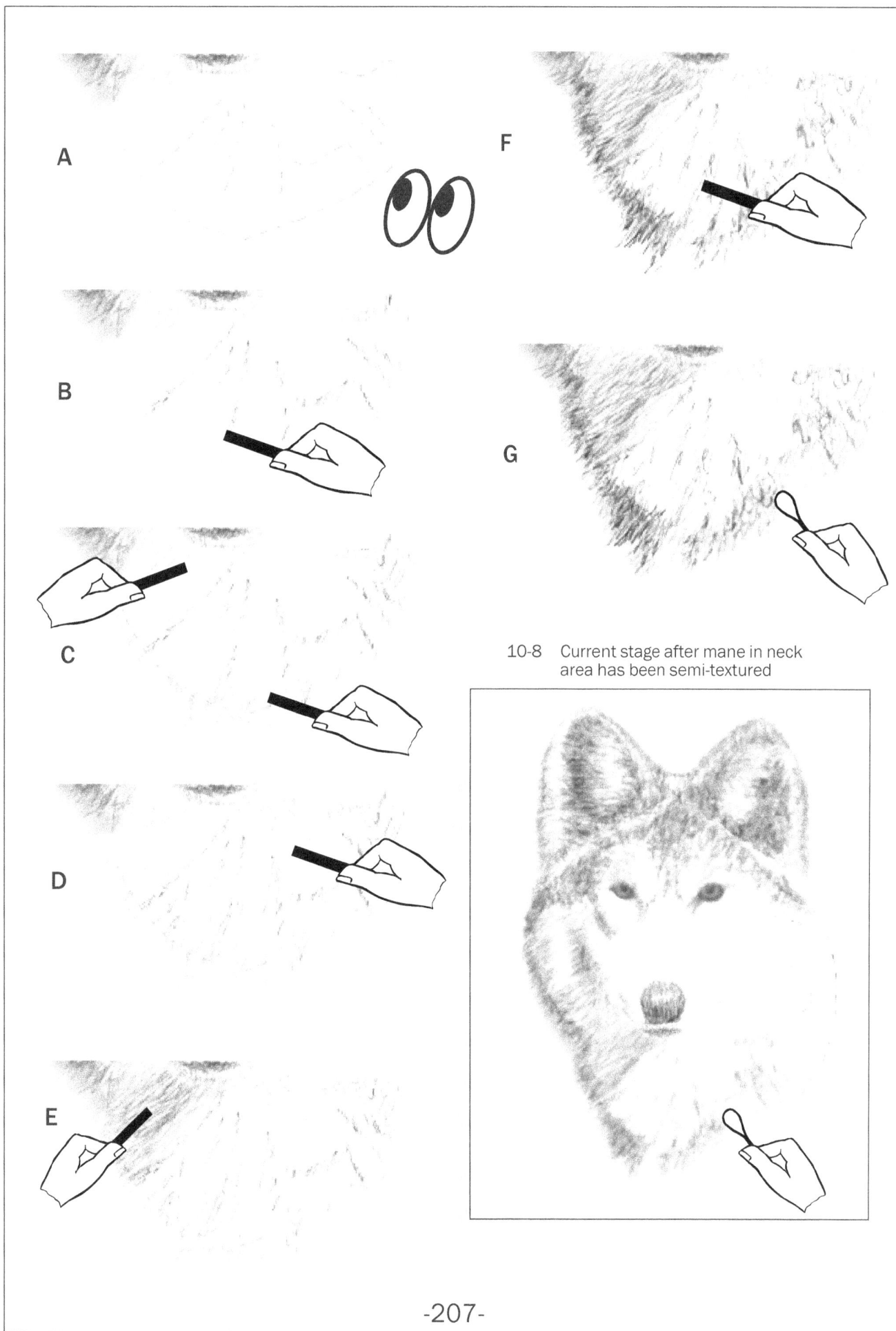

A

B

C

D

E

F

G

10-8 Current stage after mane in neck area has been semi-textured

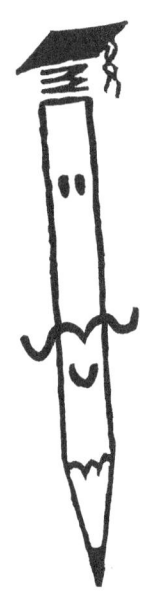

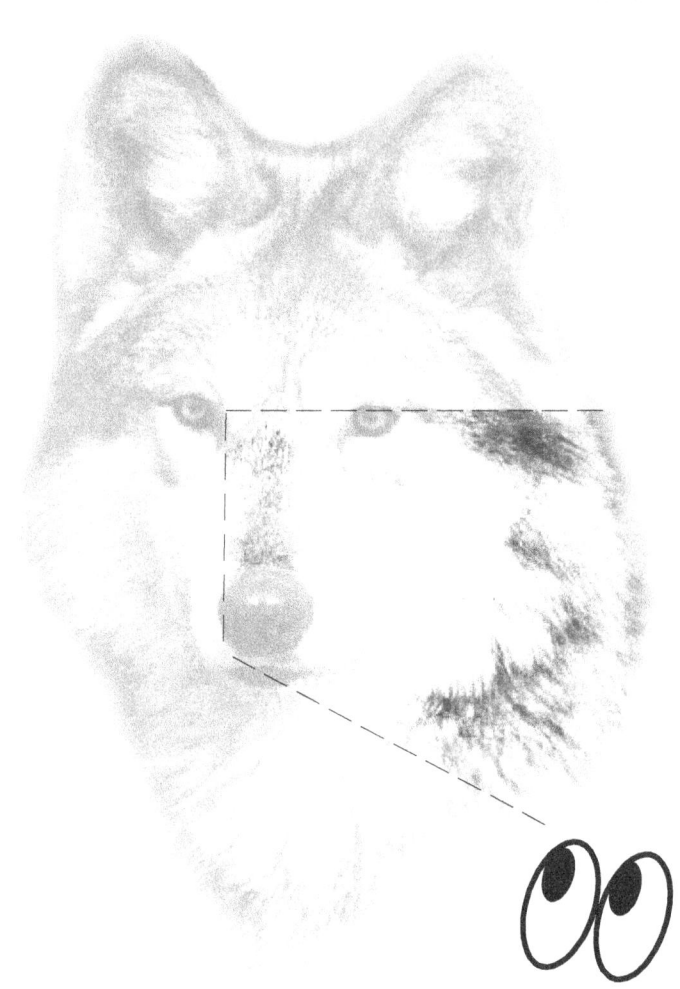

The rest of the mane, along with the adjacent cheek and the fuzz atop the muzzle, still need to be addressed.

Studying the model, we see the remaining section to be textured on our right. Since light strikes on that side, the white of the paper comes in handy again. Example (A) illustrates the present status. In stage (B), I used short angled strokes. All the while, tilting from upper left down toward the right, I made sure to follow the shapes and contour by referring to the larger version of the model on page 196. Continuing with the same process in stage (C), I added another layer to indicate the curved surface as it turns away from the light, toward the back of the mane. In stage (D), I also included some short, thin, gentle lines to replicate the look of small strands and folds on the cheek and under the eye. For the short, fuzz on the top of the muzzle, I used the side of my pencil and barely grazed the surface of the paper (E). Then, with the blender, I softened the edge separating the boundary between the fur and the background (F). Eventually my drawing appeared as shown in illustration 10-9.

TIP You can also apply a different technique for the soft fuzz on top of the muzzle by gently texturing with many, many small dots.

A

B

C

D

E

F

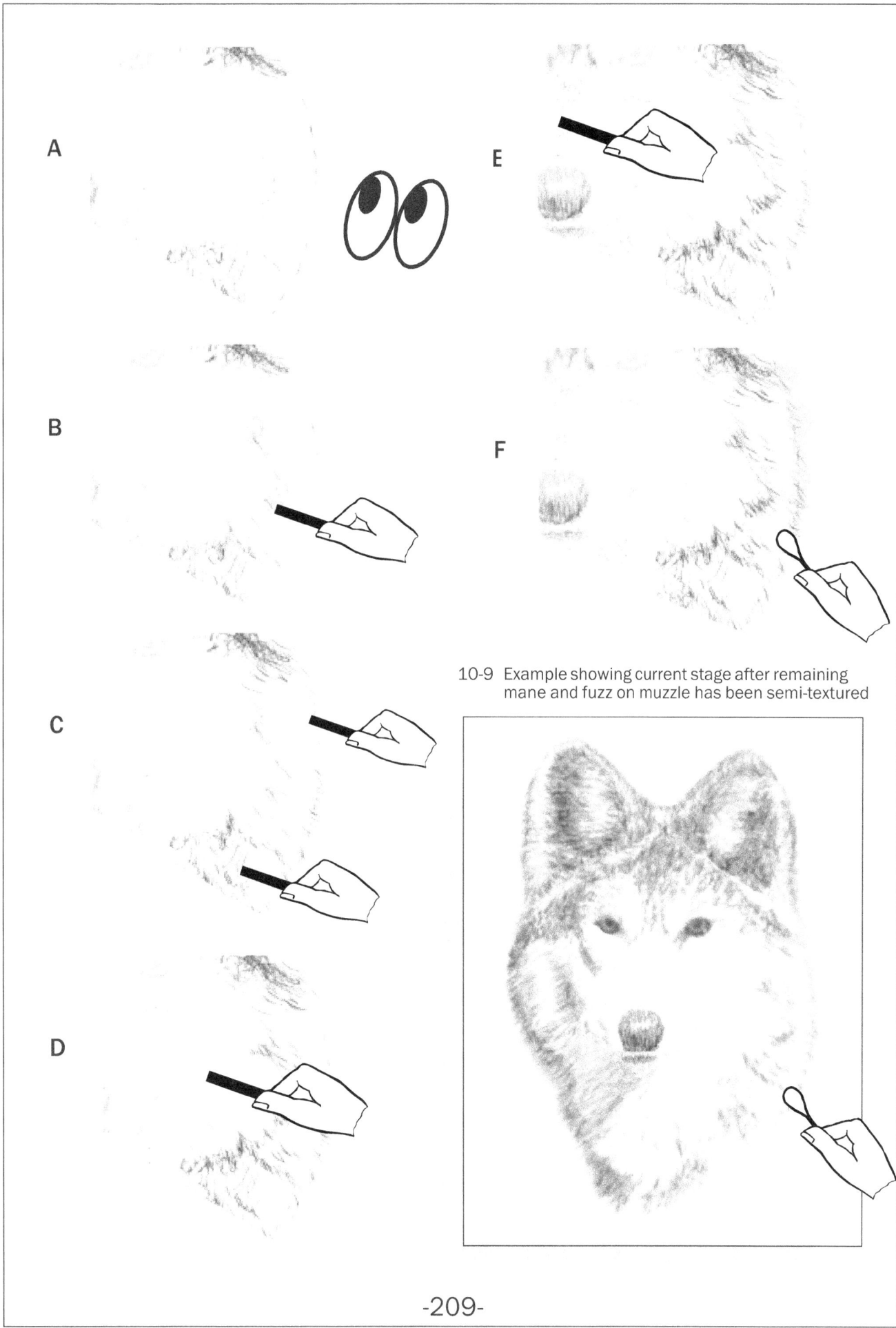

10-9 Example showing current stage after remaining
mane and fuzz on muzzle has been semi-textured

-209-

We've come a long way.
Let's review.

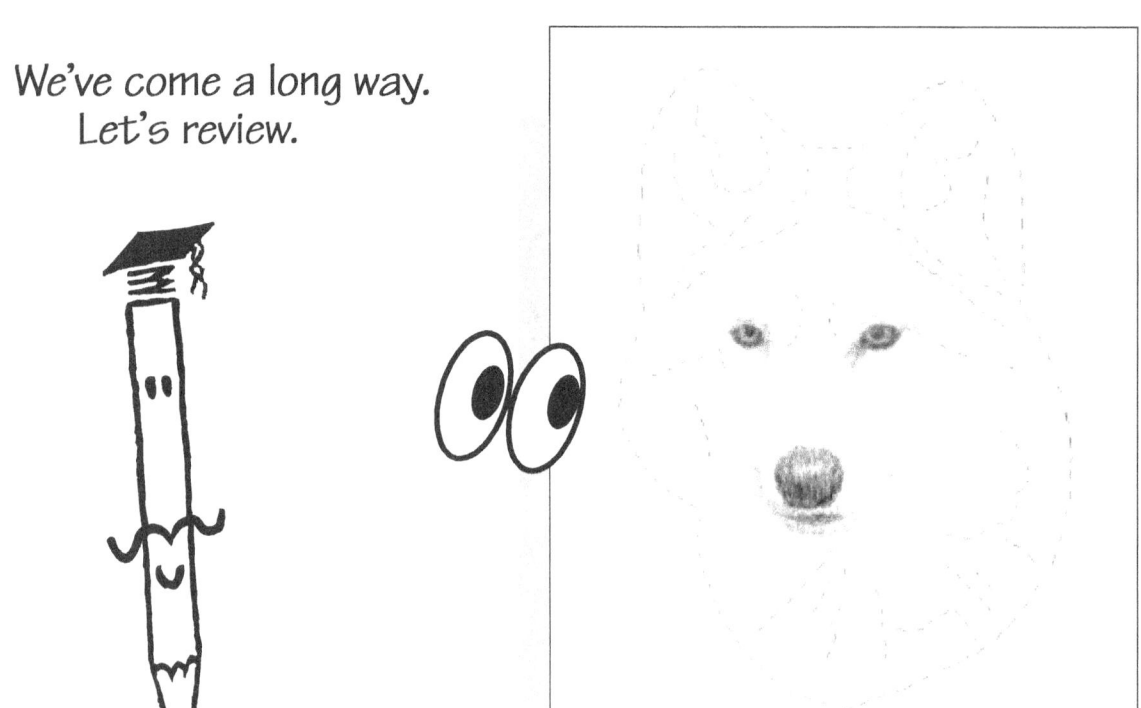

First we semi-rendered the eyes, nose and mouth,
followed by the ears and the forehead.

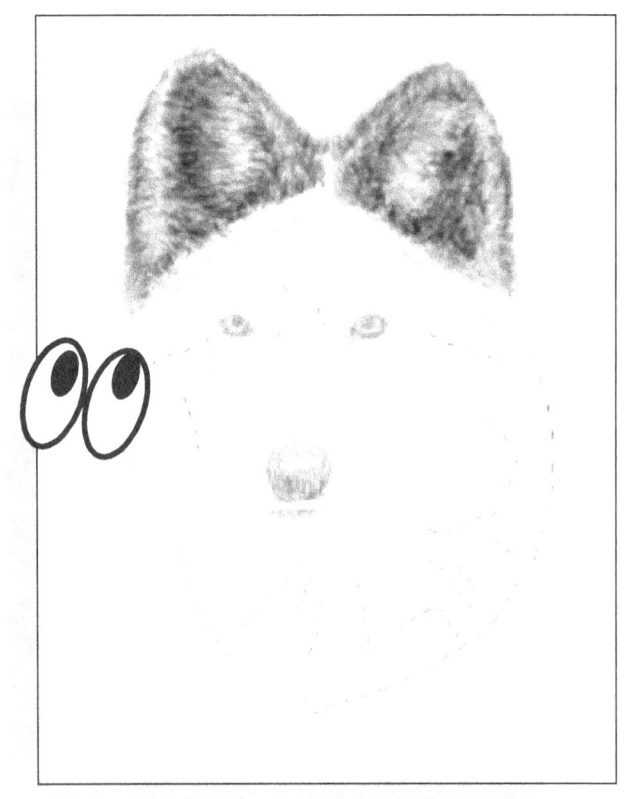

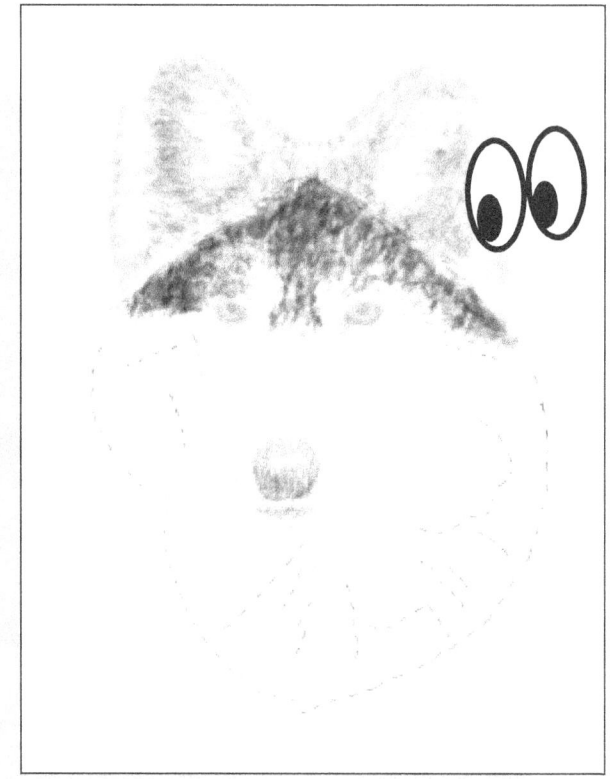

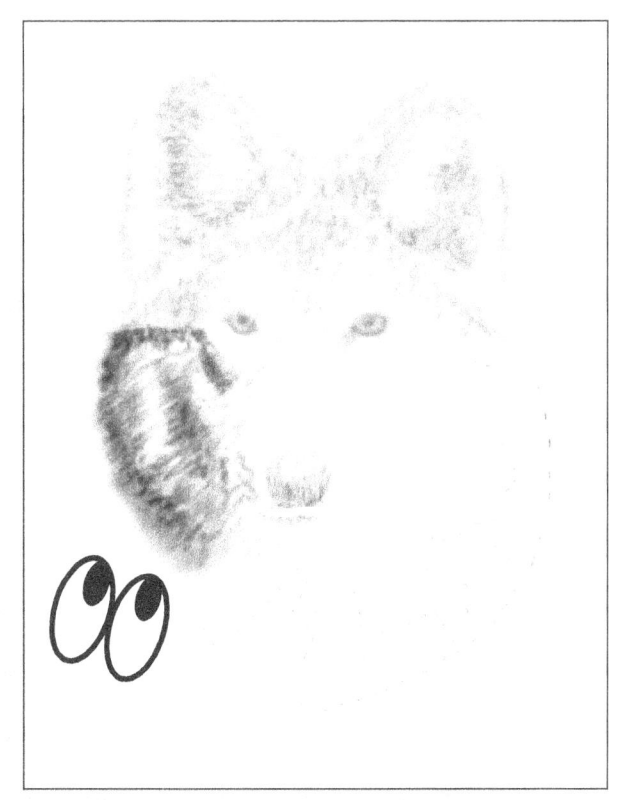

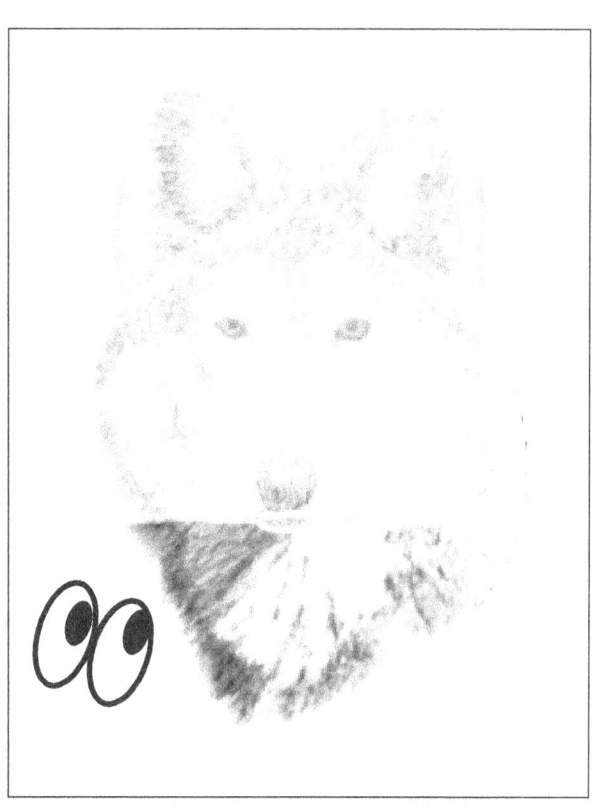

Next, working downward and around, we textured the mane, one section at a time, including the soft fur atop the muzzle. You see? Like shapes, tones and textures are also easy, when managed in segments, stages, and steps. Of course there's another factor. I'm referring to gradually developing layers.

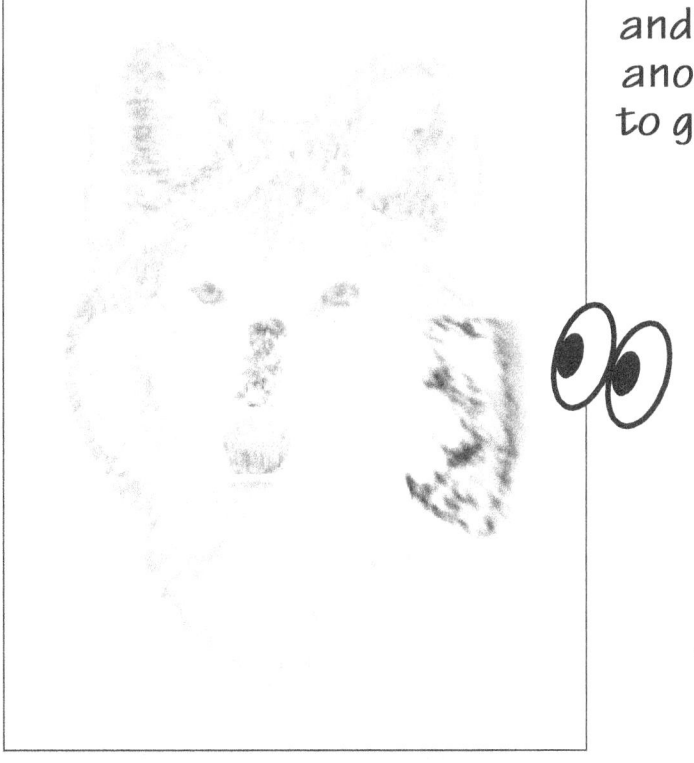

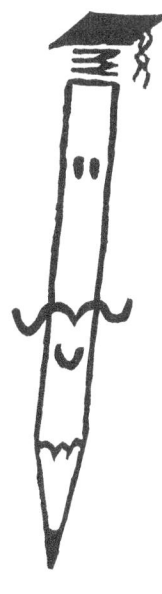

Keep going.
You're doing great.

TIME FOR A SIDE-BY-SIDE COMPARISON

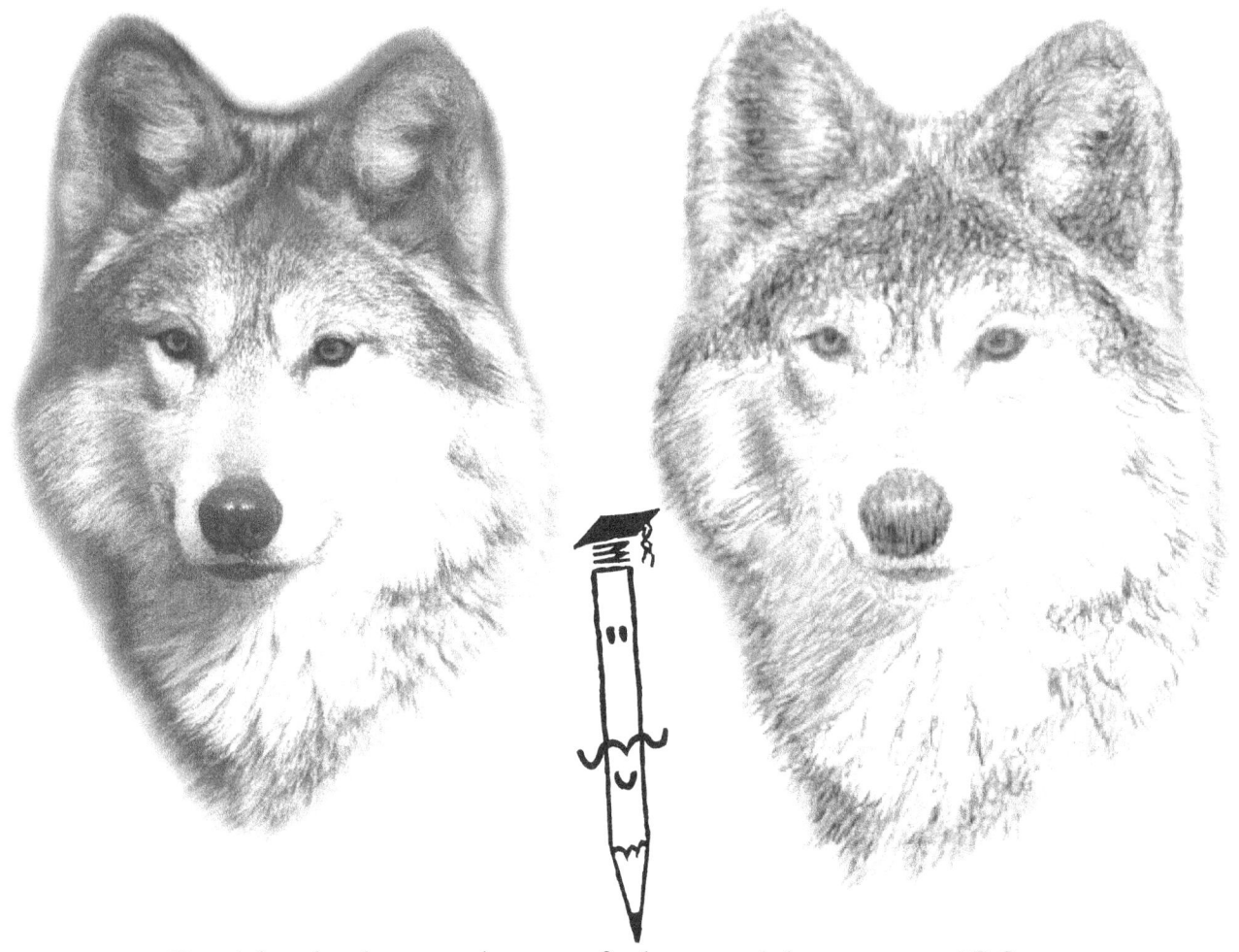

*Beside the large photo of the model on page 196,
my drawing looked much like this miniature simulation.*

Do you see a difference between the photo and my drawing? Of course you do, and that's the point. The drawing was not intended to be an exact copy of the photograph. It was meant to be a pencil rendition. In light of this, the more pertinent question is: can I call my work finished? To find the answer, first I assessed the *overall structure* and determined that the basic scale of my figure was reasonably close to the model. Switching to *random parts checks*, I zoomed in looking for smaller shape deficiencies. By comparing the wolf ears, one at a time in my drawing, to those in the model, I saw a close similarity in form. Then I studied the eyes, followed by sections of the mane, as well as the forehead, and so on. In each case, I scanned for alignments, curves, angles and proportion. Then it struck me. Apparently during texturing, I had made the horizontal span between the nose and the muzzle edge (on my left) a little too narrow. Does this mean my version is wrong? Not necessarily. When I blocked my view of the photograph with my hand, my drawing still looked convincing, even with the variation in the muzzle.

Continuing with the comparison survey, I then focused on the *shading* aspects. Searching for textures and the tone values, both overall and individual areas, I found them to be in balance for the most part, except for a few subtle things. For instance, based on the model, the fuzz texture in my drawing needed a little darkening on top of the muzzle, as did the shadow cast by it. Electing to make these changes, and since I would be in the muzzle vicinity anyway, I also chose to adjust its size discrepancy.

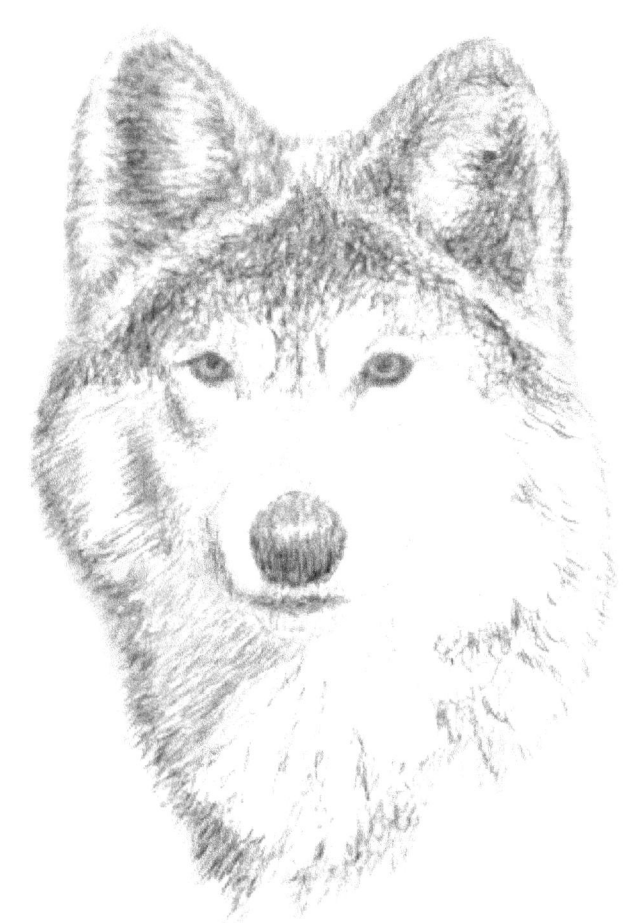

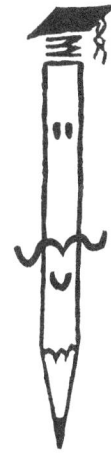

Here's how my final drawing turned out. Can you spot the change in the muzzle, before and after? Is it an improvement? Decide for yourself. Then give your drawing a full side-by-side comparison with the large photo of the model (p.196).

Do not be shocked if you discover some of your shaping and shading requires adjustment. You didn't goof! Remember that drawing is based on estimates. Modification is part of the process. Plus, the final touches were to be reserved for last, once all the parts have been semi-rendered. Then, as you have seen, it's easier to spot which areas may need additional work. Of course, the danger is that you could get carried away. My advice is *don't* - meaning don't expect your drawing to appear like mine, nor be a duplicate of the photo, and don't expect a masterpiece. Your work should represent *your unique personal touch*, with respect to your *current ability*. In the event your picture turned out other than as planned, be receptive. Your way may be more desirable. When such is the case, I suggest you enjoy the pleasant surprise and leave well enough alone. Should any of this sound new, please review pages 33 and 34 in Chapter 2, as well as pages 64, 65 and 72 in Chapter 4, along with page 156 in Chapter 8.

After your finishing touches, browse the student gallery displayed on the next two pages, and be sure to also read the follow-up.

STUDENT GALLERY

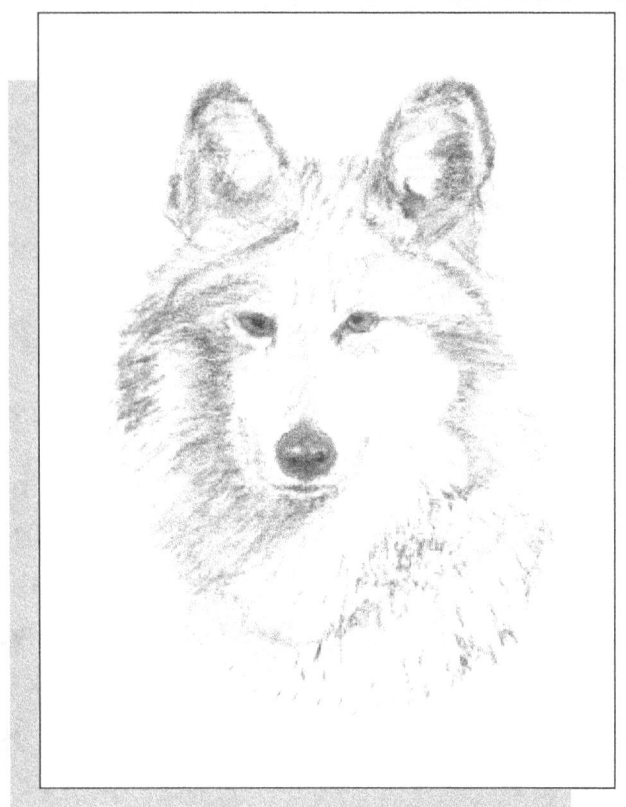

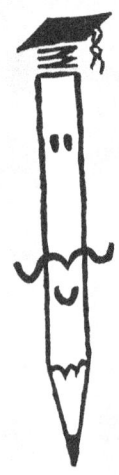

Remember that the goal was not to make a duplicate copy of the photo.

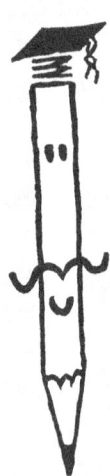

The objective was to create an interpretation.

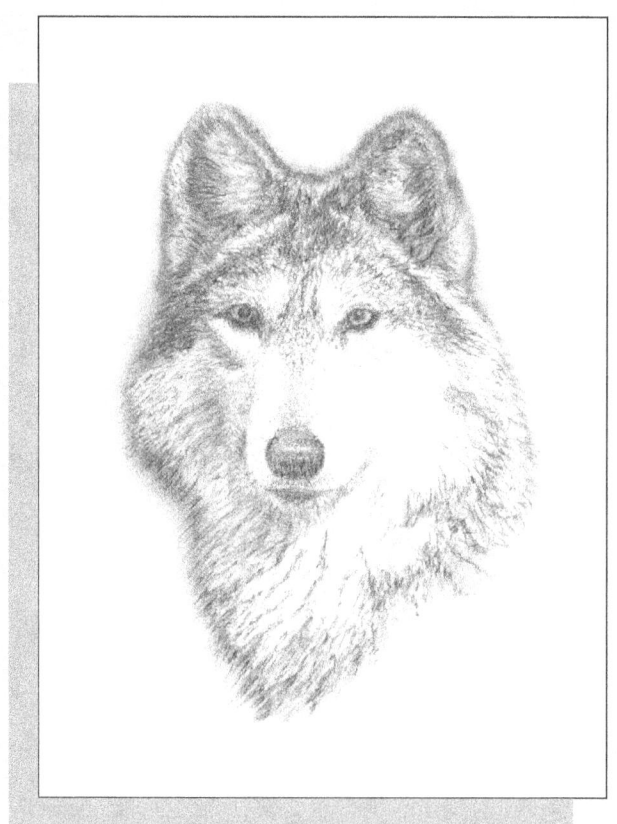

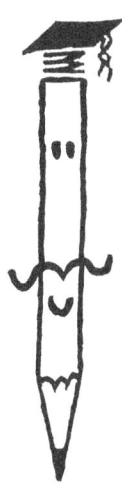

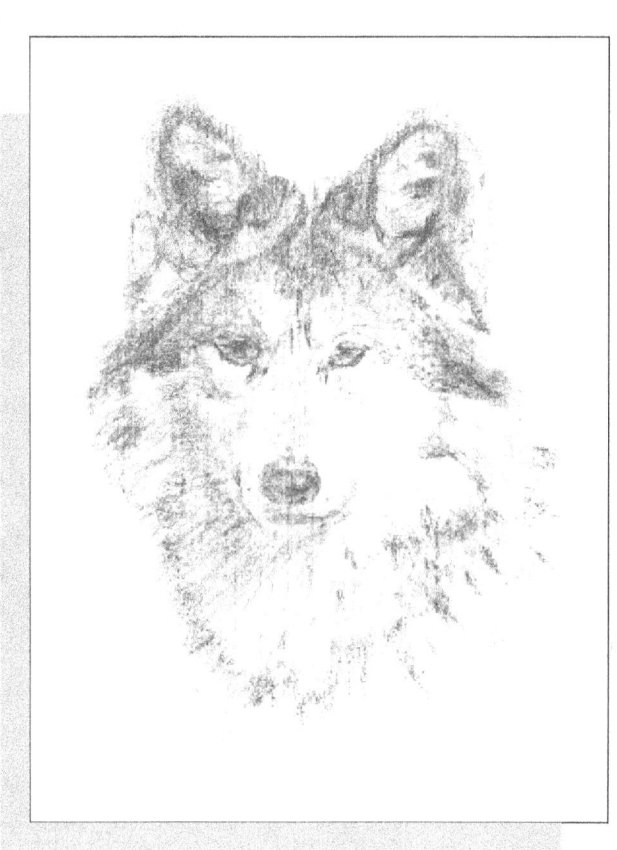

These are original, one of a kind renditions, conveying individual quality and style.

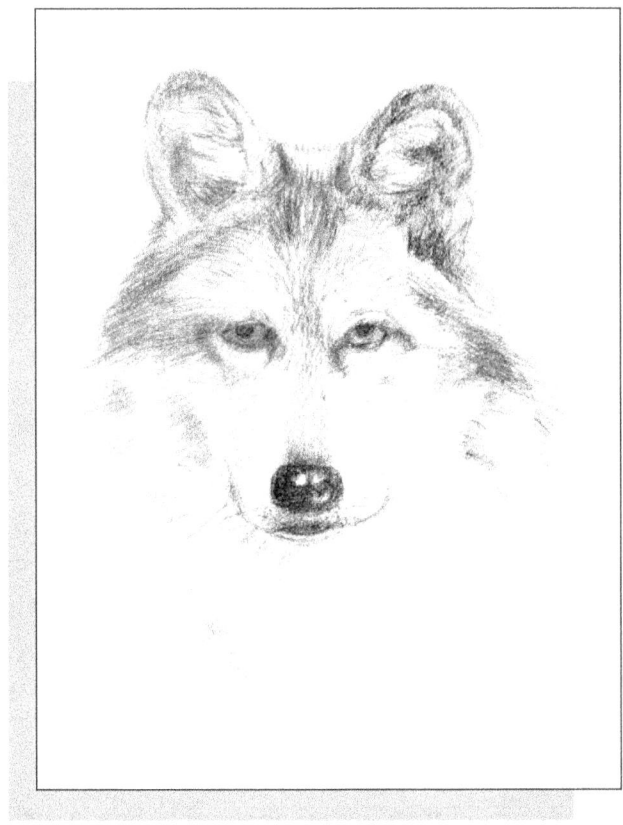

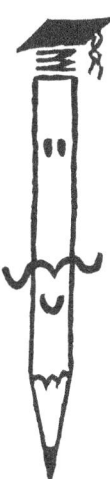

Isn't it wonderful that each creation is unique? I'm sure yours is, too. You have learned much. Take pride in your achievement.

Chapter 10
FOLLOW-UP

Well, what do you know? On this round, you discovered another important factor. You realized that the process of rendering the likeness of the eyes, nose and mouth of a living creature, such as a wolf, requires especially intense scrutiny (close study). For example, we can't assume that eyes are round, or even that they match. Careful observation enables you to notice true shapes and the subtle dissimilarities between one eye and the other. The same goes for the right and left side of the nose, as well as the mouth. Even the ears are not mirror images, as you have seen.

Above and beyond that, the fur can vary a great deal from one part of the animal to the other. Again, careful examination is necessary. When you divide the figure into sections, the array of forms, as well as textures, become easy to manage, provided they are separated into stages and gradually developing layers. Be patient. Don't hurry. Enjoy your journey as well as your destination. In other words, take your time to enjoy the experience and to ensure your success.

Since each person's vision, aesthetic appreciation and touch is different, virtually endless interpretations of the same subject can result. Thankfully, that's one of the many wonders that makes drawing so terrific. The possibilities are infinite, wouldn't you agree?

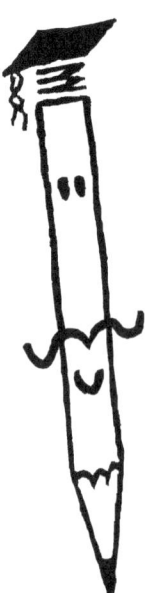

Now, it's my pleasure to say...
CONGRATULATIONS!

You have graduated Anyone Can...Arts
DRAWING MAGIC
Guidebook 2

On the next occasion when you feel inspired to shape and shade your favorite subject matter, be it a landscape, still life, human face, wildlife, or anything you desire to draw, remember to look for the distinguishing features. Then, choose an effective approach. You have many options. For example, you can select the random method, the squiggle method, the overall method, or a combination of these. You are also encouraged to invent procedures. There are techniques galore, not only for capturing the image of form, but also for laying down tones and textures. Having already experienced lots of marvelous possibilities, rejoice in your phenomenal success. Think of all the exciting ways you will be applying your advancing skills, and keep exploring that special artist in you.

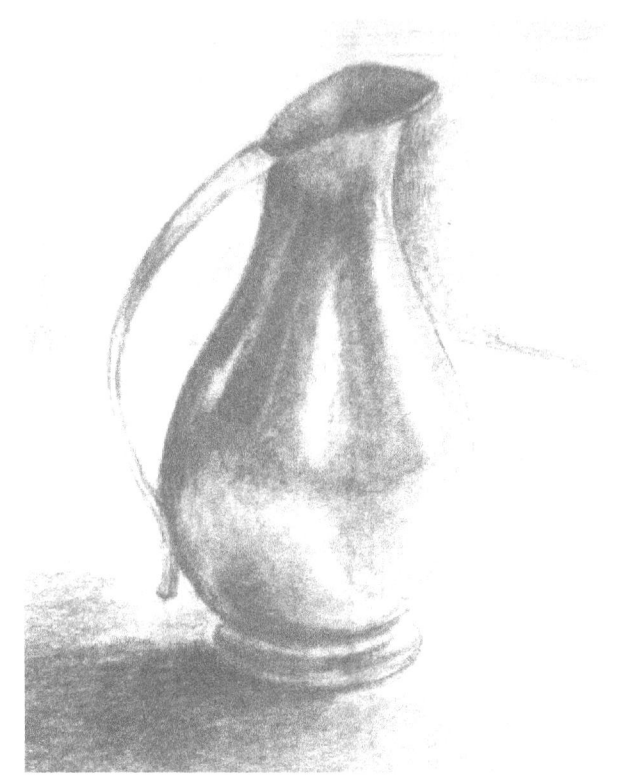

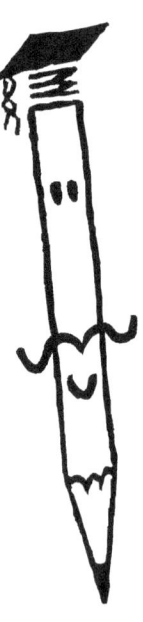

Here are some delightful things students found to draw: A pitcher, a cat and an old pair of tennis shoes.

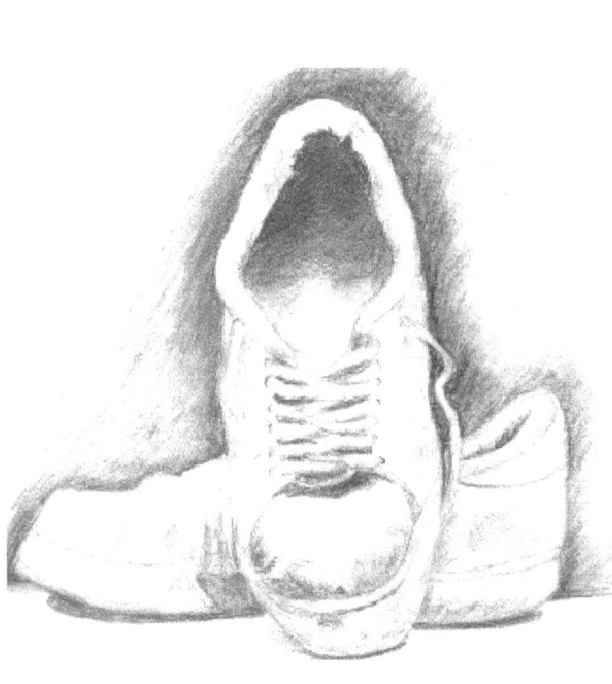

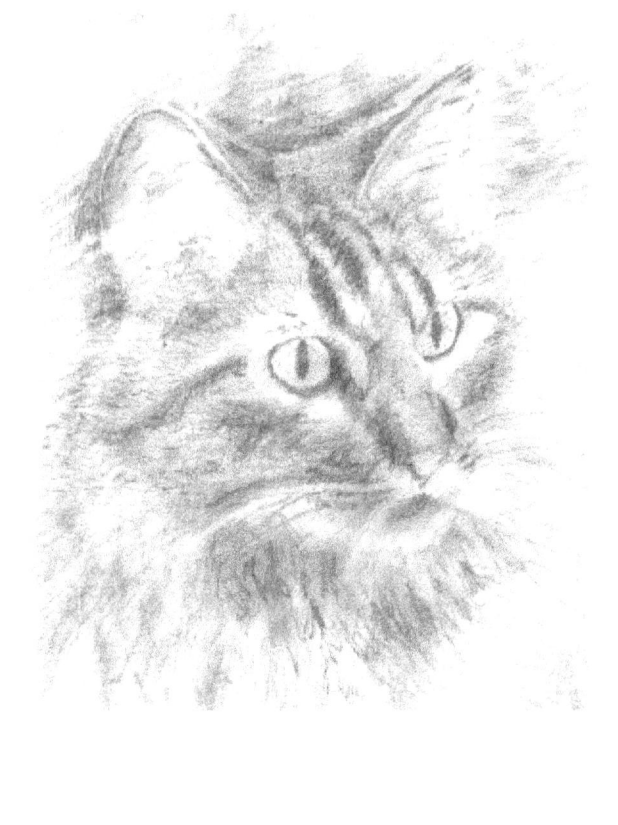

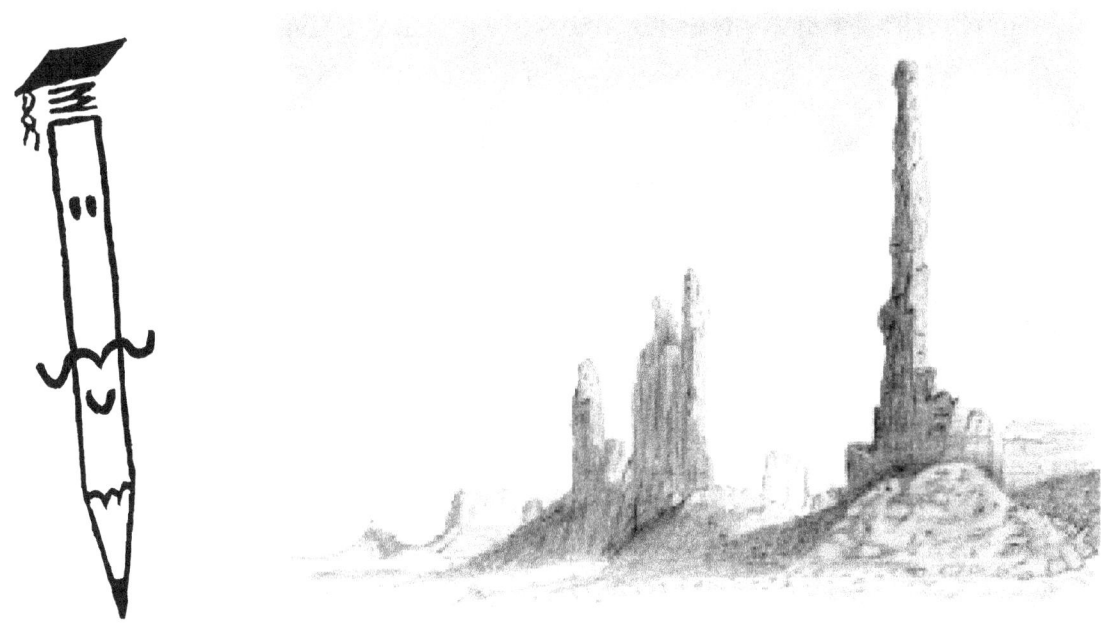

The mesas in the distance and the pepper mill were also terrific sources of inspiration.

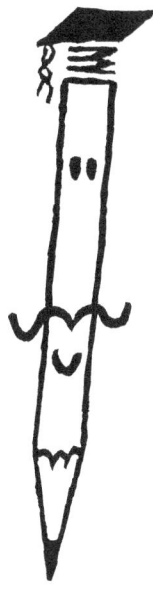

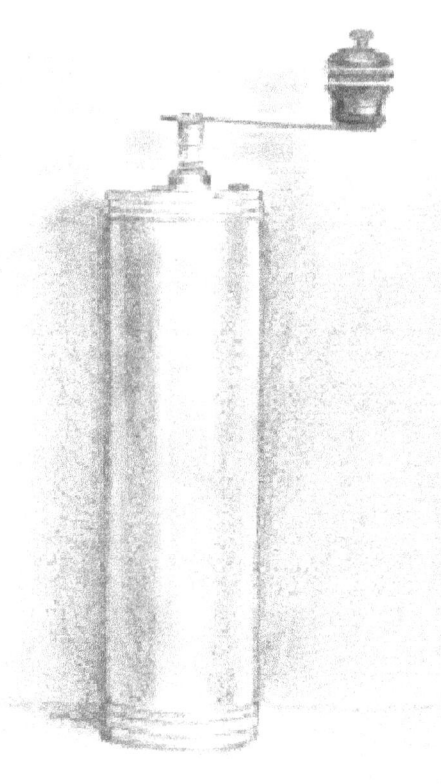

See what wonderful results you can achieve. Pick the subject matter you like, and keep it simple.

ARTIST'S GLOSSARY

Terms and Phrases as defined by Professor Pencil

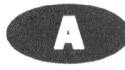
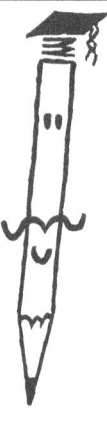

ACCENT - emphasize, increase, heighten, or improve

ACCURATE - reasonable likeness, but not expected to be a perfect or exact match

ADEPT - skillful or capable

ADJACENT - next to or beside something

ADJOINING - next to or beside something

AD-LIB - figure out or find a way to make things work

ADVERSE - not wanted

AESTHETIC - beautiful

AFFIX - attach

AGILITY - move easily and effectively

AKIN - alike, similar

ALIGNMENT - when two or more things, or reference points, locate along a straight line

ALTER - change

ALTERNATIVE - replacement

AMISS - not in proper order or accurate appearance

ANGLE - any direction other than plumb or level
 Other words with similar meanings: SLOPE, INCLINE, DIAGONAL, SLANT, TILT

ANTICIPATE - expect or foresee

APPARENT - visible to the naked eye, or obvious

APPEAL - attraction

APPREHENSIVE - feel nervous, anxious, uneasy

APPROXIMATE - almost, or nearly accurate

ARC - a curve; or to bend, as in a curve

ARTIFICIAL - imitation

ASCEND - move upward in a straight direction, or at a slant

ASPECT - visible characteristic or appearance

ASSESS - survey, examine, evaluate, study

ASSET - advantage, or valuable possession

ASSIMILATION - a process of merging various tones by blending them, or by viewing them from a distance

ASTIGMATISM - uneven curvature of eye lens causing view distortion

ASTRAY - moved away from

ASYMMETRICAL - irregular, uneven, not precise in shape

ATMOSPHERIC PERSPECTIVE - method used to indicate distance by showing things far away with less detail and softer edges

BACKGROUND - visible scenery behind something

BASE LINE - shortest line between two ends of a curve

BISECT - divide in half

BLEND - combine or mix together

BLOT - dab or pat (tap lightly)

BLOTCH - patches or spots of tone values

BLUNDER - accident or goof

BOUNDARY - a limitation showing where something starts or ends
Other words with similar meanings: BORDER, PERIMETER, EDGE

BOW - amount of bend or flex in a curve

BRISTLE - rough, coarse, stiff

CAPABLE - able (to do something)

CHARACTERISTIC - appearance

CHECKERED - spotted pattern resembling a checker board

CHIAROSCURO - variation of tones to help give the impression that a subject has light shining on it

CLOSURE PRINCIPLE - tendency to connect gaps or spaces visually

CLUMP - group, bunch

CLUSTER - gather, bunch or group

COARSE - rough

COINCIDE - two things in the same place

COMPONENT - part or portion

CONCAVE - curve that bends inward

CONCEPT - thought, idea, principle, approach, procedure or method

CONDENSE - compress or make compact (smaller, shorter, less)

CONFIGURATION - arrangement or format

CONFIRM - make sure something is accurate by checking

CONSECUTIVE - follow one after the other without any gaps

CONSIST - made of

CONSISTENT - regular, not varying or changing

CONTINUOUS LINE - a line that starts at one point and moves nonstop until finished

CONTOUR - boundary between planes

CONTRAST - visible difference between 2 or more things (for example - black and white)

CONVERGE - come together

CONVERT - change

C

CONVEX - curve that bends outward

CONVEY - show, communicate

COORDINATE - a position, or reference point, where a vertical and horizontal alignment intersect

COORDINATION - two or more things that work together, like hand and eye coordination

CORNER GUIDE LINES - horizontal and vertical lines that help draw curves

COUNTERACT - reduce, reverse, or undo

CREATIVE FREEDOM - ability to change, or modify by choice

CREST - maximum, or furthest extent of bend in a curve

CURVE - bent line

CYLINDER - tube

CYLINDRICAL - tube-like

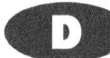

D

DAB - tap lightly

DAUNTING - discouraging

DECLINE - downward direction, at a slant or angle

DEFORMITY - distortion

DELETE - remove or take away

DENSE - close together

DEPICT - create a likeness

DESCEND - move downward in a straight direction or at a slant

DESIGNATE - specify, point out, identify by name

DESTINED - meant for

DEVIATE - stray, go past or away, or to change

DEVISE - figure out or invent

DILIGENT - careful

DIMINISH - reduce or make less

DISCREPANCY - difference

DISREGARD - ignore

DISSIMILAR - not alike, different

DISTINCT - stand out, different, or easily visible

DISTINGUISH - make visible or stand out

DIVERT - change course, turn direction

DWARF - small, or make small

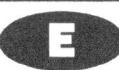

EDGE - where one shape stops and another begins

EFFECTIVE - able to achieve accurate result

ELABORATE - fancy or stylish

ELEVATION LINE - imaginary guide line along a curve crest

ELLIPSE - symmetrical or asymmetrical egg shape

ENHANCE - improve or emphasize

ENTAILS - involves or requires

EQUIDISTANT - equal distance

ESTABLISH - bring something into being or cause it to appear

ESTIMATE - a reasonable opinion or judgment based on observation (best guess)

ETCH - cut

EVALUATE - examine accuracy

EXACT - reasonably accurate

EXEMPLIFY - show by example

EXPANSE - distance, or span between two reference points

EXTREMITY - furthest distance

EYEBALL - estimate visually, without the aid of mechanical devices, rulers, etc.

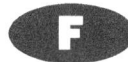

FACSIMILE - reasonable likeness or similarity to something else

FADE - gently or gradually change a tone from dark to light, or from light to dark

FAINT - barely visible

FEASIBLE - likely to work well or be useful

FEATHERING - sweeping pencil strokes in 1 direction, with gradually reduced pressure for blending tones

FEATURE - characteristic or special attraction

FIDGET - unable to stop moving

FIGURE - a shape; also the ability to think through, calculate, or estimate

FLAIR - style, knack

FLAW - not accurate, defective, undesired

FLEX - to bend a curve; or amount of bend or "bow" in a curve

FLUB - goof, botch, bungle, flaw, inaccurate, undesirable result

FLUSH - two or more things that line up (or are aligned) evenly

FOLIAGE - group of leaves

FOOLPROOF - always works

FORESHORTENING - apparent change in proportion of shapes as they turn into line of sight

FORETHOUGHT - think ahead

FORM - a shape or the procedure which makes it
Other words with similar meanings: FASHION, DEVISE, DRAW, PRODUCE

FORMAT - shape, template, or foundation, made with guide lines, to serve as a *flexible* boundary from which to develop a drawing

FREEHAND - draw without a straight edge, ruler, or any other artificial or mechanical device

FUNDAMENTAL - basic

FUSS - overwork or overdo

FUSSY - too precise or exact, difficult to satisfy

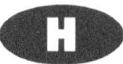

GAUGE - strength, intensity, or amount of something; or to observe, survey, figure out, estimate, judge, assess, analyze

GIRTH - form seen as both front and side view in order to give the *impression* of not only 2 dimensions (height and width), but also suggest distance around via a 3rd dimension known as depth

GLANCE - look quickly

GLIDE - smooth, easy movement

GLIMPSE - quick look or observation

GLITCH - problem or malfunction

GRAPHITE - soft carbon used for lead pencils

GROUND - visible area that something is on

GUIDE LINES - temporary lines that help draw a shape

HALO EFFECT - where two contrasting tones meet, the tone between them appears to intensify

HARD EDGE - sharp, crisp boundary

HAZE - foglike or unclear

HIGH CONTRAST - much visible difference between 2 or more things (such as tones or textures)

HITHER - here

HORIZON LINE - boundary between surface and sky

HORIZONTAL - sideways

HYPOTHETICAL - playing "what if," or imagining how things would turn out if they happened

I

IDENTICAL - visibly alike, apparently the same

ILLUSION - a visual effect, or amazing prank played on the eyes

IMAGINARY ALIGNMENT - invisible line between two or more reference points

IMPACT - effect or result

IMPLEMENT - tool, or put into action

IMPLORE - strongly request

IMPLY - communicate indirectly, suggest

IMPRESSION - feeling

IMPROVISE - figure out, or to find solutions by applying resourceful thinking

IMPULSE - urge or whim

INCLINE - upward direction at a slant

INCONSISTENT - varying, changing, or irregular

INCREMENT - division, or section of distance, equal to the one before it

INDELIBLE - not erasable, not able to be undone

INDENT - leave a slight gap, space or margin between one location and another

INDISTINCT - not easy to see

INFINITE - limitless

INITIAL - first or original

INITIATE - start or make a choice/decision and act on it

INITIATIVE - willingness to make decision or choices, plus act on them, or carry them out

INSIGHT - understanding

INSTILL - communicate to the mind or feelings

INSTINCT - natural behavior

INTACT - remain whole or as is

INTENSITY - strength, stress, pressure, force, rate, measure, or amount of something

INTENSIVE - strong pressure, force, rate, measure, or amount of something

INTERLUDE - time between events

INTERMEDIATE - between

INTERPRET (ation) - translate, change, convert, depict, or replicate

INTERSECT - cut across or through

INTERVAL - a span, space, or distance

INTRICATE - delicate, or something having many parts

INTRIGUE - interest or curiosity

INTUITION - an impulse or hunch based on feeling rather than thought

INVERT (INVERSE) - position upside down, reverse, backward, or in the opposite direction

ISOLATE - set apart

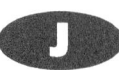

JAGGED - sharply notched, many pointed edges

JUT - extend past, or stand out

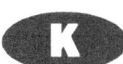

KILTER - something that appears to be in proper position, size, or condition (see "out of kilter")

KNACK - ability, talent

KNOLL - small pile or mound

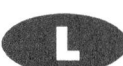

LATERAL - sideways position or direction

LATTER - second, recent, or closest to the end

LAX - not careful

LAYOUT - a written or illustrated plan

LEEWAY - extra space, or amount of freedom

LEVEL - horizontal (sideways) position without apparent angle

LIMBER - not rigid, flexible, able to move easily

LINEAR PERSPECTIVE - method used to portray distance by making far away things appear smaller and closer things larger

LOPSIDED - larger, higher on one side, or tilted

LOST AND FOUND LINES - lines with gaps or spaces

LOW CONTRAST - little visible difference between 2 or more things (such as tones or textures)

MALFUNCTION - not working well (inaccurate)

MANUALLY - by hand

MARGIN - a distance, or interval, inset from the edge; or a space between two locations

MARVEL - appreciate or admire

MAXIMIZE - get the full benefit, or to increase as much as possible

MAXIMUM - most amount, distance, or intensity

MAZE - many passageways offering a variety of choices

MEDIAN - center or middle location between two reference points

MELD - combine, mix, diffuse, blend, fade, or merge

MESH - fit together

METICULOUS - very careful

MIMIC - imitate or copy

MINIMIZE - reduce to the least strength or amount

MODEL - subject, or picture of a subject you intend to replicate

MODELING - blend variations of gray, or tone

MODIFY - change

MOMENTUM - movement

MULL - think about, ponder

MULTITUDE - many

MUZZLE - combination nose and jaw in some animals

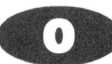

NEGATIVE SPACE - area that borders the edge of a shape

NIMBLE - flexible, quick, agile and skillful, such as with the hands

NOTCH - a gap or interval of space

NUANCE - barely visible difference

OBJECTIVE - goal/purpose, or judge by facts rather than by personal feelings

OBSERVE - look carefully

OBVIOUS - easy to see, stands out

ODYSSEY - an adventure in learning and experiencing new things

OMIT - take away

OPT - choose

OPTION(al) - choice

ORB - ball or sphere

OUT OF KILTER - not in accurate condition
Other words with similar meanings: AWRY, ASTRAY, ASKEW

OUTLINE - the surrounding shape of something revealed by a line

OUTSET - beginning or the start

OVAL - symmetrical, or asymmetrical egg shape

OVERALL PROPORTION - comparison of entire length to entire width

PACE - speed

PARALLEL - two or more things that are the same distance from each other at both ends

PEEPERS - eyes

PERCEPTION - understanding based on observing and thinking

PERIMETER - boundary of a shape

PERIODIC - occur at intervals or spans of time

PERIPHERY - edge or outer margin, like the perimeter or maximum boundary of a shape

PERSPECTIVE - point of view, or method by which to portray 3 dimensional forms on a 2 dimensional surface

PHENOMENON - unusual event or occurance that can be observed

PINPOINT - locate, or place accurately

PITFALL - danger, problem or difficulty

PITTED - surface with holes or pores

PLANE - surface as it appears in line of sight (front, top, side, bottom)

PLEASANT SURPRISE - unexpected result that turns out well

PLOT - devise or plan a course of action, such as to locate reference points

PLUMB - VERTICAL (upright) position/alignment without apparent angle

POLYGON - a shape made with three or more STRAIGHT lines that connect

PONDER - think carefully

PORE - small hole, or examine carefully

POST - after

PRECAUTION - action to prevent unwanted result

PRECISE - reasonably accurate

PRELIMINARY - first, or starting point

PREMISE - an assumption that something makes sense

PREVIOUS - before

PRINCIPLE - a basic truth, rule, or a way to do things

PRIORITIZE - select steps in *order of importance or effectiveness* - these can be a choice to proceed from large to small, or from basic to more elaborate refined stages

PROCESS - a method, or an ability to figure out and understand

PROFICIENT - skillful

PROMINENT - stands out

PROPER - reasonably accurate

PROPORTION - a comparison of length to width; or a size comparison of one thing to another

PROXIMITY - nearby or close

PUSH-PULL EFFECT - use of contrast to cause a figure to appear more prominent (stand out) and to cause the background to recede (appear to be further away)

Q

QUADRANT - quarter section

RAGGED EDGES - rough boundaries

R

RANDOM - action by choice or preference rather than logical sequence

RATIO - proportion, or scale estimation by comparing how big something is to something else

REBOUND - bounce back

REFERENCE POINT - a location or position

REFINE - improve

REFLECT - think back or relate to, represent

REFLECTED LIGHT - light that reaches a surface and bounces back, striking another surface

RELATIVE PROPORTION - size comparison of one shape, or one part of one shape, to another

RELY - trust

REMINISCENT - similar to something or reminder of something

RENDER - create, such as by drawing

RENDERING - finished drawing

RENDITION - a creation that resembles something but is not an exact match

REPLENISH - put back, or supply again

REPLICATE - create a reasonably accurate likeness

RESOURCEFUL - ability to choose best methods to use
Other words with similar meanings: AD-LIB, IMPROVISE, INVENT

REVERSE SPACE - The adjacent area at the edge of a shape
Also called: NEGATIVE SPACE, OPPOSITE SPACE, INDIRECT SPACE

REVISION - adjustment or change

ROTATE - turn, pivot, twirl

ROTUND - big, fat, or round

ROUGHS - practice or unfinished drawings

RUNG - bar on a ladder

S

SCALE - comparison of size

SECTION - part, or portion of the whole

SECTOR - specific part or location

SEE - observe and understand

SEGMENT - division or section

SEISMOGRAPH - machine that measures earthquakes and movements on or in the earth

SEQUENCE - a particular order, or procedure arranged one after the other

SERRATED - saw-tooted, jagged edge

SHADING - toning by creating variations of gray

SHAFT - body or pole section of an arrow

SHAPE - visible boundary of something

SIGNIFY - indicate or show

SILHOUETTE - a shape, filled in with one tone

SIMPLIFY - streamline; or make the drawing process easier by reducing forms to very basic
shapes with straight lines

SIMULTANEOUS - at the same time

SKETCH LINE - a freehand line made with overlapping strokes

SKIM - glance through quickly, or stroke gently on the surface

SLEW - many

SMEAR - blur or spread by rubbing

SMUDGE - blur or spread by rubbing

SOFT EDGE - blurry or vague boundary

SOLUTION - way to remedy or solve a problem

SPACE - shape or area that borders a figure

SPAN - distance (or expanse) between two reference points

SPIKED - pointed

SPONTANEOUS - unplanned, or to act without much forethought

SPORADIC - occasional

SQUIGGLE - draw impulsively by following your whims, feelings, or mood

SQUINT - observe with your eyes partly closed

STARK - harsh, sharp, clear

STATUS - current situation

STILL LIFE - scene consisting of non-living or non-moving objects

STIPPLE - dot

STIPPLING - technique using groups of dots to form tones

STRAIGHT (freehand) LINE - line made straight as possible without use of ruler or other device

STRATEGY - plan

STRICT - too precise, fussy

STRIDE - pace, rate of advancing speed

STRUCTURE - a shape, or a combination of several shapes which total one entire shape

SUBDIVIDE - divide into smaller parts

SUBJECT - item/model to be replicated, or a topic

SUBORDINATE - secondary or something not as important as something else

SUB-PROPORTION - size comparison of one span to another in a shape or figure

SUB-SHAPE - part, portion, or section of a larger shape

SUBTLE - slight, barely noticeable difference between one thing and another

SUCCESSION - organize in a particular order, or sequence (one after another)

SUPERIMPOSE - place in front or on top

SUPPLEMENTAL - additional

SURFACE - exterior, or top layer of something

SURPASS - improve, outdo

SURVEY - examine, study, observe

SWEEPING METHOD - harder stroke at the start, then ease up in one continuous motion

SYMMETRICAL - even, balanced, uniform, consistent, regular,

SYNCHRONIZE - work well together

TACTIC - action based on a plan

TALLY - examine, evaluate, assess. count up, total

TANGIBLE - something real or touchable

TAPER - gradually narrowing, or two lines that come together at a point

TECHNIQUE - method or procedure

TEMPLATE - temporary shape (or format) made by guide lines which serve as a flexible boundary in order to plot (or locate) reference points

TEMPO - speed

TEXTURE - surface appearance of materials (rough, smooth, or soft for example)

TONE - range of light to dark color or gray

TOOTH - texture or surface quality of paper

TRAIT - visible characteristic or feature

TRANQUIL - calm

TRANSFORM - change from one appearance to another

TRANSITION - the in-between stages during which something changes from one appearance to another, or a switch from one procedure to another

TRIO - group of three

TRUSTY SEVEN - basic structural components used to help draw shapes (reference points, alignments, proportions, straight lines, curves, angles, reverse space)

ULTIMATE - last or final

UNCONVENTIONAL - unexpected or unusual

UNIQUE - different, unusual, extraordinary

UTILIZE - use

VAGUE - not clear, indistinct

VALUE - visible difference in the intensity of tones

VARIATION - slightly different, not an exact match

VARY - differ, or change

VERIFY - check to be sure

VERSATILE - able to apply skills in many ways

VERSION - translation or interpretation

VERTICAL - upright

VIA - with, or by way of

VIABLE - likely to work

VICE VERSA - other way round, reverse sequence

VIEW FINDER - frame

VIRTUALLY - mostly accepted or believed, seemingly real

VISIBLE - able to be seen

VISION - eyesight, or understanding based on observation and thinking

VISUAL - relating to eyesight, such as estimating sizes or proportions by eye

VISUALIZE - picture in your mind, imagine, pretend, or make believe

VIVID - very bright, intense

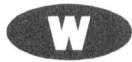

WHIM - act with little or no forethought

WITHIN RANGE - apparently near the desired size or area

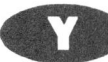

YON - there

ZEAL - enthusiasm, interest

"Drawing isn't just for some, it's for everyone."

"Just as there are methods by which to learn how to read and write, there are methods by which to learn how to draw."

Peter Kraus

ABOUT THE AUTHOR

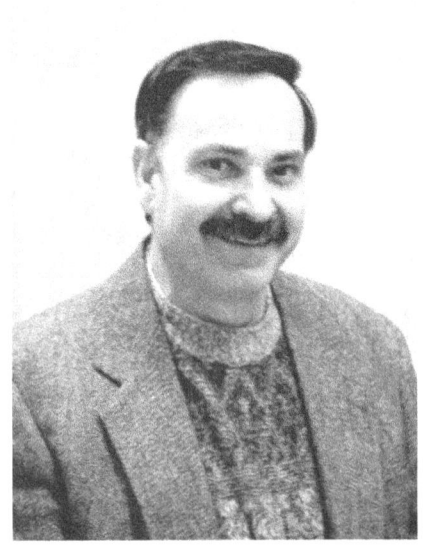

Accomplished fine artist, speaker, graphic designer, and instructor with over thirty-five years of excellent teaching experience, Peter Kraus is the founder of the ANYONE CAN...ARTS SCHOOL and the author of the *Drawing Magic* series of books. Born in Hungary, Peter emigrated to the United States as a child in 1956. Following graduation from high school, he opened his studio and gallery where he created commissioned pieces and fine custom frames. Studying psychology and art education, he earned his degree from California State University, Northridge. In addition to his dedication to *Anyone Can...Arts,* Peter Kraus is also an eminent instructor in a Los Angeles Community College. Highly proficient with multi medias and styles, Peter's aim is to bring out the expressive quality of each student. His unique approach to teaching is remarkably successful with not only the artistically inclined, but also with the artistically challenged, special needs children and adults, senior citizens and at-risk-youth. Proven correct time and again, his conviction that drawing skill CAN be learned is the heart of his ANYONE CAN...ARTS philosophy. "When we are growing up, we are taught that a very small percentage of people have the ability to draw well, but I'm convinced the opposite is true," confides Peter. While he was busy studying psychology, he questioned why some people have the talent to draw well and others don't. Was it in their DNA, did they have an extra gene? Something inside told him it was more than talent and his investigations led him to conclude that people were not only not getting the right encouragement, but that they were also getting instruction based on faulty premises. Schools teach that art comes from "intuition" and it simply flows from us. If a child isn't showing any artistic instincts from the get go, he never will. Peter doesn't deny the existence of artistically gifted individuals, but he believes drawing should be taught analytically as a skill. Instead of using the historically great artists as absolute models, our learning should start from the basics and evolve step-by-step at one's individual pace. This method gives the student a fair chance to discover he or she can actually draw well and do something with the skill. In fact, Peter prefers to look at drawing as "functional and we can use it any way we want."

www.ingramcontent.com/pod-product-compliance
Lightning Source LLC
Chambersburg PA
CBHW081112170526
45165CB00008B/2421